Liberals, Radicals and Social Politics

1892 - 1914

Liberals
Radicals and
Social Politics

1892 - 1914

H. V. EMY
Lecturer in Politics, Monash University

CAMBRIDGE
at the University Press
1973

Published by the Syndics of the Cambridge University Press
Bentley House, 200 Euston Road, London NW1 2DB
American Branch: 32 East 57th Street, New York, N.Y. 10022

Library of Congress Catalogue Card Number 72-85435

ISBN: 0 521 08740 6

Printed in Great Britain by
The Eastern Press, Limited
of London and Reading

Contents

v

Preface

This is a study of the movement of opinions and ideas within the pre-1914 Liberal party, the intention being to chart the process of internal conversion by which the party came to favour an advanced social policy. It is a study directed to the changes taking place within the character of Liberalism and the Liberal party, to the emergence of the New Liberalism and its impact upon the course of party politics. Conversely, it is not an exercise in charting the rise of the welfare state, or the emergence of specific social policies.

In so far as the two can be separated, the emphasis falls upon the political rather than upon the purely administrative debate over social reform. This period has scarcely lacked its historians, and the majority of them have concentrated upon the rise of the Labour movement and the administrative origins and history of the welfare state. This being so, an effort has been made to avoid retracing known and recorded ground. This may leave certain gaps where the administrative details of certain bills are concerned, or where some background information is desirable, but this it is hoped, does not detract from the chronological development of the argument, and reference may be had to the authorities cited.

The implicit assumption is that the history of social politics in these years is of especial significance for the understanding of modern British politics. The inter-related issues of the relationships between state and individual, individual and society, state and economy, came to assume a direct political significance by 1914, in that the individual's personal resolution of such issues was becoming a principal factor in determining his political allegiance. Modern collectivist politics involves a complexity of related issues, but the basis for any collectivism is the entry of the state into economic affairs in general, and into the market economy in particular. As such, the relation between the state and the economy is the critical nexus, far more so than the relation obtaining between the state and society at large. Whereas the latter is essentially regulative, the former is interventionist in character and will almost certainly involve the invocation of a positive goal which the economic process has hitherto been unable to secure. This study will therefore suggest that the significant factor present in the pre-1914 debates upon social policy was the economic factor; that the political struggle was being waged in terms of the state's right and ability to intervene in a market economy

hitherto adjudged to be self-sufficient, and that the willingness of the
Liberal party, under pressure from a growing and powerful Radical
wing (especially after 1906) to support such intervention, initiated a
deep divide between themselves and the more orthodox Conservative
party. This divide, moreover, marks the origin of the post-1918
'fundamentalist' division between Conservatives and Labour over
the proper organisation of economic society, and the proper extent of
the state's responsibility for redefining the basis of that society.

Because the emphasis has to fall so firmly on social politics, and
because only cursory treatment can be provided for other, major,
issues within the period, including those that are complementary to
this study, some element of historical distortion must inevitably
intrude. Conclusions based upon the evidence provided must still be
re-interpreted by the reader within the wider context of the period.
The Liberal Radicals must, in particular, be established within the
mainstream of progressive politics and their continual relationships
with and proximity to the Labour movement must not be forgotten.
Equally, the conventional substance of political debate within the
period, Home Rule, the House of Lords, tariff reform and the
ascending debate upon foreign policy, must be borne in mind. These
themes intruded continually into the arena of social politics, and
this is not an implicit attempt to minimise their importance. What is
claimed here is that the substance of political debate was altering, the
rules of the game were being redrawn to take account of new con-
testants and vastly different interests and perspectives, and in consequence political activity, the behaviour of the players, the conduct
of elections, the content of legislation, was responding to a new set of
stimuli whereby programmes, commitments and policies denoted a
direct and continuous link between values, expectations and goals
upon a national scale.

This is to argue (with P. F. Clarke) [1] that the entry of social reform
in general into politics marks a qualitative change in the substance of
politics; and in so far as previous accounts have paid too little attention to the significance of such a change upon patterns of electoral
support, and the nature of the ensuing division between the two
major parties, there is room for revision of the real strength and
electoral appeal possessed by the Liberal party before 1914. If the
emergence of class politics does not in itself afford a sufficient ex-

---

[1] P. F. Clarke, *Lancashire and the New Liberalism* (1971).

planation of the rise of Labour to replace the Liberals, a better answer
may be found by examining the impact of the New Liberalism, or
Social Radicalism as it is called here, upon the traditional bases of
Liberal support./By examining the changing nature of the party's
composition in parliament, and the relationship between composition
and policy, it should be possible to discover something of the strains
inherent in the transition from the Old to the New Liberalism. This
in turn may explain why the party was unable to accommodate itself
to becoming either a party of the left or a party of the right/If the
strains in the parliamentary party are reflected again by similar strains
amongst the organisation in the country at large, then paradoxically
perhaps, what we have is a picture of a party whose political achievements are at least a partial cause of its own long-term decline. This
is the kind of argument advanced here; in particular, that the commitment to an advanced social programme was made possible by
changes in the composition of the parliamentary party, that the programme was in part shaped by the friction generated by the struggle
between the orthodox (business) interpretations of state and economy,
and the Social Radicals as exponents of a broader, ethical, commitment to legislative intervention and planned social change; finally,
that this friction had serious consequences for the ability of the party
to function as an efficient electoral organisation in the country.

This is, as indicated, to support the kind of interpretation offered
by Clarke of the New Liberalism. It must be said, however, that this
book began life as a Ph.D. thesis in 1966, and both the reading and
my practical interest in this period finished in late 1969. At that point,
emphasis in the literature upon the idea of a New Liberalism was
both cautious and scanty. Since then, the idea has emerged almost to
the status of conventional wisdom.[2] Yet there is some danger that the
term will simply become a convenient shorthand way of referring
to the changing emphasis in Liberal policies after 1906, and this, I
think, would be to minimise its significance. So although I clearly
cannot pay tribute to all the new material that has emerged in the
last three years, I offer the following reflections in the light of the
more important contributions.

Together with Clarke's suggestion of a change in this period from
the politics of status groups to class-based politics, I would append
D. A. Hamer's emphasis upon the change from ' great causes ' to pro-

---

[2] See, e.g. K. O. Morgan, *The Age of Lloyd George : The Liberal Party and
British Politics, 1890–1929* (1971) p. 45.

grammatic politics.[3] These two points bring out the changes in scale and interest that occur in the period. Both the ambit of politics and the role of politicians as the agents for deliberate change were widened. In writing this, however, Hamer's own insistence upon examining the Liberals largely in terms of their sections and the shortcomings of their leadership can be misleading. This approach is clearly valuable in the 1890s in showing just why the Liberal party was unable to make a single, concerted step towards ' real ' (i.e. social) reform, but tends to obscure the change from traditional politics and the issues and causes of the nineteenth century, to the priority of social politics after 1902. Hamer is driven by the form of analysis he adopts to interpret the Liberal Imperialist interest in efficiency as being a (if not the) most significant catalyst in moving the Liberal party towards a commitment to social reform. This to my mind obscures the critical fact that there was, due to the efforts of a few ' Social Radicals ' in the 1892–5 parliament, a movement of opinion and ideas concerning the merits of collectivism, the rights of property and state intervention in regard to wages and hours, which was ' advanced ' in a way that few Liberal Imperialists' views were. It was this advanced opinion which was the more significant long-term influence upon Liberal thought and policy, and although individual Liberal Imperialists were committed social reformers, they contributed very little to the theoretical discussions which were so important in these years. Hamer, I think, fails to distinguish adequately between the Radicals associated with the progressive, anti-imperialist camp, and the efficiency school, which did not make much significant headway in Radical politics. I think he also fails to appreciate the extent to which the Social Radicals were active in the N.L.F. after 1898, while his point that it was more logical for those who supported intervention abroad to support it at home hardly seems to comprehend the kind of argument J. A. Hobson was advancing. Finally, I think Hamer's commitment to a ' sectional ' explanation of Liberal politics does not adequately account for the rôle and significance of organised Labour. The question of whether Labour was a section or an interest (posed by Hamer but not answered) is surely crucial to explaining the course of Liberal politics, and has to be answered in two parts. First, there is the rôle of Labour as a parliamentary pressure-group, and secondly there is the rôle of

[3] D. A. Hamer, *Liberal Politics in the Age of Gladstone and Rosebery : A Study in Leadership and Policy* (1972). See esp. Clarke, *New Liberalism*, Intro., pp. 16–18.

Labour in the country, as the most significant social force making for political change. It is surely inaccurate to explain even parliamentary politics in terms of the relationship between the party representatives alone; it is the three-dimensional relationship between Labour, Liberals, and Labour and Liberals in the country which must form the basis for any model of explanation.

This suggests two points (both made by Clarke).

1./The fortunes of the Liberal party cannot be understood except in terms of the relation between policy and electoral organisation, in the context of social reform. The degree to which the Liberal commitment to programmatic social policies offended traditional interests, polarised their own supporters and helped to bring about class-based politics, is a critical factor./The extent to which it took place, and correspondingly, the extent to which a Liberal organisation, increasingly denuded of money and influential help, had to surrender working-class seats to a still embryonic Labour machine, is the crucial indicator of Liberal decline by 1914. To concentrate upon such an indicator is the best way to avoid the temptation to write off the Liberal party in terms of ' inevitable decline ', and an inability to come to terms with ' the climate of opinion '.[4] To write in terms of a simple relationship between an ascending scale of demand for reform, and a declining Liberal will to provide such reform is really facile, and quite ignores the structural changes taking place in the economy and society which had the initial effect of solidifying the defenders of property-rights and the traditional social order, while fragmenting the supporters of change amongst several groupings, movements and parties, diffusing the strength of the demand for reform. It also ignores such factors as the strength of working-class traditionalism, apathy and ignorance, and the discriminatory effects of the electoral system for working-class voters.

2. The second factor is the phenomenon of progressive politics. This refers not only to the kind of alliance common amongst reformers and radicals (especially at municipal level), and to the introduction of a new ethic of social and moral responsibility into politics. It also serves as an umbrella term referring to the movement of new ideas and of new people into the existing political arena. The ' progressive ' is, I think, a different kind of political animal from either the popular radical or the Labour (i.e. trade-union based)

---

[4] E.g. P. Rowland, *The Last Liberal Governments* (Vol. 2) *Unfinished Business 1911–1914* (1971).

politician. Social Radicals in the Liberal party are one large sub-grouping within the progressive umbrella. If we could obtain a more accurate picture of who these men were, what motivated them and what they hoped to achieve, this would undoubtedly improve our sense of what was really happening in Edwardian politics and society.

This leads me to suggest that as ' class politics' is clearly not a sufficient explanation of the rise of Labour to replace the Liberals, we should attempt to qualify this emphasis upon social movements by stressing both the importance of the intellectual's motivation to politics in this period, and the theoretical arguments and proposals which were so much a feature of Edwardian politics.

This brings me back to my point that to concentrate upon the New Liberalism as a purely parliamentary phenomenon is inaccurate. The context of the change from the Old to the New must be stressed, because the search for system and for a new social philosophy which occurs within the Liberal party is only a particular example of what is taking place in society at large. The certainties of Victorian assumptions about society and progress evaporated in the late nineteenth century in a mood of uncertainty, personal crisis and intellectual insecurity. There was a level of change, of intellectual challenge and response, which was a more significant force shaping politics than any movement for change taking place within the Liberal party alone. It is the manner in which the party became the vehicle for this broader level of change which is the more interesting phenomenon. It is the passage into the Liberal ranks, in fairly considerable numbers, of men who were concerned to use political tools in order to reverse the primacy of economic assumptions, to replace the rôle of political economy by a form of moral economy, in the course of working out a consistent personal philosophy, that largely explains the content of Liberalism and the Liberal party after 1906. This historical perspective that seems to me to be necessary is to see how the movement of thought, particularly social and economic thought, encouraged changing views of the scope for political change, and thereby facilitated the movement of a certain kind of individual into politics. Possibly, these individuals were being drawn from a certain articulate and self-conscious section of society that was experiencing a crisis of identity at the personal level as secularism flourished in a post-Darwinian universe, and the new realism of empirical sociology and psychology made for a searching reassessment of the precise relationship between the individual and his society.

Social dislocation is then to be seen as bringing intellectual fragmentation, as providing specific motivations for individuals, as well
as broader inducements to groups and classes to review their objective
interests in a market economy. The relations between politics, the
decline of religious commitment, and the bubbling of an intellectual
ferment in the period have always been evident in the diaries of
Beatrice Webb or, for that matter, in the literature of the time
(especially in the writings of G. K. Chesterton and H. G. Wells). It
has also been admirably spelt out in M. J. Wiener's study of Graham
Wallas.[5] To perceive the kinds of influences that were at work upon
Wallas, to see his intellectual response, which was intimately bound
up with his political response, to see his equivocation between Labour
and Liberal, is to see the kind of moral and political dilemma
characteristic of so many progressives in the first quarter of the
twentieth century. The significance and meaning of modern British
politics is to be found in careers such as his; it is these Radicals and
progressives who hold the key to much that follows. The articulation
of a radical strain of dissent which is non-ideological and which is
' social ' in the sense of drawing upon a civil religion formed by a
curious mixture of idealism and empiricism, which is also with but
not of Labour, is an important strand within the formation of modern
British political culture. Progressivism is a strand quite apart from
either socialism or trade-unionism; its affinities and empathies are,
indeed, closest to Liberalism; especially in its views upon social
harmony, its distaste for class politics, and its belief that conflicts are
ultimately reconcilable. The relation between progressivism (or
Social Radicalism) and the Liberal party on the one hand, and the
relation between progressives and class politics upon the other, are
certainly important. The movement of earnest, committed and im-
pecunious young men into the Liberal party after 1895, the circumstances which allowed so many to penetrate into the House of Commons after 1906, and the degree to which they thought and acted
independently of either any established social interest in the country,
or even of their party in parliament, is surely one of the best examples
of the rôle of the intellectual in politics.

Of course, it must be said that it was not as simple as this either.
The relations between progressives, Radicals and Labour formed a
very complex mesh indeed, and if we need area studies to bring out

5 M. J. Wiener, *Between Two Worlds : The Political Thought of Graham Wallas*
(1971).

the particular way in which Liberal social policy strained Liberal organisation in the country, then we need too studies of policy-making, either from an administrative or party-political point of view, to show how theory was converted into practice and by whom. Certainly, in attempting to discover the movement in Liberal political thought, this book by-passes such detailed matters as the Labour party's contribution to the question of unemployment,[6] or where the ideas came from for such very detailed matters as insurance. All that can be said is that this book attempts to give some insight into the kind of theoretical problems that dogged the politicians, on the assumption that political change in large part depended upon solutions to such problems being found prior to the formulation of specific policies. The key point in this study is therefore to show how the Liberal party came to possess a sufficient theoretical commitment to change for it to override economic and practical obstacles which to its critics seemed such overwhelming reasons for doing nothing. The way to show this is to concentrate upon social politics and the issues it embraced. Where this does some injustice to a balanced account of party politics (e.g. by ignoring the free trade – tariff reform debate in the context of financing social reform), I can only leave it to the reader's own perspective to adjust the balance.

Finally, I would like to record my debt to all those who have, at one time or another, given me assistance in regard to sources: to Lord Harcourt, Sir Steven Runciman and Mrs Elizabeth Clay for permitting me to examine the private collections of papers in their care, to Mr Mark Bonham Carter for giving me permission to see the Asquith papers, to the trustees of the Beaverbrook Library and Mr A. J. P. Taylor for permission to see the Lloyd George papers. Also, to the trustees of the British Museum in respect to the manuscripts in their charge, to the staff of the House of Lords Record Office for their help in regard to the Herbert Samuel papers, to the National Library of Scotland in regard to the Haldane and Elibank papers, and of course to the staffs of the various libraries concerned (especially to the British Library of Political and Economic Science).

[6] But see K. D. Brown, *Labour and Unemployment, 1900–14* (1971).

1

Prelude to Power

The cumulative effect of research has qualified the drama of *The Strange Death of Liberal England*,[1] although a sense of uniqueness still remains. The years between 1886 and 1914 still seem remarkable for the self-conscious assessment of principles and the reformulation of convictions and ideas experienced and recorded by so many of the personalities involved. The atmosphere of doubt and uncertainty which Dangerfield described so vividly, surely is an important factor in its own right, and ought to be so considered in analysing the replacement of older certainties by new and awkward questions. In particular, the accumulation of purely empirical evidence has obscured the significance of the theoretical debate upon the rights and duties of the individual in society and the relationship of the government to the individual; and it was the theoretical arguments which were also important in affecting the course of politics at Westminster.

There is a temptation to impose a false simplicity upon the period. Sometimes, for example the period appears to hold no more than a contrast in inevitabilities, the rise of Labour and the decline of Liberalism. Or the Liberal party may appear as a fading anachronism; its principles of individualism outmoded, its policies dictated by electoral exigencies, its leadership a coincidental assemblage of personalities lacking the internal coherency necessary to link supporters, values and goals together within a national organisation. Or it may be suggested that the real insights are provided by a study of the changing electoral patterns and allegiances in the constituencies, or by a study of the process of 'unconscious' administrative growth. But a changing electoral pattern is not a first-order condition for change. It may either confirm an initial change or presume further change, but it is itself caused, and any interpretative judgement of the period cannot be founded upon electoral change alone. Similarly, the argument for 'unconscious' administrative change fails to make allowance for the growth of a 'conscious' political movement. Qualitative problems of scale are involved; for example, the fact of an expanding bureaucracy may of itself cause a range of political

[1] Cf. G. Dangerfield, *The Strange Death of Liberal England* (1935).

problems which would have a profound impact in an age highly sceptical of the values of bureaucracy (e.g. how to control the bureaucracy and its further growth, how to pay for it). The sudden realisation of any one such problem might transform the nature of the political argument.

This is to argue that the conclusions of empirically motivated research must be offset by some interpretative analysis of the movements taking place in the realm of ideas and opinions, into what people were thinking as well as into what they were doing. It is to argue too that it is not possible to do justice to this period except by treating the Liberal party as a primary, self-conscious political organism, deliberately trying to come to terms with events, demands for social reform and internal conflicts over policy amongst supporters. It is to argue that a consideration of Liberalism is integral to any account of the fortunes of the Liberal party. The party from 1886 to 1914 must be seen as possessing an independent character; its values and policies as providing an enduring contribution to the evolution of English party politics; the nature of its involvement with social reform as providing a testing ground for these same values, and the party's internal relationship between supporters and policies as providing the crucial variable upon which the party's longer-term fortunes hinged. More than any other organisation, the Liberal party in this period provided the forum within which values, theory and action were linked, and herein lies a story to be told.

THE NATURE OF LIBERALISM: INDIVIDUALISM

The Liberal party has commonly been described as an ' individualist ' party, although individualism is as much a matter of degree and attitude as a substantive political creed. In the first place, individualism referred to the Victorian respect for character, thrift and self-help as the criteria for defining individual progress; and, secondly, individualism included a belief in limited government, and a trust in an individual's responsibility and rationality. The best society was that which aimed at providing for its members the greatest measure of individual freedom compatible with their common good. Governments were therefore responsible for providing either those services which individuals could only provide for themselves at undue cost, or those that were only advantageous when operated for the equal interest of all; while, economically, the self-interest of calculating individuals was regarded as securing the most efficient disposition of resources amongst society at large.

In these terms, individualism appeared primarily as a statement of desirable behaviour rather than an explicit political statement on behalf of a particular party. Indeed, the more closely one questions the abiding influence of individualism upon the Liberal party, the less does this influence appear to be the decisive consideration in Liberal politics, and to argue that the Liberals were unsympathetic to social reform in the 1880s and 1890s because their own individualism clashed with the new collectivism is quite misleading.

The type of political individualism outlined above, and whose origins stemmed in large part from the utilitarian calculus, had never finally committed its adherents either to the exclusion of all governmental action or to a constant level of such action. As legislation and social rights were alike subjected to the test of utility, and as the criterion of the ' greatest happiness ' was to be measured over time as a legislative guide in a changing society, the element of paternalism, in health and sanitation for instance, was never absent. Similarly, within classical economic policy, individual choice and self-regulation emerged as a distinct norm to which activity should be directed, rather than as an ethic to which activity should be subjected.[2]

Although emphasis upon such an ethic was ' something quite exceptional in the history of social philosophy ',[3] such an emphasis admittedly prospered after 1865 with the joint impact of Social Darwinism and the work of Spencer, in whose hands the law of natural selection operating as the prime evolutionary force within society came to oppose any political activity which might obstruct the free play of adaptable individuals in a natural environment. In seeking to give a systematic form to the ideal of a competitive social structure, Spencer tended to identify Liberalism more completely with the defence of individual liberty, with a regime in which individual relationships were governed by contractual obligations freely incurred. By appealing to fundamental laws which he perceived arising from the fibres of social history, ' laws which over-ride individual wills ' and to which all human law should be subjected, Spencer attempted to define an underlying path of social evolution whose dynamic principle of natural selection encouraged an inflex-

---

[2] L. C. Robbins, *The Theory of Economic Policy in English Classical Political Economy* (1952) pp. 178–93 *passim*.

[3] *Ibid*. p. 182.

ible morality: 'the individuals of most worth will prosper and
multiply more than those of less worth.'[4] Such ideas clearly enforced
the concept of an intuitive moral sense which the individual was
expected to exercise, and such ideas were reflected in the kind of
exaggerated scope for individual morality outlined by a group of
avowed Liberals in 1891.[5] But their statements cannot be considered
truly representative of Liberal thought, including as they did a
principled opposition to both free education and free libraries,
although certain elements within their case did strike responsive
chords within contemporary Liberalism: the dislike of bureaucracy,
fear of unlimited authority, a belief in abstract principles whose meaning was extracted from chosen historical examples rather than from
contemporary contextual definition, the sense of the ideal and the
fear of fettering a natural progress. Yet these appeared quite free
from any systematic individualist philosophy,[6] and while there were
undoubtedly severe individualists amongst Liberal M.P.s, it would
be misleading to stress that these were the products of any particular
influence. Non-conformity produced the benevolent Quaker tradition
of William Fowler as well as the teetotal, Wesleyan, self-made image
of old Sir Walter Runciman. Joseph Chamberlain could support the
virtues of individual enterprise, as well as expressing a practical belief
in municipal Radicalism. He, and John Morley, could believe in
'positive humanistic values and high secular ideals', derived above
all from Mill.[7] In 1885, the Radical programme of free primary
education, reform of the land, local government, the churches and
taxation, conjured up a vista of public assaults upon property, but
the men who drew up the programme were basically individualists.[8]
It was of the nature of late Victorian Radicalism that the presence of
system-builders was so absent from its thinking. Bradlaugh, his
disciple J. M. Robertson (later an 'advanced' social reformer),
Labouchere, Sir Wilfrid Lawson and James Stansfeld were certainly
individualistic in their theories of state and society, but they neither
held a brief for Spencerism nor supported any doctrine of 'the
survival of the fittest'.

[4] H. Spencer, *The Man Versus The State* (1888) p. 105.
[5] T. Mackay (ed.), *A Plea for Liberty: An Argument Against Socialism and
Socialistic Legislation* (1891). Introduction by Spencer. This book gained a
favourable review from the Conservative *Quarterly Review*, 172 (1891) p. 489.
[6] Cf. A. Reid (ed.), *Why I am a Liberal* (London, n.d.).
[7] P. Fraser, *Joseph Chamberlain* (1966) pp. xiii, 25.
[8] For 'The Radical Programme' see the *Fortnightly Review*, 35 (1884) and 38
(1885).

Within the world of ideas, individualism amongst Liberal ranks was mitigated by the pragmatism of the economists, the teachings of the Idealists, of Arnold Toynbee, of Jowett and the University movement, and by the humanistic influence of Mill. Indeed, it might be primarily to Mill that one would look for an implicit expression of the individualist ' norm '. Aware of the limits of the ' majority will,' especially in ignorant hands, and favouring private rather than state management, closely orthodox in his economic views, yet he still managed to convey a belief in a broader interpretation of utilitarianism than many of his premises would have seemed to imply.[9] To Arnold Toynbee, state interference was justified where individual rights conflicted with the interests of the community, or where the people were unable to provide ' a thing of *primary social importance* ' for themselves. Practicable schemes were permissible; public authorities might buy land and let it below the market-price for the provision of houses, subsidising any deficit themselves. Above all, he opposed materialism and emphasised ' the spiritual ideal of life ', the development of the collective intelligence, fostered by the social conscience, an early echo, perhaps, of Hobhouse.[10]

Spencerism, and Spencer's ensuing criticisms of the Liberal party, may be seen in the context of a growing intellectual disillusionment with Liberalism. The Liberal Unionists and Conservatives were gaining ground in Cambridge after 1886,[11] Anson, Dicey and Sidgwick were moving rightwards, while James Stephen, Maine and Lecky had already gone.[12] But it is possible that the dislike of an expanding state activity was but one cause among several: dislike of the caucus and democratic politics, of the Irish Land Act of 1882 and Home Rule, of attacks upon the liquor or landed interests.[13] There are grounds too for believing that attacks by the academics upon what they termed ' collectivism ' were attacks upon the form rather than the substance of Liberal legislation, their chief fear being of the future abuse of precedents now created. Sidgwick, for example, disbelieved in socialism and believed self-interest to be an irreplaceable

9 M. Cole, *Makers of the Labour Movement* (1948) p. 117. J. Bowle, *Politics and Opinion in the Nineteenth Century* (1966) pp. 198–203.
10 A. Toynbee, ' Are Radicals Socialists? ' in *Lectures on the Industrial Revolution* (4th edn., 1894) pp. 117, 218 (original emphasis).
11 J. Roach, ' Liberalism and the Victorian Intelligentsia ', *Cambridge Historical Journal*, 13 (1957).
12 Cf. B. E. Lippincott, *Victorian Critics of Democracy* (University of Minnesota, 1938) p. 250.
13 Cf. ' The Conservatism of Today ' in *Quarterly Review*, 180 (1895).

motivating force, but he also rejected any system of abstract individual rights, and any attempt to realise non-interference as an ideal end in itself.[14] In 1891, he defined the 'individualistic minimum' of legislative intervention as 'the distribution of legal rights and obligations among private persons that results from applying the individualistic principle, as strictly as seems practically possible, to the actual conditions of human life in society'.[15] Yet this statement did not exclude governments from undertaking a wide range of services: reclamation schemes, banking and insurance for the poor, providing for scientific research and public education. Furthermore, the rights of property and labour and the need for personal security and legal equality within any society, called for continuous interpretation and enforcement by government agency. It was doubtful whether governmental functions could ever be adequately defined at one point in time, and any moderately progressive society should be prepared to countenance the expansion of such functions as population and felt needs alike increased.[16]

By the beginning of the period, there was also reason to believe that the teachings of the Idealists may have begun to nourish a tradition of behaviour which taught the responsibilities of citizenship, the need for social enquiry and the conscious treatment of felt needs. While Idealism could not, in political terms, be mistaken for anything remotely collectivist, and while T. H. Green himself thought in terms of voluntary action and the freedom of contract, there did come a new emphasis upon the positive duty of the state to secure the greatest happiness of the greatest number by acting according to the interests of the community, rather than according to the interests of the individual.[17] This in itself was a challenge to the behavioural assumptions of individualism, and by shifting the criterion of enquiry to the community at the very time when social reformers were challenging the traditional interpretation of social progress, represented an important change in scale.

If individualism was really no more than one aspect of the calculus

---

[14] H. Sidgwick, *Economic Socialism* (1886) reprinted in R. L. Smyth (ed.), *Essays in the Economics of Socialism and Capitalism* (1962).

[15] H. Sidgwick, *The Elements of Politics* (1891) p. 40.

[16] *Ibid*. pp. 143–4. Also W. S. McKechnie, *The State and the Individual* (Glasgow, 1896) for an 'organic individualist' arguing in terms of national growth requiring progressive modifications of individualism.

[17] Cf. M. Richter, *The Politics of Conscience* (1964) p. 294. Richter records that in 1906, 31 old Balliol men were elected, including 22 Liberals.

of an empirical utilitarianism, and was unable in itself to provide a sufficient explanation of Liberal political behaviour, neither was its economic twin, the principle of laissez-faire, able to provide an exclusive link between Liberalism and the competitive society. The point has been made that the Manchester school was not the most important inspiration of mid-century Liberalism.[18] It is arguable as to what extent the Liberal party in the 1870s was the party of business and was therefore opposed to the interests of labour. Against the tradition of Cobden and Bright stood the early Liberal links with the trade-union junta, and against Bright's opposition to Factory Acts stood the Rathbone–Mundella tradition of enlightened ownership. In the 1880s and 1890s, Liberalism fought shy of any identification with Manchesterism; true Liberalism was interpreted as a belief in liberty tempered with 'wholesome restrictions'.[19] It was denied that the classical economists had argued for a fully competitive existence,[20] while individualists of the Manchester school like Goldwin Smith did not exclude a paternal influence on behalf of the state, and considered that a community of interest amongst the social sections could best be developed by just such an influence.[21]

To argue that economic individualism was the sole prerogative of those business interests who preferred the Liberalism of the Manchester school to the paternalism of mid-century Toryism is not borne out by the relative composition of the two parties after the 1870s. J. A. Thomas recorded that by the late 1860s the fundamental interest difference between commercial Liberalism and landed Toryism had begun to disappear. By 1865, the share of industry and finance represented amongst the total interests of Tory M.P.s had risen to 42 per cent,[22] and this figure continued to rise steadily.[23] This accords with Kitson Clark's impressions of the changing foundations of party

---

[18] Cf. J. Vincent, *The Formation of the Liberal Party 1857–68* (1966). Also H. J. Hanham, *Elections and Party Management* (1959) ch. 6, ss. 2 and 3 for the rise of Birmingham to challenge Manchester, which was Tory in 1874.

[19] 'Liberalism Philosophically Reconsidered' in *Westminster Review*, 132 (1889) p. 336.

[20] 'Political Economy and Social Reform', *ibid*. 133 (1890) p. 634.

[21] E. Wallace, *Goldwin Smith, Victorian Liberal* (Toronto, 1957) pp. 19–20, 166–8.

[22] J. A. Thomas, *The House of Commons 1832–1901* (Cardiff, 1939) pp. 10–11.

[23] Cf. B. McGill, 'Parliamentary Parties 1868–1885', unpublished Harvard doctoral thesis (1952) p. 224. R. C. K. Ensor also pointed to the tendency for financial opinions to move, with those of the City of London, rightwards after 1870. 'Some Political and Economic Interactions in Later Victorian England', *Transactions of the Royal Historical Society*, 4th Series, XXXI (1949).

strengths between 1865 and 1885,[24] and with a more recent emphasis
upon Conservative gains in the urban areas in the 1880s and onwards,
commensurate with an effective decline in the importance of the land
and the gentry within the Conservative party.[25] The dominant impression is of a complete lack of any clear-cut interest differentiation
between the parties such as would explain either the predominance
of a particular viewpoint within one party, or the accustomed linking
of commercial laissez-faire and the Liberal party.

THE NATURE OF LIBERALISM: THE POLITICAL FACTOR

If, within the context of historical explanation, individualism has
been over-emphasised, the reverse applies to the prevailing views
upon the nature of both politics and the legislative function. Restrictions upon the extent of legislation were not only inherent within the
utilitarian calculus, but were equally implicit in the character of
nineteenth-century political thought, which was above all concerned
with a government's relationship to individuals. The state became the
government of the moment, which militated against any idea of
continuous central responsibility for social affairs. Because development was either self-evident or evolutionary, there was little sustained
challenge to belief in a political order whose problems were basically
structural (institutional reform), external (foreign policy), or the outcome of specific and limited circumstances (corn-laws and Chartism).
The significance of the social problem, however, was that as it grew
in size, so it appeared totally exogenous to the existing order. It was
a challenge not only to the internal, institutional manner of government, but also to the social structure on which the government was
based. It posed not one, but a whole series of questions: how much
responsibility could a government safely absorb? What number could
it effectively control in its own employ, and what would be the effect
of such employment upon private industry? How far had any class
a right to demand limitations of interests upon other classes? And if
Liberalism was more nearly attuned to arguments for reform couched
in institutional terms, then it was far harder for it to appreciate the
contention of more advanced social reformers that institutional

---

[24] G. K. Clark, *The Making of Victorian England* (1962) pp. 43, 241.
[25] J. Cornford, ' The Transformation of Conservatism in the Late Nineteenth
Century ', *Victorian Studies*, VII (1963); and ' The Parliamentary Foundations of
the Hotel Cecil ' in R. Robson (ed.), *Ideas and Institutions of Victorian Britain*
(1967).

reform was a secondary matter, and what really mattered was legislation upon social and economic problems. The Liberals certainly doubted their own ability to deal with the problems and furthermore they doubted the implications of such legislation upon the structure and assumptions of the limited government in which they believed.

The surface unity of late nineteenth-century politics lay not only in its deferential character and electoral anomalies, but equally in the nature of the parties and the character of representation. The Whig–Liberal creed of redress of grievance and legislative scrutiny within a balanced constitution was linked to a political structure which placed much weight upon pressure-groups and extra-parliamentary activity. A characteristic of Liberal politics was the flexibility of the channels of political communication, and the attempts by the leadership and the party centre to control factional challenges from amongst their followers. Within the Liberal party, for example, the Welsh members, the United Kingdom Alliance or the Radical Committee existed as bodies competing for priority in policy-making. Party majorities were not sacrosanct, they might alter rapidly in an age of frequent by-elections. Twice in this period, 1895 and 1905, effective loss of confidence forced a government to resign, and in both cases party schism was responsible. In that the relations of both main parties to their electoral organisations were often undecided, a party which lurched alternatively from the importance of the rank-and-file to the importance of the leadership (as the Liberals did between 1891 and 1902–3), was likely to suffer as confusion delayed the development of policy.

Policy-making was a curiously uncertain activity before 1914. For M.P.s in general, parliament was a responsive cog in the whole social machine. Its rôle was circumscribed by the belief M.P.s held that their action was of a secondary nature – a final resort available when daily processes and voluntary self-help had failed. M.P.s might lead deputations, present petitions, chair protest meetings, indulge in an assortment of campaigns. Individually, they were the ultimate articulators of dissatisfaction amongst the community, but collectively in parliament they were only involved as the last step; and in parliament, the Radical ideal of fully representative government met the Whig legacy of responsible government upon equal terms – the two were complementary and not opposed. The Radical believed in widening the electoral basis and the general interest which politics subserved, while the Whigs

believed that Government was ' *a practical thing* ', and did not exist to
furnish a spectacle of uniformity, nor to comply with logic, arithmetic or
the theories of visionary politicians. They were for Liberty, with a big L,
for toleration and for justice, but they never confused inequalities with
injustices and never desired to see administrations come and go by chance
majorities or by the changing humours of millions of uninformed
voters.[26]

The Radical was also concerned with causes and with an initiative
which was at once personal and in keeping with his individual duty
to his constituents. Radicalism and Whiggism coalesced in a trust in
deliberate government. Programmes were discouraged because it
was feared they might encourage irresponsibility, and, in a highly
principled age, political argument was firstly a dispute over principles,
and only secondly over policies.

This was a view which later Radicals (and Labour supporters)
with their desire to replace political individualism and disinterested
government with the politics of commitment, had first to break.
Witness the older schools: ' We have no need for a cry. Let us go on
in the consciousness of . . . ample power . . . inevitably ours . . . freely
and fearlessly to work out, one by one, the problems before us as
rapidly as may consist with good legislative results.' [27] Or Spence
Watson's reaction to the Newcastle Programme: ' Some of us are
afraid that the declarations (i.e. of policy) partake somewhat of the
character of a programme. Some of us look back to the good old time
when we took up one great burning question and fought it '.[28]

From property, intelligence, and status to the modern trinity of
interest, commitment and efficiency, the idea gradually gained
credence that parliament was itself the driving-wheel, and to the
dispute over the rôle of government was added the dispute over what
government (and politics) really involved.[29] And these were critical
disputes to be resolved, for merely to support the desirability of social
reform was of little practical use until the possibility of such reform
was evident. The Liberals, and the age in general, found it hard to
conceive of a change in the primary rôle of parliamentary government. It was not, said Haldane, the function of M.P.s to mould ideas,

[26] A. E. Pease, *Elections and Recollections* (1932) p. xiii, original emphasis.
[27] J. Stansfeld, M.P., ' Liberal Programmes ', *Contemporary Review*, October 1885.
[28] *Proceedings of the 14th Annual Meeting of the N.L.F.* 1891. Presidential Address.
[29] Cf. S. Letwin, *The Pursuit of Certainty* (Cambridge, 1965) Introduction.

that belonged to the universities and intellectuals. M.P.s were simply to give critical effect to what the informed, majority, opinion wished them to do.[30] Matthew Arnold, Goldwin Smith and John Morley also believed informed opinion to be of more importance than that of government or parliament: the thinkers held the real influence, ' not the men who come in at the eleventh hours and merely frame the bills for parliament.'[31] This view provided scope for the ' unofficial ' policy-makers, to the voluntary social enquirers, to the teams of writers associated with the press, and to extra-parliamentary sources in general.[32] The phenomenon of pressure-group politics never aroused attention until it was itself regarded as an aberration from the norm.

The M.P.s' limited views of their own rôle was accentuated by a belief that parliament as a whole was unfitted to intervene in problems whose basis was ' simply a question of economics '.[33] An essential point in this context was the influence of the informed few in the face of the ignorant many, several of whom might have agreed with the confession of Robert Wallace, a Progressive in matters of the eight-hours day and the feeding of school-children, that ' in the presence of a man of business I feel like a piece of putty '.[34] There was an affinity between the practical man of affairs, the businessman whose distate for abstract speculation directed against the existing order was well-known, and the deliberate Whig approach to legislation which, given the parliament of 1892, added up to a considerable barrier of inertia. If the Whigs, representing in general the propertied classes, were ' naturally averse to change ', so the Whiggish Liberal Cabinet of 1892 believed in practical rather than theoretical politics, disliked the unduly populistic appeal of the Newcastle Programme, for democracy was still ' a delicate experiment ' and appeals to overt class interest could easily upset it. Respectable politics was responsible politics, devoid of imagination but full of character, and even Radical politics subdued its force within its respect for character.

---

[30] R. B. Haldane, ' Social Problems ', Address to the 80 Club, 30 May 1891. *80 Club Year-Book* (1892).

[31] D. Hamer, *John Morley : Liberal Intellectual in Politics* (Oxford, 1968) pp. 77–8.

[32] Cf. J. A. Spender, *Men and Things* (1937) p. 63.

[33] According to Sir L. Playfair, *The Speaker*, 4 January 1890.

[34] R. Wallace, ' The Psychology of Labour and Capital ', *Fortnightly Review*, 1 November 1893.

THE NATURE OF LIBERALISM: THE ECONOMIC FACTOR

In conjunction with the emphasis upon ' practical ' politics there was the prevailing belief in a tightly-drawn theory of industrial production, the combined effect of which was to emphasise that economics and economic affairs were a special and somewhat esoteric field of enquiry, a craft and a mystery removed from the tamperings of the uninitiated.

It has been suggested that the noticeable growth in pragmatism amongst economists such as Jevons, Cairnes, and Marshall had, by the 1880s, provided a significant qualification to the principle of laissez-faire.[35] Such economists now admitted to ethical implications for their discipline, and admitted too that production solely for profit was rightly being challenged.[36] But it would be altogether incorrect to assume that this change of emphasis amounted to a significant change in outlook amongst informed opinion. The economists' reappraisal was not equivalent to the socialistic emphasis upon the need for both a new study of distribution and for a profoundly different system of production. There was a growing recognition that production and distribution were two halves of the same process, but while neither was subordinate to the other, the progressive claim in favour of the primacy of distribution was implicitly rejected. The unity of economic teaching was undisturbed, and the requirements of the productive process still pointed to capital as *primus inter pares* amongst the factors of production.

Given that the Liberal party did contain a sizeable business element, and given that explanations dealing in general terms with laissez-faire are inaccurate, it is accordingly desirable to understand precisely how the business-cum-economic community viewed demands for legislative interference with wages and hours, as by 1892 such demands constituted the crux of the progressive argument for reform. This necessarily involves some reference to the lasting influence of the theory of the wage-fund.

In its most rigid form the theory stated simply that wages depended on the relation obtaining between the population and that part of the total capital fund available for their satisfaction in the form of wages. In that the total fund was itself pre-determined by the past

---

[35] E.g. H. Lynd, *England in the 1880s* (Oxford, 1945) pp. 104–5.
[36] Cf. A. Marshall, *The Present Position of Economics* (1885) and W. Smart, ' The Old Economy and the New ', *Fortnightly Review*, 1 September 1891. See also D. Winch, *Economics and Policy* (1969) pp. 37–46.

level of industrial activity, and particularly by the past level of savings, it was a finite sum. As any division of the fund had to be made
in accordance with the priority of maintaining productive capacity
in the immediate future, the claims of capital (depreciation, new
plant, entrepreneurial ability), plus fixed costs (payment of interest
and rent) had priority, the wage-fund itself becoming a residual.[37]

The demise of the theory was commonly dated from Mill's retraction in 1869, but it is apparent that the theory, as regards practical
application, had been only modified. The retraction was in the first
instance concerned with the position of the single firm and the single
employer, where the wage-fund was now understood to be ' co-
extensive with the whole proceeds of his business, after keeping up
his machinery, buildings and materials, and feeding his family; and
it is expended jointly upon himself and his labourers '.[38] The price of
labour was determined by what the employer had to bid in the labour
market, and in the sense that his fund was seen in the form of his
existing cash and credit balances, and by his personal decision as to
what sum of money would pay him to hire labour, so ' the real limit
to the rise [in wages] is the practical consideration, how much would
ruin him or drive him to abandon the business: not the inexorable
limit of the wage-fund '. So, ' the right and wrong of the proceedings
of trade unions becomes a common question of prudence and social
duty '; i.e. they should refrain from pursuing a selfish or short-sighted
wages policy.[39]

Such qualifications were echoed by the friends of labour, by
Arnold Toynbee and the Webbs,[40] and they possessed immediate
significance for the bargaining power of trade unions. If labour was
not always paid out of the proceeds of past sales, the indeterminate
nature of the capital fund implied that wage rises need not at once or
automatically impinge upon the share of profits. If wages could
depend upon the manner of the production of the national dividend
and its distribution, unions might benefit at the expense of higher
prices to the consumer, by exploiting rising profit margins, rents of
ability or a labour scarcity.

[37] J. S. Mill, *Principles of Political Economy* (W. J. Ashley's edition, 1909) pp. 343-4,
349-50. For a full description of the wage-fund – S. and B. Webb, *Industrial
Democracy* (2nd edn., 1902) Part 3, ch. 1.

[38] Mill, *Principles of Political Economy*, p. 992.

[39] *Ibid.* p. 993.

[40] Toynbee, ' Are Radicals Socialists? ', pp. 114-16. S. and B. Webb, *Industrial
Democracy*, p. 618.

Yet the introduction of such flexibility did not imply any serious breach in capital–labour relationships. In that the emphasis remained upon capital accumulation (savings being automatically rendered into ' productive ' resources), there was an assumed justification for a form of distribution which favoured the saving classes (i.e. the middle classes), and related any income advance amongst the working classes to a gradual but continual increase in the production of material commodities. Given the strong assumptions made regarding the use of income by these two classes, the vital difference between productive and unproductive expenditure, there was no possibility of income being raised by ' artificial ' wage increases which went beyond the limits imposed by the immediate production of marketable wealth. A man could only be paid out of the value of his production – measured by market prices. This was axiomatic: 'How can any man have a *right* to a wage unless he produces something worth the wage, and who is to decide whether his work is worth the wage or not but the people who buy what he makes? ' [41]

The classical emphasis upon the almost-perfect laws of the market remained; omnipotent supply and demand schedules working through a highly responsive price mechanism made the consumers' market peculiarly aware of cost changes, while the disposition of highly mobile capital resources were directed by an equally sensitive interest rate. Wages could not deviate for long away from a ' natural ' equilibrium without resultant changes in either prices or profits causing compensatory movements in the demand for labour which would bring the wage-level back to its point of equilibrium. In this manner, a minimum wage-level could not be figuratively defined, and high wages could only be related to improvements in efficiency, rising profit-levels, and changes in the relative supply of labour. [42] While the economists were prepared to qualify the idea of a predetermined wage-fund, they still believed that there existed a technically-fixed level of employment, related to, and pre-determined by, investment in capital assets, and consequently, that wages could only move within narrow limits. [43]

Marshall, in 1885, considered that the change in wage-theory ' has not been very great. Although a good deal of new work has been

---

[41] W. Smart, *The Living Wage* (Glasgow, 1893) original emphasis. Also A. Marshall, *Elements of the Economics of Industry* (1892) pp. 405 and 406.

[42] W. Smart, *Miners' Wages and the Sliding Scale* (Glasgow, 1894).

[43] A. Marshall, *Economics of Industry*, p. 408.

added and the old work has been developed, yet but very little has been destroyed '. ' There has been a great change, but it has not been in the theory itself, it has been in understanding how it is to be applied.' [44] He sought to redress classical theory by pointing out that remarks concerning population pressing on a finite limit to production (especially on food) were made under a semi-empirical assumption that the law of diminishing returns, especially relevant in the context of the land, would also be prevalent in industry. Hence the classicists' concern for the scarcity of capital, and the importance of securing continued capital resources. The idea of a determinate wage-fund was a ' vulgarisation '. What was really meant was that in the division of production into rent, profits and wages, the reward of labour was linked more or less to a ' profits-fund ' whose security was crucial. If labour saw that its real interest lay in helping to stimulate the productiveness of industry, then in the ensuing competition for resources, the rate of interest would necessarily fall, hence increasing the share of total product which capital was ' compelled to resign to labour '.[45]

Marshall thereby confined the legitimate trade union wage-policy firmly within the limiting factors of the state of trade, state of the labour-market, and the return on capital.

Of course there is a Normal Value about which the wages of each kind of labour tend to fluctuate ... but at any given place (or age), the general relations of the wages of one trade to those of others are determined by the operation of broad causes; and any attempt to keep wages much above or much below their natural level will be opposed by strong natural forces, and will fail.[46]

Any attempt to raise wages nationally, he believed, must involve a policy of restriction, either of hours, or of the supply of labour. Such a policy would diminish profit-margins, reduce incentives to produce, diminish the national dividend, and lower wages and employment. Payment must be proportionate to effort: for wages to keep rising beyond what was due to increased effort, would be an increasingly severe burden to throw upon profits, which would have to finance a higher level of productivity. The interests of production

---

[44] *Report and Proceedings of the Industrial Remuneration Conference* (1885). Appendix D, A. Marshall, ' Theories and Facts About Wages '.

[45] *Ibid.* pp. 189–92.

[46] From A. C. Pigou (ed.), *Memorials of Alfred Marshall* (1925), ' A Fair Rate of Wages ', p. 224.

called for flexible wage-rates; minimum wage-rates, in particular, imposed on industry, would impinge upon the employers' freedom to decide whom they might employ at varying states of trade.[47]

Informed opinion seemed generally close to Marshall's position. A writer like Auberon Herbert could claim in 1891 that the theory of the wage-fund ' has never been substantially shaken ',[48] while the Webbs recorded in 1897 that lingering devotion to wage-fund ideas lay ' at the root of most of the current middle-class objections to Trade Unionism '.[49] Nor is there any reason to believe that ' practical ' business views differed from the academic, and indeed, they may well have been even slower in admitting any flexibility.

In 1877, Sir William Rathbone had foreseen an imminent challenge to British commercial supremacy. The answer, he felt, lay in increasing the savings of the working classes, and he censured a labour audience for an apparent fall in their savings: ' if those who are ... working for weekly wages save so small a proportion of their increased share of the national income, the fund available for wages will be so diminished that serious distress will ensue '. The workers were ' now receiving ... so large a share of the wealth of this country ' that their obligation to save was paramount.[50]

Employers at the 1885 conference took the same view. Sir Thomas Brassey thought ' wages must follow the fluctuations in profits '. He discounted disproportionate capital accumulation through high profits, for the latter attracted competition which would speedily reduce prices and profits to the norm.[51] Sir Lyon Playfair assumed a state of highly elastic demand within the consumers' market, where the least price-change was reflected throughout an industry's sales. ' The selling-price of the commodity is the governing wheel of trade.' Sound wage-increases were the outcome of the security of capital, efficiency, or expanding markets. The tie between effort and reward was crucial; if hours were to be reduced, employers could only pay (for example) for eight hours' work (and interestingly enough, would only hire those who were capable of producing the previous output in the reduced time).[52] These views spanned both parties: Sir Hugh

[47] *Ibid.* also *Economics of Industry*, pp. 386–92

[48] A. Herbert in T. Mackay, *A Plea for Liberty*, p. 392.

[49] S. and B. Webb, *Industry and Democracy*, p. 604.

[50] Sir W. Rathbone, *The Increased Earnings of the Working-Classes* (Liverpool, 1877).

[51] *Report and Proceedings of the Industrial Remuneration Conference*, p. 12.

[52] Sir Lyon Playfair, *Wages and Hours of Labour* (1891).

Bell, analysing the accounts of several companies, thought that as the percentage going to wages was by far the largest single element of cost, even a small percentage wage-rise would involve a far greater, and totally unacceptable, decrease in the return to other factors. He accused the unions of practising restriction of hours and the restraint of trade in attempting to force up wages.[53] Enlightened Liberal employers were beset by the same limitations – Mark Oldroyd reluctantly expressed his belief in 'a practical recognition of the economic laws'. The worker could not claim for more than the amount of labour he expended in increasing the utility of an article – measured at market prices.[54] William Mather, a supporter of an optional eight-hours' law in which wage-increases were justified by increased output, emphasised a labour policy recognising the essential harmony of production.[55] Similar views were held by Radicals like Bradlaugh, who thought all hours legislation undermined profit margins – he believed in voluntary limitations according to the state of trade [56] – and Labouchere, who defended the high income of the commercial classes on the grounds that it formed an essential contribution to 'the entire wage-fund of the country'. The system of competition for resources lowered interest-rates, and the cheaper capital could be obtained, the more there remained for the wage-fund.[57] Bradlaugh also expressed to perfection the Liberal disbelief in the efficacy of state management as certainly inefficient and probably corrupt, and not the least of his case was a refusal to believe that the state could allocate scarce resources or maintain incentives and invent a better system of distribution than could be achieved by the cautious manipulation of the market economy.[58]

Similar views recurred within the Cabinet. Morley was quite content to denounce the complete equality of distribution as 'against human nature', and when he claimed that 'wages are the great master-key of social improvements at this stage', not only an innate individualism but also a belief in the natural authority of the cost–output ratio prevented him from supporting hours limitation.[59]

[53] Sir Hugh Bell, ' The Living Wage ', *National Review*, February 1894.

[54] M. Oldroyd, *A Living Wage* (1894).

[55] W. Mather, ' Labour and the Hours of Labour ', *Contemporary Review*, November 1892.

[56] C. Bradlaugh, *Labour and Law* (1891) pp. 31, 34.

[57] A. Thorold, *Life of Henry Labouchere* (1913) pp. 417–18.

[58] C. Bradlaugh, *Socialism : Fallacies and Dangers* (1887).

[59] J. Morley, *Liberalism and Social Reforms* (1889).

Harcourt too, steeped in the traditions of public economy, differed
little in essentials from Morley.[60]

THE APPROACH TO REFORM: THE LABOUR FACTOR

The rise of a political labour movement in the 1880s is best interpreted in terms of the accumulation of political fragments and
themes which marked the English labour tradition in the nineteenth
century.[61] By the 1880s the labour legacy was being catalysed by at
least three factors whose significance sprang as much from their own
self-evident appearance of permanence as from the varied apprecia-
tions of contemporary observers. The first factor was the re-emerg-
ence and further clarification of the intellectual critique of the
existing order whose origins dated formerly from Owenism and
Chartism and latterly from the critics of Victorian materialism,
Arnold, Ruskin and Morris. This factor is almost inseparable from
the second, namely, the growth of empirical enquiry into the precise
nature of the Victorian order, its premises, its requirements and its
consequences. Such a spirit drew increasingly from the teachings of
positivism, scientific socialism, and from the writings of Henry
George. Thirdly, there was the growing pre-occupation with the
observable consequences of the Victorian order after 1879, with the
phenomena of falling prices, recurrent cycles of unemployment, and
the grim awareness of poverty. Each factor has received a host of
chroniclers, and each possesses its own especial perspective. For
present purposes, therefore, the repetition of familiar ground will be
kept to a minimum, but a working knowledge of the context within
which the Liberal party operated is necessary. The next two sections,
therefore, deal with the rise of an empirical tradition amongst the
labour groupings, and the initial impact of unemployment as a
political issue requiring legislative treatment, the extent of whose
implications amongst the related issues of hours, wages and poverty
provided the substantive case for the argument upon social reform.

The growth of empiricism was ultimately fatal to the kind of
natural, evolutionary laws purveyed by Victorians, but initially, the
rejection of *a priori* reasoning was not always antagonistic to the
prevailing order. Many empiricists wished to support the order, and
accordingly drew heart from the enquiries of Sir Robert Giffen, who

---

[60] A. G. Gardiner, *Sir William Harcourt* (1923) Vol. 1, pp. 229, 232–3.
[61] J. Saville, ' The Background to the Revival of Socialism in England ', *Bulletin
of the Society for the Study of Labour History*, Autumn 1965.

found that ' the " poor " have had almost all the benefit of the great material advance of the last fifty years ', and of Viscount Goschen.[62] Until Arnold Toynbee and Sidney Webb established themselves as authorities, the spirit of empirical enquiry operated in favour of the politically orthodox, and this balance of advantage did not swing quickly as may be gathered from the furious collisions of facts and figures which marked contemporary political encounters, and from the complete denial of reformers' figures not only by their political opponents, but also by government departments.[63] The practical men strongly resented losing the empirical argument, for to lose that argument was to expose one's premises to unwelcome probing. Until the 1890s, at least, the empirical argument had scarcely dented faith in the ' single science ', and knowing that debates about society had been conducted upon its terms for a century, its strength was entirely predictable.[64]

Would-be empirical reformers laboured under the patent unreality which often characterised their associates. Socialism, for example, in the 1880s and 1890s was more a statement of hope and faith than a coherent system. To Hardie, socialism was ' not a system of economics. It is life to the dying people . . . the higher ideal which underlies the socialist movement '.[65] While to Alfred Marshall ' all socialist schemes, which have any claims to be practical, avowedly involve a compromise : they do not venture entirely to dispense with material reward as an incentive to industrial energy; they rely . . . more on the sense of duty '; and Marshall believed in harnessing the strongest human motives, rather than the highest, to the social goal.[66] State socialism was in many ways a reaction to the mythical identity called forth by Spencer between an individualist ethic and Manchesterism. In its attempts to reform the scheme and the assumptions of society, it was political rather than economic. Collectivism involved above all the universal and compulsory application of state power; the socialists assumed economics to be a question of organisation, and before the effect of either education or Marx could be felt,

---

[62] R. Giffen, *The Progress of the Working Classes in the Last Half of the Century* (1884) p. 28. Viscount Goschen, *Essays and Addresses on Economic Questions 1863–1893*, 2 Vols. (1905).

[63] See next section.

[64] Cf. R. L. Meek, *The Rise and Fall of the Concept of the Economic Machine* (Leicester, 1965).

[65] D. Lowe, *From Pit to Parliament* (1923) p. 104.

[66] A. C. Pigou, *Memorials of Alfred Marshall*, pp. 212, 310.

a deeper analysis was simply beyond them. Typical was the romantic socialism of Morris with its emphasis upon fellowship and a vague, communistic ideal : ' so far as Society has any conscious organization, it will be the instrument for the arrangement of labour so as to produce wealth from natural material, and to distribute the wealth when produced without waste of labour '.[67] Or the harmony of Blatchford, ' the new religion of Socialism ', which looked to a tradition of Darwin, Carlyle, Ruskin, Dickens, Thoreau and Walt Whitman.[68] Strands of Christian Socialism, the Labour Church Movement, an older reaction from materialism and inequality, were very typical of socialism as an intellectual force in the 1890s.

English labour thinking as yet placed little weight on Marxian labour value theories; the Fabian Society early rejected abstract labour as the basis of value, and adopted the Jevonian idea of value measured in terms of marginal utility.[69] This idea stressed the inherent tendency for any factor of production to want to secure an exact equation between effort and reward, such that each factor-unit employed would gravitate to its optimum situation of employment.[70] Through Marshall (1891) and Wicksteed (1894) this idea was linked to a substitution effect which was concerned with an employer's attempt to maximise the resources at his disposal in order to obtain an exact balance between the marginal contributions of each factor to production.

The significance of the theory lay in its teaching that no productive agent alone was the single cause of value; the contribution and substitution of each factor within the productive process took place upon the same principles. This dealt a blow to all residual theories of distribution and was instrumental in depicting returns to any factor as due instead to relative supply and demand schedules, and to the conditions governing their operation within the market. The theory of marginal productivity, collectively embodying these ideas, then first marked the demise of those schools of thought associated with the pseudo-panaceas of the single-tax, land nationalisation, and the

---

[67] R. C. K. Ensor (ed.) *Modern Socialism* (1903) p. 82.

[68] Cf. A. Reid (ed.) *The New Party* (1895).

[69] G. Wallas, *Men and Ideas* (1940) pp. 103–4.

[70] I.e. each factor sought to maximise its advantage such that equilibrium was reached when the return (cost) to the final unit of a factor employed was exactly equal to its net contribution to output. In complete equilibrium, the net returns to the last unit of any factors employed would be equal in all uses, and the sum of all returns would exactly exhaust the total product.

wage fund.[71] As theoretical explanations of the process of distribution, these theories (and their supporters) were effectively doomed
to obsolescence before 1914 although Liberalism, at this stage, was
still identified with them, and where both economic orthodoxy and
the English labour tradition were thereafter able to provide themselves with continuing theoretical interpretations of the economic
nature of society, it might be argued that Liberalism found such an
interpretation increasingly elusive.

Although it was the case that Labour rejections of ' economic
man ' were often accompanied by statements that labour deserved
' the full reward ' of its productive services,[72] it was left to H. M.
Hyndman, almost alone, to insist that the reward of labour was
crucially dependent upon the social value of the product.[73] Sidney
Webb totally rejected the Marxian reaction to the apparition of the
pre-determined wage-fund, ' the assumption of the potential illimit-
ability of the class of wages, not stopping short of the entire aggregate product ', and he regarded ' the category of wages, at any rate
in the scientific analysis, as rigidly determinate and limited as the
others. Nor is the result arrived at by any clap-trap as to the product
of labour.'[74] Webb made full use of the marginal approach, aiming
to develop that aspect of the theory which stated that the return to
any factor, in equilibrium, would be equal to its marginal net product. In this respect, his own use of this theory underpinned his
practical suggestions regarding the policy organised Labour should
follow, and may have seemed both more consistent and more
realistic to his associates than the Fabian political record might by
itself otherwise imply.[75]

Marginal productivity, as a theory, was mainly concerned with
relative wage-levels and relative factor rewards. It did not shed much
light upon the aggregate reward of labour, and Marshall's belief
that wages in the long run would tend to equal the net product of
labour offered cold comfort when there was still so little idea of

[71] The theory possibly had little influence before 1914 beyond academic circles.
T. W. Hutchison, *A Review of Economic Doctrines 1870–1929* (Oxford, 2nd
edn., 1962) p. 24.

[72] Cf. A. Morris, *Discussions on Labour Questions* (1890).

[73] H. M. Hyndman, ' The Final Futility of Final Utility ' in *Transactions of the
Political and Economic Circle of the National Liberal Club*, Vol. 2 (1894).

[74] S. Webb, ' On the Relation between Wages and the Remainder of the Economic
Product ' (1889) in R. L. Smyth, *Economics of Socialism and Capitalism*, p. 68.

[75] See A. M. Macbriar, *Fabian Socialism and English Politics 1884–1918* (Cambridge,
1962).

improving the efficiency of labour, and allowing labour to benefit from the resultant improvement in total production. Webb now related the idea that the reward of an entire factor was determined by its utility at the margin of production [76] to an imperfect labour market where unemployment and price competition created a margin governed by the normal return to the unskilled worker. To Webb, this invoked the apparition of ' marginal man ', working for a wage that was just sufficient to maintain him as a viable economic unit, the cost of whose hire did just equal his worth to the productive process (i.e., the Ricardian normal wage, which Marx interpreted as the inevitable ' norm ' of capitalism).

In the market economy, differential advantages, scarcity, rents of ability, might weaken this analysis with regard to local markets, but the prevalence of the unskilled, the casuals, within an industrial system where bargaining strength lay with employers, did set a real drag upon the progress of labour, either collectively or as individuals; ' the ordinary labourer cannot permanently obtain, in a system of competitive wages, more than his potential individual product at the very margin of utilization of land, capital and skill '. In such a situation, productivity increases only benefited the labourer in so far as they raised the margin of utilisation of industry in general, and allowed more employment, more opportunities for better jobs. But so long as wages were regarded simply as a residual or as the one flexible element in total cost, the productivity of the labour force remained incidental. Until a specific policy to raise the margin was applied, aggregate wages could not rise, although in so far as a single union was concerned, the employer's range of choice could be influenced by changes in the quality, quantity and disposition of the labour force available to him.[77]

Yet Webb's diagnosis demonstrated that, collectively, working conditions could not improve without some collective regulation of the labour market, in particular, the regulation of hours and wages. And by the late 1880s the theoretical statement was very closely paralleled by empirical studies of working-class conditions and by trade-union

---

[76] I.e. that the price which obtained for the last unit of the factor employed under the most unfavourable conditions of hire would tend to be the normal prevailing price in the market.

[77] Cf. S. Webb, ' The Rate of Interest ' in *Transactions of the Political and Economic Circle of the National Liberal Club* (1889) Vol. 1. Also E. J. Hobsbawm, ' Custom, Wages and Work-load in Nineteenth Century Industry ' in A. Briggs and J. Saville, *Essays in Labour History* (1960).

experience. From their joint articulation emerged the policy of the minimum and its collectivist overtones.

It has been suggested that to see the 'New Unionism' as a force dating purely from 1888–9 is misleading: trade union outlook had been changing after 1886 as the new methods, machinery and the increasing division of labour constituted a first challenge to the crafts, bringing concern to such moderates as Knight (boilermakers), Mawdsley (cotton-spinners), and Burnett (engineers).[78] It is, indeed, unlikely that the unions had ever accepted *in toto* the economic determinism of the wage-fund, with its inherent hostility to the crucial union concept of a 'just wage'.[79] The older craft unions were cautious in the protection of their own structures; leaders like Howell, Burt and Broadhurst did accept the virtues of the 'indivi-dualistic norm', of thrift and co-operation with the employers, and looked askance at entering into full co-operation with those socialists who had held up their own efforts for ridicule.[80] The older school of union leaders challenged in the 1880s, Burnett and Robert Austin, George Shipton and John Wilson, were dubious of formulating an industrial programme and embarking upon independent labour politics; yet their political quiescence concealed the beginnings of a rift within the industral process between, on the one hand, the orthodox 'business' interpretation, and on the other, the world of labour.

A policy of safety-first, a reluctance to invoke overt political aid for labour except for cases of special helplessness, reluctance to deviate from official Liberal policy – such was the character of the T.U.C. until 1885, at least.[81] But by 1892, quite apart from the dockers, the gas-workers and the general labour unions, it was noticeable how the organised industries were adopting specific economic policies. By 1889, the Amalgamated Railwaymen had a National Programme demanding a guaranteed weekly wage, hours limitation and overtime rates.[82] The formation of the Miners'

[78] A. E. P. Duffy, 'New Unionism in Britain, 1889–90. A Reappraisal', *Economic History Review*, 24 (1961) No. 2.

[79] R. V. Clements, 'British Trade Unions and Popular Political Economy, 1850–1875', *Economic History Rev.*, 24 (1961) No. 1.

[80] E.g. T. Burt, 'Labour in Parliament', *Contemporary Review*, May 1889. (Hours and wages were so closely connected that any reduction in hours would always mean a proportionate diminution in wages); also G. Howell, *Trade Unionism, New and Old* (3rd edn., 1900).

[81] S. and B. Webb, *The History of Trade Unionism* (2nd edn., 1920) p. 369.

[82] P. S. Bagwell, *The Railwaymen* (1963) pp. 132, 149.

Federation of Great Britain heralded the decline of the old National Union and an attack upon the sliding scales, together with the coming of the eight-hours movement. Even the Durham miners, despite Burt and J. Wilson, were challenging a scale which gave them little security of earnings, a challenge culminating in the strike of 1892,[83] while in South Wales a similar strike erupted in 1893. Mann and Burns were making headway amongst the engineers, criticising the leadership of Austin and Anderson. Within the T.U.C., although traditional loyalty beat off Hardie's challenge to Broadhurst, 1887–90, and the challenge to Fenwick in 1892–3, the speakers displayed a tendency to favour positive legislative action. In 1887, the President, Bevan, condemned ' the unrestrained, unscrupulous and remorseless forces of capitalism ', and called for support for state intervention in a speech which might fairly be described as typical.[84] A definitive measure of land nationalisation was passed in 1887, the miners' eight-hours day in 1889, a complete eight-hour day in 1890, and the complete collectivist programme in 1894.

The significance of the clash between the skilled ' aristocrats ' of labour and the unskilled remains arguable, but it does seem that the clash involved a real difference between the old unionists and the new over the desirability of a more aggressive labour policy. Two views of the industrial process were involved, each view being a product of a particular stage of development in the market economy. The older generation saw the T.U.C. as ' a federation for obtaining, by parliamentary action, not social reform generally, but the particular measures desired by its constituent trade unions '. It saw advances as dependent upon industrial conditions largely outside its control, and it saw each industry separately. Mann, Tillett and Thorne differed because they were concerned with aggregate distribution in the entire labour market, and saw the impossibility of any general improvement in conditions unless there was action on a market-wide scale, literally collective in scope. They realised, with Webb, the essential interdependence of labour, the effect of the marginals (or casuals) upon the prevailing wage, and the unity within the many-headed problem of poverty. In essence, the significance of the labour debate of the late 1880s lay in the change in scale that was

83 G. Best, *Bishop Westcott and the Miners* (Bishop Westcott Memorial Lecture, Cambridge, 1966).

84 B. Roberts, *The T.U.C., 1868–1921* (1958) pp. 117–18.

being discussed. And the change in turn was eased and gained an impetus from the emerging consciousness of a common problem.[85]

For the older trade unionists, the orthodox teachings that labour was to be seen as 'cost', that wages were the one predominantly flexible element in the cost structure, rested on certain assumptions remaining relevant. For the skilled, it assumed an average rise in real earnings over time, such that a worker, with the help of his trade society, could protect himself against periods of misfortune or declining wage rates provided such periods were periodic and not endemic. This suggested a labour market which balanced uncertainty due to trade fluctuations against the security of knowing that certain skills could always claim a more or less certain reward. The artisan's reliance upon a trade society, especially in regard to old age, also suggested a certain stability amongst occupations, such that a work-man might expect to earn a constant livelihood extending over many years. This implied his ability to secure some say in the determination of his working conditions, perhaps through exploiting a scarcity or local monopoly, while a union of skilled men might reckon to indulge in some restrictionism to maintain a stable relationship between the supply of capital and the demand for labour within an industry. For the unskilled, it was of more importance that the conditions for labour mobility existed; not only in travel, but in the existence of housing or lodgings at reasonable prices. It might also require a certain reservoir of jobs to which they could turn – the railways, the docks and hitherto, the seasonal demands of agriculture.

In the last quarter of the nineteenth century, significant economic structural changes were undermining such assumptions. 'The sur-vival into the second half of the nineteenth century of the conditions of domestic industry . . . had an important consequence for industrial life and the industrial population which is too seldom appreciated. It meant that not until the last (twenty-five years) did the working-classes begin to assume the homogeneous character of a factory pro-letariat.' After 1875 the final decline of 'the individualist traditions of the artisan and the craftsman, with the ambition to become himself a small employer', removed another obstacle to the wider growth of trade unionism.[86]

[85] Cf. E. J. Hobsbawm, *Labour's Turning Point 1880–1900* (1948); H. Pelling, *Popular Politics and Society in Late Victorian Britain* (1968) p. 37. Also T. Mann and B. Tillett, *The 'New' Trades-Unionism* (1890).

[86] M. Dobb, *Studies in the Development of Capitalism* (1947) pp. 265–6.

The collective impact of such changes may have been considerable. Between 1881 and 1901, the population grew from 25·9 million to 32·5 million, and whereas in 1851 half of the population lived in towns, by 1901 the figure had risen to 77 per cent.[87] The 1891 census discovered chronic overcrowding in the towns; over one-tenth of the population lived two or more to a room while in London this figure rose to one-fifth, and on the north-east coast to one-third. This resulted in pressure on working-class rents. A survey in 1893 of 30,000 working-class dwellings found the average rent to be 23·5 per cent of income, a disproportionately high figure.[88] Between 1881 and 1911, there were marked changes taking place in the occupational distribution of workers, a great growth of employment occurring in mining, public utilities and commercial categories, and marked falls in agriculture, textiles and amongst general workers.[89] Social distress received increasing publicity throughout the 1880s, with estimated figures of those affected creeping inexorably upwards. Giffen reported in 1885 that 82·6 per cent of adult male labourers were earning less than 30s a week, and whatever benefits the working classes may have gained from falling commodity price levels, these could scarcely qualify Booth's conclusion that working-class conditions were utterly miserable.[90]

Whatever the economic reality of the great depression, the bitter experience of unemployment brought home to trade unionism the weaknesses of their position. In particular the ideas of the ' standard rate ' and the ' normal day ', which together formed the bargaining reality behind the expression ' a fair day's wage for a fair day's work ', were threatened by the competitive downward-forcing of wages. Increasingly, the unions found it difficult to gain recognition for their semi-empirical, semi-normative concept of a ' just wage ', and justice itself seemed alien to the mechanisms of the market economy.[91] From the 1880s, the older unions came under pressure from further mechanisation, a greater division of labour and the consequent encroachment of semi-skilled grades upon the position of the skilled. Such was the experience of the iron trades, shipbuilding

---

87 T. J. Marshall, ' The Population of England and Wales ', *Economic History Review*, 5 April 1935.

88 W. Smart, *The Living Wage* (Glasgow, 1893).

89 D. C. Jones, ' Some Notes on the Census of Occupations for England and Wales ', *Journal of the Royal Statistical Society*, January 1915.

90 Cf. M. Bruce, *The Coming of the Welfare State* (1961).

91 S. and B. Webb, *Industrial Democracy*, pp. 281–3.

and the boot and shoe industry. Equally, unions were under a continual pressure to extend hours, which they resisted on the grounds that the corollary was a reduction in standard rates when employers saw that earnings could be made up by men working longer hours. They were opposed to the increased demand made for payment by results which threw the emphasis in many craft industries from time-rates to piece-wages, or to time-rates with premiums and bonuses attached specifically to stimulate output.[92] Unions disliked the tendency for the standard to be set according to the fastest man, with the ensuing claim by employers that the earnings of the exceptional represented the average wage for the industry. Such a system, they claimed, undermined quality and skill, used men up too quickly, and had a severe effect in undermining the level of security within a given employment. The Webbs noted a tendency, as mechanisation spread, for craftsmen and workers of intermediate skills who previously had enjoyed a degree of liberty in the time and place of their employment to turn increasingly to the device of the ' normal day ' in an attempt to strengthen their bargaining position. The attempt by employers to attain a highly exact relationship between work and pay, called forth complaints that the ' quantum ' of output demanded in return for the weekly wages kept increasing, thereby ' nibbling ' again at the average level of earnings.[93]

By the 1880s, the infringement of the ' normal day ' in part foreshadowed the coming disputes over hours. Union opposition to overtime hardened; the employers' demand for flexibility in the face of competition was seen as a device for extorting more work from the men, who, once dependent on overtime earnings, lost the protection of the ' standard rate '. ' Built-in ' overtime evaded the checks of the factory inspectors; employers could make a practice of encouraging it to offset fixed costs and minimise charges resulting from idle machinery.[94] Long hours and the exhaustion of the labour force, together with increasing unemployment, led the unions into the ' fallacy of the fixed work-fund ', the idea that the amount of

---

[92] D. F. Schloss, *Methods of Industrial Remuneration* (3rd edn. revised, 1898) p. 87.

[93] D. F. Schloss, *Industrial Remuneration*, p. 59. An enquiry into skilled trades in Liverpool in 1894 found that all preferred the certainty of regular weekly wages, and most made attempts to equalise the distribution of work in order to attain it. (*Commission of Inquiry into the Unemployment of Liverpool*, 1894; Beveridge Collection on Unemployment, Vol. 2.)

[94] S. and B. Webb, *Industrial Democracy*, pp. 345-6.

work available at any time was both known and limited, and that in the interests of security of employment and of earnings, it had better be shared by as many men as possible.[95] This was vigorously attacked by economists and business men as implying a restriction upon output, which could only reduce aggregate earnings in the long run.[96]

The 1885 Industrial Conference revealed trade unionists emphatic in their scepticism towards semi-official estimates of wages and possible rises in standards of living. Giffen's figures were repudiated by Ben Jones of the Co-operative Wholesale Society, and by Mrs Ellis, of the Huddersfield pattern weavers; James Lynch from shipbuilding, W. G. Bunn from The Hearts of Oak, and G. Sedgwick of the boot and shoe industry condemned mechanisation, the subdivision of labour, the spread of home-labour, the undermining of the crafts, and the emphasis upon piece-rates. They and Mawdsley protested their instability of earnings, while Mawdsley considered co-operative production to be a failure and H. W. Rowland of the Cabbies disliked Marshall's moralistic attitude towards unemployment. Toyne of the Miners' National Union supported John Burns in rejecting official calls for harmony in capital–labour relationships, and Burnett, speaking for the T.U.C. parliamentary committee, said he and his colleagues believed the existing system to be derisory; any reward labour gained, it had to fight for.[97]

The same complaints were made with similar force ten years later, relating now to the breaking down of the old crafts, the tendency for boys at machines to replace skilled men and the continual passage of semi-skilled youths or young men into the casual labour market. A goldsmith condemned the ' intolerable ' team-system and the decline in quality. A book-binder spoke of ' commercialism ', a wood-engraver disliked the onset of steam-printing. Steadman in shipbuilding and Swift of the engineers were pessimistic over the implications of mechanisation.[98] Evidence before the 1894 Royal Commission on Labour revealed a uniform demand for greater stability in earnings, although there was little support for a ' General Act ' to regulate wages – it was admitted that a fixed minimum would tend to increase unemployment, but there was a great deal of

---

95 Cf. J. Burnett (Report and Proceedings, p. 166): ' Every man who works over-time 4 quarter-days takes away a day's work from another man.'
96 A. Marshall, Economics of Industry, p. 380.
97 Report and Proceedings of the Industrial Remuneration Conference, passim.
98 F. W. Galton, Workers on their Industries (1895) pp. ix–x.

Labour thinking in favour of measures to improve the security of the wage-earners' position – employers' liability, a more systematic enforcement of the Factory Acts, the prevention of excessive hours and the regulation of employment. The Minority Report, signed by W. Abraham, T. Mann, Mawdsley and Michael Austin indicated a basic consensus amongst trade unionists for a single department of Labour, legislation against sweating, an eight-hour day in government employment and dangerous trades, and a general condemnation of private profit as the sole motive in a competitive system.[99]

Undoubtedly there was a growing disposition amongst Unions to challenge the employers' *diktat* regarding the manner of employment and the conditions of work. They objected, for example, to competitive employers arranging forward contracts at low prices (particularly in the mines). In 1886, the Window–Glass Workers stated that such a practice meant the employers were 'legally pilfering a portion off each of their workers' weekly earnings'.[100] Unions opposed the lowering of prices as a cure for general depression; the only effect was that one employer engrossed a portion of existing demand from another – total product stayed the same.

If the unskilled were making a first challenge to the conditions which condemned them to perpetual 'marginalism', the older unions were more concerned with the issues posed by the changing scale of capitalism,[101] and in attempting to strengthen the 'normal day' and the 'just wage', there might not have seemed a very great gap between these concepts and their socialist equivalents, the eight-hours bill and the living wage.[102] The Webbs based their device of the national minimum upon the broader definition of the 'common rule' and its extension throughout industry. It was a device to secure labour efficiency and bargaining strength. Embracing a physical sufficiency wage, minima of hours, education, leisure and sanitation, the 'minimum' was intended to demonstrate to employer and

---

[99] T. G. Spyers, *The Labour Question : A Digest of the Evidence to the Royal Commission on Labour* (1894) p. 52.

[100] S. and B. Webb, *Industrial Democracy*, p. 444.

[101] E.g. the engineers' strike, a skilled union disturbed by recurrent unemployment and attempting to re-assert some influence over hours, machines, etc. (Marshall feared the effects of a union victory upon the economy.) R. O. Clarke, 'The Dispute in the British Engineering Industry 1897–98', *Economica,* n.s. May 1957.

[102] E.g. *Socialism and Trade-Unionism : Wherein Do they Differ ?*, Socialist Group of the London Society of Compositors 1897.

union alike that their real interest lay in the regulation and organisation of the market – above all, of the labour market. Personal interest
could not always be best secured by a person enjoying a position of
relative security, since it was precisely because security was, at best,
only relative, that the market could only maintain a few in comfort,
and these few had often little economic claim to be so maintained.
To create a ' minimum ' throughout the market would be to eliminate the inefficient, the sweated and the casuals, to end the continual
under-rating of labour, to transfer competition to the quality of
production rather than to prices and wages, to provide a spur to
technical progress as a means to reducing costs, and to ensure that
wages based upon the principle of utility would provide a continual
incentive to improvement; a price for the man instead of a man for
the price. The whole community may, ' by a persistent and systematic use of the device of the common rule, secure an indefinite,
though of course not an unlimited rise in its standard of life '.[103]
As contempt for materialism merged in scorn for commercialism, so
' the desire for cheapness, and the great mass of unskilled labour in
the market, fight against the trade unionist ideal of the living wage.
Yes! The living wage that is proclaimed from the pulpits of the
churches now is only the old trade union doctrine of a minimum
wage, coming back to us in another form '.[104]

THE APPROACH TO REFORM: UNEMPLOYMENT

The empirical argument was a powerful stimulus to change, not only
because it gradually excluded the alternatives to legislative intervention, but because it exposed contrasts; in particular, it contrasted the
experience of one class with the increasingly doubtful assumptions of
another, and the keening of this contrast supplied sharpness to the
political confrontations. The intensity of experience, and the intensity
of personal involvement, gave the cause of reform its inspiration and
turned the commitment to reform into a major test of political
sincerity.

For Liberals, the factual argument could affect their sense of what
was practicable, but in the early 1890s the party had not developed the
same sense of commitment which was to be displayed by an
important wing of the party after 1906. To be fair, this would also
apply to early Fabianism. Moral indignation was no substitute for

---

103 S. and B. Webb, *Industrial Democracy*, p. 795 (original emphasis).
104 Quoted by Galton, *Workers on their Industries*, p. 150.

passion, and Mrs Webb was a very different political animal to Annie Besant. In a highly emotional period, to divorce facts from feelings could seem not only insincere but sterile, and the Liberals' deliberate and cautious approach between 1892–5 contrasted strongly with the optimism of reformers. The party's aloofness, which amounted almost to a sense of embarrassment, of being surprised on stage when the curtain went up, was illustrated in their initial attitude towards the unemployment issue.

Necessarily, the Liberal response must be seen within the wider context of unemployment, deterrence and the Poor Law. In 1892, responsibility for the unemployed still lay with the Local Government Board (L.G.B.) and the Poor Law Guardians, but the previous unity of the Poor Law was in the process of modification. The major obstacle in the way of any change in the treatment of the unemployed lay in the opposition to increasing the provision for out-relief as this, it was thought, might amount to condoning the position of the unemployed who should rather be encouraged to lift themselves out of their own unfortunate predicament. The work-house test, whereby anyone actually prepared to perform certain stringent tasks within the work-house was adjudged to be in real need of relief, specifically discouraged out-relief. The able-bodied and their families might be relieved out of the work-house if they were prepared to perform some acceptable task, such as stone-breaking, to indicate their utter destitution, but if a person refused such a task he could be deemed idle and disorderly and punished accordingly. In some agricultural districts and small towns an outdoor relief prohibition order applied which forbade all forms of out-relief.[105]

Since 1886, it had been admitted that the local sanitary authorities might hire men for some nominal wage, from the unemployed, upon such schemes as it lay in their power to perform; the making of roads and bridges, and in London the care of parks and hospitals. The circular calling for the provision of such work, first issued by Chamberlain in 1886, was re-issued by both Fowler and Shaw-Lefevre. However, the Guardians were not allowed to finance such schemes from the Poor Rate, even though such expenditure was with a view to reducing the numbers who would otherwise apply for poor relief in the usual manner. All expenditure by the local

---

[105] Cf. Sir H. Owen, ' The Powers and Duties of Guardians ', *Third Report from the Select Committee on Distress from Want of Employment* (1895) Parl Papers, Reports from Committees (3) Vol. IX.

authorities for schemes of work had to be sanctioned by the L.G.B., which was scarcely extravagant.

As long as it was natural to look for causes of poverty in the man rather than in society, the system worked, for the assumptions of individualism coupled with the stigma of poverty together furnished the moral Plimsoll line above which everyone strove to remain. Under these assumptions, categories of the unemployed were classi-fied on strong moral grounds – ' the workless, the thriftless and the worthless '. As unemployment was, for the individual, a state assumed to be transitory and one determined by natural, seasonal, causes, then the minimum of interference with its causes and con-ditions was the order of the day, for quite apart from the cost of the interference: ' to undertake unnecessary and expensive works to provide precarious employment for the unemployed would tend to bring about the disorganization of labour, the thriftlessness and the shiftlessness. . . .'' [106]

By the late 1880s, the growth of empirical investigations had begun to underpin the formulation of a demand that unemployment be seen, not as an individual aberration caused by personal, moral deficiencies, but as a social aberration, the outcome of measurable socio-economic factors. Unemployment was beginning to emerge as a distinctly new theme of social anxiety, linked to the plight of the unskilled and individual insecurity within the market economy, calling for further information, for a Department of Labour, for a new emphasis upon out-relief and public works, and in general, culminating in a demand that legislative action be taken to counteract the wastage of industrialism. Sidney Webb was able to provide statistics to counter the charge of thriftlessness; one-third of the paupers were children, one-tenth were insane, half were infirm or aged. The rising cost of the Poor Law helped to bring about its own re-appraisal. The overall cost, which had been running (annually) at some £5 million in the 1880s, passed £10 million in the early 1890s and had risen to £14 million by 1905. Concern at such figures was reflected in attempts by the Charity Organisation Society (C.O.S.) to commend as ideals those poor-law unions, Brixworth, Bradfield and St Georges-in-the-East, which had almost entirely abolished out-relief within their limits. And it was reflected in governmental fears of incurring fresh expenditure upon schemes, such as relief works, which might be purely alleviatory. As the

106 *The Times*, 13 December 1893.

recognition grew that much Poor-Law expenditure was wasteful, and as working-men themselves were able to be elected as Guardians after 1894, so the utility of the Poor-Law system was exposed to increasing attack.[107]

From the relief of pauperism, informed opinion began to consider the relief of poverty, and after 1885 came a progressive relaxation in the previously strict administering of Poor-Law rules. By 1893, the Board of Trade was clear that the phrase 'unemployed' was a highly complex one composed of several distinct categories. To the incapable and sub-standard groups with their moralistic connotations was added the problem of seasonal, cyclical and short-term trade fluctuations which affected the 'steady and capables'. And to these were added further problems of underemployment, casual labour at the docks, the twilight of the apprenticeship system, and the multiplicity of men without training, education or hope. In 1894 came the first official admission that it was no longer to be assumed that an able-bodied man could generally be relied upon to find work to support himself and his family,[108] and in 1895 the select committee report supported this view. Yet still officialdom dispatched remedies with unceasing regularity. An 1893 report made an extensive survey of foreign farm and labour colonies, and discovered that permanent labour colonies usually became receptacles for 'undesirables'; 76 per cent of the inmates of German colonies, it was noted, had been imprisoned. Temporary relief works were justified as long as they too did not encourage the work-shy, and while some attempts to distribute public work to counteract fluctuations in the seasonal demand for labour were justified, 'measures of prevention rather than cure' were to be preferred. Labour bureaux had a limited function, being least useful when the need was greatest and providing no answer for the unemployables. The real problem was how to prevent 'the economic deterioration of the casually and insufficiently employed', and 'any proposal which sets out with the idea that the evils resulting from want of employment are capable of immediate remedy on a large scale should ... be regarded with the greatest caution '.[109] This was very much the attitude of the 1894 Labour

---

[107] M. Bruce, *The Coming of the Welfare State* (1961) p. 86.

[108] *Report on the Unemployed of Scotland*, C7410, LXX, 1894.

[109] *Board of Trade Report on Agencies and Methods for Dealing with Unemployment*, C7182, LXXXII, 1893. See also *The Government Organisation of Unemployed Labour*, published by the Fabian Society, 1886. (Copy in the British Library of Political Science.)

Commission, which concentrated a little more upon questions of hours regulations and municipal employment, both of which the Majority Report, however, rejected as remedies, preferring to see unemployment as an economic adjunct of the existing theory of production and therefore as incapable of serious treatment:

> It is work which creates demand for work, and diminished production cannot cause any general absorption of the unemployed without either trenching on the wages of those employed already or diminishing the rate of profits and interest to an extent that will recoil on the working-classes themselves.[110]

The Minority Report fought shy of such issues, preferring to treat them as one with the issue of the eight-hour day, agitation for a single department of labour, the control of casual labour and the payment of trade union wages in such public works as existed.

The Liberals did establish one Select Committee on unemployment, which reported in 1895. With regard to remedies, Keir Hardie suggested financing relief works equally between a special (local) rate and a government subvention, while John Benn suggested, for London, that all relief should be a charge on a Common Poor Fund. In its Third Report, the Committee were agreed that the Guardians should be empowered to agree with any sanitary authority within their Union that in consideration of the latter employing a certain number of the unemployed, the Guardians would contribute up to half the cost of such employment. The report also saw suggestions for a small tax to be levied by municipal authorities upon ground values, to provide a fund applicable to permanent public improvements; for governments to grant loans free of interest during exceptional distress; for afforestation and roads, for some machinery to assist men in finding work, for public grants to voluntary agencies for the relief of distress, and a whole series of measures, ranging from old age pensions and the sale of food below cost, to emigration, allotments, and swifter loans from the L.G.B.[111]

Such proposals did represent some advance in the climate of opinion by 1895, although the Liberal party was defeated before it could consider actual legislation. Nevertheless, their response had been cool –

---

110 *Fifth and Final Report of the Royal Commission on Labour*, C7421, xxxv, June 1894.

111 *Third Report from the Select Committee upon Distress from Want of Employment*. See especially Appendix 33, a summary of proposals by the Chairman, Sir Henry Campbell-Bannerman.

their fears regarding the economic and political implications of intervention outweighing their knowledge of distress. Official opinion, moreover, as represented by Sir Hugh Owen remained sceptical. Owen believed the Guardians had already sufficient powers to grant relief, and opposed Exchequer grants-in-aid to municipalities for relief works. He denied that it was the duty of any public department to provide work for the unemployed; the work-house test, he said, operated in the interests of the rate-payers (a point of view which remained that of J. S. Davey).[112] The officials refused to credit Hardie's figures for the unemployed. The Board of Trade thought it 'quite misleading' to suggest that the percentage unemployed amongst trade unionists was an accurate guide for the whole working population: Llewellyn-Smith suggested that the character of the trades, and their respective rates of fluctuation in their own labour-demands defeated Hardie's simple averages. At a time (January 1895) when the percentage of unemployed trade unionists was approximately seven, and at a time when Hardie was insisting there were a million unemployed, Smith claimed that 'the percentage of unemployed spread over the whole field of industry is probably not over three, giving roughly ... 300,000 adults out of about 10 million adult workers'. However, having regard to the evidence of various unemployment registers and local authorities, the Board of Trade eventually decided on a figure of 150,000 'as our outside limit; a large body of persons, it is true, when taken in the aggregate, but inconsiderable when scattered over so vast an area. The figure is certainly over-stated'.[113] The 1895 Committee found 44 per cent of the total population making returns complained of severe distress, much of it due to a severe winter.

The fact that ministers received this kind of information is some excuse, but at the L.G.B. neither Fowler nor Shaw-Lefevre gave much indication of any difference of opinion with their officials. In April 1895, Hardie pointed out that the Rotherham Board of Guardians were paying men upon relief works only 7d a day, with 2d a day for wife and each child. Shaw-Lefevre refused to interfere. In the same month, the Conservative member for Wandsworth, Kimber, pointed out a certain reform was necessary in his constituency. Under the Local Government Act of 1888, the parishes and unions of London were allowed a grant of 4d a day for each indoor pauper,

112 *Ibid.* pp. 929–32.
113 Cabinet Memorandum, Cab. 37/38, 8 January 1895 (Public Record Office).

the limit for such payments being calculated on a certificate based on the average number of indoor poor so maintained during the five years previous to 25 March 1888. In Wandsworth and Clapham, the average was 1,624, whereas by 1893 the actual number chargeable was over 2,800. Would Shaw-Lefevre amend the necessary certificate, as he had the power to do? Shaw-Lefevre refused to intervene on the grounds of insufficient information. Furthermore, he refused to prepare a digest of the statutes relating to the Poor Law for this ' would require a great amount of time and labour '.[114]

By the early 1890s, the debate upon unemployment had begun both to clarify the nature of future political debate upon the manner and the scale of legislative intervention, and to catalyse trade union opposition to the orthodox interpretation of the market economy. Within this dual context, the reaction of the Liberal party to the demand for reform has to be seen as involving (at least) a two-fold response. First, there was the implicit conflict between the behavioural assumptions of individualism, respect for the established practices of the constitution and the deliberative, responsive qualities of legisla-tion; and the need to assert a concept of social or collective responsi-bility, in which the government would undertake the conscious direction of change, together with a positive, deterministic approach (rather than evolutionary) to the pursuit of progress. Secondly, there was the more explicit conflict between the orthodox theory of pro-duction which stressed saving and the sanctity of capital, managerial freedom of production, labour-as-cost and flexible wage-rates, and the trade union repudiation, based on experience, of the assumptions of perfect competition, and their ensuing demand for minima of wages, hours and working conditions to be imposed by legislation upon the market, not only for their own good, but as an essential condition of the market's own progress. Furthermore, the union challenge, while amounting to a repudiation of ' individualism ' in name, was not a challenge dependent upon a sharp antithesis between a systematic individualism and a fully-fledged collectivism. Theirs was a challenge to individualist assumptions and to the economic and social conditions which harboured them; a demand for a changing scale of political activity and governmental responsibility. This was a demand to which the Liberals with their variety of internal influences, Utilitarians, empiricists, humanitarians and individualists, but with a lack of any one overriding influence, could adjust. But as a party,

114 Parl. Deb., 4th Series, V32, C571, C581, C918, 1 and 4 April 1895.

such adjustment needed time, needed changes in the composition of the party, needed conscious enquiry into the meaning of familiar catchwords, ' social harmony ' and ' the balanced constitution '. The Liberals were faced with an economic problem in politics which was an entirely new phenomenon. Unlike the Conservatives, they were quicker to admit its existence; but to explain their caution in terms of a single, simple, factor is to miss the essence of the very complicated, semi-empirical, semi-normative debate in which all political activity was enmeshed before the first world war.

2

The Liberals in Office 1892-5

In July 1892, the Liberals and their Irish allies gained a majority of 40 over the 315 Conservatives and Liberal Unionists. The majority was a small one, dependent upon the umbilical cord of Home Rule and open to a host of speculative interpretations. If the Home Rule policy occupied the first place in politics, the amorphous bulk of the social problem constituted, after Newcastle, a strong contender for second place. The test questions had already emerged. The entry of local Labour associations into politics had brought widespread attempts to secure fair-wage clauses in local contracts,[1] and the Liberals faced an articulate demand that the government create a precedent in the struggle for wage-justice by establishing minimum wages in government departments. Wages were further entwined with the issue of hours, particularly in the case of the miners whose demand for an eight-hour day was now strong enough for them to expect legislative attention. Labour leaders placed a heavy emphasis upon hours' legislation in general: 'the legal eight-hour day is the grappling-iron between the competition of today and the co-operation of the future '.[2] The Liberals, however, were concerned with the implications of such legislation, for in 1892, social reforms for the working classes were not yet identical with the claims of labour.[3] Social reform involved measures that were recognisably national, were not the single prerogative of a political party and were open to discussion by men of goodwill on all sides of the political spectrum. Whereas the claims of labour were not only economic in nature, so arousing the susceptibilities of a particular (propertied) class, but implied a new emphasis upon sectionalism and self-interest which was unwelcome to traditional Liberal views upon disinterested government.[4] According to Burns, ' the worker today has no politics but what is embodied in his own material interest '. According to the Liberals, such materialism

---

[1] Cf. H. A. Clegg, Fox and Thompson, *A History of British Trade Unions Since 1889* (Oxford, 1964) Vol. 1, pp. 287–8.
[2] John Burns at Battersea, October 1891 in JBP, Add. Mss 46305 f. 131.
[3] E.g. S. Buxton in the *Daily Chronicle*, 2 July 1892, who made a firm distinction between the two.
[4] JBP, Add. Mss 46305 f. 95.

suggested an inadequate appreciation of the nature of political
activity.

Possibly, Labour programmes and candidates caused most distaste
amongst grass-roots Liberalism, but there was a general fear of being
stampeded by essentially ephemeral agitations into adopting measures
harmful to the community's own long-term prosperity. It was impossible to divorce Labour politics from the intellectual haziness of
socialist schemes whose authors ' seem like men telling their dreams
of the night, forgotten almost as soon as told '. There was a fear of the
intangible. ' While Socialism is everywhere, no system of it is erect.
Each new scheme is ephemeral. How many have we seen since 1848?
Is any, or none, the correct solution for present problems? ' [5] Hence
the hope among Liberal reformers that, by continuing with their
traditional emphasis upon electoral reform, by promoting the gradual
absorption of Labour within a more democratic political process,
there would take place a clarification of Labour's thought and ideals,
and a willingness on their part to work within the existing institutions. This would then make it possible to deal with those claims
which could be contained in a practical social programme.

The Liberal party after 1886 had moved some way to familiarise
itself with the social problem. Among their several legacies they
numbered policies for free land and allotments, and a growing
acquaintance with the ideas of Henry George, while in A. J.
Mundella and Arthur Dyke Acland they possessed two champions
of free education. The tenor of the 1885 Radical Programme stayed
within Liberal ranks, especially the suggestions for taxation reform
in order that ' the taxation of the future ought to take the character of
insurance, or of investments for the general welfare '. Liberals like
Haldane stressed a fulfilment of the just obligations of property, and
if the Tories had grievously anticipated them over free education,
small holdings and local government reform, still there were
measures for democratising parish councils, unifying London, and
for paying M.P.s.[6] Within the Liberal Reviews and the Press there
was no lack of enthusiastic discussion. Not only was there an exceptionally able school of Liberal journalists, H. W. Massingham,
W. T. Stead, J. A. Spender, C. P. Scott and T. P. O'Connor, but
the columns were freely available to advanced writers of all opinions,
Hardie, Burns, Webb, Champion and Harrison. Francis Channing

[5] *The Speaker*, 10 May 1890.
[6] R. B. Haldane, ' The Liberal Creed ', *Contemporary Review*, October 1888.

was later to claim that after the debacle of 1886, the Liberals in and outside the new parliament worked out ' in practical proposals ' ' every item of our programme ... visibly going to the root of each question '.[7] This was, perhaps, an exaggeration. Certainly, there were areas and sections where new ideas were discussed, but not all were consistent and their collective influence was much diffused.

J. A. Spender later claimed that the emergence of policy, 1886–92, was due to the National Liberal Federation rather than to the leadership, and to ' unofficial members of the party in and out of Parliament '.[8] One such ' unofficial ' group was that of Asquith, Grey, Acland, Haldane, Tom Ellis, Sydney Buxton, Augustine Birrell and Frank Lockwood, who dined together periodically and worked in concert preparing amendments to bills. Through Hudson, and through Spender's friendship with Acland and Ellis, the group was linked to the Federation and to the Press, while through Hudson's friendship with the Lib-lab James Rowlands, they gained a contact with Labour problems. Through Haldane, they were further in touch with the Fabians [9] while via Buxton they were linked to ideas for financial reform and the ' fair wage ' movement. All nominally counted as friends of Labour; Acland had links with the Co-operative Movement, had been a supporter of the ' Unauthorized Programme ' and was an early advocate of old-age pensions. Buxton was an adviser of the dockers during the strike of 1889. Lockwood was apparently willing to retire in favour of a Labour candidature at York, and regarded the Labour vote as the backbone of Liberalism.[10]

Yet their reservations were as significant as their admissions. Buxton supported the eight-hour measure only with the clause for trade-option attached and Haldane, the self-avowed ideas-man of the group,[11] was totally opposed to the measure, thinking the real aim of its supporters was to raise wages rather than to regulate hours. He was equally opposed to granting government employees legislative limitations upon their hours, quoting John Morley with approval: ' the tax-paying workmen elsewhere would ... complain that they were paying for the extra comfort of their fellow labourers '. He

---

[7] F. Channing, *Memories of Midland Politics* (1918) p. 67.

[8] J. A. Spender, *Sir Robert Hudson* (1930) pp. 18–19.

[9] But John Morley wrote to Haldane: ' The Fabians interest and suggest, but they are loose, superficial, crude and impertinent ', Haldane Mss 5903, 28 September 1891, f. 190.

[10] Sir E. Hamilton papers, Add. Mss 48658, 17 June 1892.

[11] R. B. Haldane, *Autobiography* (1929) pp. 92–3.

emphasised voluntary combination and clearly formed demands; 'politicians must be not only idealists but men of business'.[12]

It is possible that Liberal Social Radicalism at this stage saw its task in terms of administrative reform, rather than in extensive legislative enactments. *The Speaker* was quite happy to condemn 'that most wooden of all bureaucracies – the Local Government Board', and speaking of working-class hatred of the Poor Law, to describe it as 'the most serious impediment to thrift and good citizenship at present at work in the English social organism'. It could review Hobson's *Problems of Poverty* most favourably, and be gratifyingly scornful of Mackay's *Plea for Liberty*. Liberals, it thought, have 'profoundly modified their principles of action; but they cling to their old language'. Laissez-faire had served its purpose, now it was simply a rule of thumb – although something equally useful would have to replace it.[13]

Since defeat in 1886, Liberalism had undergone more or less continuous exposure to comprehensive suggestions for internal reform put forward by various 'advanced' bodies. Apart from explicitly socialist programmes, the most detailed was that printed by *The Star* on 8 August 1888, as 'The London Programme', which incorporated, initially for the London Progressives, all the measures characteristic of 'Labour' politics by this time, including the taxation to extinction of rent and interest, taxation reform, a minimum wage and a maximum working-day, factory legislation, Poor Law reform, universal pensions, temporary relief works for the unemployed, municipal housing policies and compulsory land acquisition powers for local authorities. All that was missing, in fact, was the socialist clause for nationalisation. These demands were endorsed by the Metropolitan Radical Federation, that association of London Radical Clubs which was a somewhat more advanced body than its counterpart, the London Liberal and Radical Union. *The Star's* programme was given further publicity by the Fabians, notably in Sidney Webb's broadsheet *Wanted : A Programme* which was printed for private circulation among leading London Liberals. In the same year (1888) the London Liberals agreed on a joint policy with J. B. Firth's Municipal Reform Union, forming the basis of the London Progressive Alliance, with the main emphasis upon a programme of

---

[12] R. B. Haldane, 'The Eight-Hours Question', *Contemporary Review*, February 1890.

[13] *The Speaker*, 25 October 1890; 1 August and 21 February 1891.

extensive municipalisation.[14] A last point of contact between the
Progressives, Fabians and London Liberal M.P.s was the London
Reform Union, whose secretary was Tom Mann and whose body
included George Barnes and W. C. Steadman, Ben Tillett and
Sidney Webb, and from the Liberal side six M.P.s (Haldane, John
Benn, Corrie Grant, J. T. Dodd, Fletcher Moulton, Murray Mac-
donald) together with Herbert Samuel and Sir Richard Stapley.[15]
This body was, however, apparently lethargic.

Through policies announced via the National Liberal Federation,
the party did evince a certain willingness to meet advanced demands.
Since 1887, at Nottingham, the Federation had apparently committed the party to a list of measures which included Home Rule,
Welsh disestablishment, electoral reform, free elementary education,
factory and housing acts, and the equalisation of the death duties.[16]
By 1889, in Manchester, the resolutions had been extended to cover
the taxation of land values and ground rents, the extension of compulsory powers of land acquisition to local authorities, the free breakfast table and the development of local government. In addition,
conference now passed a blanket resolution favouring disestablishment, free education, the ' direct popular veto of the liquor traffic ',
rating reform, the taxation of mining royalties, housing and factory
acts and the reform of the Lords. This pattern was repeated in 1890 at
Sheffield, while in 1891, at Newcastle, the only new inclusion was
Scottish disestablishment. In the event, the omnibus resolution,
moved that year by Sir Wilfrid Lawson and Henry Fowler, was no
different from that passed in each of the preceding four years.

At Newcastle no mention was made of a graduated income-tax,
pensions, wages or hours legislation. The miners eight-hours question
was sent up by five associations but as these contained four different
suggestions, the President (Spence Watson) claimed the N.L.F. could
not pronounce upon the issue. Leadership at the conference was
averse to giving any support to the idea of a programme, although
the impression remained that in the customary post-conference speech
by the leader, Gladstone had given a vague blessing to the programme as such.[17] From his speech, the encouragement was clearly

---

[14] J. Stuart, ' The London Progressives ', *Contemporary Review*, April 1892.

[15] Copy of a prospectus in the Herbert Samuel Papers. Also G. Wallas to Samuel,
11 March 1893, HSP A/155 (1).

[16] *Tenth Annual Report of the N.L.F.* (1887).

[17] In 1898, Hudson wrote to Herbert Gladstone that the Newcastle Resolutions had
never been intended to form a party programme, but that impression did arise

slight. He supported the reform of taxation only briefly, and referred his audience to speeches in parliament, his major emphasis lying with public economy. He thought it necessary ' to extend Labour representation in parliament ', yet this was evidently to be done through payment of election expenses and registration reform, plus the extension of local government. He welcomed the movement for shorter hours, but legislation for an eight-hour day needed ' much careful examination '. Having said so much, mentioned disestablishment and temperance, he finished at great length upon Ireland.

Official Liberalism fought shy of any explicit commitment to Labour. Francis Channing's motion to check excessive hours on the railways, and Sydney Buxton's resolution for a ' fair wage clause ' to be included in all government contracts, debated respectively in January and February 1891, received little encouragement as the basis for a Labour programme.[18] Although Schnadhorst for one was apparently in favour,

somehow this frank acceptance of a ' Labour Plank ' was shelved by timid counsels at headquarters. I have always regretted it, because I know from letters received from those who fought in the election of 1892 that many seats were won by my motion and by Buxton's probably also. I am confident that a bold acceptance of a definite Labour programme, in addition to the proposals as to rural reforms, and the stereotyped but rather hackneyed list of disestablishment, local option, registration and taxation, each appealing only to special groups, would have made all the difference.[19]

Certainly the ' hackneyed list ' of measures claimed priority. Condemned by Webb as ' political dead-sea fruit ' in 1888,[20] they were solemnly endorsed by Wemyss Reid in 1890 on behalf of official Liberalism,[21] and took pride of place in Buxton's *Handbook of Political Questions* in 1892. The supporting sections which squabbled for priority were anathema to Radicals like Robert Wallace who

when W. G. Gladstone took them as the basis of his speech. H. Gladstone replied: ' Mr. Schnadhorst . . . pressed it on my Father through the usual channels as something essential for party interests. In promulgating that policy my Father gave pretty clear indications that it was for the future and others rather than for the present and himself.' HGP, Add. Mss 40020 Correspondence dated 9 and 10 March 1898.

18 E.g. J. Bryce to A. Morley, 15 March 1892, copy, HGP, Add. Mss 46022, ' A separate Labour policy would be fatal to Liberalism '.

19 Channing, *Midland Politics*, p. 117.

20 S. Webb, *Wanted : A Programme* (1888) p. 12.

21 *The Speaker*, 11 January 1890.

referred to the lack of popular interest in the speeches of Labouchere, Alpheus Morton or Samuel Storey: ' the heart of the community is in the social question ',[22] while the *Quarterly Review* sarcastically observed that the Liberal M.P. was ' expected to provide himself with a complete outfit of opinions '.[23] On the morrow of the Liberal victory, *The Times* described the majority party as ' a motley crew – notoriously associated of ill-assorted and mutually-hostile factions '.[24]

It was, indeed, the sectionalism of the party rather than the nature of its programme which was the greater handicap, in particular, the sectional unrest amongst the Celtic strongholds. Both Welsh and Scottish Liberals were claiming a greater proportion of the time of the national legislature; both wanted Grand Committees of the House. Nonconformity amongst both sections was preponderant – 27 of the 28 Welsh Liberals were nonconformists, and since 1890, the Welsh party had been striving for disestablishment (the N.L.F. had first adopted it in 1887), while the Scottish Liberal Conferences of 1890 and 1891 had declared in favour of Home Rule all round, Scottish disestablishment, the abolition of the House of Lords, and the amendment of the Crofters' Act. In 1891, at Perth, the Scots further dropped the eight-hours issue and added instead payment of members.[25] Both countries were experiencing in these years (1892–6) strong national movements, with cultural and educational roots, and in that the Scottish contingent was 50 strong, and the Welsh contingent contained some extremely forceful M.P.s, D. A. Thomas, David Randell, Frank Edwards, Sir George Morgan, Bryn Roberts and Lloyd George, their collective discontent was likely to be a disconcerting element in a party whose nominal majority was only 40.

It would, finally, be difficult to overestimate the potency of the liquor question amongst the party – 263 out of 274 Liberals were pledged to local veto.[26] Control of the liquor traffic was an integral part of nonconformist and progressive programmes alike,[27] and the anti-drink lobby was strongly represented in the 1892 parliament. The Presidents of the United Kingdom Alliance (Sir Wilfrid Law-

---

[22] R. Wallace, ' The Future of Parties ', *Fortnightly Review*, 1 May 1894.

[23] Vol. 175 (1892) p. 538.

[24] *The Times*, 2 January 1893.

[25] J. G. Kellas, ' The Liberal Party in Scotland ', unpublished Ph.D. thesis (London, 1961) pp. 110–12.

[26] From the *Pall Mall Gazette Election Supplement for 1892*.

[27] It was important to a nonconformist progressive like John Benn in whose constituency in 1892 one out of every five places of business was a liquor shop. A. G. Gardiner, *John Benn and the Progressive Movement* (1925) p. 130.

son) and of the National Temperance League, W. S. Caine, both sat as Liberals, while amongst the Liberal vice-presidents of the Alliance were T. P. Whittaker, T. E. Ellis, H. D. Wilson, R. A. Allison and Sir Walter Foster. Still other prominent spokesmen were William Crosfield and Thomas Snape, with Henry Wilson representing the Scottish Temperance Movement. This was a collectivity with which Lib-labs like Burt (also a vice-president of the U.K.A.), Fenwick and Wilson (J.), as well as large employers, were willing to associate.[28]

COMPOSITION

The circumstances implied that the Liberal party was in strong need of firm direction, but Gladstone at the age of 82 had little thought of beginning a new phase of his career as a social reformer. Ireland was his only public pledge, and for him the Irish question was also a Labour question, for the Irish labourers were amongst the most needy and the most suffering.[29] He denounced ' the perilous course of socialistic legislation ', and declared that he had been pushed against his will into supporting the payment of M.P.s.[30] In John Morley, he had one who possessed similar views upon the undesirability of hours and wages legislation. Morley was also on record as remarking that ' the truth is we have moved much too fast and too far towards the extreme left on every subject at once, and quiet sensible folk don't like it '.[31] As Chancellor, however, Harcourt disagreed, and told Gladstone that ' mere *taxation* reforms will not satisfy the British Liberals '.[32] But while he wanted a fair balance cast between British and Irish interests, his idea for the very minimum of legislation was temperance reform (local option); village councils having control of the schools; registration reform, one man, one vote; payment of members and Welsh disestablishment.

In the House of Lords Earl Spencer agreed with Harcourt that some new stimulus was needed. English measures had to be produced ' which would be both concise and telling ', but he was pessimistic over difficulties, as were his fellow peers. As Kimberley wrote to Ripon :

[28] Cf. N. Longmate, *The Waterdrinkers* (1968) p. 225. (Before Christmas 1893, 24 private members' bills for regulating the liquor traffic had been introduced.)

[29] Cf. H. Pelling, *The Social Geography of British Elections 1885–1910* (1967) p. 415.

[30] To Sir E. Hamilton, 9 February 1893, Add. Mss 48659.

[31] Sir W. Harcourt to Spencer, 16 July 1892 WHP, Box 8.

[32] *Ibid.* (Original emphasis.)

What little has reached me in the way of rumour about the feeling in the Liberal party tends to show that there is no enthusiasm for Home Rule, and a desire to put forward at once other measures. Of course, H.R. *must* be brought forward. Besides our position and repeated pledges, the Irish Nationalists hold us in the hollow of their hand.[33]

Both peers thought Home Rule should be accompanied by a registration, ' one man – one vote ', Bill, although Ripon, as the ' Red Earl ', did apparently possess some reputation as a Labour sympathiser, being willing to invoke ' state interference in questions of wages and the like ' against ' the sacrosanct laws of political economy '.[34]

With such uncertainties in mind, it was scarcely surprising that the Cabinet of 18 revealed a distinct tendency to divide into two blocs. An ' Irish ' bloc of Gladstone, Bryce, Sir George Trevelyan, Fowler and the two Morleys was countered by an ' English ' bloc of Harcourt, Asquith (Home Office), Acland (Education), and Mundella (Board of Trade). But Asquith was still comparatively new, Acland was under something of a cloud for having ' unfrocked himself ' after taking orders in the Church of England, while Mundella was ' too commercial for Acland and Asquith '. Each therefore went his own way, and as Acland wrote: ' we have no leader now – each man manages his own department '.[35] The Liberals were also beset by a shortage of men ' fit for promotion to the front bench ',[36] and this provided some rather unlikely appointments. Amongst the junior ministers, for example, Grey was happily suited at the Foreign Office, but Sydney Buxton was strangely placed under Ripon at Colonies – and George Russell, another social reformer, at the India Office. Herbert Gladstone under Asquith and Thomas Burt under Mundella were some compensation, but there were few concessions to Radicalism, neither Dilke nor Labouchere.

Still there was room for a certain cautious optimism. It was recognised that the best hope of reform lay with the Liberals rather than the Conservatives, although ' this applies to the rank and file only, and not to the leaders, and to prevent possible misunderstanding, the less said about this " hope " the better '.[37] Not only the Fabians, but Burns and Hardie were ready to co-operate with any group moving

[33] Kimberley to Ripon, 19 July 1892, RP, Add. Mss 43526.

[34] L. Wolf, *Life of Ripon* (1921), Memorial by S. Buxton.

[35] W. H. G. Armytage, *A. J. Mundella* (1951) p. 289.

[36] Sir W. Harcourt to Rosebery, 23 May 1894, WHP, Box 8.

[37] K. Hardie to J. Burns, 23 May 1891, JBP, Add. Mss 46287.

in their general direction.[38] Atherley-Jones later claimed that Hardie
was anxious for a working-alliance between the advanced Radicals
and the pledged Labour M.P.s although ' that can only be when you
definitely sever yourselves from the Whig element '.[39] The immediate
question was to what extent the Radicalism of the elected House of
Commons was likely to coincide with advanced opinion outside it,
and whether Liberal Radicals were prepared to support any ' social '
measures.

The Liberal victory was gained mainly in the Counties. In England
the party increased from 65 to 103 seats, and by winning 46 out of 58
County divisions in Wales and Scotland, they held, overall, 149
against 143 Conservative (County) seats. In the Boroughs they did
less well; in England, from 40, they advanced to 68 against the Conservatives' 100. In London itself, they increased from 11 to 25, out of
62.[40] The moral was plain: ' Our strength now lies in the Counties,
and we must keep our hold on them.' [41] Labouchere noted that the
desire for English reforms was a mixed one:

The Borough members want a registration and a one-man Bill – the
County members want, besides this, a parish councils bill – these parish
councils have taken hold of the agricultural labourers ... The Trade
Unions want a Bill for payment of members, and throwing the expenses
of the returning officers on the rates. [Significantly, he also warned that]
' self-preservation is the first law of nature, and many of our friends
would rather be in Parliament with a Tory government in power, than
out of it with a Liberal government '.[42]

Not only is a comprehensive definition of Radicalism difficult however, but its value is problematical. The pattern was one of individuals
pursuing causes, rather than flat commitments entered into by the
party as a whole. While many declared their predominant individualism to be quite compatible with a measure of collectivism, they
defined the ensuing compromise in terms of ideals or spheres of
action, rather than in terms of policies. Hence it would be a mistake
to identify the ' New Liberalism ' which was being promenaded in

---

[38] ' This policy has done more for Socialism than all the preaching about class-war ',
JBP, Add. Mss 46305 f. 96 (c. 1890).
[39] L. A. Atherley-Jones, *Looking Back* (1925) p. 68, quoting a letter received from
Hardie.
[40] From *The Pall Mall Gazette Election Supplement for 1892*.
[41] Ripon to Kimberley cited L. Wolf, *Life of Ripon*, p. 201.
[42] Labouchere to H. Gladstone, 27 August 1892, HGP, Add. Mss 46016.

the journals with the Radicalism of the House of Commons. Rather
a distinction should be made between the advanced or ' Social
Radicals ' and the more traditional elements.

A traditional Radical might be defined as ' a would-be root and
branch reformer of the Constitution – a politician who advocates
measures which are considered " extreme "; that is, which go far
beyond the desires of the average political opinion of the day '.[43]
This would be accurate in regard to Samuel Storey or Alpheus
Morton, or as a description of the politics of Labouchere, whose own
motto was ' a fair field and no favour ', and who believed that
' Radicals are essentially practical '. It was to emphasise the means
and the structure of politics, rather than its purpose, a school which
believed that ' [The Cabinet] had no charge of souls, it was merely a
business concern running the affairs of the nation as cheaply and as
effectively as possible '.[44] It was akin to the Radicalism of Sir Wilfrid
Lawson who described himself as ' a fanatic, a faddist and an " extreme man " ', opposed to ' the peerage, the beerage and war ' [45]; or
to the views of the ' monomaniacal Gladstonian ' from Keighley,
Isaac Holden. It was closely attuned to the cry of public economy,
and because these believed in a beneficial humanitarianism interpreted by reason, it tallied with the views of those, like John Morley
or James Stansfeld, who saw Liberalism as some huge, fated,
historical force, constantly striving for the meaningful expression of
abstract ideals. As a political tradition it was allied to the grievances
of nonconformity, an opposition to landed privilege, a belief in
equality of political opportunity, and drew its intellectual inspiration
equally from Cobden and Mill – peace, retrenchment and reform.

This viewpoint was especially associated with a previous parliamentary generation, whose Radicalism, founded in opposition to the
aristocracy, predated the rise of Labour and social issues. This view
also received its reinforcements in 1892. Hudson Kearley, for example, described himself and his partner from Devonport, E. J. C.
Morton, as ' out and out left wingers ' in just such a tradition.[46]
Philip Stanhope was another, returned for Burnley in 1893, and so
too was Thomas Nussey from Pontefract, elected in June 1893. There
were, in addition, a few who, while closely associated with this traditional Radicalism, also regarded themselves as standing within an

[43] ' The English Radicals ', *Edinburgh Review*, 191 (1900) pp. 207–25.
[44] Thorold, *Labouchere*, p. 414.   [45] Longmate, *The Waterdrinkers*, p. 217.
[46] H. E. Kearley, *The Travelled Road* (Rochester, 1935) p. 54.

English Labour tradition: Dr Clark, the socialist-cum-crofters' candidate from Caithness, who introduced a bill for the nationalisation of the mines, and L. A. Atherley-Jones, son of the old Chartist leader, Ernest Jones, a recognised counsel for English miners.

Among those who belonged more distinctly to a Social Radical school were Robert Wallace from Edinburgh, whose especial concern was the feeding of starving school-children by public authorities; C. A. V. Conybeare who came from a recognised Radical family, with a concern for establishing wage-boards for sweated industries [47]; J. A. Murray Macdonald, a very advanced Radical from Bow and Bromley who had pledged himself to regard unemployment ' as second in importance to no other question whatsoever ', and who also favoured land nationalisation and universal old-age pensions [48]; and J. M. Paulton, who introduced a bill for the state promotion of industrial schools, but opposed the miners' eight-hours bill. There was a group of acknowledged Labour sympathisers, F. A. Channing, William Byles, founder of the *Bradford Observer*, Sir George Newnes, proprietor of the *Westminster Gazette*, and Henry Dalziel, a journalist much occupied with the unemployed. And there were those employers noted for adopting the eight-hour day, Sir John Brunner, William Mather, Mark Beaujoy, William Allan, Thomas Bayley and Captain Norton.[49] Finally, there were the several pensions advocates: R. L. Everett, a Liberal landowner from Suffolk, Charles Dodd, Fletcher Moulton (elected in 1894) and Captain Naylor-Leyland, who crossed the floor in 1894,[50] and those members who campaigned behind Sir Thomas Fry for the abolition of Poor-Law disfranchisement.

Sitting with the Liberals, the 11 Lib-labs were far from agreement themselves on matters of reform. John Wilson, Fenwick, George Howell, Burt and (after being re-elected in 1894) Broadhurst were opposed to hours legislation. Arch was solely concerned with his

[47] N. G. Annan, ' The Intellectual Aristocracy ' in J. H. Plumb (ed.), *Studies in Social History* (1955) p. 243.

[48] Parl. Deb., 4th Series, Vol. 8, C750: 7 February 1893. Macdonald was also an early underconsumptionist. In 1894, he asked for a popular budget, claiming that they had ' to increase the power of the poorer classes to demand commodities and to check the enormous saving powers which were given under existing conditions to those who possessed large incomes '. (V22, C96, 12 March 1894.)

[49] Cf. H. W. Massingham in *Contemporary Review*, December 1893.

[50] Everett declared in parliament that in his part of the country, ' there was not a single county address . . . which did not contain some allusion [to pensions] and a promise on the part of the candidate to give his attention to some well-considered scheme '. (V22, C1335, 4 April 1894.)

fading agricultural support, Havelock Wilson with the sailors, and Randal Cremer with efforts for international peace. None was remotely collectivist. This left only Pickard, Sam Woods, Abraham and James Rowlands to press for fair wages, employers' liability and the eight-hours principle.

The largest group of members with a common cause and policy were the 25 London members, who certainly owed something to the Labour vote in 1892.[51] Liberal gains in London were almost all in working-class areas, in Southwark West, Lambeth North, Kennington, Newington, Bermondsey and Camberwell. In 22 of the constituencies where the working class constituted over 80 per cent of the poll the Liberals won 17, and in all of them they increased their vote. There was a markedly poorer performance amongst middle-class constituencies.[52] The 25 included both Hardie and Burns, three of the Lib-labs, Murray Macdonald and three London Progressives, John Benn, E. H. Pickersgill and William Saunders. Two more, Mark Beaujoy and James Stuart, were Progressive aldermen. Sir Charles Russell and Sydney Buxton were labour advisers and sympathisers, and D. Naoroji, an early associate of the Indian Congress movement, was classed as a Liberal and Labour member. In Lambeth North, F. M. Coldwells had progressed from gardener to harbourmaster, and in Whitechapel Samuel Montagu deftly reconciled the Jewish vote with Labour claims for aliens restriction. J. S. Wallace, who had taken part as a Radical in both the match-girls' and the dockers' strikes, sat in Limehouse. Thomas Bolton was a solicitor specialising in labour cases, F. C. Frye a grocer who operated a profit-sharing scheme, Captain Norton a brewer with an eight-hours scheme, while A. Grove was an ' advanced ', and R. V. Barrow a ' Newcastle ' Radical. R. K. Causton had played a rôle in developing the Liberal-Progressive alliance, while Thomas Lough and E. H. Bayley claimed concern for the unemployed.[53]

In 1892–3, the London Liberals were asking in particular for the taxation of ground values and the adoption of the principle of betterment whereby private owners who had benefited from large improvement schemes in their neighbourhood might be taxed. Above all, the Progressives desired a more fully united metropolis, but although the Liberals appointed a Royal Commission on London Government in

---

[51] S. Webb, ' The Moral of the Elections ', *Contemporary Review*, August 1892.

[52] P. Thompson, *Socialists, Liberals and Labour* (1967) p. 96.

[53] From *P.M.G. Election Supplement for 1892*

1893, neither they nor the Conservatives adopted this scheme. In general, the Progressives were to be disappointed with the Liberal response; only Benn and Stuart spoke consistently on Progressive matters, while the government did not tackle the London water question and did not provide any stimulus for the improvement of technical education in London, or elsewhere.[54]

Elsewhere among the Boroughs, there was no similar concentration of would-be reformers. Conservatism was dominant in Lancashire, holding seven out of nine seats in Liverpool, five out of nine in the Manchester-Salford complex, and was especially strong in Birmingham and the west Midlands. The Liberals did hold two out of three in Sheffield and three out of five in Leeds, but Yorkshire and the north-east were not a breeding ground for Liberal social reformers.

There is, however, some reason to suppose that the number and the position of the Radical section within the party may have changed slightly from the position of mid-century where the pattern was of 'a massive and homogeneous right-wing', and a Radical minority of perhaps 10 per cent which did all the shouting. The right-wing was no longer quite so 'massive',[55] and the Radical element would seem to have increased in number, the problem being the divisive interpretations which the Radicals themselves put upon their various creeds. It might, perhaps, be possible to include the London group, the Lib-labs, the handful of Social Radicals and a selection of the 'traditionals' and eight-hours men within a nominal Radical grouping, but this should be interpreted more as a collective disposition to Radicalism than as a disposition to collectivism. In this way, a figure of at least 60 is attained, or roughly 21 per cent of the party. If all those who dubbed themselves 'Radical' or 'Progressive' are included, including local option and disestablishment advocates, the figure would be nearer 80, but this would weight the composition of Radicalism very heavily in favour of 'traditionalism'. Many Welsh Radicals, for example, would have thought in terms similar to those of Lloyd George: 'the danger of the Labour movement at the present moment seemed to lie in confining itself to one or two questions of what he could not help thinking to be of secondary importance. He

---

[54] A. G. Gardiner, *John Benn*, pp. 167–9.

[55] J. Vincent, *The Formation of the Liberal Party*, pp. 3–5. Between 1859 and 1874, the Liberals included 198 landowners, 151 businessmen, 84 lawyers and 49 gentlemen of leisure. There were only a score of identifiable Radicals.

considered the land ... temperance ... and disestablishment to be
equally of interest to labourers as an eight-hours bill '.[56] In summary,
what does appear is a Radical wing very much in a ferment, in which
social reform was simply one element, and where individual issues,
rather than the sense of overall policy, provided the prime political
motivation. As such, the Radicals were more likely to be a drag upon
legislation than a source of momentum.[57]

The Radical section did preserve its own loose committee organisation, ' for the purpose of keeping governments up to the mark and
for current work ', theoretically elected by an open meeting of Radicals. This lasted until early 1893, when after allegations that the
Whips had packed the meeting it was decided to have an elected
Radical Committee of 25 which could work on its own without the
need to summon the whole Radical section.[58] It seems that the core
of this body was drawn largely from the ' traditional ' Radical
element – Storey, Stanhope, Labouchere, Dilke, Dr Clark, W. S. B.
Maclaren, Kearley and Morton, who had been joined by 1895 by
Norton, Sir Alfred Jacoby, John Ellis, Sir William Wedderburn,
Logan and Strachey.[59]

Dilke, in referring to the 1890s, later wrote that

it was always understood that the whole of the section were favourable to
the miners' eight-hours bill ..., to very drastic action with regard to the
House of Lords, and to payment of members. Most of them were supporters of adult suffrage and Home Rulers. All of them took part in
ballotting for labour measures.[60]

Yet again, much depended upon emphasis and priorities. An
election address in 1895, for example, signed by 13 Radicals, listed
' three great reforms ': franchise and registration, reform of parliamentary procedures and greater powers for local authorities, and the
abolition of the legislative powers of the Lords. These were essential
preliminaries if Home Rule, disestablishment, local option, land
reform and the taxation of land values were to be gained, while they
advocated also ' the economical administration of the revenues of the

56 *North Wales Observer*, 28 October 1892.
57 Cf. J. P. Mackintosh, *The British Cabinet* (1968) pp. 213–14.
58 Memo. in the Dilke papers, Add. Mss 43919, 31 January 1906, ff. 16–17.
59 *Ibid*. (Also Kearley, *The Travelled Road*, p. 54.)
60 *Ibid*.

country ', and a ' practical advancement ' of the claims of Labour ' as set forth by its accredited representatives '.[61]

While the Radicals had increased in number, it was also noticeable that they were concentrated amongst the lawyers and professional men, and amongst the journalists and authors. It was rare for a man of business to gain a reputation as a Radical, but not exceptional. Such men showed their ' progressive ' side more by a reputation for practical philanthropy at their works – William Mather or Sir John Brunner – or more often by espousing the cause of education (particularly technical); Mundella, for example, or Caleb Wright, a self-made cotton-spinner from Leigh who was President of the Mechanics Institute. If the men of advanced ideas were more generally found among the non-business section, the significance of the business category lay not in any division into specific economic interests, but in the fact that they provided the largest single grouping whose views and experiences were most nearly uniform. While there was only one example of an economic interest acting clearly in its own defence in the 1892 parliament (the coal owners), there was a tendency for businessmen to approach issues of trade and commerce from a similar point of view.[62] As they were mostly silent men, and very few of their members either attained office or were indeed office-seekers, their voting strength was an obvious, dependable, counterpoise to the factions. Of 274 Liberals (including Hardie and Burns) at least 120 were businessmen, and in this parliament they had the support of an influential section of lawyers and professional men, scholars like Playfair and Sir Henry Roscoe, gentlemen of leisure like Leveson-Gower and the Hon A. G. Brand, large landowners such as George Lambert and T. C. Warner of Devon and Somerset, the occasional diplomat like Earl Compton – in all, one may hazard there were at least 30 such men. And these were the men upon whom the administration depended, and given the peculiar circumstances of the Liberals, the issue of the leadership, the disputes over foreign policy and public economy, depended to some considerable extent.

[61] Dilke papers, Add. Mss 43915, 9 July 1895. The 13 Radicals were Bayley, Byles, Carmichael, Clark, Dalziel, Dilke, Hoare, Labouchere, Leon, Morton, Norton, Stanhope, Wedderburn. The Labour measures included hours limitation, full right of combination, employers' liability, direct Labour representation.

[62] E.g. *The Economist* (cited Armytage, *A. J. Mundella*, p. 281): ' It is hardly fair to make the staple industries of the country the target for amateur efforts in social and industrial legislation.'

IN PARLIAMENT

Given the composition of the party in 1892, and the lack of any marked emphasis upon progressive social measures, it was to be expected that traditional issues would assume priority. This was underlined by the fact that the political initiative lay so securely with Gladstone – 'it is in an unusual degree *his* government'[63] – and by establishing firm commitments to Ireland, local government reform, local option, and church disestablishment, he shaped the entire emphasis of the Liberal ministry.[64] Home Rule completely dominated the opening session of 1893 (which lasted until March 1894), and this Bill, the Parish Councils bill and the 1894 budget engulfed over 160 sittings between them. Given also the circumstances of a divided leadership,[65] and the degree to which the various leaders, Rosebery, Harcourt, Morley, were able to indulge in their own mutually contradictory programmes, which further encouraged the sectionalism within the party, it is not surprising that the strength of the traditional elements in the party, the campaigns against the Lords, the Church, and the brewers, overshadowed the social issues.

It was noticeable, however, in those measures of social reform which were brought forward, that a division was already forming in the Liberal ranks between the Social Radicals upon the one hand and the spokesmen for economic orthodoxy upon the other. This occurred in debates upon the Employers' Liability Bill, the Bill to limit railwaymen's hours, the Miners' Eight-Hours Bills, the Factory and Workshops Bill of 1895, and over unemployment.

The Employers' Liability Bill of 1893 proposed to make the employer liable for all injuries to workmen in his employ (reversing the Act of 1880), save for those due to their own wilful negligence, and it forbade employer and employees from contracting out of its provisions by means of a private scheme. Progressive opinion (and Conservatives like Gorst and Rollit) supported the bill fully,[66] but Walter Maclaren, a Liberal railway director from Crewe, moved an amendment to exempt the employer in certain cases from being bound by the abolition, he being concerned with safeguarding the interests of the North-Western Railway's insurance fund.[67] He was supported

---

63 Campbell-Bannerman to Sir W. Harcourt, 14 August 1892, WHP, Box 9.

64 See details in W. E. Gladstone papers, Add. Mss 44648.

65 See P. Stansky, *Ambitions and Strategies : The Struggle for the Liberal Leadership in the 1890s* (1964) pp. 99-134, *passim*.

66 Parl. Deb., 4th Series, Vol. 10, C1059, 24 March 1893.

67 Also H. Pelling, *Popular Politics and Society in Late Victorian Britain* (1968) p. 8.

in debate by three Liberals; C. E. Shaw, a Staffordshire manufacturer, and two lawyers, H. P. Cobb and Bryn Roberts, while his
clause was only narrowly defeated by 235 votes to 217. (The bill was
eventually wrecked by the Lords who insisted upon provision being
made for contracting-out.)

1893 also saw the attempt by Gorst to insert a definite figure into
Mundella's Bill to limit the excessive hours of railwaymen, suggesting that the Bill as it stood would not lead to any general reduction
in hours. He wished to interpret ' excessive ' as more than eight hours
for signalmen and 10 hours for others. He was opposed by a Conservative, Sir James Fergusson, and by the Liberal industrial magnate
Sir Joseph Pease (both speaking for railway interests), who opposed
any interference ' with the freedom of contract and the labour of
adult men '. This was not a matter for parliament, but a question for
the administrative discretion of the Board of Trade, with which
Mundella concurred, upholding the ' elasticity ' of working conditions and concentrating on the ' serious, practical side '.[68] The
amendment was defeated (257–71), whereupon the Bill was further
emasculated in the Lords.

1893 saw the first skirmish over the Miners' Eight-Hours Bill. This
claim sprang from a variety of motives, health, a desire for greater
wage stability, but their case rested basically on the argument that
shorter hours and greater safety would mean increased efficiency and
the ability to maintain a stable output, although perhaps at increased
prices.[69] In 1893, Sam Woods claimed that the majority of miners
were agreed in demanding the measure, and to the argument that to
reduce hours would reduce output and thereby increase cost, he
pointed out that the miners in the north-east were already working
seven-hour shifts [70] (although this applied only to the hewers: the
transit hands, mainly boys, still worked eleven-hour shifts).

The issues raised were two-fold: the principle of state interference,
and its adjudged economic effects. Here the opponents of the measure
were divided, coal-owners from the north-east tending to oppose the
principle of interference itself, the remainder taking their stand on
more practical grounds. Sir James Joicey from Durham believed
that to legislate here would mean having to legislate ' for 50–60 per
cent of the industries in this country '.[71] He opposed parliament inter-

---

[68] Parl. Deb., 4th Series, Vol. 11, C1092–5, 24 April 1893.
[69] Cf. B. McCormick and J. Williams, 'Miners and the Eight-Hour Day 1863–
1910 ', Economic History Review, December 1959.
[70] Parl. Deb., 4th Series, Vol. 8, C1842–5, 3 May 1893.   [71] Ibid. C1854.

fering with economic laws. D. A. Thomas from Merthyr Tydfil, speaking for South Wales' coal-owners, did not object to the principle of interference, but pointed out that having introduced an eight-hour system into his own collieries, the men had so suffered from reduced earnings that they had asked him to revert to longer hours. He maintained that the real object of this Bill was to restrict output and thereby raise prices and wages. He would only support the measure if it included provision for local option. Both Joicey and Thomas were arguing from the context of an experience formed under the conditions of the sliding scale, and their opposition to a universal bill was strengthened by their sense of internal variations in the coal industry.[72]

In South Wales, Northumberland and Durham, production was geared to export markets, where the relationship of costs to prices was especially significant. The fact that wages were price-determined gave the owners an invaluable competitive flexibility, and any attempt to restrict output with the aim of raising prices in the interests of wage stability threatened a loss of markets. The alleged identity of interest between the coal-owners and the older mining leaders (Fenwick, Burt, John Wilson), was based on a belief in the virtues of conciliation and the sliding-scale, allied to the emphasis on high output to maintain a strong competitive position.[73]

Elsewhere, coal-owners were equally concerned with their competitive position in the home-market, but by 1892, owners in the Midlands and Yorkshire were having to face almost alone the pressure of the Miners' Federation for hours and wages concessions, and this may have had something to do with their greater willingness to support an approach to uniformity throughout the industry.

On 4 May 1893, the second reading of Woods' Bill passed by 279 votes to 201. As only 143 Liberals and perhaps ' a score '[74] of Conservatives were known to be committed in support, this represented an apparent triumph. Many Liberals, however, were influenced by Gladstone who deprecated that this Bill should become a party matter, and though personally favouring non-intervention, declared: ' yet I am bound to admit that the present epoch is one a little too late

---

72 The sliding-scale was a device in which the standard wage, expressed as a base calculated from the average wage obtaining over a given time period, was to fluctuate in an agreed percentage relationship with movements in the selling-price of coal.

73 Cf. E. W. Evans, *Mabon* (1955) p. 27.

74 J. Chamberlain to Dilke, 31 March 1892. Dilke Papers, Add. Mss 43889.

for urging that on the House '.[75] As the majority of miners did seem to favour the Bill, he too recorded a vote in its favour. Of the Liberals, 185 voted likewise, 33 voted against and several deliberately abstained.[76] On 11 May however, Gladstone refused to give an undertaking as to the Bill's prospects, and on 18 August he politely extinguished Woods' hopes of a committee stage.[77]

In 1894, the Bill was introduced by H. J. Roby, and although the weight of the speakers lay with the Bill, Asquith admitted that it had ' strong and formidable opponents ' amongst the Liberals whose opinions ' must be respected '. After the Bill passed its second reading comfortably, the government reluctantly afforded it Committee facilities, but after a fierce debate, largely amongst the members of the Liberal party, an amendment in favour of local option moved by D. A. Thomas passed by five (112–107), effectively wrecking the Bill.[78]

The Bill's supporters undoubtedly fell at the economic hurdle, never agreeing amongst themselves as to whether the Bill would raise prices, wages benefiting through sliding-scale adjustments, or whether existing output could be maintained in shorter hours through increasing efficiency. Liberal opinion was not enthusiastic about the ' universal ' bill. The *Daily News* rejected Joicey's arguments, but sided with D. A. Thomas [79]; local option was the key, based on voluntary district agreements possibly with some legislative backing. William Mather's draft bill of 1893 was a fair example of Liberal opinion. His object was ' to render Parliament free from all responsibility of rigidly fixing the hours of labour per day or week '. He aimed at establishing a minimum 48-hour week, and gave authority to the members of a trade union to call a meeting within a particular area or region, and to agree upon such a limitation of hours within their area as the Bill allowed. They were then to approach their employers, and in the event of disagreement with them, would approach their local authority who could directly enforce the union's decision after a further referendum among its members. The agreement was to last

---

[75] Parl. Deb., 4th Series, Vol. 8, C1858–9, 3 May 1893.

[76] *Westminster Gazette*, 4 May 1893.

[77] Letter to Woods, published in *The Times*, 23 August 1893.

[78] *The Times*, 14 August 1894. Liberals for: Dilke, Woods, Atherley-Jones, William Allen, Thomas Bayley, Charles McClaren; against, D. A. Thomas, Sir C. M. Palmer, J. Pease.

[79] *Daily News*, 4 May 1893. Also J. E. C. Munro, ' The Economic Effects of an Eight-Hours Day for Coal-Miners ' (1891), *Transactions of the Political Economy Circle of the National Liberal Club*, Vol. 2.

a year and to apply to all adult workers over 18. His suggestions were
in all essentials the same as those advanced by both Tom Mann and
Sidney Webb.[80] In the round, however, Liberal opinion was certainly
ahead of the summary of the Majority Report of the Royal Commission on Labour: ' where an eight-hour day is economically harm-
less it will come of itself, where it is economically injurious ... it is
probably undesirable '.

The last specifically Labour measure was Asquith's Factory and
Workshops Bill of 1895, which brought laundries, wharves and
docks, and dangerous trades under supervision, and proposed to
regulate the hours of work of women and young people. The measure
met a general welcome in the House and it was given an unopposed
second reading.

Asquith remarked apropos requests for extending the overtime
regulations that he had gone as far as was practicable without losing
the support of the House, and this became clearer when the Bill was
considered by the Standing Committee on Trade. This Committee
represented the bastion of the commercial interests (who had been
particularly annoyed when the Employer's Liability Bill was sent to
the Standing Committee on Law); its 50 or so members were dominated by large employers – amongst the Liberals for example, were
Sir James Joicey, Sir Joseph Leigh, Sir William Rathbone, Sir Joseph
Pease, Sir Walter Maclaren, Sir John Barran, E. T. Gourley, and
Mark Oldroyd. The attempts to broaden the scope of this Bill with
respect to hours control revealed a small minority of reformers (8–9)
opposed by an unwavering majority of never less than 30 composed
of both parties, and this type of division was of far more importance
than a straight party division. An amendment proposed by William
Allen to include all domestic workplaces occupied with work handed
out in a factory or workshop in the new regulation was defeated 48–
8; a similar attempt failed 41–9. An effort to peg the hours of work of
men in any employment to the maximum permitted to women in
that trade was lost 35–9; to reduce the maximum hours of work permitted to women and young persons from 60 (under the Bill) to 48 was
lost 36–9. But Matthews' (a former Conservative Home Secretary)
amendment to reduce the age-limit to which overtime regulations
were to apply, from 16 to 14, was carried by 40 to 14. In all attempts
to secure a greater protection for women and greater rights for the
employed, the small minority of 8 to 12 invariably consisted of

[80] *Final Report of the Royal Commission on Labour*, pp. 67–8.

W. Allen, Broadhurst, Burns, Dilke, Naoroji, David Randell and Sam Woods, and quite often included Liberals like Philip Stanhope, Charles Hobhouse, and the Irish Labour member, Michael Austin. These were occasionally joined by employers like Walter Maclaren or Sir John Barran.[81]

These years were, finally, the first in which the working conditions of labour and the social conditions of the populace formed a continuous backcloth to the administration. The years 1893, 1894, 1895 each saw an amendment to the address asking for help for the unemployed. The aims of reformers were two-fold; to insist upon the size of the problem, and to commit the authorities to invoke the responsibility and powers of the state to deal with it. The major initiative was taken by Keir Hardie, but he received only isolated support from Liberals like W. P. Byles and Murray Macdonald. Fowler consistently refused to consider a policy of hours limitation as a means to spreading opportunities for work, and refused too to admit that a central responsibility for the unemployed did exist.[82] However, the government's consistent refusal to take up such suggestions as afforestation of the highlands, the reclamation of tidal waste-lands, relief-works in general, or the provision of labour registries, steadily alienated a number of their own back-benchers, Dalziel, E. H. Pickersgill, R. L. Everett, Thomas Lough, John Benn, and the accumulation of Liberal criticism was instrumental in securing for Hardie a Select Committee in 1895 to enquire into the unemployed.[83] Liberal ministers showed themselves remote from the realities of the situation. While the percentage of unemployed trade unionists rose from 2·1 per cent in 1890 to 6·3 per cent in 1892, 7·5 per cent in 1893, and was still 6·9 per cent in 1894,[84] Shaw-Lefevre could claim that ' the average condition of the labouring people of this country was infinitely better than it had ever been in the past '.[85] Meanwhile, the Select Committee located 179 localities in the spring of 1895 where well over four million people were experiencing exceptional distress. The Liberals were also extremely dilatory in adopting the ' fair wage ' principle in government employment,

---

[81] *Reports from Committees*, x, July 1895.

[82] E.g. Cab. 37/34, 29 November 1893 (H. H. Fowler).

[83] See Parl. Debs., 7 February 1893; 19 December 1893; 7 February 1895; also *The Times*, 13 December 1893.

[84] *Tenth Annual Abstract of Labour Statistics of the U.K.*, Cd. 2491 (1905) LXXVI, p. 2.

[85] Parl. Deb., 4th Series, Vol. 30, C269, 7 February 1895.

despite consistent pressure from their back-benchers, notably Lough, Stuart, Wallace, Rowlands and Captain Sinclair. Only in 1894 did the Admiralty and the War Office adopt in principle the eight-hour day, but Liberal ministers made no advance at all towards the idea of the minimum wage.[86] This in many ways contrasted oddly with the good administrative record of Asquith at the Home Office, Mundella at the Board of Trade (before his resignation in May 1894), and A. H. D. Acland in charge of education. All three were associated with several minor but valuable reforms, Asquith with increasing the numbers and functions of the factory inspectorate, Mundella with establishing a separate Labour Department and passing a number of small acts demanded by organised Labour, while Acland had overcome a great deal of resistance in continuing the establishment of free elementary education. 'We have tried (said Asquith), to show that it is possible to reconcile the claims of labour with the reasonable exigencies of practical common-sense.'[87] Yet common-sense provided no answer to the economic and financial problems which stood in the way of social reform; nor could it prove of much help to a party whose warring sections could not agree upon a single scale of priorities, and whose various demands for Welsh disestablishment, local option and electoral reform committed the party above all to the maintenance of its own internal equilibrium.

AFTERMATH

Despite their groundwork, the Liberals had not succeeded in passing one distinctively national, social measure. While they could justifiably complain of the Lords and of the 'sharp issues' which dogged them, they confronted few or none of them squarely: electoral reform, unemployment, sweating, hours. The Commission on the Aged Poor (1893-5) reported negatively, although Liberals signed minority reports stating they did not think the report satisfactory.[88] Of nine measures requested by the T.U.C. in 1891, only three (notification of accidents, abolition of the property qualifica-

---

[86] Cf. Cab. 37/32, 15 December 1892, *Minimum Rate of Wages in Government Departments* (Shaw-Lefevre).

[87] Cited *Liberal Magazine*, August 1894.

[88] *Royal Commission on the Aged Poor* (1895) C7684. Broadhurst recommended the adoption of a universal state pension for all whose income was less than £3 a week, payable out of public funds. J. Stuart, J. Arch and Humphreys-Owen recommended that another investigation be begun.

tion for Guardians, and a factory act) had passed. Direct encouragement to Social Radicalism from the Cabinet was absent, and
concessions came only after struggles. Such was the pressure upon
the time-table that back-benchers were often frustrated; numerous
bills were lost in 1893, over 20 dealing with working-class housing
alone, only Howell being successful with three small bills for safeguarding the funds of provident societies. Bills for shortening the
hours of labour (Burns, Beaujoy, Macdonald, Mather and Samuel
Evans), for abolishing Poor-Law disfranchisement (Fry, J. Richardson, J. Wilson, James Paulton and William Allan), were constant
casualties upon the legislative by-ways. The pressure for reform was
present, but its blow-holes were limited.

And yet it would be inaccurate to deduce from this a consequent
or permanent loss of Labour support. The Liberal commitment to
Labour interests was on a different par to that of Salisbury, who saw
Parish Councils as being merely for the amusement of the working
classes. The Liberals were not devoid of credit. William Dacey, for
example, secretary to the Sheffield branch of the Railway Servants,
thought the Railway Hours Act had brought 'something like
10,000 unemployed men into the industry'.[89] The T.U.C. Parliamentary Committee welcomed the Factory Act, the Parish Councils,
and the Equalisation of Rates in London. They appreciated
Asquith's administrative reforms. In October 1894 the T.U.C. echoed
the verdict of the N.L.F. in June in calling for the abolition of the
veto of the Lords,[90] and if a new school of Labour leaders was oust-
ing the Lib-labs from their previous influence within the movement,
still Pickard was President of the Miners' Federation, Abraham was
not uninfluential in South Wales, and the recorded statements of
Burns, C. W. Bowerman, W. C. Steadman, A. Wilkie, as well as
Tom Mann and Ben Tillett, showed them to be still thinking more
in terms of trade union interests than explicitly in the interests of
political labour. While the T.U.C. had been passing collectivist
resolutions during the early 1890s, there was as yet no equivalent
advance of collectivists among the central organisation.[91] In 1895
Congress could still revise standing orders to exclude 'bounders on
the bounce'[92] and the president could still censure the I.L.P. for

---

[89] *Liberal Magazine*, May 1895, p. 156. This opinion was endorsed by the secretary
of the A.S.R.S., E. Harford.
[90] *Ibid*. October 1894, p. 322.
[91] Clegg, Fox and Thompson, *British Trade Unions*, pp. 258–62.
[92] The phrase was that of Burns.

fighting Lib-labs. The tone is perhaps best caught in the presidential address of 1894 by William Delves, who said : ' we rely upon wise, independent political action and trades unionism for the redress of the wrongs under which we labour. This Congress is an independent body. It is bound to no political party. But it means business. " Legislate " will become . . . more and more, our watchword.' [93]

Nor should sweeping attacks (for example by the Fabian Society) be taken at their face value.[94] ' To Your Tents ' was politically motivated but it was by no means politically conclusive. A year later Bernard Shaw paid tribute to the ' progressive spirit ' of the Liberals; ' the Socialists ', he said, ' were far too sectarian '.[95]

A comparison with Labour programmes in the early 1890s (if one leaves out of account for the moment the admittedly crucial issue of nationalisation), reveals that in proposals for reform, the tenor of Liberal-Radicalism as a whole was not markedly different from ' advanced ' demands. The Conference of the Labour Electoral Committee in June 1894 asked for state payment of M.P.s and election expenses, a legal eight-hour day and the abolition of the House of Lords; a living wage to be paid by all elective public bodies, a Labour minister, land law reform, municipalisation of the tramways, workmen magistrates, and for public contractors to employ only trade unionists.[96] A special meeting of the T.U.C. on 12 July 1895 agreed on 20 proposals which differed from the above by including old-age pensions, employers' liability and Poor-Law reform. These were selected by a committee on which a socialist influence was not insignificant. They were put to an assembly and voted on without discussion where they passed by 66 votes to 58. The only real concession to Socialism was land nationalisation.[97] The 1895 I.L.P. Conference differed somewhat in asking for universal old-age pensions at 50, a universal eight-hours bill, the taxation to extinction of unearned income, and provision for widows, orphans and the sick,[98] but this was scarcely practical politics.

[93] *Economic Journal*, 4 (1894) p. 740.

[94] Fabian Society, ' To Your Tents O Israel ', *Fortnightly Review*, 1 November 1893. This was written only seven months after Webb and Shaw had drawn up a progressive programme for the Liberals (*Fortnightly Review*, 1 February 1893). According to Beatrice Webb, the Fabians had acted ' for fear of being left behind ' (*Our Partnership* (1948) p. 110).

[95] *Liberal Magazine*, November 1894, p. 390 (at Westbourne Park).

[96] *The Times*, 20, 21, 22 June 1894.

[97] *The Times*, 12 July 1895 (the Committee consisted of Tillett, Curran, Entwhistle, G. Kelley, Arrandale, Woods and Mawdesley).   [98] *The Times*, 17 April 1895.

The real gap between Liberalism and the young Labour movement was more a matter of emphasis, of political opportunism at the national level; the real clash came in the constituencies where the confrontation between the two took place on grounds which were at once less sophisticated and more open. Extreme elements on both sides received the widest press. In December 1894, the Glasgow I.L.P. asked all Socialists 'to deal a crushing blow to the deceitful, treacherous Liberals'.[99] Keir Hardie often provoked outbursts, especially his claim to control 25 per cent of the total voting power of the industrial centres.[100] The patrician *Speaker* referred to the 'crack-brained and ill-conditioned schemes of the I.L.P.' – 'Vulgar and inept' – 'ridiculous body of self-seekers'.[101] Progressive journals too found the 'personal arrogance' of Hardie distasteful.[102] Often this individual dislike provoked policy differences; *The Speaker* rejected Hardie's idea for the central direction of relief in 1895 when that proposal was gaining ground in the House of Commons.[103] The extreme were remembered at the expense of the cautious. When C. H. Wilson, the Liberal ship-owner from Hull, was provoked into anti-union measures during the Hull dock-strike of 1893, this became far more memorable than Rosebery's successful mediation in the coal strike of that year in South Wales. Nevertheless, it was plain that trade union discontent with their predicament was growing; the fact that two-thirds of the annual product was absorbed by one-quarter of society was inconsistent with their sense of justice. Neither the assumptions of traditional Radicalism nor the laws of production were wholly consistent with the growing articulation of that sense, and as the unions began to demand, as of right, legislative remedies against a market economy they had increasing cause to question, so they discovered common ground with 'absolutist' criticisms of the order.

[99] *The Times*, 4 December 1894.
[100] *The Speaker*, 5 January 1895.
[101] *Ibid*. 20 April and 3 August 1895.
[102] Cf. *Daily News*, 13 December 1893: 'Keir Hardie does not understand statistics.'
[103] *The Speaker*, 16 March 1895.

3

Regrouping and Recovery 1895-1905

Defeat in 1895 left the Liberal party lacking in two respects, in
effective leadership, and in a unified programme behind which the
party could gather. The first factor is primarily the story of the
eclipse of Rosebery, the failure of Harcourt and Morley to fill his
place, and the effective consolidation of Sir Henry Campbell-
Bannerman as leader. This is the story of the South African war
and the struggle of imperialists and pro-Boers, and this is, primarily,
a well-told story. To gain a fuller appreciation of the nature and
significance of the changes occurring in the Liberal party between
1895 and 1905, it is necessary to look beneath the surface into the
movements occurring first amongst the Radicals themselves, secondly
within the organisational sphere and the recovery of Liberalism in
the country, and thirdly amongst the personnel of the parliamentary
party. When these are linked (in the next chapter) to the movement
in ideas, it is possible to see that by 1905 the Liberal party, and the
kind of Liberalism it embodied, had changed considerably from the
state of 1895.

THE RADICALS

Outwardly, the Radicals were a weak force between 1895 and 1900.
Their two most experienced leaders, Labouchere and Dilke, were
both distrusted within the party. The former was on bad terms with
Rosebery, while Dilke had voted against his party in the critical
(cordite) division which led to the fall of the Liberals.[1] Of Dilke,
Campbell-Bannerman wrote:

He has no following but three in the party (Dalziel, young [C. P.]
Allen, and McKenna) – the party *will have none of him* but he is an
insatiate intriguer. He dines and otherwise nobbles the press men in the
lobby, who sing his praises.

We have had lately the ludicrous cabal got up by him, Labby and
Philip Stanhope: each one has his own personal grudge against the
late Govt. – and would rather defeat and thwart *us* than help the Lib.
party or injure the Govt. Yet the correspondents talk of them as ' the

[1] H. E. Kearley, *The Travelled Road*, p. 91.

64

Radicals' and hold them up as patriots. That view is not taken by the honest rank and file here . . . I can only say that the whole dirty tissue of intrigue so revolts me (and others) that the temptation is great to chuck the whole affair. You should hear for instance honest John Burns or Tommie Burt giving their mind on those gentlemen.[2]

In 1895, the remnants of the old Radical Committee attempted to regroup their forces, ' which to tell the truth had become rather ragged in the last part of the late parliament '.[3] At the beginning of 1896, the Radicals combined to form the Liberal Forwards, an ' advanced' group who were primarily concerned with foreign issues, but who were later, especially after the establishment of the New Reform Club in 1898, concerned with promoting ' a vigorous propaganda of successive portions of the Liberal programme '.[4] The first decisive Radical venture was an attempt to capture the National Liberal Federation (N.L.F.) in March 1896, in which they were unsuccessful, but by May the Radical Committee, having been reconstituted into a body of 19, issued a statement of policy according to which it was ' useless . . . to recapitulate the various items of a programme, on the necessity to which all Radicals are agreed, but the legislative accomplishment of which is impossible under the existing parliamentary constitution '. The Radical section was therefore to co-operate in independent parliamentary action aimed at the democratisation of parliament; their secondary concern was to be a policy of devolution – ' Home Rule all round '.[5]

It is essential that the Liberal party of the future should cease to exclusively base its policy upon the propaganda of a middle-class political organisation, and seek to secure the sympathy of the working-classes by the active promotion of those land, labour and social reforms in which they are profoundly interested, and to which the strongest and most obstinate resistance is offered by the irresponsible and privileged members of the non-elective branch of the legislature.

The Times reported that not only was official Liberalism embarrassed by this statement, but non-confirmity and the Irish

---

2 To D. H. Saunders, 24 March 1896, CBP, Add. Mss 52517 (original emphasis). The letter was phrased in the context of foreign affairs.
3 Stanhope to Dilke, 7 August 1895, Dilke papers, Add. Mss 43915.
4 *The Times*, 17 July and 7 December 1896; 12 November 1897; 28 July 1898.
5 W. Allan, W. Allen, Atherley-Jones, Bayley, Dr Clark, Dalziel, S. Evans, Jacoby, W. Jones, Labouchere, Logan, Luttrell, Lloyd George, Maden, McKenna, Norton, Pickard, Stanhope, Wedderburn. *The Times*, 20 May 1896 (Dilke was not included as ' he did not believe in formulating programmes ').

Home Rulers were equally annoyed by the dismissal of their own demands.[6] The quarrel apparently continued in a subterranean fashion, for the following year the N.L.F. found it necessary to pass a resolution desiring ' to see closer and more cordial co-operation among all sections of the Liberal party, and all the forces that make for progress, believing that only by such mutually sympathetic action can those important social reforms be achieved which are so urgently demanded by the growing needs of the community '.[7]

The Radical Committee obtained a distinct success when the Radical wing of the National Liberal Club (N.L.C.) captured the club's organisation, in the summer of 1897, and elected a new political committee with Labouchere as the Chairman and H. J. Reckitt as secretary.[8] The committee itself included Sir Robert Reid, Stanhope, Herbert Samuel, Rufus Isaacs, and W. M. Thompson, the editor of *Reynold's News*. The Committee wrote an open letter to the constituencies asking them for their opinions on policy, designating several areas where opinion would be welcome.[9] By November, the replies indicated that the weight of opinion lay with the democratisation of parliament, involving the abolition of the Lords' veto, reform of registration and electoral law, and devolution. Amongst ' other prominent reforms ' were included all the major issues of the day (excluding nationalisation).[10] These were then drafted into a manifesto of Radical reform which was ' greatly resented by the official organisation '.[11] 38,000 copies were circulated, and a meeting of the General Committee of the N.L.F. at Derby agreed to make electoral reform a priority, a decision endorsed by Asquith a few days later.[12]

This led to renewed protests in March 1898 that the N.L.F. was not responsible for drawing up a programme in the sense of a ' fixed and definite ' course of events, and to protests on behalf of the ardent Home Rulers.[13] Morley's concluding speech struck a judicious balance between foreign affairs, the Church, Home Rule and temperance, but completely by-passed social reform.

---

6   *Ibid.* (leading article).
7   *Report of the Nineteenth Annual Meeting of the N.L.F.* (Norwich, 1897).
8   R. Stevens, *The National Liberal Club, Politics and Persons* (London, n.d.).
9   *The Times*, 2 August 1897.
10   *Ibid.* 25 November 1897.
11   Stevens, *The National Liberal Club*, p. 24.
12   *The Times*, 20 May 1898.
13   *Ibid.* 23 March 1898.

In November 1898, a meeting of Liberal Forwards under Sir Robert Reid decided on a request being sent to all Forwards for them to indicate on a postcard the three reforms which they regarded as being indispensable.[14] 'The overwhelming preponderance' stressed the abolition of the Lords' veto, while electoral reform, pensions, the taxation of land values, local veto and various minor items of social reform received a joint but lesser weighting. In December, however, the General Committee (of the N.L.F.) was once again occupied with the issue of the leadership, and discovered safety only in attacking Conservative policy abroad and in pledging its faith to the 'great and undying' principles of Liberalism.[15] In January 1899, the party held a formal meeting at the N.L.C. under Carrington to resolve differences on policy, but agreement was minimal and the occasion was marked by renewed squabbles (particularly involving Labouchere).[16]

The picture is one of a Radicalism where there still existed a tension between the traditional and the more advanced reformers, with the balance tilted in favour of the traditionals. The latter's influence was no doubt the greater in that the tendentious issues raised by the foreign policy of the Salisbury government overshadowed the prospects of a social programme. While the Jameson Raid of 1897 produced a parliamentary enquiry which exonerated the Colonial Secretary, Chamberlain, it caused a section of Liberal back-benchers to condemn the implicit support lent by both Harcourt and Campbell-Bannerman, who sat upon the committee, to its findings. In the ensuing censure motion tabled against the government, and by implication against Liberal participation in the committee, 55 Liberals voted for the motion.[17] This body included a strong element of Radicalism in which the traditionals were especially present: Labouchere, Stanhope, Lawson, McEwan, Maden, Norton, Wedderburn, Souttar, together with Burns, Broadhurst, Channing, Lloyd George, Wallace, James Stuart and Yoxall. Sufficient Radicals abstained, however, to make it evident that the Radical bloc was not a cohesive entity. The challenge to imperialist leanings abroad did stem mainly from the traditional Radicals led by Labouchere, Lawson, Dilke and Stanhope, and while it might be possible to date the growth of that anti-capitalist body of opinion later associated with

[14] *Ibid.* 22 November 1898.
[15] *Ibid.* 17 December 1898.
[16] *Ibid.* 24 January 1899.
[17] J. Butler, *The Liberal Party and the Jameson Raid* (1968) pp. 204, 302.

opposition to the Boer war from 1897,[18] at this time the Radicals did not have any kind of constructive alternative policy to present, and their reliance upon a negative condemnation of Imperialism ensured their own relative isolation in 1900.[19]

The strength of traditional Radicalism and the particular views of the leadership complemented each other's initial remoteness from the ' New Liberalism ', a term which had begun to flourish in the press after 1895. Fowler still ' did not believe in programmes for any political party '.[20] John Morley in December 1895 declared to his audience the paramount urgency of social questions, but in the course of a long speech, he never quite managed to mention any. Harcourt in a speech to the Home Counties Liberal Federation in March 1896 dwelt entirely upon the House of Lords, temperance, electoral reform, peace and retrenchment; *The Times* thought it quite clear that the New Liberalism did not flourish in the Home Counties. Haldane claimed that in this ' epoch of social progress ', the Liberal party had reached ' the stage of putting the community first and class second ',[21] but he too believed the New Liberalism to be more a tendency than anything specific. The ' New Liberals ', he wrote, ' esteem a progressive policy in social matters more highly than anything else at present in Liberalism ', and he noted, with reference to T. H. Green, that ' the language of the social good ' was used by ' a growing number of the younger Liberals '.[22] Still he did not mention reformist issues, and Asquith was only slightly more specific, being willing to condemn ' the optimism of averages ' by pointing out that with a rising standard of comfort, more glaring contrasts of inequality existed than ever before.

A contemporary division (made by *The Speaker*) of the party into two, the Forwards, and ' the great body of the party ', was seemingly accurate. The weight of this body, ' anxious that in grasping at shadows we shall not lose the substance ',[23] was decisive in anchoring the party's commitments broadly to the base of 1892–5. So temperance and Welsh disestablishment remained prominent, despite warnings from *The Daily News* that the former excited the maximum of

18 *Ibid*. p. 287.
19 Cf. B. Porter, *Critics of Empire* (1968) pp. 69, 84.
20 *The Times*, 9 December 1897.
21 *Liberal Magazine*, December 1895, p. 492 (all reports of speeches taken from this source).
22 R. B. Haldane, ' The New Liberalism ', *Progressive Review*, November 1896.
23 *The Speaker*, 6 May 1899.

hostility for the minimum of good.[24] Despite Herbert Gladstone's attempts as chief whip to slacken the party's hold upon local option, the United Kingdom Alliance was still sufficiently influential with Liberal and Radical opinion to make his task a difficult one.[25] In 1899, the Liberation Society were also urging disestablishment upon Campbell-Bannerman as the best way to recover dissentient Liberals.[26]

Despite Radical energy, there is little sign of a positive advance on their behalf within the parliamentary party. A 'New Radical' described the Liberal predicament in 1897: effete organisation, internal indiscipline, the inapplicability of stale and traditional cries, and 'an Illingworth wing in the North [which], with the tacit support of a majority of the front bench, treats the whole movement towards a change in the relation of Labour and Capital as a mere predatory revolution'.[27] These difficulties were compounded by the Boer war; in 1901 the party still had 'no clear aim and no firm purpose in relation either to foreign or to domestic policy'.[28] In this vein, the Liberals failed to gain any permanent advantage from the Conservatives' inability to enact an Old Age Pension Bill, and were further unable to capitalise upon the favourable by-election trend which persisted right up to the outbreak of war in October 1899.[29] The Liberals further failed to fashion any links with organised labour, although the two were probably closer in 1899 and 1900 than three years previously. An I.L.P. programme outlined in 1899 was very similar to the Radical emphasis of these years, and it would appear that both Labour and Liberal politics were facing similar problems of direction and definition.[30] A writer in 1900 identified three separate schools of thought amongst contemporary social reformers: the modern radical and the land law reformers, the labour or new trade unionist school and thirdly the definitely-avowed collectivists. All three schools had four measures in common; pensions, the land for

---

[24] *Daily News*, 30 December 1897.

[25] Sir C. Mallet, *Herbert Gladstone : A Memoir* (1932) p. 156; Gladstone to Campbell-Bannerman, 12 December 1899, CBP, Add. Mss 41215.

[26] CBP, Add. Mss 41241, Minutes of a Deputation from the Executive Committee of the Liberation Society, 12 June 1899.

[27] *Contemporary Review*, October, December 1897; August 1898; January 1899.

[28] J. A. Murray Macdonald, ' The Liberal Party ', *Contemporary Review*, May 1901.

[29] Cf. *The Speaker*, 7 October 1899, talking of ' a great redistribution of power at hand '. Also F. H. Stead, *How Old Age Pensions Began to Be* (1909) pp. 107–13.

[30] K. Hardie and R. MacDonald, ' The I.L.P. Programme ', *Nineteenth Century*, January 1899; E. R. Pease, *A History of the Fabian Society* (1916) p. 156.

the people, a shorter working-day and railway nationalisation.[31] Even allowing for necessary and important differences in emphasis, this does suggest that progressive politics had acquired an underlying unity by the late 1890s which had been lacking before. The Liberals, as a party, had made certain gestures in the progressive direction, but had failed, through their internal indecisions, to take any initiative. The bulk of the party apparently supported the miners' eight-hour day,[32] and individual Liberals, such as H. J. Tennant, had attempted with some success to broaden the provisions of the 1897 Compensation Act. The party opposed the attitude of Lord Penrhyn towards his strike-bound quarrymen, and Liberals and *The Daily News* declared in sympathy with Labour during the engineering strike, Vaughan Nash (private secretary to Campbell-Bannerman) raising a fund for the women and children. A. H. D. Acland probably expressed the majority Liberal opinion when he wrote: ' if the demands of the employers are conceded, much of what we have always considered of the essence of Trade Unionism is at an end. I do not see how a prolonged warfare and bitterness on the part of the [Trade] Unionists throughout the country is to be avoided '.[33]

Yet there was little or no official Liberal support for trade unionism in its legal battles in the 1890s,[34] and an equivalent commitment to the eight-hour day and the regulation of hours, fair wages, the condition of the agricultural labourer, factory acts, the payment of members and relief works for the unemployed, which appeared regularly in Labour programmes, was missing from Liberal speeches and Liberal priorities. Campbell-Bannerman, for example, varied little from a staple diet of electoral reform and the House of Lords, temperance, housing ' for the very poor ', reform of the land laws and, of course, foreign issues.[35] Asquith added the extension of the Employers' Liability Act and promised ' a complete and direct attack upon the whole problem of old age ',[36] but from the end of 1898, Morley spoke only on imperialism, and after Rosebery at the City Liberal Club on 5 May 1899 had called for a renovated Liberalism based on ' a new Imperial spirit ' and the virtual abandonment of

---

31 W. Diack, ' Radicalism and Labour ', *Westminster Review*, August 1900.

32 *The Times*, 6 May 1897.

33 Acland to Ripon, 7 December 1897, RP, Add. Mss 43637.

34 Cf. J. Saville, ' Trade Unions and Free Labour ' in Briggs and Saville, *Labour History*, ch. 9.

35 *Liberal Magazine*, April and June 1899, for reports of Liberal speeches.

36 *Ibid*. January 1899 and June 1899.

Home Rule, domestic issues were at a further discount. Kay-Shuttleworth told Campbell-Bannerman soon after his accession that ' the party expect much more activity and initiative from the future leader of the front bench. . . . They want an earnest lead on the home questions of the future '. Before the 1900 election, he thought ' domestic and constructive questions are what we can best unite upon ', recommending education, licensing, the Lords, retrenchment, and electoral reform.[37] But at that stage, the party was neither inclined to admit the primacy of social questions, nor had it advanced much in its understanding of them. For all the Radicals' attempts to draw up a programme, for all the contemporary recognition that the individualistic school of Radicals had been superseded, the ' Forward ' policy, in parliament at least, had advanced little beyond the admission that the old Liberal philosophies were inadequate.[38] As to issues which involved the principle of state action or collective control, there was little indication as yet of a programme explicitly based upon that principle.

LIBERALS AND RADICALS IN THE COUNTRY

In the country, the picture emerges of a tension between Radicalism and the established or orthodox supporters of the party. This tension was expressed in struggles between the two within the organisational structure of the party, notably the N.L.F.; the rise of the Radicals to a position of influence within the latter body being a contributory factor in the emergence of demands for social reform after 1901.

The success of the parliamentary party depended firstly upon the Liberal Central Association (L.C.A.), which was the direct responsibility of the chief whip, and dealt ' with that part of political organisation which is concerned in every respect with membership of the Commons '.[39] The function of the L.C.A. was to guide the local associations in the selection of candidates, and to act as agent in the provision of speakers and funds, and further, to pass on official policy. This combination of activities assured for the L.C.A. the theoretical predominance within Liberal organisation,[40] but theory did not always coincide with practice.

---

[37] To Campbell-Bannerman, 24 January 1899 and 13 October 1900, CBP, Add. Mss 41221.

[38] Cf. C. B. Roylance Kent, *The English Radicals* (1899) pp. 429–31.

[39] R. S. Watson, *The N.L.F. 1877–1906* (1906) p. 64.

[40] H. Gladstone termed it ' an inner political circle of great power '.

The effectiveness of the L.C.A. depended upon the ability and the influence of the chief whip, who necessarily had to be a man of some standing, both within the parliamentary party and as regards the dignataries who staffed the local associations. The formal control by the L.C.A. over the constituencies themselves was slight; this was a responsibility of which the Liberals, with their emphasis upon the autonomy of constituency associations, deliberately fought shy. The responsibility for the maintenance and formation of local organisations was held to rest with the National Liberal Federation, which, in fact, lacked the centralised and permanent apparatus through which to act.[41] The aim of the N.L.F. was ' to establish a general political organisation ', but effective power was to lie in the component parts ' which shall be strong and independent '. The L.C.A. controlled the bulk of the party's funds, through both its own private subscriptions and through the passage of money, raised by occasional N.L.F. campaigns, into the chief whip's account. Liberal organisers in the country looked to the L.C.A. and the chief whip for payment and instructions, although in practice, their main focal meeting-point seems to have been through the N.L.F., especially on the occasion of the annual conference.

If the L.C.A. was concerned with the parliamentary party, the popular party in the country looked to the N.L.F. as the vehicle for their aspirations. The delegates from the federated associations met once a year at the Council (i.e. the annual conference) of the N.L.F. The Council in turn elected the General Committee which met two or three times a year on average, supervised the administrative work of the N.L.F., and before 1890 drew up the agenda for the annual conference. This Committee consisted of the officers and the representatives from each of the federated associations.[42] After 1890, a smaller General Purposes Committee was established, to be chosen by election from the General Committee, and this new body was to have the final say over the agenda for the conference.[43] The General

---

41 F. H. Herrick, ' The Origins of the National Liberal Federation ', *Journal of Modern History*, XVII (1945).

42 On the basis of three delegates from each constituency. The General Committee was therefore a large body of upwards of 300 to 400 people on average.

43 In 1896 this Committee became known simply as the Executive Committee. This was a body of 18 (later expanded to 20) members plus two ex-officio members, the President of the N.L.F., and the Treasurer. M.P.s were ineligible for this Committee. The Executive met at least one month before the N.L.F. Council met, and asked for the opinions of the federated associations ' in order that the Committee may be guided in framing the resolutions to be submitted to the Council '. (*Daily News*, 10 March 1896.)

Committee was to assist in the formation of new Liberal associations, and, with the N.L.F., was to partake in the work of political education and propaganda. Co-ordination with the work of the L.C.A. was assisted after 1886 when the N.L.F. and the L.C.A. shared common premises and a common secretary (Schnadhorst) at 41 and 42 Parliament Street. In 1887, the two departments jointly established the Liberal Publication Department, and from 1886, N.L.F. constituency surveys were made available to the L.C.A., while in 1888 the N.L.F. itself established a new department to deal with registration.[44]

This dual structure could be criticised on two counts, the efficiency of the organisation, and the character of the men who operated it at local level. The first factor is more a matter for the next section, but the second is relevant here.

There was an inherent conflict between the style of 'popular democracy' favoured by the caucus-model, and the men and the supporters who possessed both the time and the means to give direction to this model. Ostrogorski recorded that after 1885 the attendance at ward meetings was poor, with only a small minority contributing anything to the expenses of the association. Hence the importance of a Secretary, but 'the great difficulty of many associations is . . . to afford a (full-time) Secretary ', and they accordingly relied upon an honorary figure who was either an amateur – a businessman who could not afford to devote much time to politics – or a zealot, possibly non-conformist, probably lower middle-class, and possessed of a very narrow political horizon: shopkeepers, clerks or superior artisans whose struggle for success and security 'makes them look with admiration on those a few steps better off ', and strongly influenced their views in selecting candidates.[45]

While making due allowance for Ostrogorski's dislike of the caucus, his observations were in accord with accusations made by emergent Labour politicians. He stressed that temperament inclined to orthodoxy which prevailed among Liberal party machines, not so much 'immured in an unchangeable creed ' but displaying ' rather . . . a constant inclination towards conformity with the attitude of those who are supposed to be the depositaries of the faith ' (and he also noticed ' the vehement and aggressive style ' of non-conformist

[44] B. McGill, ' Francis Schnadhorst and Liberal Party Organization ', *Journal of Modern History*, xxxiv (1962).

[45] M. Ostrogorski, *Democracy and the Organisation of Political Parties*, Vol. i (1902) pp. 332–3, 342–8.

deacons and tradesmen).[46] The combination of small personages in a small community might well make for illiberality, and Ostrogorski does suggest certain conclusions: that Liberal party organisation was built upon the implicit admission of fundamental social differences, and was not, of itself, exposed to any internal movements which might have changed its character. The only real effectiveness it possessed was the transmission and expression of traditional Liberal principles, which was most easily accomplished within the familiar context of policies aimed at liberty for the subject and the control of unpopular interests and institutions. It was not, therefore, surprising that the N.L.F. failed to touch on controversial matters to reform at least until the 1890s – the effective inclination to do so from below was slight.

A great burden undoubtedly rested on the voluntary activities of those men willing to assume the effective responsibility for organisation. Men such as Robert Spence Watson, President of the N.L.F. from 1890 to 1902, or his predecessor Sir James Kitson. Of Watson, J. A. Spender wrote:

He belonged to a political order ... which was immensely important to the Liberal party in these years. This consisted of men who stood outside Parliament but who were the political leaders of their localities and had the purely disinterested object of keeping their fellow-citizens in the right path. Most of them were business or professional men to whom politics were necessarily a side-issue, but they were the mainstay of the local clubs and associations, and gave generously of their spare time and all the money they could afford for the support of the cause, on which they genuinely believed the welfare and progress of the country to depend. The local newspapers treated them with great deference and reported their speeches at length, and it was everywhere recognized that they had to be consulted before a candidate was ' sent down ' or any serious development of policy proposed. The dissent of any one of them was recognized at once as a matter of grave import which might entail the loss of a seat or indeed of several seats. ... The Federation was the special organ of these men.[47]

In the 1890s, and especially after 1895, this structure came under a great deal of criticism from the Radicals, who asserted that the L.C.A. had too great an influence in the internal counsels of the N.L.F.,

[46] *Ibid.* pp. 350, 352.

[47] J. A. Spender, *Sir R. Hudson*, p. 65. (Hudson succeeded Schnadhorst in 1893 as secretary to both L.C.A. and N.L.F.)

that the N.L.F.'s effective initiative with regard to the suggesting and drafting of policy was seriously circumscribed both by the formal control of the whips, and the informal degree of power exercised by the men of influence within the N.L.F.[48] After 1895, the Radicals were demanding a more active role for the N.L.F. This demand conflicted with the views of influential members of the N.L.F., not only in the specific demands made, but in the break made with the essentially Whiggish style of politics affected by these members. It was a paradox of the caucus model that the power given at local (constituency) level to popular committees was never formally transmitted to the national level, and the role of the annual conference as regards the parliamentary party and the enunciation of policy remained ambiguous. While the Liberals invariably stressed that ' the essential principle of the Federation is the participation of all members of the party in the formation and direction of its policy ', at the same time they declared that, in conference, ' no formal political programme is submitted for general acceptance, but the opinion of Liberals on current questions is . . . authoritatively ascertained. Thus the whole strength of the party may be concentrated upon the promotion of such legislation as is by general consent deemed of the first importance.'[49] The power of first the General Committee, and secondly, of the General Purposes Committee, to vet the resolutions reaching them from the constituencies, and the maxim that conference only dealt with those questions on which the sense of the party was apparent, acted as a political sieve through which unwelcome particles of Radicalism were effectively strained. It was in this way that the N.L.F. was precluded from discussing the eight-hours issue in 1891, and upon these grounds that the 1891 Newcastle Resolutions were rejected as either in themselves a programme for the parliamentary party, or as constituting a precedent for the future activities of the conference.

This conflict between Radicalism and officialdom emerged into the open after the defeat of 1895. In August 1895, a deputation from the Radical Committee led by Dilke, Labouchere and Stanhope met

---

[48] Watson, *The N.L.F.*, p. 64, admitted that the administrative work of the two bodies was carried on jointly ' but there has never been any attempt upon the part of either to influence the action of the other in its own department. The work, the direction, the finances of each have been kept entirely separate '. In his speech to the conference in 1896 (below): ' I assert that not a single resolution has ever, at all events since 1886, been suggested, hinted at or drawn, altered or manipulated by any Whip or leader whatsoever '.

[49] *Proceedings of the 10th annual meeting of the N.L.F.* (*1888*), *Annual Report*.

Harcourt and the chief whip, Ellis, to protest that two bodies sharing the same offices and staff could not in any sense be independent. Harcourt rejected the accusation.[50] On 9 March 1896, just prior to the meeting of the N.L.F., the Radical Committee called a meeting of the party which some 90 Liberals attended, and the specific complaint involved the manner in which the Executive Committee was chosen.[51] The discussions were apparently inconclusive, and a compromise resolution was passed: ' that the (Radical) Committee be instructed to summon a meeting of the Radical and Labour members after the (N.L.F.) Conference to consider the future organisation of the party '. Many Radicals, however, remained dissatisfied and claimed that the meeting had been packed.[52]

Also on 9 March the annual report of the N.L.F. was issued. It defined the duties of the Federation as the discussion of the report itself, the transaction of general business, and the expression, through resolutions, of previously agreed policies. Full and proper discussion of policy should take place in the General Committee and ' the Council must remain largely an assembly of a declaratory nature '. However, some concessions were made. In this year (1896) before the annual report was put to the Council, it was decided that ' the Council shall be open for the free discussion of any matter affecting the policy and principles of the Liberal party '. New rules for the selection of the Executive Committee were announced. Henceforth, there would be, each year, compulsory retirement of the three members who had attended the fewest meetings during the past year, and one month before the meeting of the General Committee at which the Executive was selected a list of all those offering themselves for office would be sent to the federated associations, who were now to be entitled to add their own nominations. If the number of nominations exceeded the number to be elected, the vote was to be taken by ballot at the meeting of the General Committee. This proposal was evidently in answer to the Radical claim that both the General and the Executive Committees were too much the preserve of the influential and official. The Report asked for two

---

50 *The Times*, 10 and 11 March 1896.

51 *Ibid*. The gist of the Radical complaint seems to have been that although the Executive Committee was nominally elected by the General Committee, the ' wire-pullers ' within the latter body were able so to control which members stood, and how many, that the election became meaningless.

52 *Westminster Gazette*, ' The Case for Separation ' by ' Independent Radical ', 11 March 1896.

considerations to be borne in mind – a balance between the regions within the organisation, and for ' a considerable proportion ' of the Executive to consist of the Presidents or Officers of the affiliated associations.[53]

At the Conference itself, these proposals were adopted, and the Radical revolt seems to have fizzled out. R. Winfrey did propose that the entire Executive Committee should be elected by the N.L.F. but he obtained little support, and Watson's speech (cited above) clinched the issue. The Radicals were, according to Stanhope, disgusted with the Conference, and fell back on the usual accusations of packing by the wirepullers.[54] It was true that the Radical charges had obtained very little support. Of the earlier meeting, *The Daily News* observed : ' Who and what are the " Radical Committee " that they should dictate what is best for the affiliated Liberal associations without even so much as asking the advice of the persons concerned? ' The paper pointed out that the local associations possessed the power of initiative, for any five of them could convene a meeting of the General Committee, and they could submit what resolutions they pleased to the Executive Committee (without necessarily getting them accepted). ' With such power in their hands, surely it is the fault of the Federated Associations if they do not get their own way; and if they are fettered, as their critics contend, then it is in the local associations ... that the work of emancipation should begin.' [55]

The Radicals did not take immediate advantage of the change in the rules. The 1896 Executive did represent some alteration from the personnel of the previous six years, which was a combination of powerful businessmen like Kitson and relatively insignificant figures from the constituencies, but the change was mainly a consequence of M.P.s defeated in 1895 now becoming eligible for membership, William Mather, for example, although C. P. Allen, Corrie Grant and Dr Clifford were all elected for the first time in 1896.

One good indication of the rising interest in the Executive is provided by the number of unsuccessful aspirants for election. In 1896, there were three, in 1897 only one, in 1899, the number rose to ten (including C. H. Roberts, Ryland Adkins, a Radical land-owner and a Radical lawyer respectively, and L. T. Hobhouse). By 1900,

---

[53] Proceedings of the 18th annual meeting of the N.L.F. (1896), *Annual Report*. Also *Daily News*, 10 March 1896.

[54] *The Times*, 28 March 1896.

[55] *Daily News*, 10 and 11 March 1896.

the Executive numbered several Radicals, including Hugh Fullerton, a retired merchant, G. H. Radford, a writer, and W. H. Lever. With the exception of Hobhouse, all the above five were Radical M.P.s after 1906. 1901 saw a rise in the number unsuccessful to 22, and in 1902, to 25. In 1901, A. Birrell, W. H. Dickinson, J. F. L. Brunner and J. Stuart were elected, in 1902, Murray Macdonald and W. S. Rowntree, and in 1903, R. C. Lehmann and D. M. Mason. Thereafter, numbers standing declined with the increasing interest in parliament itself, but from 1903 to 1905, the Radicals amongst the writers, lawyers and ' independents ' were in a majority upon the Executive Committee, which also argues for some increase in Radical support amongst the General Committee itself. It was possibly more than coincidence that in 1903 the N.L.F. declared social reform to be imperative and called for increased labour representation. In 1904, the primary resolution again dealt with social reform and the issue of the land, and 1905 saw Fenwick and Lever's motion for establishing permanent machinery for the unemployed.[56] After 1906, with a Liberal government in office, the N.L.F. confined itself largely to re-affirming support in Liberal policies, and the Radical activities were concentrated in parliament.

ORGANISATIONAL RECOVERY

To study the Liberal organisational base is to gain an insight into the effect of the parliamentary debate upon the party's grassroots support. Although central party organisation before 1914 had not yet assumed a fully modern significance in terms of enforcing party discipline or mobilising a mass vote, the characteristics of the organisation, the relationships between the centre and the constituencies, the efforts to raise money, to locate possible candidates, placate local notables, together with the role of the N.L.F., do jointly provide an indication of how influential sources within the party viewed the New Liberalism and its affiliations with progressive politics. The conclusion that emerges is tentative and must wait upon the more detailed studies of constituency politics,[57] but it would appear that the strength of the ' New Liberalism ' at the centre was not duplicated *in any depth* amongst the constituencies, and that there existed considerable

[56] This is perhaps an exception to A. L. Lowell's description of the N.L.F. as an ' opaque sham '. (*The Government of England*, 1 (1908) p. 570.)

[57] See P. F. Clarke's comments (*Lancashire and the New Liberalism*, ch. 1, Parts 3 and 4, *passim*).

tension between the old and the new (especially in the case of making conciliatory gestures towards the Labour party). It appears too that the entry of a number of Social Radicals into parliament after 1900, and again after 1910, was in part made possible by a slide away from a dependence upon the local notables. In this sense, the parliamentary party might almost be described as a party living upon borrowed time, in that the entry of a large Radical element composed of journalists, authors, social workers, etc. into the party, without any equivalent increase in the means and methods to support them (which might be deduced from the fall in the business element in parliament), placed an increasing strain upon two key factors. First, the ability of local constituency organisations to mobilise on the basis of belief in and support for a cause; secondly, the ability of the central organisation to provide sufficient financial support to give local organisations a measure of viability.

With both factors, the Liberals had traditionally experienced difficulty. The sectionalism of the parliamentary party was reflected in individual constituencies, such that the abiding problem for the organisation was how to appeal to the separate enthusiasms of the sections and induce them all to the poll. This was difficult enough in the days of temperance, education, celtic sectionalism and the non-conformist conscience, but when the new issues emerged, reform of the Poor-Law and aid for the unemployed, and when a profound sectional difference emerged between those who were to benefit from social reforms and those who were to pay for them, it became increasingly difficult to mobilise upon the basis of a uniform incentive.[58] As the Liberals became increasingly identified with a programme of social reform and as their need to appease the claims of labour increased, so their efforts in turn cost the constituencies the tangible support of local contributors and forced them to rely further upon the centre, both for finance and the provision of candidates. After 1900, as contests grew in size, so too did their style alter, and from the politics of personality, of local influence and personal claim, there arose an awareness of the new principles of politics with some further linkage between supporters, their expectations and definitive goals over time.[59] Principles were expressed within issues, especially in the cases of land and taxation, and when the new principles were

[58] Cf. J. Howarth, ' The Liberal Revival in Northamptonshire, 1880–1895 ', *Historical Journal*, 12 (1969) 1.
[59] Cf. P. F. Clarke, ' British Politics and Blackburn Politics, 1900–1910 ', *Historical Journal*, 12 (1969) 2.

capable of touching men in their pockets, there too was a further reason for being deliberate in one's choice of party. It would, of course, be hard to separate the consequences of defects within Liberal party organisation from the consequences arising from defects within the electoral system itself, and it would therefore, be unwise to gauge popular strength simply as a reflection of votes cast or seats won. The electoral register was scarcely inclusive, registration anomalies militated against the working-class voter, and there was always the issue of the plural voter.[60] Yet this qualification apart, one may still see the variations in Liberal candidatures, and in their share of the vote won, as reflecting structural failures indicative of shifting patterns of allegiance.

The inefficiency of the Liberal organisation was well remarked upon by contemporaries in the 1890s. In comparison with the Conservative structure, 'the scheme of Radical organisation (lacks)... the comprehesnsive net-work of divisions and sub-divisions...contains frequent gaps, and the party managers can never be certain of getting into immediate touch with the wavering and irresolute voters until these gaps are filled '. The defect of the caucus was to place virtually its whole emphasis upon popular participation, and very little upon a permanent structure to control the popular vote, so that the final structure was necessarily incomplete: ' Many of the villages and smaller towns are without committees of any kind, and even in populous centres it sometimes happens that the only centres of propagandism are clubs, which exist as much for recreation as for political education.'[61] A strong indictment of the apathy and indifference of Liberal constituency politics was made by the *Westminster Review* in 1887.

Many associations have become more or less close bodies representative of a few, and out of touch with the bulk of the Liberal party. It has been ... common ... for small ward meeting to elect more members to the association than there have been persons present at the meetings. Selected lists of names have been put to the meeting, and carried as a matter of the commonest routine. . . . There exist only vague and superficial relations between the associations and the electors; the central body takes little or no trouble to ascertain the opinions of the masses ... the association in effect represents ... no one at all but the members themselves.[62]

[60] N. Blewett, ' The Franchise in the U.K. 1885–1918 ', *Past and Present*, December 1965.
[61] *The Times*, 14 September 1895.   [62] Vol. 128 (1887) p. 393.

This view was strongly underlined in a paper read by the secretary of the South Wales Liberal Federation in 1888,[63] and was further repeated by *The Times* in 1895.[64] In Wales, organisation was similarly deficient, Lloyd George claiming that 90 per cent of Welsh Liberals were ' outside the pale ' of Liberal associations; [65] after 1895 when the Conservatives won 9 out of 34 Welsh seats (a record), in 8 or 9 constituencies Liberal machinery ' crumbled into obsolescence ', while Liberalism here proved especially vulnerable to labour troubles.[66] In Scotland, the same picture prevailed; the Scottish Liberal Association was a largely titular body which pursued a policy of ' no interference with local associations ', and was further hindered by the difference in outlook between Radical Glasgow and a Whiggish Edinburgh.[67] The lack of effective central control resulted in the steady narrowing of the gap in the popular vote between Liberals and Conservatives, with the Conservatives winning 36 seats to the Liberals 34 in 1900.[68] Scottish Liberalism also faced an early challenge from organised labour, with which it consistently refused to co-operate. Financial difficulties were acute,[69] the 1900 election gave every sign of having been fought ' on the cheap ',[70] and the recovery of Scottish Liberalism after 1900 found the party managers embarrassed for funds in England with which to help, and unable to exploit any sizeable resources in Scotland itself. Part of the trouble was that the Liberal imperialists were busy building a fund of their own which was not available to Gladstone, but the roots of the trouble went deeper. In August 1901 Sinclair told Gladstone that a by-election in north-east Lanarkshire would cost up to £1,500, and he could get nothing out of an almost entirely working-class constituency. On 22 May 1903 the Scottish Liberals made a formal request for the recontinuance of a previously-allotted national grant of £200, while in November 1903 the need for money was apparently acute and there was too a shortage of candidates.[71]

[63] R. N. Hall, *Liberal Organisation and Work* (1888).
[64] *The Times*, 14 September 1895.   [65] *Carnarvon Herald*, 4 November 1894.
[66] Memo by H. Allgood, 20 March 1903, LGP, A/3/3/6; K. O. Morgan, *Wales in British Politics*, pp. 168–9.
[67] J. G. Kellas, *The Liberal Party in Scotland*, pp. 116–20.
[68] Cf. D. W. Urwin, ' Development of Conservative Party Organisation in Scotland Until 1912 ', *Scottish Historical Review*, October 1965.
[69] Sinclair to Gladstone, 5 February and 22 May 1903, HGP, Add. Mss 45995.
[70] Munro-Ferguson to Gladstone, 25 August 1899, HGP, Add. Mss 46057.
[71] Sinclair–Gladstone correspondence, HGP, Add. Mss 45995.

If the situation in Wales and Scotland suggests that in their areas of strength the Liberals relied on traditional issues and the tradition of Liberalism itself to sway the results, such a policy in an area such as London was little short of disastrous. By 1885-6, the London and Counties Liberal Union, set up in 1881, was in great financial difficulties.[72] In 1887, the L.C.L.U. was replaced by two separate bodies, the Home Counties Liberal Federation, and the London Liberal and Radical Union (L.L.R.U.) the latter including the 58 constituencies in metropolitan London itself. It aimed to establish a candidate in every constituency, and at establishing a liaison between Liberals and Progressives over a programme for the forthcoming L.C.C. elections.

In 1888, however, Sidney Webb severely criticised the shallowness of Liberal organisation in London. In most associations, he asserted, there were not enough Liberals to be found to man the General Council at a ratio of 1 for every 25 electors. Of the members of the General Councils, less than 10 per cent did any work or subscribed any money. The Liberals had lost the respect and the allegiance of many of the 300 working-men's clubs that existed, and the clubs themselves had joined with the Metropolitan Radical Federation (M.R.F.) in organising for political work upon the L.C.C. Every man, he pointed out, who joined one of these 'Labour Unions' (as the joint committees were called), represented an active political worker lost, even temporarily, to the Liberals.[73] Meanwhile, the L.L.R.U. established a new committee on organisation under W. S. Caine and Renwick Seager, and this, with the help of James Stuart and R. K. Causton was instrumental in procuring the Liberal recovery in 1892.[74] Yet the recovery itself was not used as a base from which to improve organisation; B. Costelloe told Samuel that the London seats 'are simply going to pieces ... we shall save very few of them'.[75] The Daily News reported on the eve of the 1895 elections that there were no Liberal candidates in at least five seats, while in Kennington, a temperance candidate, supported by Caine and Lawson, was opposing Beaujoy. By 1900, only three London constituencies had a competent Liberal agent, as against 30 in the case of

[72] *Liberal Yearbook* for 1887.
[73] S. Webb, *Wanted : A Programme* (1888).
[74] Also HGP, Add. Mss 46022, L.C.A. circular dated 23 December 1891 signed by Schnadhorst stating London organisation to be in a lethargic state, and asking for every possible help from leading Liberals.
[75] HSP, A/155 (1) Costelloe to Samuel, 10 December 1893.

the Conservatives. The vital work of registration had so lapsed that the number of constituencies in which the lodger vote exceeded 15 per cent of the electorate fell from 15 to 9 by 1899, while Liberal apathy in Bow and Bromley and West Ham had allowed the growth of strong local Labour parties.[76]

The Liberals were not completely impervious to this process. The N.L.F. in 1886 urged ' the necessity of energetic efforts in the county constituencies for the purposes of political education and organisation ', and in 1887 the N.L.F. sponsored a series of conferences to this end. In 1887, the annual report recorded that 405 new associations and clubs were either in the process of affiliation or had affiliated since the great split. The 1888 Conference dealt with the charge that Labour candidates were too infrequent. Spence Watson claimed: ' This charge can rarely be sustained, but it is of the highest importance that the officers of Liberal associations should take care to make their associations so thoroughly representative as to give no ground for such a complaint.' [77]

He also pointed out the difficulty of both influencing the constituencies in this matter and of financing those Labour candidates who emerged. This issue was fast becoming the prime bone of contention between London and the constituencies. 1886 had seen the formation of Threlfall's Labour Electoral Association which, even if it desired to work in harmony with the Liberal organisation, still expressed a strong claim for working-men candidates.[78] Schnadhorst, upon the L.C.A.'s Committee on Candidates, found himself opposed at constituency level by such individuals as Kitson and Illingworth when he tried to influence the associations in their selections, and in 1891, when faced with a request from the Secretary (Tims) of the M.R.F. for the withdrawal of 50 Liberal candidates in London so that these constituencies might be contested by the direct representatives of the unions and the L.E.A., Schnadhorst had to point out that he had no direct power over individual associations.[79] The action of independent Labour candidates in 1892, such as Tillett's opposition

---

[76] P. Thompson, *Socialists, Liberals and Labour : the Struggle for London* (1967) pp. 71, 76, 91f., 104f.

[77] *Proceedings of the 11th Annual Meeting of the N.L.F.*

[78] A. W. Humphrey, *A History of Labour Representation* (1912) p. 96.

[79] B. McGill, ' F. Schnadhorst and Liberal Party Organisation '. (Although Arnold Morley and Schnadhorst were possibly considering helping over 40 Labour candidates in 1892, but they were relying on Andrew Carnegie for money which did not arrive.)

to Illingworth in Bradford, the Fabian call in 1893 for 50 candidates with a fund of their own to fight Liberals, and the I.L.P.s unsuccessful electoral strategy in 1895 exacerbated an already tender relationship. John Morley, for example, who in 1890 specifically favoured increased Labour representation, announced in Newcastle in 1894 that ' for special representatives of labour to make war upon the Liberal party is insanity and is suicide '. He did not disagree so much with the new principles or ideals as with the new methods.[80]

In 1891, the General Committee of the N.L.F. appointed eleven district agents, grouping the constituencies throughout the country (with the exception of those which came under the more immediate purview of the H.C.L.F.) in order to make a complete investigation of the party organisation.[81] On balance, however, there seems little doubt that the poor showing of the Liberal party in the 1890s was due in considerable part to their inability in the decade after 1886 to rationalise their organisation in the country, to give it both depth and clarity; and it was also due to the beginnings of friction between headquarters in London and the leaders of constituency politics over the degree of central direction permissible, especially over the problem of Labour candidatures.

It is also likely that official Liberalism felt the effects of 1886 far harder and for longer than they would admit.[82] Since 1868, the Liberal financial inferiority to the Conservatives had been evident and 1886 itself was only one of a series of steps which saw financial and landed support moving rightwards.[83] By 1886, the Liberals had lost a whole array of titled wealth – Hartington, Derby, Northbrook, Selborne, Carlingford, Argyll, Fitzwilliam, Yarborough – and they had lost Birmingham and with it valuable influence in the west Midlands. After 1886, most landed men supported the same party.[84] These losses were doubly serious, for they denied the Liberals an important source of money at the very moment when they needed to

80 J. Morley, *The Liberal Programme* (1894).

81 Watson, *The National Liberal Federation*, p. 123. (He had to stress that no interference with local affairs was intended.)

82 Cf. *The Times*, 14 September 1895.

83 H. J. Hanham, *Elections and Party Management, 1868–1885* (1958) ch. 17; W. B. Gwynn, *Democracy and the Cost of Politics* (1962) p. 94.

84 F. M. L. Thompson, *English Landed Society*, p. 122, also A. E. Pease, *Elections and Recollections*, pp. 39–40, for the declining base of landed Liberal support in the north. G. L. Goodman, ' Liberal Unionism and the Revolt of the Whigs ', *Victorian Studies*, December 1959. D. Southgate, *The Passing of the Whigs 1832–1886* (1965) pp. 412–13.

redevelop their organisation and possibly to provide finances for poorer (labour) candidates, and they were denied too the influence of a landowning class which was still significant.[85] Although the cost of elections had been reduced after the 1883 Corrupt Practices Act, it was still a cheap election which cost under £1,000, and as the number of contested elections rose gradually with the growth of the electorate, the Liberals found themselves at a further disadvantage in being unable to raise a campaign fund fully adequate to the occasion. Not only were the Liberals unable to afford as many agents as the Conservatives, but after 1885, the salaries for their agents were often low, behind hand and even uncertain.[86] When to this picture is added that of the Liberal party suffering, even marginally, from a decline in the support of such important sections of the party as the non-conformists,[87] the pattern of small tradesmen and superior artisans moving to the suburb,[88] and the growing antipathy between the Liberals and a significant section of the middle-class,[89] the structural basis of the Liberal party takes on a very fragile air indeed. Such fragility was particularly expressed in the difficulty the Liberals experienced in contesting sufficient seats in parliamentary elections, and this was very much a long-term factor; the Liberals were rarely able to approach the number of Conservative candidatures, and in 1895 for example, the Liberals failed to contest 112 seats, in 1900, 145, but in 1906, only 5. The Conservative figures were 7, 12 and 15 respectively.[90]

After 1895, the Liberals attempted to revitalise their constituencies. Extensive instructions were issued for improving the work of registration,[91] while the annual report presented to the N.L.F. in 1896 urged the constituencies to mobilise all the local support they could, especially financial, in order to reduce the strain upon head-

---

[85] Cf. H. J. Hanham, ' British Party Finance 1868–1880 ', *Bulletin of the Institute of Historical Research*, 27 (1954). Also Ostrogorski, *Democracy and the Organisation of Political Parties*, Vol. 1, p. 365.

[86] *The Times*, 16 February 1894.

[87] J. F. Glaisier, ' English Non-Conformity and the Decline of Liberalism ', *American Historical Review*, LXIII (1938).

[88] J. P. Dunbabin, ' Parliamentary Elections in Great Britain 1868–1900 ', *English Historical Review*, LXXXI, January 1966.

[89] H. Pelling, *The Social Geography of British Elections 1885–1910* (1967) pp. 31, 37.

[90] T. Lloyd, ' Uncontested Seats in British General Elections 1852–1910 ', *Historical Journal*, VIII (1965).

[91] *Notes and Hints for the Guidance of Liberals* (1896).

quarters.[92] In 1898, the N.L.F. approved the creation of a special fund 'for re-organising those constituencies in which the party machinery is at present defective', which raised £11,000 by 1900.

Meanwhile in April 1899 Herbert Gladstone had succeeded Ellis as chief whip. Time was too short to remedy the deadweight debt he inherited from Ellis of abandoned and empty seats, and he found the financial situation little better. Because, he stated, 'the ordinary sources of supply are nearly dried up', he intended asking 30 friends to become guarantors each to the tune of £2,500. He did not, in the first place anticipate having to ask for more than £1,500 each, but this sum soon rose to £2,000 for, as he told Ripon, only 7 of his 30 had responded. Ultimately, it seems, the campaign fund depended on the contributions of a score of prominent Liberals, and it was noticeable how many such Liberals were beginning to complain of the financial strain upon them.[93] In the circumstances, Gladstone indicated to Ripon, the Liberals had done as well in 1900 as might have been expected:

We shall have to wait for the reaction. Until it sets in pretty strongly we shall never get candidates to face these tremendous majorities in the big towns.

The war and the personal troubles inside the party have given the Tories every opportunity of using their great preponderance in the press, in money and in candidates to the greatest advantage.

The one element of hope in it all is the solidity of the Associations and Liberal workers. Local defections ... seem to have been rare, and in many constituencies we have had for the first time the active help of men who left us in '86.[94]

1900 saw something of a turning point, for the clash between the Rosebery and Campbell-Bannerman wings, whatever the drawback at national level, does seem to have stimulated fresh interest amongst the constituencies. After 1900, it was the Liberals who stood to gain as the successive issues of education and free trade rallied again to

---

[92] *Proceedings of the 18th annual meeting of the N.L.F.* (1896).

[93] Gladstone to Ripon, 12 and 24 September 1900, RP, Add. Mss 43543. Charles McClaren, Lord Brassey each gave £2,500. Sir James Joicey £2,000, McEwan and Lord Overtoun £4,000 each, Tweedmouth over £9,000, A. Morley £1,000, and J. Horniman 10,000 guineas bringing his total of contributions to 'nearly £28,000'. Cadbury was helping '7 or 8 constituencies', and the I.L.P. where there was no Liberal. Sir Joseph Pease was contributing up to £4,000 for 5 seats. Sir Joseph Leese had spent £4,850 in 4 elections since 1886, and could not afford more than £200 now. (HGP, Add. Mss 46022, 46058, 46017.)

[94] RP, Add. Mss 43543, 7 October 1900.

their support sections whose active allegiance to the party had been in decline. At the L.C.A., Gladstone initiated a further drive for reorganisation. In a survey probably published after the 1900 election, it was noted that the local associations were still resting too heavily on a few wealthy supporters; losses in this respect having been heavy in 1886, since which time there had also been a 'slow but sure consolidation of the Tory forces in the villages'.

There are hundreds of Associations at the present moment which are moribund and useless ... It is impossible to lay too much stress on the necessity ... of making the annual election of the Committees of these local associations a matter in which the whole party in the area shall take an active share or interest.[95]

New units of organisation had to be established at local level with an agent in every constituency. The District Agent would have to see that as many Liberals as possible were 'activated' and as much monetary support as possible raised, for organisation was far too dependent on small groups of wealthy supporters. The ideal to work for ' is the self-supporting local organisation, with a Resident Agent working in the constituency all the year round. M.P.s should spend more time in their constituencies, and more speakers should be available.' The survey suggested an effective division of England into 12 to 14 districts under the District Agents who would in turn be supervised by an Advisory Committee of Liberal M.P.s, candidates and leading party members within each district. The initial difficulty was to raise the £8,000–£10,000 required to equip the districts and to provide for an annual expenditure of some £14,000 to keep them going.

At the beginning of 1903, a National Liberal Campaign Fund was established, aiming at a minimum of £50,000. It was specifically to be devoted towards bringing party machinery up to scratch and ' to render such financial aid as may be necessary to ensure that constituencies which are running poor men as their candidates are not handicapped ... by lack of money'. By 4 October, 1905 this fund had reached £40,000, and in that year the annual report of the N.L.F. noted that the Federation lacked a permanent subscription list and remarked that ' a yearly income of £5,000 should be assured if the organisation is to be maintained in a condition of proper

[95] *Memorandum on Liberal Re-organisation*: (Most Private) C1900 (British Museum estimate).

efficiency '. This fund too was established, and met with reasonable success.[96]

Although it is uncertain as to whether the organisational scheme outlined above was ever inaugurated, the emphasis upon a subscription-based income, upon fighting as many constituencies as possible, and upon encouraging popular participation in local politics, was of great benefit to the party not only in providing for the numbers eventually returned in 1906, but in allowing particularly for Radicals to fight in constituencies which would previously have been rejected as hopeless. The Home Counties Liberal Federation was itself in desperate need of money – practically every constituency needed an immediate grant of from £200 to £600 to make its fighting at all even a possibility. In the final event, the Liberal ability to fight virtually every constituency in the Home Counties must have been a factor in their successes in that region [97] – Abingdon, Brentford and Dartford were won, double victories were recorded in Southampton and Brighton, Whiggish candidates were successful in Salisbury (E. P. Tennant), East Grinstead (C. H. Corbett), Bedford (P. Barlow), Cheltenham (J. E. Sears), Eastbourne (H. G. Beaumont), New Forest (Sir R. H. Hobart); while amongst the Radicals were W. H. Cowan (Guildford), E. H. Lamb (Rochester), T. B. Silcock (Wells), V. H. Rutherford (Brentford), F. E. N. Rogers (Devizes), F. Mackarness (Newbury), and A. A. Acland (Christchurch).[98]

Nor can the Home Counties be properly considered apart from London, where so large a proportion of Radicals were returned. The first emphasis upon reform in the capital came when Gladstone realised that the reform and overall co-ordination would have to lie with the L.C.A. for the local organisation was so poor, and so much necessarily depended upon the candidate. The Liberals, he held, in London, ought normally to hold at least 18 constituencies.[99]

---

[96] By March 1907, £4,727 had been collected. Gladstone later recorded that he had great difficulty in maintaining a policy of small contributions over a period of years before an election. The party ' was in dead opposition to anything in the shape of endowment. Liberals could not give money without knowing what policy and what leader they were called on to support at an election still distant.' HGP, Add. Mss 46118, f. 63.

[97] L. Harcourt to Gladstone, 5 February 1904, HGP, Add. Mss 45997. In the Home Counties, only four seats had no Liberal candidate.

[98] Radicals receiving regular help included Chiozza Money, Alden, F. Acland, Grant, Outhwaite and Vivian.

[99] HGP, Add. Mss 46058, Memo. November 1901, also stressing need for agents and younger men. Also, Memo. by Seager who thought 33 constituencies were winnable and 8 more were worth fighting, HGP, Add. Mss 46023, 4 October 1901.

Throughout the summer of 1901, a large registration drive was mounted in London, and by 27 June £925 had been given in grants for registration work to 27 London constituencies, although in 9 constituencies the work was apparently regarded as hopeless.[100] In July, the report of a special sub-committee on reorganisation in London found throughout a general weakness in the voluntary organisation and a shortage of funds. Reform, it said, must be a matter of reinvigorating the grass-roots.[101] Following these recommendations the London Liberal Federation was established to replace the L.L.R.U., and a number of full-time agents were appointed, but it is clear that the lack of funds was an almost insuperable burden upon the reorganisation.

Not the least of Gladstone's achievement was securing a close and effective relationship with the officials of the N.L.F., notably through its Secretary, Sir Robert Hudson, although Hudson made it quite clear that the N.L.F. could provide no financial help. Gladstone used his opportunity between 1899 and 1902 as official speaker to the N.L.F. to drive home to both constituency workers and to agents two of his priorities – grass-roots organisation and the acceptance of Labour candidates. To conference in 1902, he deplored the tendency to rely increasingly on central party resources; and while paying tribute to the work of the N.L.F. he ' respectfully put the question ... has it altogether moved with the times? ' Discussions and resolutions meant nothing unless there was ' real material power behind them '. Perhaps the N.L.F. could start ' new undertakings in political work and organisation '. For the Federation, the new President, Birrell,[102] pronounced himself ready to accept the advice and to ' organise public opinion in every constituency '. To the breakfast given to the Liberal agents, Gladstone went on to say:

You can do a great deal to make the path of Labour representation somewhat easier ... whatever some distinguished Liberals say.

[100] HGP, Add. Mss 46105 Memo. dated 27 June 1901. (Seager had tracked down 11,366 outvoters.)

[101] HGP, Add. Mss 46105 Memo. dated 19 July 1901 (a sub-committee of the 1899 enquiry). Also Memo. 5 February 1902, suggesting two alternative schemes for London organisation, choice depending on cost: either the Liberals might finance 16 agents in charge of 34 constituencies at an estimated expense of nearly £5,000 p.a., or they might depend on 8 agents over 31 constituencies at a cost of £3,300 p.a. (which was more likely). Both schemes relinquished at least 20 constituencies to the Tories or Labour.

[102] Birrell succeeded Watson in 1902, and was succeeded himself by A. H. Dyke Acland in 1906, by Sir William Angus in 1908, and by Sir John Brunner in 1911.

Too many men say ' I want to be a candidate ', but the constituency has a terrible record, or no organisation.... There are hundreds ay, hundreds – of constituencies that ought to put their houses in order.[103]

Gladstone also urged the agents to accept the Labour movement as a great new progressive force, although Birrell, in his Address, had again pointed out that Labour representation was a matter for the constituencies who were not to be ' bullied ' by ' independent labour parties '. Liberalism as a force now seemed far more inclined to fraternise with Labour, and indeed, Gladstone explained himself as merely continuing official Liberal policy, Hudson and Ellis having promised Richard Bell support in 1898, while Ramsay MacDonald and Sam Woods had previously contacted Gladstone in 1900 with regard to some concessions to Labour.[104] But there was still plenty of evidence that constituency Liberals were unwilling to surrender any ground. Gladstone recorded that the surrender of seats to Labour provoked ' much local disfavour '; *The Speaker* noted that the party's attitude in such affairs was often selfish and short-sighted: ' middle-class Liberalism has been sadly corrupted by years of prosperity. Manufacturing families once identified with the school of Cobden and John Bright have too often turned Tory or Jingo.' [105] Gladstone implicitly recognised the gap between the notables and the organisation when he told Campbell-Bannerman: ' the Liberal party has got out of touch with the great class of industrial managers. One has to quarry deep for information.' [106]

The loss of north-east Lanark in 1901 due to Labour intervention, Gladstone's support for Tom Richards as successor to Sir W. Harcourt in South Glamorgan, and for Arthur Henderson as successor to Sir Joseph Pease in Barnard Castle in 1903 provoked considerable feeling.[107] Barnard Castle brought about the resignation of Samuel Storey as chairman of the Executive of the Northern Liberal Federation, and opened the way for his conversion to tariff reform. Before he resigned, Storey outlined his position in a letter to *The Daily News*, in which he pointed out that there were then at least four other Labour candidatures pending in the north-east:

103 *Proceedings of the 24th Annual Conference* (1902).
104 R. MacDonald to Gladstone, 14 March 1900, HGP, Add. Mss 45986.
105 *The Speaker*, 8 September 1900.
106 4 January 1905, CBP, Add. Mss 41217.
107 See P. Poirier, *The Advent of the Labour Party* (1958) pp. 181–200 *passim*, and F. Bealey, ' Negotiations Between the Liberal Party and the L.R.C. Before 1906 ', *Bulletin of the Institute of Historical Research*, xxix, November 1956.

We will not consent to have forced upon us candidates chosen only by one class and salaried by and responsible to outside societies, which begin by forbidding their candidates to identify themselves with . . . Liberalism.

The effect of surrendering to this new policy will be the destruction of organised Liberalism here in the North. . . . Depend upon it, there are thousands of middle-class Liberals, thousands of Radical Workmen, who, if they are not encouraged to fight for their own . . . will perforce retire to their tents and watch with dismay the process by which some of the Liberal leaders and Whips are nursing into life a serpent which will sting their party to death.[108]

Storey claimed he had written support from 19 out of 23 constituency Presidents,[109] and he certainly had the support of Sir Charles Furness, then President of the Northern Liberal Federation, the which body had launched a campaign against independent Labour representation in 1903, while in 1900 Alfred Illingworth had relinquished his links with the Liberal party as a protest against the encouragement given to Jowett in West Bradford.[110] In such circumstances, it behove Gladstone and the L.C.A. secretary, Herbert, in contemplating an electoral pact with Labour, to weigh up the growing Liberal organisational weakness in harnessing the working-class vote, against the known prospect of alienating powerful supporters. On balance, with the knowledge that the L.R.C. would in any case fight at least 35 constituencies, and being fearful of Labour otherwise splitting the vote in many hitherto safe constituencies, the prospect of utilising Labour organisation as complementary to the Liberal proved sufficiently attractive for an agreement. It seems fair to conclude that the electoral agreement of 1903 upon the Liberal side was viewed primarily as a short-term answer to Liberal weaknesses in the constituencies, and not as part of any longer-term readjustment of Liberal and Labour aspirations. Gladstone did desire a union of progressive forces, but he desired votes even more, and in 1906 he attributed the abnormality of the Liberal victory largely to the success of this agreement.[111]

Gladstone's treatment of Labour underlines a wider, if less certain,

---

[108] *Daily News*, 6 July 1903.

[109] *Daily News*, 8 July 1903.

[110] *Daily News*, 16 February 1903: ' He carried with him a certain number of the older men, who still stand aloof.'

[111] See F. Bealey, ' The Electoral Arrangement Between the L.R.C. and the Liberal Party ', *Journal of Modern History*, xxviii, December 1956. Also HGP, Add. Mss 46021, f. 186.

criticism of his electoral policy, and that is that it may have been weighted too heavily on the side of attaining victory in 1906 and thereby passed by the deeper problem of ensuring that a permanent responsibility for constituency strength existed. Although Gladstone himself had established a reallocation of responsibilities in 1899, he had not solved the nebulous position of the N.L.F., and it was reasonably certain that a chief whip, when in office, would not be able to give the same amount of time to the organisation at large. Gladstone's period as chief whip was perhaps exceptional in that respect. At the beginning of 1903, Harold Spender began a survey for *The Daily News* of Liberal organisations. He found Liberalism in west Scotland to be very dispirited, on bad relations with Labour, and in the 37 seats held by the Tories in Scotland, there were only 13 probable Liberal opponents. The Liberals had only one great morning daily in Scotland, *The Dundee Advertiser*, and here the one efficient force the party seemingly possessed was the Young Scots under J. M. Hogge.[112] In Northumberland and Durham, there were a lack of candidates, with labour complications in the big towns. In Yorkshire the position was better, although the Liberal organisation in York depended over much on the Rowntrees,[113] and Spender noted that ' Mr A. Illingworth at Bradford represents a certain class of opinion that is vocal in most Liberal clubs of the North '.[114] In the populous areas, the Midlands and the Sheffield region, the Liberals were without any press support; in Worcestershire, Warwickshire and Staffordshire, in most of the divisions ' there has been no Liberal organisation for many years '.[115] Everywhere, he remarked on a lack of candidates – there were none as yet in Glasgow, Manchester, Sheffield or Newcastle; there were still 32 vacancies in London, and in the Home Counties (where at that time the Liberals held only 5 out of 73 seats), 58 vacancies.[116] Clearly, a great deal must have happened in the following two years. In May 1902, there were over 250 seats without candidates in England and Wales, and Gladstone was gloomy over the prospects.[117] By November 1903, the situation had so improved that he could then classify

112 *Daily News*, 7 and 10 February 1903.
113 *Ibid*. 12 February 1903.
114 *Ibid*. 16 February 1903.
115 *Ibid*. 28 January 1903.
116 *Daily News*, 16 and 23 January 1903.
117 HGP, Add. Mss 46105, Memo. dated May 1902.

282 seats in England and Wales as a certain or probable win,[118] although it seems unlikely that such an improvement was the fair measure of revitalised constituency parties alone.

Gladstone himself was later to claim that 1906 had been won in the constituencies,[119] and in comparison with the party as it was in 1922 he noted that between 1899 and 1906, when the party was certainly struggling, there still came a stream of requests from the constituencies for meetings, speakers, candidates and assistance, and in Gladstone's opinion, it was the world war which broke Liberal constituency organisation. He summed up his own efforts as follows:

When I became Chief Whip the Liberal party . . . was in low water and great economy was necessary. The normal annual charge (i.e. the years in which there was no general election) was about £16,000. At the General Election of 1900, we put into the field 397 candidates. The cost was £60,000. At the General Election of 1906, the number rose to 518. The cost was £100,000. I inherited £15,000 and handed £20,000 over to my successor. It was difficult to make ends meet and twice I had to borrow £5,000 from a near relative. Altogether, I received during the six years £260,000.[120]

To place the Liberal machine of 1900 into running order for the victory of 1906 was no mean achievement, but it remains uncertain as to how far this represented a positive gain in Liberal strength, and how far it was a matter of capitalising on favourable electoral circumstances. The victory of 1906 was certainly explained by the great increase in the Liberal vote,[121] and it was to Gladstone's credit that the candidates were there and in a position to make use of it. Whether or not Liberalism after 1906 was able to continue the improvement at grass-roots is altogether more doubtful, and in order to attain some perspective herein it is necessary to remember that 1906 was fought at a moment when Conservative party organisation, a model of efficiency as late as the later 1890s, had declined almost to its nadir before the war.[122]

[118] HGP, Add. Mss 46106, 21 November 1903. (Certain losses=96.)
[119] HGP, Add. Mss 46480, Memo., 18 November 1922.
[120] HGP, Add. Mss 46021, Memo., November 1922.
[121] Cf. A. K. Russell, ' The General Election of 1906 ', unpub. Ox. D.Phil. thesis (1963).
[122] Cf. N. Blewett, ' Free Fooders, Balfourites, Whole-Hoggers ', *Historical Journal*, XI (1968) pp. 95–124; R. B. Jones, ' Balfour's Reforms of Party Organisation ', *Bulletin of the Institute of Historical Research*, XXXVIII, May 1965.

CHANGES IN THE PARLIAMENTARY PARTY

Defeat in 1895 had reduced the party's parliamentary strength to 178, as opposed to a Conservative and Liberal Unionist strength of 411. Although by-election successes did reduce the gap and infuse the Liberals with a little spirit, a party of between 180 and 190 M.P.s under a divided leadership and relying heavily upon the support of certain geographical areas (each area possessing its own priorities) just did not have the propulsion to confront issues which only promised further discord. And until a sufficient consensus of opinion had emerged in the party circles with regard to policy, the Liberals were not prepared to commit themselves unreservedly to a particular leader, to a particular political emphasis, or to a political programme. Such commitments only became feasible as both circumstances and the composition of the parliamentary party altered.

In 1895, not only was the scale of defeat overwhelming, but its incidence was also of some consequence. The geographical pattern of support that was emerging after 1886 saw Conservatism dominant in London and the Home Counties. In 1885, 1886 and 1892, for example, the Liberals did not win a seat in Berkshire, Surrey, Middlesex, Kent and Sussex; and in Hampshire, Bedfordshire, Huntingdonshire and Essex, the Liberals won only four seats in three elections. Conservatism was powerful in the west Midlands, East Anglia and Lancashire, while Liberalism was centred in Wales, Scotland, Yorkshire and the north-east, the north-west and the east Midlands. In 1892, Liberal strength lay in the constituencies running up the very centre of England, in the line roughly taken by the Cotswolds and the Pennine Chain. This long stroke was crossed in the form of a T where the Liberal grip upon the north-east and West Riding ran over into East Lancashire and the north-west. In 1895, the Liberals lost the north-west, their gains in Lancashire, the south Midlands, Gloucestershire, much of the east Midlands and Central Wales. The Tory predominance in south and central England spread up the flanks of the Pennines, snapping the Liberal spine and leaving a somewhat emaciated body pinned to the geographical extremities.

As the party was forced into its electoral strongholds and besieged, a crucial problem arose in that its safe seats were often dominated by long-established industrial interests. This was especially the case in Yorkshire and the north-east, where opinion inclined in favour of the local candidate of established reputation, rather than towards the progressive with advanced and unfamiliar ideas.[123] In general, this remark is more relevant to the case of England than to Wales and Scotland. In the English boroughs, for example, the Liberals after 1895 held only 42 seats out of 168, and only 66 out of 234 English county seats, and hence the party's capacity for introducing new blood to parliament was extremely circumscribed. The failure to make any impression in the Boroughs also meant that the Liberals lost an immediate source of contact with urban problems between 1895 and 1900, which further tilted the balance within the party towards the ideas and interests of its safe regions.

In these regions, before 1900, representation was largely in the hands of businessmen, lawyers and professional men, and men of independent means. Amongst these were very few Social Radicals. Wales and Scotland, for example, contributed together a third of Liberal M.P.s between 1895 and 1900, but only J. H. Dalziel, Robert Wallace or Dr Clark could be described as Social Radicals, and all came from Scotland. Welsh Radicalism in the 1890s remained very much an expression of traditional ideals. In England, the story was even gloomier for progressives. In London, in 1895, the Liberals were reduced from 25 to 8 seats out of 62, and indeed, only 5 Liberals managed to hold their seats throughout 1892, 1895 and 1900. In Lancashire, the Liberals were reduced from 22 to 9 out of 58 in 1895, and although this number now included C. P. Scott for Leigh, only Charles Schwann could lay any claim to be a progressive social reformer amongst the remainder.

The one area in England where Liberalism held its own in 1895 was Yorkshire and the north-east. In Yorkshire, the Liberals held 35 out of 52 seats in 1892 (including 17 out of 19 in the West Riding); in 1895, the number fell to 27, and in 1900 to 26. Again, the Conservative advance was most marked in the Boroughs, winning 17 out of 26 by 1900. Amongst the Yorkshire Radicals beaten in 1895 were W. P. Byles and Havelock Wilson, while A. H. D. Acland retired from the House owing to ill-health, to be followed in 1897 by Mundella, and in 1898 by the death of Frank Lockwood. Fred Maddison succeeded Mundella from 1897 to 1900, and in 1899, C. P. Trevelyan was returned for Elland, otherwise the domination of the great industrial magnates was complete. Sir James Kitson in Colne Valley, Charles Wilson in Hull, the Illingworths in Bradford, the

---

[123] See P. F. Clarke, *Lancashire and the New Liberalism*, ch. 9.

Peases in North Yorkshire and Durham, and Alfred Hutton (textiles) in Morley. In Durham, in 1892, the Liberals held 15 of the 16 seats, of whom 10 were industrial magnates, including Sir Charles Palmer, Sir James Joicey, and Sir Joseph Pease.

The stability of representation amongst these areas in the 1890s was in contrast to the turn-over of Liberal M.P.s as a whole, suggesting perhaps, the continuation of Whiggish interpretations of politics, and explaining the lack of coherent effort amongst the party. In 1892, *The Times* noted that 38 per cent of the Liberal intake (103 out of 274) had not been sitting in the immediately preceding parliament [124] (although some, like Dilke, were old hands returning). In 1895, only 140 Liberals of the previous parliament retained their seats (including 17 who had entered at by-elections 1892–5), (although some like Morley, Harcourt and Woods re-entered at by-elections). In 1900, another 35 Liberals entered the House who had not sat there before, and of the 399 Liberal M.P.s in the House at the end of 1906, 205 had been elected for the first time. Of the remaining 194, only 73 had been elected in 1892, 16 had been first elected in 1895, and roughly 100 had entered the Commons between 1895 and 1905.

The Liberal candidates in the north, at least until 1900, were much of a type in their experience and qualifications, local men of long and impressive standing. In 1892, E. T. Gourley had held Sunderland since 1868, Thomas Fry had held Darlington since 1880. J. C. Stephenson, in South Shields, first won the seat in 1868, and Sir Joseph Pease had been sitting for South Durham or Barnard Castle since 1865. Sir Charles Palmer, whose company employed 15,000 men, and who was the founder of Jarrow, was known as 'The Grand Old Man of Tyneside'. Samuel Storey had been three times Mayor of Sunderland and its M.P. since 1881. Joicey was the director of the two largest collieries in County Durham. A typical list of qualifications for these men included the offices of J.P., local councillorships and inevitably, President of the Chamber of Commerce. Sometimes a political alliance was underpinned by marriage; Alfred Illingworth, for example had married the daughter of Isaac Holden, the Liberal M.P. for Keighley (1882–95).

The Liberal dependence upon such established families was in terms of constituency influence, contributions to organisation and funds, and also in the provision of candidates. From 1892 to 1906

124 *The Times*, 1 July 1892.

the Pease family provided four M.P.s – Sir Joseph in Barnard Castle, his younger son, J. A. Pease (a later Liberal Chief Whip) first in Tyneside and then in Saffron Walden; H. F. Pease in Cleveland, succeeded by A. E. Pease from 1897 to 1902. At the same time Herbert Pike Pease, a nephew of Sir Joseph (and also a director of Pease and Partners) sat in the House as a Liberal Unionist. Sir Joseph told Herbert Gladstone in 1900 that if the five seats in which he was helping were all contested, it would cost him £4,000 at least,[125] and in 1903, J. A. Pease found himself close to being declared a bankrupt as Pease and Partners had been so neglected for politics.

If the Peases were exceptional, this type of political network was not in itself uncommon, e.g. the Brunner–Mond complex in Cheshire. The father–son relationship was indeed, a common one. The two sons of Briggs Priestley, a worsted manufacturer, were both sitting as Liberals after 1906, Sir Arthur Priestley for Grantham and Sir W. E. Briggs Priestley for Bradford East. The sons of Russell Rea, Sir Charles McLaren, Sir C. M. Palmer, Alfred Illingworth, Weetman Pearson, Sir Charles Furness, C. E. Schwann, Sir John Benn and Sir George Newnes all followed their fathers onto the Liberal benches. R. H. Barran and Sir John Barran were nephews. Family relationships extended across party lines; C. E. H. Hobhouse was a Liberal, his brother a Liberal Unionist. When George Whiteley became a Liberal after the Agricultural Rating Act of 1897, his brother continued to sit as a Conservative. Campbell-Bannerman's brother had also sat as a Conservative. The two Wason brothers were on opposite sides until the Free Trade crisis when Eugene Wason became a Liberal. The same pattern was repeated when Captain Seely from the Isle of Wight joined the Liberals; his brother C. H. Seely, continued as the Liberal Unionist at Lincoln. Again, in the Conservative party, at the turn of the century, there were at least eight pairs of brothers.

The family tradition remained powerful until the first world war, suggesting that the essential character of the House had changed little in half a century. (In 1864, *The Economist* estimated that a political career was effectively open to only about 5,000 men),[126] and in terms of a political tradition, one has only to think of the Gladstones, the Chamberlains, Churchills, Harcourts, Aclands, Buxtons and Trevelyans. The tightly-knit character of the House, allied to

[125] 19 September 1900, HGP, Add. Mss 46058.
[126] W. L. Guttsman, *The British Political Elite* (1963) p. 80.

the essential similarity of experience enjoyed by many of its members (particularly by groups of its members), may have constituted an inherent barrier to change for some considerable time.

Reform, in the sense of legislation stemming from the growth of progressive sentiment in the House, was in general dependent upon changes in party composition, and in particular, in changes in the relative size, influence and uniformity of the ' business ' groupings.[127] By this is meant not merely the link between an economic interest and voting behaviour, but rather the type of experience which may have influenced attitudes broadly towards issues of a social and economic nature. The question is really two-fold: first, whether personal economic interests and views were sharp enough for members to wish to defend them by ignoring the official party line in any possible conflict; secondly, whether in the absence of an official ' line ', members' opinions were strong enough for them to seek to form an implicit alliance with others of a like opinion. In the case of the Liberal party, given that social reform did pose a challenge to existing views, the question becomes to what extent did Liberal M.P.s oppose reform by allying explicitly or implicitly with the party of the *status quo*, the Conservatives?

As the Liberal party did not officially champion any ' advanced ' social or economic issue before 1906, the explicit link can scarcely be adequately tested. It is also inadequate in that it tends to assume a direct personal motivation on the part of M.P.s which, at the risk of seeming naive, is missing from their arguments which were couched exclusively in terms in defending the staple industries of the country, and the ' economic fundamentals ' as they saw them. It fails also in that no interest was ever completely agreed in the manner of its defence. In 1892, of seven coal-owners, two (Bayley and J. E. Ellis) favoured hours limitation,[128] and D. A. Thomas was prepared to support local option. After 1906, Joseph Walton, A. B. Markham and J. C. Rickett, all coal-owners, declared in favour of an eight-

---

127 Assuming, of course, that the ' business ' outlook stayed relatively constant in its orthodoxy. After 1900, and especially after 1906 when a group of more ' progressive ' businessmen were elected, there was probably some change amongst the ' business ' outlook itself.

128 Ellis had been a previous opponent of limitation (A. T. Bassett, *Life of J. E. Ellis* (1914) p. 39). Allowance must be made for the business concern in that the three staple industries of coal-mining, iron and steel, and textiles, then accounted for 46 per cent of net industrial output, and supplied 70 per cent of all exports. (D. H. Aldcroft, *British Industry and Foreign Competition, 1875–1914* (1968) p. 23.)

hours day. By 1908, none of the previous coal-owning opponents to the miners' eight-hours bill remained in the House.

A strong case can be made out, however, for the implicit alliance, as it appeared in the 1895 Factory Act, and continued to exist amongst the coal-owners. In 1901, for example, an unofficial 3-line Whip was issued against the miners' eight-hours bill by eight members, of whom two were Liberals, Joicey and the Hon. W. C. B. Beaumont.[129] Joicey was also known for his extreme laissez-faire sentiments (he opposed workmen's compensation as socialistic [130]) and his opinions were perhaps, more in line with Conservative rank and file opinions than Liberal.

This implicit alliance might well have been fostered by the character of the House, for often party differences existed in spite of business ties. John Dewar, of whisky fame, was a Liberal M.P. for Inverness, and Alex Dewar held South Edinburgh for a year (1899–1900) for the Liberals. Thomas Dewar, however, the managing director of the firm, was Conservative for Tower Hamlets, 1900–6. The Peases provided another such example, while George Palmer, the Liberal M.P. for Reading 1892–5 and 1898–1900, succeeded his father in the town, and was a director of Huntley and Palmers (biscuits). His brother, Walter Palmer, also a director of the firm, was Conservative M.P. for Salisbury 1900–6. Sir W. H. Wills and Sir Frederick Wills were both directors of the tobacco firm; the former fought East Bristol as a Liberal, the latter sat for North Bristol as a Liberal Unionist. Or, there might be common regional economic ties. The board of the North-Eastern railway included Sir Joseph Pease, Grey, Joicey and Kitson as Liberals, while Meysey-Thompson was the Liberal Unionist for Handsworth (Staffs), and the Right Honourable Sir John Wharton was the Conservative for Ripon.

In such a context, it is not easy to suggest why a man might choose to be a Liberal rather than a Conservative. The choice certainly points back to non-economic factors, to differences over electoral reform, to family traditions, to religion and the impact of ' great issues '. In the north-east, a point of difference might have been the Liberal tradition of conciliation and arbitration in labour matters, their stress upon co-operative methods of production, as exampled

---

[129] Copy LGP, A/2/2/1, 26 February 1901.
[130] J. A. Thomas, *The House of Commons*, p. 148.

in the career of a man like Sir David Dale,[131] or in the North-East railway company's recognition of the Railwaymen's Union, but, as will become apparent, this did not mean that their regard for Labour was founded in anything other than a strictly business (and orthodox) view of the labour market.

The existence of an implicit alliance might have been the more tangible in that the Conservative party by the end of the century could lay a real claim to being a party of business itself. Although the category of landholders and men of private means still occupied a distinctive place within Conservatism (and in the overall House, the men of commerce, industry and finance seem to have been little in excess of the numbers of lawyers, landed men and professionals throughout this period[132]), by 1892, the distribution of business interests was reflecting in some cases a Conservative lead. J. A. Thomas shows that in 1900 70 per cent of the Tory party possessed business interests of some sort. In 1895, the *Banking Almanac* listed 26 M.P.s as directors of joint-stock banks and finance companies in the U.K.; 7 were Liberals, and 19 were Conservatives. In 1900, the Liberals had 9 such directors against the Conservatives 28, while after 1906, although the Conservatives had dropped to 7, the Liberals could only claim 11. Similarly, as regards the railway interests: railway directors in the Commons numbered 76 in 1895 (before the election), of whom 22 were Liberals; in 1906, the Liberals numbered 16 out of 63, and by 1910, 11 out of 42.[133]

It would appear that after 1892, the Liberals, proverbially short of candidates, were falling back upon two sources, men of standing, of landed families and independent means, often having connections with the law or the armed forces; and journalists, especially men having literary and academic qualifications. From 1895–1900, when Liberal candidates were successful in 36 contested by-elections, the landowning element was distinct: Courtenay Warner, Emmott Barlow, Lord Edmund Fitzmaurice, A. W. Soames and Sir William Brampton-Gurden. This element was also strong in 1900, and was

---

131 Sir E. Grey, *Sir David Dale* (1911) with a memoir by Howard Pease.

132 Guttsman, *The British Political Elite*, p. 82; J. A. Thomas, *The House of Commons*, pp. 10–11; also see the composition of the Commons in 1892 according to a letter to *The Times*, 22 July 1892. The 'business' element = 226. Barristers, gentry and landowners = 227. The balance was held by the armed forces and the professional men. Also *P.M.G. Election Supplement for 1900*. Of 400 Conservatives, 112 might be classified as 'land and independent means', and 135 were purely business.

133 *Bradshaw's Railway Manual* for 1895; 1906; 1910.

re-inforced by the influx of free-traders after 1904, and the coming of age of young scions of noble houses.[134]

The second category was especially marked in 1906. Practically the whole of *The Daily News* team entered parliament, Masterman, Belloc, Lehmann, Whitwell Wilson and Chiozza Money, and they were accompanied by a considerable group of journalists and newspaper proprietors. Sir Henry Norman of the social magazine *The World's Work*, Sir George Newnes of the *Westminster Gazette*, Franklin Thomasson of *The Tribune*, G. P. Gooch, George Toulmin, William Byles, J. Massie, Charles Mallet, Dalziel, H. L. Lea, Sherwell and C. P. Allen. These were accompanied by a number of 'progressive' writers such as Alden, Clem Edwards, J. M. Robertson, W. C. Steadman, A. H. Scott (ex-secretary of the Bolton shop-assistants), W. H. Dickinson, Henry Vivian and T. J. Macnamara.

With this influx, two consequences ensued, the first being the relative decline in the business component of the Liberal party, measured as a percentage of the party as a whole, and the second being the absolute decline in the numbers of the long-established magnates holding Liberal seats in the party's safe regions, and their replacement by, in several cases, Labour and Social Radicals.

The business proportion of Liberal M.P.s dropped steadily throughout the period. Whereas in 1892–5, it had been of the order of 43–4 per cent of the party, after 1906 it had declined to 36–7 per cent and after December 1910 to 33–4 per cent.[135] This decline was also associated with an influx of businessmen in 1906 who had not sat in the House before (78 out of 146 who could be classified as business were new to parliament) suggesting some decline in the degree of influence wielded by the magnates who had tended to dominate the party in the 1890s. This impression is heightened by looking at the regions.

In Yorkshire, roughly half (17 out of 35) the Liberal M.P.s were 'business' in 1892, and 16 out of 26 in 1900. But of the 38 Liberals

---

[134] Cf. H. R. G. Greaves, 'Personal Origins and Interrelations of the Houses of Parliament (since 1832)', *Economica*, June 1929. Table 1, for the persistent aristocratic element present in the Commons before 1914. Also M. Kinnear, *The British Voter. An Atlas and Survey Since 1885* (1968) p. 100 for Unionist Free Traders in 1904. Between 1904–6, 11 such free-traders joined the Liberals and 9 stood as Liberal candidates in 1906, 6 being successful (Churchill, Poynder, Ivor Guest, T. W. Russell, J. Seeley, A. Taylor).

[135] On the basis of the tables given.

and Labour returned in 1906, the business element remained at 16, while of the 35 Liberals elected in 1892, a bare half-dozen still sat after 1906. There were now 3 L.R.C. M.P.s, 4 Lib-labs, and a group of Liberal Social Radicals: Herbert Samuel, C. P. Trevelyan, Noel Buxton, Francis Dyke Acland, A. J. Sherwell, Hamar Greenwood and C. N. Nicholson. In Durham, after 1906, there were only two (Furness and Palmer) of the ten former industrial magnates left, and here too there were 3 L.R.C. M.P.s, 2 Lib-labs and James Stuart. In Lancashire, the 1906 intake included 11 L.R.C. M.P.s, the Lib-lab Maddison and, amongst the Radicals, William Byles (accompanied by Hilaire Belloc), Ryland Adkins, Henry Vivian, George Toulmin, N. W. Helme, and Winston Churchill. Finally London, which showed the greatest success, 42 Liberals being returned with 3 L.R.C. members. Thirty-one Progressive members of the London County Council were also returned (not all for London constituencies), while previous London Radicals, such as John Benn and Murray Macdonald, now re-entered parliament.

Significantly, these Radicals provided the party with a source of junior administrative talent which had been lacking in 1892. There was, in fact, a distinct 'second tier' of young Liberals emerging after the turn of the century. Herbert Samuel was under-Home-Secretary in 1906 and Postmaster-General in 1911. Francis Acland was Financial Secretary to the War Office in 1906, to be succeeded by Charles Mallet in 1910 and by H. J. Tennant in 1911. T. J. Macnamara served first under Burns and afterwards at the Admiralty, and Masterman succeeded him at the Local Government Board before succeeding Samuel at the Home Office. C. P. Trevelyan served at the Board of Education 1908–14, J. M. Robertson at the Board of Trade after 1912, and McKinnon Wood became Financial Secretary to the Treasury in 1912. Lewis Harcourt was exceptional in receiving an initial Cabinet appointment in 1906, and by 1909 this younger generation had completely replaced the more long-serving members who received junior offices in 1906.[136]

In sum, the entry of a sizeable bloc of Social Radicals into the party by 1906, accompanied by a relative reduction in the effective influence possessed by the business grouping, was instrumental in forwarding the emphasis upon social politics. While it would clearly be simplistic to see the course of social reform as shaped too precisely

---

136 Thomas Lough (Board of Education); H. E. Kearley (Board of Trade); E. Robertson (Admiralty); Lawson Walton (Attorney-General).

Changes in the Internal Composition of the Party 1892–1910

	January 1892	December 1895	December 1905	December 1906	December 1910
Business:					
Light manufactures	17	10	12	23	25
Iron, steel, rail, shipbuilding	31	15	18	33	28
Collieries, mines	7	7	4	6	5
Merchants	25	17	14	35	24
Textiles	22	15	15	27	12
Banks, finance	13	6	15	22	11
Brewers, distillers	5	3	1	1	1
Total business =	120	73	79	147	106
Non-business:					
Barristers, solicitors	63	47	45	87	60
Land, independent means	27	20	27	41	23
Armed forces	4	1	14	27	17
Professionals (doctors) etc.	15	10	10	27	26
Authors, journalists, publishers, etc.	32	18	25	45	35
Lib-labs	11	9*	11	24	5
Independent Labour	2	—	3	30	43
Total non-business =	154	105	135	281	209
Totals†	274	178	214	428	315

* Now includes Burns.

† Figures obtained from: *The Times*, July 1892; *Pall Mall Gazette Election Supplement* for 1892, 1895 and 1906; *Dod's Parliamentary Companion*, 1895, 1906 and 1910; *The Liberal Yearbook* for 1905, 1906 and 1910.

by the conflict between business and non-business views – some businessmen were highly radical, e.g. Josiah Wedgwood, and equally, non-business was far from being in complete alignment with Radicalism – it was certainly the case that the dominant lines of the reformist debate were shaped by the Radical challenge to established (business) orthodoxy. The writings and speeches of the Radicals, after 1900 especially, were in marked contrast to the caution of the leadership, and it was the ideas of Radicalism which increasingly served as the touchstone for party debate. In so far as their writings publicised the social problem as the pre-eminent political issue, and in so far as they were able to lay claim to candidatures in the Commons, so the nature of the Liberal recovery before 1906 represented a significant shift in the internal balance of the party from the orthodox to the radical.

4

Recovery 1900-5

With defeat in 1895, with the parliamentary party overshadowed by its internal political dissensions, the 'crystallising' of 'dreams and ideals'[1] became a matter for the hidden party of intellectuals and journalists. Liberalism in the 1890s divided, in effect, into two halves which did not come together until after 1900, when a younger generation in closer contact with progressive ideas penetrated the parliamentary party.

If the administration of 1892 had been content to garnish a traditional emphasis with a progressive tinge, there were those sources amongst the grass-roots of the party which attempted a more basic examination of Liberalism itself, thinking to broaden its political programme and win for it the leadership of the avowed progressive elements. At Oxford, the teaching of Green and Jowett was developed by young Liberals like Herbert Samuel of Balliol and Leonard Hobhouse of Merton. They led a group of Liberals who, in connection with Mann and Tillett of the General Labourers' Union, held a series of meetings in the Home Counties (although mainly in Oxfordshire) from 1890 to 1895 on social and political reform, dealing with hours and wages and the formation of the 'New Liberalism'; speakers included Seebohm Rowntree and Mackinnon Wood.[2]

A second source of contact amongst Oxford University Liberals was the Russell Club, founded in 1880. Its members included, apart from Hobhouse and Samuel, C. H. Roberts and J. A. Simon (both elected in 1906), F. W. Hirst, J. Massie and J. L. Hammond. Both Samuel and Hobhouse were close to the Fabians, Shaw, Graham Wallas and the Webbs, and both had strong labour sympathies.[3] By 1895 Samuel was secretary to the Home Counties Liberal Federation, while Hobhouse had moved to *The Manchester Guardian* and with C. P. Scott, and the leader-writers Arnold and Montague, was dealing sympathetically with Labour aspirations. Not all, however,

---

[1] F. Channing, *Memories of Midland Politics* (1918) p. 173.

[2] HSP, A/2.

[3] HSP, A/3, also H. Samuel, *Memoirs* (1945) p. 13.

moved in the same direction. With Hilaire Belloc, Simon, Hirst and Hammond collaborated in a statement of Liberal principles which owed much to John Morley, and repeated a dislike of state control and municipalisation, with an emphasis upon public economy and free trade. Hammond, however, echoed T. H. Green in the stress he gave to the positive development of civic virtue and the promotion of an ideal of citizenship through the development of state educa-tion.[4] Cambridge was not so avowedly political, although C. F. G. Masterman was President of the Union in 1896. The Liberal party did retain a relatively enlightened Press. Massingham, of *The Daily Chronicle*, and Spender of *The Westminster Gazette* remained critical of the parliamentary party's isolation from movements in the country, while Liberals in the Reviews expressed similar senti-ments. Later Liberal M.P.s were sometimes identifiable amongst the world of labour and Unions. Clem Edwards was secretary to the Federation of Trades and Labour Unions; J. H. Yoxall and T. J. Macnamara led a 'ginger group' upon the teachers' executive called the 'Indefatigables', pressing for better pay and conditions.[5]

In 1893 the Rainbow Circle was formed by William Clarke and Murray Macdonald to include progressives of all shades of opinion; Liberals like B. F. C. Costelloe and Sir Richard Stapley, clergymen like the Reverend Lilley and Dr Morrison, and later M.P.s such as Samuel, Charles Trevelyan, Russell Rea, and Percy Alden. It included intellectuals such as John Hobson and John MacKinnon Robertson and several Fabians, Pember Reeves, Olivier, Burrows and Ramsay MacDonald.[6] Ten of its 25 members were elected to parliament in 1906.[7] The aim of the body was 'to provide a rational and comprehensive view of political and social progress, leading up to a consistent body of political and economic doctrine which could be ultimately formulated in a programme of action . . . for social reformers'.[8] According to Hobson, the founding by the Circle of a journal, *The Progressive Review*, in 1896 marked the origins of the 'New Liberalism'.[9] The immediate intention of the 'New Liberals' was to unify the 'multiplicity of progressive movements', to come to

---

[4] *Essays in Liberalism*, by Six Oxford Men (1897). See also F. W. Hirst, *In the Golden Days* (1947).
[5] Clegg, Fox and Thompson, *A History of British Trade Unions*, Vol. 1, p. 225.
[6] H. Samuel, *Memoirs*, p. 24, also HSP, A/10.
[7] P. Thompson, *Socialists, Liberals and Labour*, p. 148.
[8] Preface to *The Rainbow Circle, papers 1910–1911, Second Chambers in Practice*.
[9] J. Hobson, *Confessions of an Economic Heretic* (1938) p. 51.

grips with 'that huge unformed monster', the social question, and to implement 'a specific policy of reconstruction' based on a new conception of 'economic freedom...the conscious organisation of society', and 'an enlarged and enlightened conception of the functions of the State'.[10] Hobson and Robertson were also members of the London Ethical Society in 1896–7, attempting to give a further formulation to rationalist interpretations of society.

The two figures most closely associated with the intellectual growth of Social Radicalism were John Hobson and Leonard Hobhouse, who together provided for the Liberals a distinctive treatment of the economic problem in politics, viewing the inter-related issues less as a matter for separate and independent disciplines than as an essay in distributive justice. The scheme of their studies provided a crucial development in the simple idealism of much reformist thinking, and provided too an alternative analysis to both the cost-conscious business school and to such social theorists as believed in the supremacy of voluntary action to reliance upon the state.

Hobson's initial and prevailing concern was with the thesis of under-consumption, which placed him immediately beyond the pale of orthodoxy.[11] Yet he was more than an under-consumptionist, for his analysis of market imperfections and the inequality of distribution was linked to conceptions of social utility and wealth to which, in his 'humanist economics', he strove to impute an altogether ethical content. Due partly to the influence of John Ruskin, he tried to broaden the basis of political economy, to elevate the economic status of consumption to equal that attributed to production. His ideals shaped the manner of his analysis as well as its content. He rejected the search for 'common denominators' in economics, for a body of undeniable first principles, although if economics was concerned with life as well as with wealth, it was incapable of exact terminology, and his definitions accordingly were tinged with imprecision.

The idea that inequality of income distribution was to be judged not merely against a standard of social (or even natural) justice, as the socialists seemed to claim, but against an economic equilibrium where a direct and constant relationship obtained between rates of consumption and saving, was the core of his thesis.[12] In an ideally balanced society, industrial progress in its most efficient form involv-

---

[10] *Progressive Review*, October 1896, no. 1.

[11] E. E. Nemmers, *Hobson and Under-Consumption* (Amsterdam, 1956) p. 26.

[12] J. A. Hobson, *The Industrial System* (1909) pp. 45, 53–4.

ing the complete elimination of waste, depended first upon the empirical discovery of this ratio, and secondly, in preventing any deviation from this norm in either consumption or savings, which would otherwise cause disequilibrium. Hobson viewed the evil of depression in his own society as the result of ' over-saving ', but his approach was equally condemnatory of both over-spending and ' unproductive expenditure '.

Under-consumptionist theory conceived it fallacious to suppose that the power to consume and the desire to consume were necessarily to be found in the same persons. By itself, however, the identification of a fundamental imbalance between the ability to produce and the power to consume was neither new [13] nor particularly useful. It did lead to a greater emphasis upon raising wages, and it did provide an implicit challenge to the assumption that the function of low income-earners (i.e. the working-classes), lay solely within the productive sphere, and so possessed little economic significance for consumption and equally little for savings. But a policy of raising wages, or even of redistribution, was no real reply to an orthodox standpoint which admitted the desirability of such an attempt, but stressed the fundamental limitations set by the cost–output ratio and the imperative of preserving the ' profits-fund '.

As Hobson's basic premise always rested upon the desirability of the price-mechanism in the market economy, he never denied such limitations. What he did deny was their deterministic application. He believed the social consequences, the human costs and strains, fostered by the extremes of inequality were weakening the market-economy itself. The true art of industrial, as well as of social progress (for in the ideal society the two were inextricably linked) required as great an emphasis upon justice and equality, as upon the dictates of economic self-interest. Hence his condemnation of a society in which strength prevailed over right, in which value was expressed only in monetary terms, and where a completely unregulated price-mechanism could only direct resources according to the will of the strongest, i.e. the wealthiest. His economics were continually directed towards the elevation of human efficiency, the satisfaction of human needs, the recognition of ability and the provision of incentive. He wished to substitute for a mechanical, totally-

[13] Nemmers, *Hobson and Under-Consumption*, pp. 15–16 for under-consumptionism in Marx, and B. A. Corry, ' The Theory of the Economic Effects of Government Expenditure in English Classical Political Economy ', *Economica*, February 1958, for earlier under-consumptionists.

objective, science of the productive process, an all-inclusive study of the organic welfare of industry, where the criterion would be production according to social utility. His conceptions of wealth and ' illth '; of the organic nature of society, although used as a subjective weapon against the commercialism of orthodox political economy, should not obscure the fact that his stress was upon the refurbishing of the economic process, the restatement of its underlying precepts in wider terms. In this sense, his thought was a logical extension of previous interpretations, and condemnations, of the social and economic system. He was, perhaps, appealing to sentiments in progressive thought which were more than half-formed, and which had never been truly the province of any one group or party. The due proportion of effort to reward, equality and economic security, were together to be seen as the only basis for economic expansion. Equality of opportunity should mean the right of equal access to natural resources, to the use of the land, to the proper enjoyment of one's labour. The insistence upon minimum standards of income and of employment, whether attained by private means or through productive investment by the state, was the only basis upon which a society could develop as a highly-integrated organism.

The notion that the creation of wealth was a social process led him naturally to the idea of social value, itself akin both to the progressive conception of betterment, and to the ' unearned increment ' of the socialists; and the notion that the growth of capital value, especially with regard to property and land, could be regarded as due in part to the action of the community itself was a major justification for policies of progressive taxation. Hobson's identification of social value was entwined with his discovery of an unproductive surplus born of monopoly and social inequality. He drew strongly from Henry George's stress upon the importance of economic rent within distribution,[14] but in common with the marginalist approach, he rejected residual theories of distribution in favour of his own analysis which divided cost and reward into necessary and non-necessary elements. The existence of rent, i.e. a payment over and above what was economically necessary to call forth a factor's services, was again seen as the outcome of any factor's monopolistic situation, and not as due simply to that factor's unique or inherent

---

14 J. A. Hobson, ' The Influence of Henry George in England ', *Fortnightly Review*, 1 December 1897.

qualities. The rewards of land, labour and capital were determined by the economic circumstances of their own bargaining positions.[15]

Although rent might accrue to all factors, it was peculiarly identified with the predominant position of capital, which expressed itself in the form of continual increases in the size and strength of firms, and in the existence of a class which benefited from a privileged social position within the market to extort increasingly favourable bargains for itself.[16] Hence, as the market was distorted by the very nature of its economic growth, so its inequalities were further accentuated by the facts of its social composition. Although it was possible to adduce evidence to show that poverty measured in terms of rising real income was perhaps diminishing, 'felt poverty' was growing with the widening gap between 'legitimate human desires and present possibilities of attainment'.[17]

Although Hobson provided the justification for a policy of income redistribution, and although he too believed in the necessity for creating a minimum standard of income throughout the community, he did, in fact, reject the marginal theory of distribution in favour of a similar but far more unwieldy concept of his own. He rejected the attempt to impose any absolute concept of value upon the industrial process, for to regard production from the sole stand-point of consumers' utility was only the obverse of regarding the economic process in terms of cost-of-production theories. Both views exhibited ' an almost materialistic conception of value as a property or force stored in material forms of wealth and transmitted from one end or other of the chain of industry '.[18] Concerned as he was with the fluidity of the market economy and with combining a realistic appreciation of its processes with an ethical explanation of its purposes, Hobson preferred to define value in terms of the economic importance of a good or service, and to demonstrate that such value could only be found through a complicated equation whereby supply-factors (problems of production, economic and human costs) were weighed against demand-factors (utility and purchasing power): ' only by turning to the actual play of economic forces in a market can we perceive the organic relation between cost and utility, operating through supply

---

[15] *Economics of Distribution*, pp. 66–9, 119, 306; *The Social Problem*, pp. 153–4; *The Industrial System*, pp. 76–80, 226–7.

[16] J. A. Hobson, ' The Monopoly Rents of Capital ', *Transactions of the Political and Economic Circle of the National Liberal Club*, Vol. 2 (1892).

[17] J. A. Hobson, ' Is Poverty Diminishing? ', *Contemporary Review*, April 1896.

[18] *Economics of Distribution*, p. 66.

and demand, which is required to establish the truth that value is determined by the interaction of the two '.[19] The ' organic relation ' in turn led him to the notion of a ' vital value ' to be expressed and measured by the application of a standard of social utility, and this was the ' final ' principle to which he committed himself in *Work and Wealth* in 1914. Hobsonian thought and terminology provides, overall, a revealing insight into the predicament of the self-conscious Liberal intellectual trying to reconcile the practical and omnipotent world of economic science with the idealism of the social reformer. The resultant mixture, at once both meaningful and cryptic, empirical and utopian, may be said to be typical of both the ' betwixt-and-between ' stance of the radical reformer and of the Wellsian nature of contemporary visions of the new realities.

Meanwhile, ideas of social value and the surplus entered into politics increasingly after 1900, particularly in the spheres of taxation and the land. In the 1890s, Hobson's concern lay with inequalities of bargaining power which led him to repudiate alike the commodity view of labour and moralistic explanations of unemployment. Unemployment, the waste of resources, was the living proof of underconsumption : ' no reform will be of the least avail in securing a net increase of employment unless it can be shown to increase the proportion of the general income of the community that is applied in demand for commodities '.[20] Hence his support for attempts to expand the rôle and functions of trade-unionism, advocating ' the economy of high wages ', shorter hours and increased leisure as a means to stimulate output and efficiency.[21] With the identification of the surplus within distribution, he supported both trade-unions' attempts to secure for themselves part of that surplus, and any policy to secure for labour either the rent due to ability, or differentials due to skill.

The emphasis upon state-sponsored schemes to redistribute income, developed in book-form in 1900 and 1902, was not fully systematised until 1909, but the argument was sufficiently well developed by 1900 to give it a coherent form. In that the division of the product was into a maintenance or subsistence fund (minimum wages and efficiency, depreciation, basic costs), a productive surplus (rents due to ability, skill, incentive payments, progress efficiency payments), and the

19 *Ibid*. p. 62.
20 J. A. Hobson, ' The Economic Cause of Unemployment ', *Contemporary Review*, May 1895.
21 J. A. Hobson, ' The Economy of High Wages ', *Contemporary Review*, December 1893.

unproductive surplus (the economic rent of land, surplus profits), so redistribution involved an attempt to divert the unproductive surplus to a better economic use, and away from those people who would save too high a proportion of it. In the same way that a tax upon the economic rent of land would not affect its supply, so the unearned increment might be taxed to extinction, thereby providing funds for public consumption by way of social reform. The taxation of high incomes was itself partly justified on grounds of accelerating the use of income by labour in the demand for goods, but Hobson was also concerned to clarify that taxation should not impinge upon productive investment, incentives or ability; he had reservations as to how far graduated taxation might be pushed, and he dissociated himself completely from such socialists or single-taxers as refused to distinguish adequately between the various elements of cost and surplus.

Hobson never did suggest an avowedly collectivist policy. The state might either regulate industry by way of arbitration boards, factory acts, or by imposing obligations like workmen's compensation. It might directly operate such industries as he designated ' routine ' i.e. those subject to tendencies towards monopoly through economies of scale, for example the railways and transport systems. State control could be justified in terms of favourable income-effects, or in the provision (for example), of cheap credit and subsidised housing. The state had an overall responsibility to secure the optimal use of a society's resources.[22]

The basic premise still remained, free co-operative effort amongst individuals. This was especially the case for organised labour. The state would engage to bolster the normal wage-system through pensions and unemployment insurance. It would do what it could to eliminate economic friction and congestion in the labour market, for the creation of economic security and ' adequate public provision against destitution will enable Trade Unionists to struggle for the " surplus " with better chances of success than they would otherwise possess '.[23] Indeed, the growing trade union disposition to favour allegedly collectivist policies in regard to land, pensions and industrial legislation ' is not attributable to any distinct theory of state functions or any preference of public to private enterprise. These projects are

[22] *The Social Problem*, pp. 175–6, 194–5; *The Industrial System*, pp. 270–2.
[23] *The Industrial System*, pp. 207–10.

primarily viewed in their bearing upon the bargaining power of the workers.' [24]

Hobson's attack upon the classical assumption that saving could only do good was paralleled by the independent investigations of J. M. Robertson, a later Liberal minister, who went further than Hobson and attacked the savings–investment link itself, seeing more clearly than Hobson the existence of what came to be called the savings paradox. The stock of money saved, he wrote, was not necessarily a productive fund; the idea that 'the net amount of annual savings ... always equates exactly with a mass of tangible " saved " materials ' was an ' extraordinary hallucination '.[25] Saved wealth was merely a deferred demand for resources and only became an actual (or effective) demand once it had been translated into money-credit, and was available to stimulate the demand for goods.[26] In that ' industrial confidence is notoriously commensurate with activity of demand, the creation of wealth can obviously be promoted by the substitution of an ideal of consumption for an ideal of parsimony '.[27] Again, if saving represented a delayed demand, an excess of savings could lead to unintended stockpiling, falling prices and a lack of incentive to exploit the credit available. For savings to be continually channelled into investment ideally implied a constantly rising rate of consumption, else it either involved Hobsonian underconsumption or an element of forced obsolescence, as the competitive system constantly rejected the old and the marginally inefficient.[28] Fluctuations within the system became continuous as industries found their products superseded, and waste and unemployment became endemic. ' Production can never approach to being theoretically maximized under an individualistic system ', but it might be under a more socialistic organisation.[29] Finally, to insist that all provision for old-age pensions and sickness should be met by individuals' saving could only result in further restriction of present consumption, whereas state pensions, when spent would boost demand, and the increase of wealth (incidentally broadening the base for further taxation). His analysis brought him to endorse a programme of public works for the unemployed, the nationalisation of the railways, and the reduction

[24] *Ibid*. pp. 210–12.
[25] J. M. Robertson, *The Fallacy of Saving* (1892) p. 74.
[26] *Ibid*. p. 86.
[27] *Ibid*. p. 90.
[28] *Ibid*. pp. 105, 111.
[29] J. M. Robertson, *Saving and Waste* (1896) p. 4.

of the National Debt as a way of reducing the investment incomes potentially available to the rich.[30]

The connection between increased wages and the demand for goods was familiar in both trade union and Progressive circles.[31] There is some reason to believe that the Rainbow Circle acted as a point of contact for disseminating such ideas, in perhaps the same way as *The Nation* lunches after 1906 were also influential in linking informed progressive opinion.[32] Herbert Samuel's restatement of Liberal principles in 1902 certainly owed a great deal to the influence of Hobson and Hobhouse; in that political behaviour rested upon ' a science of ethics ', he advocated a positive use of the law by government in order to remove the distortions from the competitive process. Individualism as an ethic was rejected in favour of the organic interdependence of society and the individual. A system of progressive, graduated taxation was advocated to finance productive social investment by the state.[33] Furthermore, Hobson wrote Samuel a long explanatory account of his economic beliefs (although this was possibly after the publication of the book).[34]

If Hobson was concerned with formulating an answer to the prevailing economic determinism, and with improving the productive efficiency of the community, Hobhouse attempted to redefine the principles of association upon which the community depended. Their spheres of interest overlapped, and their respective approaches were similar in that each depended in argument upon analogies drawn from the natural sciences, and both rested their arguments upon ethical premises to make plain their aversion to mechanistic or fatalistic interpretations of social progress.

Leonard Hobhouse's study of the Labour movement reflected the influence of both Hobson and the Webbs.[35] Hobhouse identified the producer's surplus as income he received in excess of this costs (including normal profit), and this became a legitimate target for unions in their attempt to maintain standards of comfort and to attain a living

---

[30] J. M. Robertson, *The Future of Liberalism* (Bradford, 1895) pp. 20–3.

[31] Cf. H. Samuel: ' High wages tend to increase the wealth of the community in two ways; by raising the efficiency of labour and by increasing the demand for goods.' HSP, A/6 (notebook) p. 5. And evidence of J. Mawdsley before *The Industrial Remuneration Conference (1885)*, Proceedings, p. 163.

[32] J. A. Hobson, *Confessions*, p. 83.

[33] H. Samuel, *Liberalism* (1902) pp. 5, 8–12, 18, 183–5.

[34] J. A. Hobson to H. Samuel, undated, *c.* 1902–3, HSP, A/155 (iii).

[35] L. T. Hobhouse, *The Labour Movement* (1893).

wage. He followed Sidney Webb's use of the margin in suggesting that low wages were the refuge of the weak employer and the sweater; an efficient industrial system needed rising wages as a spur to its own progress and qualitative advancement. Through the example of the co-operative movement he attempted to harmonise the interests of producers and consumers over possible conflicts (e.g. price), for an organisation like this, based on the principle of equal advantage and directed towards the satisfaction of the real (basic) needs of a small society, suggested an analogous treatment for the wider association of the state, wherein divisive interests could be ' harmonised ' through the central authority. A union, a co-operative, a state, were all alike in structure and in having the same internal relationship of ends to members. In each, authority was based on an elective principle, justified on broad utilitarian grounds, with spheres of responsibility rationally defined upon ethical as well as upon economic premises. This approach related compulsion to the common good, and collective control to the common interest.[36]

Before it could be accepted that state help was practicable, the proposition that state help was desirable had to be agreed upon. Hence the disputes over the nature of social bonds that accompanied the investigation of social phenomena, and the need felt for a clear theoretical formulation of the purpose and the expected consequences of social reform before a political programme could be attempted. Where social progress and economic growth were seen as the spontaneous by-products of an ideally self-regulating society, Hobhouse desired to substitute the rational comprehension of social evolution and the conscious direction of future growth. Where Spencer had believed social growth to be natural, but denied the analogy of organic life to be applicable to that of an organised society, Hobhouse (and Hobson) believed in the conscious affinity of mind and body, government and society.

Spencer held the spatial separation of individuals, their mobility in space and time, to be removed from the cellular life of units in an organism. He refused to admit that society had any equivalent to an organic brain.[37] Hobhouse was critical of Social Darwinist tendencies in Spencer's thought and of its fatalism, its implicit acceptance of inequality, and especially of its willingness to place instinct and

---

[36] *Ibid.* pp. 33, 40, 42–3, 46, 50.
[37] H. Spencer, *The Man Versus the State* (1888) p. 76.

mechanical development above rational thought and a sense of values.[38] All life was admittedly governed by some selective process, but the higher the life-form and the more the rational replaced the arbitrary, the more could such life rise above its own environment, and nurture, not only the individual intelligence of its members, but the collective intelligence that stemmed from their common purposes and their similarities of life. The more developed the organism, the greater the inter-dependence of the cell-life. Instead of a development confined by the crudity of natural selection, Hobhouse postulated an evolution regulated by the biological law of compensation, through which each individual member of society could consciously select the qualities and virtues to shape his own environment and development.[39] Instead of confusing the animate with inanimate life (the mistake of Social Darwinism), instead of being bound by the capacity to survive alone, he imbued the existence of an intelligence with choice and free-will, and the ability to create the criteria of conduct through which it might realise its own good. Through the inter-dependence which existed amongst a single life-form, the ideal of a collective humanity emerged, seeking that form of government and organisation through which its highest good might be continued through 'a purposive and intelligent organisation of life'.

By ascribing to the collective intelligence (or 'mind') of a society, an idealised personality of its own which was both continuous and dynamic, a government was seen to act for the best in promoting the development of this collective or 'social intelligence' by expressing such ideals as were patently in accord with the common good. These ideals, or maxims, formed the criteria governing its legislative activity. The essence of authority was not that it was drawn briefly from a majority decree, nor was the voicing of the maxims to be a matter of simply providing a legal or institutional basis for such abstract rights as were admitted: liberty, nationality, or property. Rather, as government became the very personification of a 'mind' that was expanding deliberately over time, so its authority stemmed from the continuous responsibility to protect the interests and improve the functioning of the social intelligence. All ideals and maxims were relative to the common good, but the government's responsibility to

[38] L. T. Hobhouse, *Social Evolution and Political Theory* (Columbia, 1911) pp. 28–9, 75–7.
[39] L. T. Hobhouse, 'The Ethical Basis of Collectivism', *International Journal of Ethics*, January 1898.

society for the preservation of this dynamic intelligence was an absolute upon which the common good depended.[40]

If political individualism was a view of political activity which regarded government as a corporate institution acting within a field of legally-defined, finite relationships, and where the rights, duties and responsibilities of individuals and governments were alike assessed and treated beneath the auspices of an independent (and neutral) legal system, then except in respect of certain 'withdrawn' spheres (defence, crown privilege), there was a basic assumption of equality between the two. The criterion governing social bonds and behaviour was, in the last resort, a legal one, and the limiting definitions were also legal; adjudication, arbitration and legitimacy. Now, however, instead of rights and duties in the sphere of political activity being controllable within a legal context, Hobhouse, by providing for each an ethical justification, removed the ultimate interpretation of each from the law and gave to governments a potentially almost infinite field of activity.

A recognition of this process lay behind much of the individualism of the day (e.g. A. V. Dicey), and fear of the implications of this process constituted the principal limitation upon interventionist legislation amongst that part of the Liberal party most in accordance with the Whig-legal legacies of a balanced government and an individualist 'norm'. The real indictment brought by their opponents against the individualistic Liberals was more that their view of the proper scope of a government's activity was too narrow, than an outright condemnation of Liberalism itself.[41] Where Hobhouse-type views took hold they marked a distinct broadening of political conceptions. For instance, the Trade Disputes Act of 1906 may be seen in terms of a conflict between the upholders of a strictly legal definition of equality, and those who believed social and political considerations were superior in such circumstances to a legal definition.

While Hobhouse had not adopted the socialist criticism of the law as being purely a subjective weapon within the class-struggle, his analysis, coupled with Hobson's ethical studies of the economic process, did lead to an emphasis upon a 'just' wage, a 'right' to minimum standards of life and work, a condemnation of anti-social,

---

[40] *Social Evolution and Political Theory*, pp. 147–8, 164–5, 201–2. Also L. T. Hobhouse, *Democracy and Reaction* (1904) pp. 160–1.

[41] Cf. Ramsay MacDonald, *Socialism and Government* (1909) p. 43: 'The individualist basis of Liberal political philosophy requires to be replaced if the political principles of Socialism are to be brought into harmony with its social theories.'

sectional (or class) behaviour, and to the formation of a criterion of an ideal society with which to judge the desirability of legislation; an approach which was akin not only to socialist idealism, but to the tone of social Radicalism expressed by Masterman and Massingham, Lloyd George or Winston Churchill.

It would, furthermore, be more accurate to see such enquiries as a prominent strand within the evolution of a progressive ideal rather than as a purely political response on behalf of the Liberal party. Evolutionary concepts were not only akin to Fabian gradualism, for Ramsay MacDonald, in rejecting class-warfare, also believed firmly in the organic interdependence of society, in socialism as a movement of social and economic betterment. 'Socialists should think of the State and of political authority, not as the expression of majority rule or of the will of any section, but as the embodiment of the life of the whole community.' [42] The state became the personification of something like the product of all past experience and habits, which was closer to Hobhouse than to those doctrinal elements who wished to reject the past teachings of society. In England, in fact, materialistic interpretations of history resolved themselves into aesthetic-religious denunciations of materialism. Graham Wallas ' never believed in an inevitable, automatic and scientific process by which a social revolution would come to itself '.[43] Few English socialists were concerned with the inevitability of a proletarian uprising, and scientific socialism expressed itself in social analysis and inquiry rather than in goading the workers towards the dialectical fulfilment of their historical rôle.

Yet while the identity between social Radicalism and moderate socialism was founded at heart upon their joint sense of how society was developing and the social ideal which was desirable, there was less agreement upon the immediate transitional period and the necessary political remedies. Radicals disliked both the bureaucratic manifestations of socialism, and Fabian assumptions that institutional reform was a solution in itself. Where Hobhouse emphasised that the democratic machinery had to be perfect before new powers devolved upon it, MacDonald thought electoral reform ' a red herring '. Hobson disbelieved in nationalisation as a panacea; his concern was for the state to socialise those industries where productive efficiency could be improved by eliminating human costs. In their belief in the harmony

[42] *Ibid.* p. 91.
[43] G. Wallas, *Men and Ideas* (1940) pp. 103–4.

of social interests, in their perhaps more realistic sense of the industrial processes at work, the two Liberals condemned sectionalism, either by classes or by trade unions. By its very nature, distributive justice, involving a system of rewards at once functional in its emphasis upon incentives to effort and the necessity of wage-differentials, and ' social ' in the support given to minimum standards, had to imply a heavy reliance upon co-operative methods of production.

IDEAS IN CONTEXT

Such ideas were, however, only one strand in the development of the progressive cause before 1906, and before they could be linked to the level of concrete policy, before they could be embodied in a political programme, they had to be accepted as relevant to the actual conditions of labour. This relevance grew as the theoretical speculations of writers such as Hobson and Hobhouse were paralleled by the increasingly sceptical experiences of organised labour, and the emergence of a concerted demand on their behalf for state intervention in the market economy. As Radical and Labour support for such a policy became both urgent and specific, so they came further into conflict with the orthodox business view over the degree and kind of social reform which might be safely achieved in the market. This conflict, first evident in the debates over the Miners' Eight-Hours Bill, 1893-4, grew further before 1906, and was a prime influence in determining the bounds and the response to Liberal reforms after 1906.

The ' New Unionism ' had focused attention upon the economic problems of labour, and paved the way for a broadening of trade union functions and responsibilities. Unemployment was discussed regularly as an economic problem by the T.U.C. from 1894, the year that Delves had called for the legislative redress of labour grievances. With the growth of the unions, and the ensuing counter-attack by the employers, came a hardening of bargaining positions. The unions were still primarily concerned to improve their own structure and attain a unity of their own for industrial purposes – four out of five men still made their own bargain with the employers.[44] Industrial defeats and the legal attack through the courts, culminating in Taff Vale, was in the first place an attack upon their bargaining strength, and their first response was an industrial one, the formation of the

---

[44] E. H. Phelps-Brown, *The Growth of British Industrial Relations* (1960) pp. xxvi, 272.

General Federation of Trade Unions 'to render mutual assistance in disputes, strikes and lock outs' to its members. Both the engineers and the cotton-spinners, defeated in 1897–8 and 1893 respectively were amongst the 44 unions who joined, and if political attitudes were mainly a response to economic problems, it is worth remarking that the older unions, who had affiliated to the L.R.C. prior to Taff Vale, were mostly concerned with the impact of mechanisation; brass-workers, fancy leather workers, boot and shoe operatives, ship-wrights and London book-binders.[45]

The initial demand that the unions support an independent Labour party offered little to those whose object it was to get trade unionists into the Commons to promote union interests there. George Howell's view of the good 'a few, diligent, active and able men'[46] could do was echoed in 1896 by the T.U.C. President, Mallinson, who first praised the work of propaganda done by socialists:

By all means let us have a workers' political party, only let it be kept outside Trade Unionism. There is plenty of work for such a party, and though it renders valuable assistance to Trade Unionism it could not take the place of the latter ... The strength of Trade Unionism hitherto has lain in the fact that it formed a common ground where workers of all shades of political opinion ... could meet to take united action to improve their conditions of employment.[47]

So the trend was firstly towards the emergence of trade unionism as an independent force. By 1898, the railway servants had decided upon political representation through their General Secretary, Bell, to act in the same way as Havelock Wilson had done for the sailors, or as the miners' representatives (whose unions established a political fund in 1901).

Trade unionism had to establish, according to Mallinson, that labour was the chief factor in production, and that the 'remuneration of labour should be the first charge on production'. This was the cry of the 1890s, the rejection of the dictates of the 'buy in the cheapest, sell in the dearest market' school.[48] It was noticeable that the main strikes in the period made the same claim. In the coal-strike of 1893, the men rejected the employers' view of arbitration in which wages

---

[45] E. J. Hobsbawm, *The Labour Aristocracy* in Briggs and Saville, *Essays on Labour History*.

[46] A. W. Humphrey, *History of Labour Representation* (1912) p. 118.

[47] *The Times*, 9 September 1896.

[48] E.g. Clem Edwards, 'A Policy for Labour', *Contemporary Review*, August 1894.

were to be absolutely regulated by prices. A trade union in itself was
'a living denial of this claim', and arbitration should henceforth be
based upon the recognition of a living wage.[49] The miners claimed a
greater share in the determination of selling prices and condemned
the employers' acceptance of forward contracts at low prices. The
employers' view that it was more important for the collier to have
plenty of work rather than a high rate of wages (his earnings being
tied to the amount of coal produced), was resented by miners in view
of the wage fluctuations they had to endure.[50] In South Wales 'a new
generation' had arisen who rejected the view of wages as being
always price-determined, and in the stoppage of 1898, they overthrew
the apostle of the sliding scale, Mabon, and claimed a minimum
wage.[51] In 1902, the scale in South Wales was replaced by a conciliation board, and the selling-price became only one factor in the determination of wages. When W. J. Ashley observed the coal industry in
1903, the fixed relations of prices to wages had been weakened, the
sliding scale as an implicit defence of profits had gone, and even
Burt was arguing that the demand for labour should constitute a
factor in arriving at a wage-level. The miners' claims were conflicting
with the policy of cheap coal for British industry: 'ultimately, the
quarrel of the miners with the dependence of wages on prices is a
quarrel with the practice of unrestrained competition'.[52]

In the cotton strike of 1893 over the employers' proposals to reduce
wages by 5 per cent because of price-falls, the men refused to accept
that there was an obligation on their part to accept wage-falls in time
of depression, in return for rises in prosperity. In this case labour was
willing to work short-time (but this represented an increased cost of
production to employers), rather than reduce their rate of pay, and
this was an indication that they viewed the maintenance of the
standard as a principle upon which they were not prepared to compromise. It was observed that this was not a mere fight about wages:
'it involved, above all, the testing of a theory as to the best method of
dealing with an adverse condition of trade'.[53]

In cotton and coal, the situation was aggravated by the orthodox
insistence that there could be no artificial maintenance of a price-level

49 Clem Edwards, 'The Coal Strike', *Economic Journal*, 3 (1893) p. 650.
50 The owners' point of view was expressed in a letter to *The Times*, 17 July 1896,
   by T. Ratcliffe-Ellis, the Secretary of the Federated Coal-owners.
51 E. W. Evans, *Mabon* (Cardiff, 1955) p. 64.
52 W. J. Ashley, *The Adjustment of Wages* (1903) pp. 46-7, 61.
53 E. Helm, 'The Cotton Dispute', *Economic Journal*, 3 (1893) p. 342.

in an industry whose structure of costs was directly related to, and in part determined by, the costs of international competitors. Although between 1893 and 1906, wages were slowly asserting a claim to be considered at least as important as the advantages of flexible wage rates, still the latter was the norm. The living wage, although more nearly linked to notions of efficiency, was not yet 'economic'. In 1905, for example, A. C. Pigou accepted that wages should be related to output and profit levels, but still the general conditions of trade formed a limiting factor.[54] In the long run, he assumed normal wages would tend towards the efficiency-wage, for in accordance with the 'economic harmonies',[55] wage movements would always cause a re-assessment of the relative attractiveness of an industry to enterprise and capital. Wages could not be kept for long above an 'economic' level, and for wages to fluctuate according to temporary movements in demand and supply meant more work and a larger national dividend available for distribution than through fixing minimums.

Wages were partnered as an issue by trade union attempts to exert a say in conditions of work, over hours and the employment of non-unionists. The Hull shipping dispute was an example of the latter in 1893, and the boot and shoe stoppage in 1895 and the engineering strike were prime examples of the former. 'The masters have fought far more against interference in regard to machinery and the claim of Trade Union officials to "boss" their workshops than against the demand for an eight-hours day', and F. W. Hirst for one reacted strongly against attempts to 'lower the productive capacity of labour in order to absorb the unemployed'.[56] Although the bulk of employers were willing to meet the men's representatives, and although collective bargaining was apparently capable of preserving the chief interests of the men, still there were instances which caused resentment e.g. the non-recognition of the railway unions and Lord Penrhyn's dismissal of the Board of Trade's 'outside interference with the management of my private affairs'; but increasingly this extreme laissez-faire attitude was suspect to all who wished for a more harmonious and efficient industrial system. A logic implicit in the situation began to unfold: 'Unless...the State be prepared to assume the active regulation of wages it may be doubted whether

[54] A. C. Pigou, *Principles and Methods of Industrial Peace* (1905) pp. 96, 99.
[55] *Ibid.* p. 54.
[56] F. W. Hirst, 'The Engineers' Strike', *Economic Journal*, 8 (1898) p. 124.

in industrial quarrels it can exert any compulsion beyond that of persuasion.' [57]

The consequences of the market economy were open to inspection – the competitive basis which put a premium on strength, a profit motive which incited employers and men to cut corners, lower quality and indulge in petty restrictions. Reports from the factory inspectors suggested that often, only the barest essentials of the Factory Acts were complied with, ' enforcement . . . showed the State as having to intervene not only to make employers less rapacious but to make them more competent ', and so possibly ' public ownership would substitute not justice only, but efficiency ', for competitive muddle. [58]

Apart from defeat in the courts, the unions might also feel they were not receiving their due protection from the law. The T.U.C. in 1898 condemned victimisation by the railway companies (who had forbidden their men to accept representative positions on local councils), and censured the Post Office for dismissing union officials. They feared ' the despotic system of espionage practised in the engineering, coalmining and other industries ', whereby employers obtained very detailed character notes from one another on prospective employees. [59] Again, following the South Wales coal strike, 6,000 men, in one or two districts alone, had been disqualified from voting for accepting poor relief, [60] while after the 1897 Compensation Act at least one company established that no man over 50 would be engaged, and any man receiving compensation from the company would have to receive the approval of general management before being re-engaged. [61]

The presidential address to the T.U.C. in 1900 remarked upon the change occurring within the union movement. Ten years ago the question had been ' how best to determine the rights and duties of the working-classes in the existing social order? ' Now the probing was directed against the order itself. There was indeed ' a struggle for existence ' within society, and Social Darwinian assumptions prevailed; it was the survival of the fittest and not of the best, a fact surely open to debate. The President ' thought he was justified in saying that in all forms of social evolution the economic factor was the dominant one, and that it was the factor which conditioned the

[57] L. L. Price, ' Industrial Conciliation – A Retrospect ', *Economic Journal*, 8 (1898) p. 471.   [58] Phelps-Brown, *British Industrial Relations*, pp. 74-5.
[59] *The Times*, 2 and 3 September 1898.
[60] *The Times*, 6 October 1898.   [61] *Liberal Magazine*, January 1899, p. 574.

struggle for existence and this determined which should be the fittest to survive '. The ending of this struggle through the socialisation of production and the development of social responsibility had to come before man could become master of his own environment, or could truly sway the path of his own evolution.[62]

While the trade union world had changed little in outward appearance by 1900, there had certainly been a growth in support for ' such laws as will put an end to a system under which the producer of wealth has to bear an enormous burden in the shape of rents and profits, which go to the non-producers '.[63] Experience hardening within the confines of the market economy had begun to produce a new political accord, and although ' the L.R.C. was in no way committed to socialism but only to common action on a labour programme of which the content was still undefined ',[64] the pressure for social change had become more specific. Ideas had become more significant in that sufficient doubt had been aroused by the turn of the century for a positive commitment to action to emerge. A subtle transformation was taking place and from old dogmas, empiricism and experience brought forth new emphases. From a traditional concern for environmental regulation sprang the principle of social responsibility, from which in turn sprang collective action for the common good. Once unemployment could be traced to socio-economic causes, then the conclusion emerged that the responsibility for a national evil rested with the government; if the cause was determinate, then so might be the cure. And if it was unjust to leave a man to bear the financial responsibility of an accident or circumstances for which he was not responsible, so the government was expected to devise a protective remedy.

The unions were approaching the same conclusion as Hobson and Webb i.e. the strength of their bargaining position depended upon the degree of security they could win from the state in the market, security against underselling, against the sweater, against bad housing, high rents, casual labour and an unregulated labour market, above all, perhaps, against the old Poor-Law. Individual or parental responsibility, arguments based upon cost, paled before the immensity of the problem. They were in accord with Hardie's emphasis

---

[62] *The Times*, 5 September 1900 (speech by Pickles).
[63] L.R.C. Resolution, quoted in J. H. S. Reid, *The Origins of the British Labour Party* (Minnesota, 1955) p. 91.
[64] Cole, *British Working-Class Politics 1832–1914*, p. 168.

upon the principle of national responsibility, and for elective administrative councils to be set up to undertake public works under a
Ministry of Labour.[65] Barnes and Henderson demanded a system
of public labour exchanges, and the regularisation of the demand for
labour by municipalities and employers.[66] By 1905, the T.U.C. were
asking ' as a vital principle ', for the recognition of the right of
labourers to demand employment from the state without forfeiting
any of their civil rights. And certainly they would have agreed with
Hardie when he said in 1905:

One real cause of unemployment was the lack of effective purchasing
power. They were told it was want of demand in an economical sense, but
the demand was really ineffective owing to the under-payment of the
workmen. If the workman were paid the value of his labour he would be
able to purchase with his wages what his labour produced. The consequence was what was called over-supply, but was really under-
consumption, and the evil was increasing.[67]

The specific demands of the unions after 1900 were indeed directed
towards their own economic security: pensions, hours and housing
legislation, electoral and educational reform, the abolition of child
employment.[68] In this sense, interventionism and socialism had
become interchangeable terms, and at stake was ' the fundamental
question of the economic organisation of industry, in which lie
embedded the roots of social problems, of which unemployment is
the greatest '.[69]

Upon this question the orthodox business school were unprepared
to compromise, and the nature of the implicit alliance between men
of like views in either of the major parties becomes of major significance. In office, the Conservatives were closely identified with the
moralistic views of the Charity Organisation Society, represented in
the party by the group associated with Sir Elliott Lees and Sir
Frederick Banbury.[70] At least until 1904, the Conservatives refused

65 Keir Hardie, *John Bull and His Unemployed* (1905).
66 G. Barnes and A. Henderson, *Labour Exchanges*. Copy in the Beveridge Collection on Unemployment, Vol. 2.
67 *The Times*, 26 January 1905 (L.R.C. Fifth Annual Conference).
68 See *Infancy of the Labour Party 1900–1912*, Minutes of the L.R.C. (London
School of Economics), Vol. 1, f. 234. Also Cole, *British Working-Class Politics*,
p. 185, for election manifestoes.
69 J. Burgess, ' What Labour Wants ' in W. T. Stead (ed.), *Coming Men on
Coming Questions* (1905) p. 399.
70 Mowatt, *The Charity Organisation Society*, pp. 72–3. Also *The Times*, 6 May
1897 and 13 March 1902 for Conservative opposition to hours legislation.

to consider schemes involving public expenditure upon pensions or relief-work, partly due to the Boer war, and partly due to more inherent obstacles. A. J. Balfour, for example, apparently regarded the unemployed as a kind of ' hardy annual ' to be dealt with accordingly,[71] and there is too Masterman's commentary upon the effect of Will Crooks' most moving speeches in the Commons during 1904–5: ' nothing particular was done. There was no obvious reason why anything should be done. No one expected that anything would be done.' [72] The Duke of Argyll produced a defence of a very orthodox political economy in 1893, attacking the new-fangled marginalists and justifying economic inequality: ' the natural, necessary and legitimate result of diverse, various and unequal gifts ', an approach much publicised in the 1890s by W. H. Mallock.[73] According to Argyll, ' the reservoir out of which wages came belongs wholly to the employers (plant, capital and enterprise), exclusively from (their) resources . . . and they have an absolute right to regulate the terms on which they will carry on the work '.[74] He and Mallock believed that ' the individual brain is the original seat of genius and enterprise '. If the original predetermined wage-fund was gone, still there was a fund dependent for its increase on the ability of management and the security of capital ' and you strike fatally at these conditions when you make any unreasonable demands either as to rates of wage, or as to hours of work, or – most of all – as to powers of interference with the delicate machinery of industrial management, towards which the wage-earning classes have contributed nothing except manual skill '. Such opinions coincided with those of Sir George Livesey, Alex Siemens, Lord Wemyss or Sir W. Lewis, the backers of the National Free Labour Association and the founders in 1898 of the Employers' Parliamentary Council.

As contemporaries became increasingly disturbed at British vulnerability in the face of foreign competition, the unions proved a ready scapegoat. From November 1901, *The Times* carried a series of articles on ' The Crisis of British Industry ', condemning ' ca' canny ', the reduction of hours, and union restrictions on new machinery, as all part of a movement which was forcing up the costs of production. Conservative opinion inclined to the belief that the condition of the working classes was improving steadily, while pauperism as an

[71] H. Russell Wakefield to S. Buxton, 27 July 1905 (S. Buxton papers unsorted).
[72] ' Liberalism and Labour ', *Nineteenth Century*, 1906.
[73] Duke of Argyll, *The Unseen Foundations of Society* (1893) pp. 23, 578.
[74] Letter in *The Times*, 6 January 1898.

economic burden was declining.[75] While such opinion was ready to condemn views which saw the problem of social reform as simply irremediable, it warned that there was no heroic remedy and supported Sir Robert Giffen – ' so high an authority in regard to all questions of political economy ' – in his pessimism regarding ' economical experiments affecting the poor '.[76] For *The Times* ' The modern economists have . . . thrown an air of mystery over the source, movement and incidence of wages. They have destroyed the fiction of a wages-fund, a fixed amount not to be increased, only, in some cases, to create other fictions '.[77] For labour, the assumption that the proceeds available for distribution were still limited suggested that wages and profits were mutually hostile. What one gained the other lost, and mutual dependence was obscured.

The tenor of such Conservatism was remarkably similar to Liberal views which emanated either from the whiggish or the practical traditions of politics. Alfred Pease, for example, considered it folly:

to attempt to fix wages at a higher rate than the rate fixed by demand and supply, the rate which distributes the whole circulating capital of the country among the entire working population, (for) it can only be accomplished by keeping a like proportion of their number permanently out of employment.

He denounced

The delusion, from which the Victorians were free, that it is possible to remove the questions of wages or the cost and standard of living outside the operation of economic laws, or that you can free a community from the consequences of defying the law of supply and demand in relation to labour.[78]

If it was not a question of ' natural ' versus ' just ' wages, it was the claim for the freedom of management. D. A. Thomas believed in conciliation boards and collective bargaining, was sympathetic to a minimum wage, and admitted:

The State has a perfect right to prevent (an) individual from treating badly those whom he employs, and it has an equally perfect right to take

---

[75] Cf. *The Times*, 18 November 1901.
[76] *The Times*, 8 December 1899.
[77] *The Times*, 16 September 1897.
[78] A. E. Pease, *Elections and Recollections* (1932) pp. 43-4.

from him in the shape of taxes a part of the wealth he earns by his energy. . . . But the State has no right to control his creativeness.[79]

Under a progressive taxation system, the rich employer was only ' a tenant for life ', and meanwhile it was in everyone's interest that he should set about making full use of his abilities to create as much wealth as possible; the more the individual made, the more would the community have to share out in social reforms. Meanwhile, freedom of production, ' the laws of commerce ', were opposed to socialistic attempts not only to regulate the environment of work, but to impose upon its internal nature, its costs, its capital and profits, unworkable ' non-economic ' demands. Both Thomas and Weetman Pearson (the later Lord Cowdray), stressed that the working of an enterprise and the economic function of management would be the same whoever was the owner; deciding the return due to capital, the division of any ' surplus ', or the return due to specialised ability. And they considered the claim that total product would be increased if private profit was either limited or extinguished to be altogether unproven.[80] The strength and prevalence of these views, the degree to which their holders regarded them as axioms provided the element of rigidity, the one constant factor to which all other positions were related, in a political debate fast gathering momentum.

IDEAS AS POLICY

The period between 1900 and 1905 possesses a deceptive simplicity. J. A. Spender later remarked that to look at these years in the retrospect of a rising Liberal tide could be misleading: ' they were a period of exhausting labour and baffling uncertainty. There were many weeks in 1904 and 1905 when the downfall of Mr Balfour's government seemed a matter of days, or even hours, but time after time it miraculously survived and went blandly on.' [81] Hence, when victory finally came it was difficult to decide whether it had really been won upon the resurrection of old issues, or the emergence of the new. E. R. Pease, for example, thought Liberalism between 1895 and 1905 ' had no policy, and it seemed incredible then . . . that a party with so little to offer could sweep the country.' [82]

Certainly, the criticisms of Liberal aimlessness current before 1900

[79] Viscountess Rhondda, *D. A. Thomas* (1921) pp. 125, 278.
[80] J. A. Spender, *Weetman Pearson* (1930) p. 291.
[81] J. A. Spender, *Sir R. Hudson*, p. 70.
[82] E. R. Pease, *A History of the Fabians*, p. 117.

continued after the party had recovered some apparent unity, and it
was a sign of how fast opinion was moving when it became increasingly difficult to judge the Liberal party upon its merits, rather
than in terms of a highly stylised interpretation of politics in which
the economic interpretation of society became the criterion for
deciding political allegiance. There was a general agreement that the
Liberal radicals had fallen into two sections:

The one holding up, with much constancy and energy, their ancient ban-
ners over a part of the field from which the combatants seem to have
disappeared; the other gravitating towards Socialism, with the ideas of
which they are largely infected, but towards which they are in a very
perplexed attitude of mind.[83]

The truth of Sidney Webb's jibe that 'a Liberal reform is never
simply a social means to a social end, but a campaign of good against
evil ',[84] lived on when the Liberal revival after 1902 patently owed
so much to traditional radicalism and to non-conformist demands.
The latter made it very plain that they regarded the first duty of a
Liberal government to be the redress of educational (and later
licensing) grievances.[85] There was little doubt that in Wales, for
example, ' without the organisational spearhead and spiritual dedica-
tion of dissent in 1906, Liberalism would never have emerged from
the shadows '.[86] Progressives found the implications disturbing: Cecil
Chesterton thought the Radical wing of the Liberal party had
degenerated into a political committee of the Free Church Councils.[87]
Even worse, the Home Rule, anti-Imperialist, free trade influence
had so shackled the Labour Representation Committee (L.R.C.) that
it too was in danger of losing its identity amongst a swamp of amorphous radicalism. The Liberals were continually fighting shy of a
commitment, and despite their prolific output, men like Masterman
had ' no hold on any section of the electorate that counts politically '.
This was a general charge. ' We want to know what the Liberal
intelligence is thinking, not what 42 Parliament Street is compiling ',
wrote Ramsay MacDonald in 1903. Liberals too remained sceptical of

[83] J. W. Mackail, *Socialism and Politics* (Hammersmith, 1903).
[84] S. Webb, *Twentieth Century Politics*, Fabian Pamphlet 108 (1901).
[85] Cf. J. G. Rogers, ' The Nonconformist Uprising ', *Nineteenth Century*, October
1903.
[86] K. Morgan, *David Lloyd George : Welsh Radical as World Statesman* (Cardiff,
1963) pp. 36–7.
[87] C. Chesterton, *Gladstonian Ghosts* (1905) p. 12.

the party in parliament. The only Radicals there, according to Massingham in 1904 were Lloyd George, Dilke, Burns, Lough, J. H. Whitley, Labouchere, Macnamara and Cremer, plus a handful of Scottish, Welsh and Labour members.

In the aftermath of 1900, the political situation was confused in that Conservative unpopularity began long before the real Liberal recovery arrived. When income tax touched 1s 2d in May 1901, and in 1902 a registration duty was imposed on imported corn, arousing fears of a bread tax, this aggravated discontent over the spiralling cost of the war, giving the Liberals a surprising win at Bury, on 10 May 1902. Despite the arrival of peace in June, the by-election trend was never reversed as the combined effects of the 1902 Education Bill, the 1903 free trade controversy and the 1904 Licensing Bill gave the Liberals new rallying cries.

It would be difficult to give a very precise date to the passing of the shadow of Rosebery, and the effective reunification of the Liberal ranks, but the evidence would point to a date not before the end of 1902 and not later than 1903. Before this date, official Liberal policies and emphasis had changed little. In 1902, Samuel recorded that the Liberals had not made up their minds on the eight-hours day issue: ' The question is still in the stage of discussion and experiment, and the measure has not been given a place among the acknowledged aims of the party ', although they were agreed on the regulation of hours for mines and shops, and the limitation of child labour. ' Liberalism ', he claimed, ' is no stereotyped collection of fixed proposals ',[88] but the only spheres where Liberalism could in fact be said to have made any advance were in land and taxation reform. On pensions, no definite plan had as yet commended itself to the Liberal party as a whole; with regard to unemployment, Samuel recognised the primacy of economic over moral causes, but was very cautious with regard to state responsibility, or relief works, and did not mention labour exchanges at all. Sidney Webb to his wife described the book as ' a collection of platitudes ', although to Samuel himself his criticism was more instructive:

you are weak and vague in the *connection* between your fundamental principles of Liberalism, and some of your particular projects – you need more accepted ' axiomata media '. Thus, without such, Factory Acts and Housing Schemes are apt to be *merely* empirical.

[88] Samuel, *Liberalism*, pp. 31, 86.

The sort of middle axioms you need . . . are such as: To Raise Com-
pulsorily the standard of life, to enforce a National Minimum on each
important point, Collective Regulation of all matters of common concern,
and so on. These are the instruments by which your fundamental principle
can be applied.

The reply to your projects, by a reasoning Liberal of the old school,
would be: ' I do not see that the proposed remedy would not be worse
than the evil to be cured.' He says this because he is unconsciously
assuming quite a different set of ' axiomata media ' from yours. Thus he
believes that ' The Standard of Life ' can only be raised by individual
action, that the enforcement of any national minimum is bad as infringing
liberty, that Individual Freedom is the basis of any healthy state; and so
on.

I wonder what John Morley says of your idea of Liberalism.[89]

Samuel, as a Liberal imperialist and a one-time member of the
Co-efficients was curiously shy of avowing doctrines such as the
' minimum ' and the ' carefully-constructed bottom ' to the state.
Perhaps this was due to the character of social imperialism, wary of
allowing efficiency as a goal to degenerate into collectivist priorities,
and perhaps it was due too to Samuel's sense of the practical. His
book, in fact, sold badly. On 13 July 1904, the publishers told him
that sales, 2,250 to date, had been very slow, and they proposed
remaindering 700 copies. Meanwhile, A. J. Sherwell's book, *Temperance and the Social Problem*, had sold 90,000 copies and gone
through ten editions since 1899.

The connections between the evil of poverty and its separate manifestations amongst the old, the under-employed, the sweated and the
sick, while admitted by many Liberals still seemed to mean to many
piecemeal reform, housing, land and taxation. With regard to pensions, for example, F. H. Stead had written to all M.P.s at the end
of 1902, and had received only 47 replies, Liberals showing no marked
eagerness for the reform. Sir William Robson refused to support
pensions ahead of a reduction in the food taxes. In the House, Channing, Burt, Burns, Broadhurst and Sir Walter Foster had promoted
a bill to provide pensions of 5s a week for all over 65 on a non-
contributory basis, but Stead looked to five Liberals not yet in parliament for his main help (W. T. Wilson, Chiozza Money, W. H.
Lever, E. W. Davies, Alden) and to a sixth, Stopford Brooke.[90]

[89] 20 March 1902, HSP, A/15.
[90] Stead, *Coming Men on Coming Questions*, pp. 154-6.

In 1902, Gladstone's call to the N.L.F. for more effort in the constituencies was interrupted by a call of ' Give us a policy first ', but it was not until March 1903 that the N.L.F. ceased to concentrate upon a negative condemnation of the government's policies – the corn tax, the war and the education bill – and passed a positive resolution in favour of the ' imperative ' need of social reform. In 1904, conference advanced a little further and mentioned ' particularly ' the housing question, the reform of the land laws, the equality of rating and kindred matters. 1904, in fact, saw the largest meeting held since Newcastle in 1891. It was not until 1905 that a resolution (moved by Fenwick and Lever) was passed for ' the restoration of effective combination ' and the creation by the state of ' permanent machinery applicable to the whole country for investigating and alleviating the lack of employment caused from time to time by exceptional trade depression ' (this in response to the severity of the 1904 winter). Lever also expressed a hope that such machinery could be allied to the provision of pensions. During the whole of these five years there was an absence of any evidence to suggest that either the N.L.F., or the Liberal Central Association in conjunction with the whips office, made any attempt to instruct candidates in regard to policy, either by way of meetings or by way of establishing priorities. This manner of behaviour, highly reminiscent of the nineteenth century, was in marked contrast to the activity of the L.R.C.[91]

Yet the dilatoriness in official channels does not tell the whole story. The economic interpretations of the war, allusions to rampant capitalism on the Rand, made not only by Hobson, Lloyd George, Labouchere and C. P. Scott, but by Channing, A. B. Markham and F. W. Hirst, did denote a change in the character of Radicalism. ' So far as discussion of Imperial questions was concerned, the character of the Radical left had undergone an almost total transformation.'[92] No longer purely Cobdenite, relying on peace and retrenchment and an exclusive interpretation of imperialism from the criterion of the Liberal tradition, Radicalism began to develop a more constructive view of foreign affairs, and this process did have repercussions for domestic politics.

The revelations with regard to the ' State of the Nation ', the concern for the physical condition of the race that accompanied the war,

---

[91] *The Daily News*, April 1903. Interview with Barnes and Ramsay MacDonald. Also *The Times*, 15 and 16 April 1904.

[92] Porter, *Critics of Empire*, p. 295.

did provide some impetus to social reform. No nation could rule an empire if it bred only degenerates. The Report of the Committee on Physical Deterioration indicted the condition of the urban poor, the standards of nutrition and hygiene, and supported school medical inspection and the feeding of necessitous schoolchildren. This concern for ' efficiency ' was repeated in the commercial awareness of a challenge from Germany and America, and further found expression in industrial demands for state help.[93]

The turn of the century also witnessed a good deal of publicity and propaganda for and by the progressive cause. In July 1899, the Chaplin Committee had given the first positive official support for a state-supported pensions scheme. In 1901, the Minority Report of the Royal Commission on Local Taxation gave a cautious approval to the principle of taxing land values on the grounds of betterment, while Rowntree's study of poverty in York, fully bore out Booth's investigations a decade earlier.[94] The publication of a collection of essays by a group of Liberals, under the editorship of Masterman, and including Noel Buxton, Whitwell Wilson and A. C. Pigou, dwelt upon the conditions of the urban poor, overcrowding, drink and a lack of every conceivable facility; they advocated town-planning, extensive housing schemes and drastic land policies giving compulsory powers to the municipalities, ' frankly recognising that such undertakings must be of an unremunerative character '.[95] Masterman agreed with the diagnosis of social ills provided by Hobson, and with the reliance upon the power of the state to enforce a conception of social utility.[96] A speech at Hastings in October 1901 on ' The Abyss ' was the forerunner of his continual emphasis upon the national responsibility to create a civilisation worthy of the name. Amongst his proposals were the feeding of schoolchildren, the reform of taxation, pensions, a Ministry of Labour and public works for the unemployed – the whole amounting to the conscious pursuit of ' the organic whole '.

The Liberal press were devoting a great deal of space to these and related ideas. When Massingham left *The Daily Chronicle* for *The*

---

[93] B. Gilbert, *The Evolution of National Insurance in Great Britain* (1966) pp. 81, 88–90.

[94] S. Rowntree, *Poverty : A Study of Town Life* (1901) drew an initial distinction between primary and secondary poverty, and estimated that 40 per cent of the working class of York lived in one or the other.

[95] C. F. G. Masterman *et al.*, *The Heart of the Empire* (1901) p. 147.

[96] *The Speaker*, 13 July 1901 (a review of Hobson's *Social Problem*).

Daily News in 1899 (Harold Spender and Vaughan Nash accompanying him), he formed a team of advanced writers and reformers, which, with the backing of George Cadbury, campaigned continually for social politics, for social justice and for unity amongst the Progressive ranks. In January and February 1903, the paper ran a series of articles on pensions; from 7 February, Harold Spender wrote upon the state of Liberalism in the country. The paper gave a great deal of support to the land question, to the garden city movement (then in its infancy), raised over £2,000 for the Bethesda quarrymen, and finally staged the sweated trades exhibition in 1906.

In 1899 *The Speaker* also changed from the pro-Rosebery, Whiggish editorship of Wemyss Reid, to the radical, J. L. Hammond, whose contributors included F. W. Hirst and John Simon. Again the emphasis was upon Progressive unity; gratitude was expressed for the role of the L.R.C. during the war, and even more for the behaviour of prominent socialists. Massingham contributed a series of critical portraits of the Liberal leaders in 1902, Percy Alden detailed the problem of the unemployed, and Masterman dwelt on the reform of the Poor-Law. From 15 October 1904, *The Speaker* ran a series of articles on social policy which represented the conclusions of a committee which consisted of L. T. Hobhouse, J. A. Hobson, J. L. Hammond, F. W. Hirst, Masterman, Charles Buxton, Vaughan Nash, J. H. Morgan and H. C. Fairfax-Cholmely.[97] In sum, this represented the most detailed programme any Liberal group produced. It dwelt upon the reform of the taxation system to introduce a scheme of graduated taxation, discriminative where it applied against the unearned increment or the wasteful use of land. The guiding principle – ' private benefits must not be divorced from public burdens ' – applied equally to land reform, stressing compulsory powers for local authorities, a better organisation of production including access to markets and distributive outlets, co-operative banks backed by the state, government finance for co-operative farming methods and agricultural research, a state forestry department and the taxation of land-values based upon a separate site valuation. They proposed that if a landlord was unable to supply the capital for cottage building, he should have to provide an adequate site, and the local authority would build and let the requisite cottages, which was supported by an Hobsonian suggestion that this would indirectly boost wages. The state should provide such

---

[97] Later published by *The Speaker* as *Towards a Social Policy* (1905).

remunerative work for the unemployed as was sufficient for their maintenance, and powers should be given to central committees to carry out works of reclamation (or to joint-committees of a county council working under a new Labour Department). They suggested the abolition of workhouses, the establishment of organised labour bureaux, and the physical sustenance of every child in elementary schools. They advocated a Trade Disputes Act, Factory Acts, while in the matter of pensions, ' it should be among the first duties of a Liberal administration to keep in view the production of a pensions budget as soon as financial order had been obtained '. Finally, they recommended administrative reform to incorporate advisory departmental committees responsible to parliament to watch the progress of bills and the activities of the departments, especially those dealing with home affairs. ' Productive expenditure upon measures of social reform ' could not be refused, retrenchment was a means and not an end in itself within a modern Liberal administration. ' No progressive nation can live upon a policy of public parsimony; no fixed level of expenditure is feasible.' [98]

This was the most explicit formulation of state activity; usually, the existence of such a programme was only hinted at, the responsibility only glimpsed. But individual Liberals writing in the reviews were beginning to make personal statements of faith as a prior commitment to future political action. The Christian Social Union, for example, believed there was ' no private action which has not a social value '.[99] To its magazine – *The Commonwealth* – Liberals and Socialists alike contributed: Webb, Lansbury, Hobson, Masterman, G. W. E. Russell, C. R. Buxton, and they were certainly not distinguishable from one another by their writings. Liberal-Radicals undoubtedly believed they were closing the gap between themselves and socialism; they were eager to protest their willingness to ally with practical reformers, while maintaining their hostility to militant socialism. Alden and Pickersgill agreed with the L.R.C. in asking for the use of public credit, national and local, to provide schemes of development to employ labour, and T. J. Macnamara could ask that the state act as foster parent to working-class children, enforcing parental responsibility, feeding schoolchildren, providing medical inspection, free tram rides, and free baths. That it ' sounded like rank Socialism ' he admitted, but declared he was ' not in the

[98] *Towards a Social Policy*, p. 119.
[99] *The Commonwealth*, January 1896.

least dismayed '.[100] Another manifestation of this goodwill was the increasing support for labour representation, particularly if it was trade unionist rather than socialist, although this must be seen in the context of the next election, of uniting to defeat the Conservatives. It is, in fact, doubtful whether Liberalism at this period did understand either the nature of labour's political aspirations, or the nature of the divide between themselves and the political labour movement.[101] Many Liberals continued to interpret socialism as meaning simply a policy calling for the increased use of the resources of the state. In interpreting such a policy in terms of either pragmatism or empirical social enquiries, they perhaps failed to see that their own ideal of refurbishing and renewing a previous balance of forces and interests, social and economic, within the existing state, would grow the more difficult the more such a balance depended upon the permanent fulcrum of the state.

In 1899, the Lib-labs had formed a parliamentary group of their own under Burns, Woods and Fenwick to act together upon labour questions.[102] After 1900 it was apparently this group which became the focus for liaison between the various Radicals and the L.R.C., especially on the issue of aid for the trade union movement. The moving spirit was Dilke, who gave luncheons for the members, and it was he, in company with Sam Woods, who arranged for the T.U.C. Parliamentary Committee to meet Asquith and Haldane over the Taff Vale case; as the latter were both dubious of fighting the decision, this Radical alliance (which continued after 1906 for the purpose of securing the Trade Disputes Bill unaltered), may be credited with a measure of effectiveness.[103]

The Radical committee was itself maintained after 1900, and in March 1903, a conference of Labour and advanced Radical M.P.s agreed to take joint action over the private members' ballot (although Keir Hardie refused to attend).[104] Dilke claimed that as a result of this alliance, the group ' invariably (secured) a place for the Miners' Eight-Hours Bill, frequently a place for two miners' bills '. ' By a weekly meeting and the consideration of subjects for ballot for

[100] T. J. Macnamara, ' In Corpore Sano ', Contemporary Review, February 1905.
[101] Cf. a letter by S. G. Hobson to The Daily News, 17 February 1903 stressing this point in reply to a leader on 16 February which asked why Liberals and Labour wished to quarrel over names.
[102] Cole, British Working-Class Politics, p. 159.
[103] Dilke papers, Add. Mss 43919, Memo, ff. 24–7.
[104] The Times, 12 March 1903.

private members' rights on motion or resolution, it has successfully brought a very large number of Radical subjects before the House.' Samuel later recorded that, once elected, his first duty was to assure the Labour members of his wish to co-operate with them on labour questions. He joined with Hardie in pressing for consideration of the unemployed, and at the end of 1904, he wrote to Balfour suggesting a commission on the unemployed to consider setting up some permanent machinery. The government, however, did 'not think the present moment... opportune '.[105] The Radical Committee was enlarged from 25 to 40 in 1904, and a further emergency committee of four established.[106] Their actual successes were not many but were significant, being largely confined to securing increasingly favourable votes for both the miners' Eight-Hours Bill and Shackleton's Trade Disputes Bill. However, on 18 April 1905, they did gain a victory when the House approved, against the wishes of the government, a resolution approving the state feeding of necessitous schoolchildren.

A realisation did exist amongst the younger Radicals that a Liberal policy had to be seen to be developed. Samuel wrote to Charles Trevelyan in 1904 suggesting a Liberal amendment to the Address if no measure of social reform was announced. Either they, or J. H. Whitley, or Runciman, or ' one or two others ' might speak. ' It would make a good many people realise that there is a young group who are in earnest in pushing these questions to the front as parts of a large policy.' [107]

Part of their motive was the desire to provide a constructive alternative to tariff reform. So Trevelyan, an ardent land reformer, urged the taxation of land-values upon Campbell-Bannerman, but the latter, although certainly aware of the possibilities here, did not encourage him. Spencer thought Trevelyan's manifesto in favour of a detailed policy of land reform ' has little sense of proportion as to the fitness of subjects at the present time '.[108] Bannerman was also being pressed by Sir Walter Foster on behalf of the Land Law Reform Association, who urged the importance of practical measures of rating and housing reform, and by Sir John Brunner who urged the benefits of developing ' a vigorous home policy '.

[105] A. J. Balfour to H. Samuel, 9 December 1904, HSP, A/155 (iii).
[106] Dilke papers, Add. Mss 43919, ff. 24–5. The four were Stanhope, Dilke, L. Harcourt, Norton; Labouchere joined later. [107] 18 January 1904, HSP, A/14.
[108] CBP, Add. Mss 41229, Spencer to Campbell-Bannerman, 11 October 1903, CBP, Add. Mss 41229. See also Chapter 6.

Brunner's advice formed part of a larger design for 'active government aid to trade', and for shaking off the restrictions of laissez-faire type attitudes. In 1904, Brunner and a group of Liberal business M.P.s forwarded a memorandum to Bannerman. A Liberal government, they believed, must positively assist trade by developing the internal resources of the kingdom, so providing a constructive counterpart to 'extravagant expenditure abroad'. 'We regard it as sound policy to spend national funds on the promotion of local interests provided that such expenditure contributes to the national welfare.' The memorandum suggested government expenditure on scientific research, instancing the example of the German metallurgical industries, and on ports, harbours, and internal transit, thereby aiming to reduce the goods-rates for businesses. 'There is, at present, we are aware, a strong reaction manifesting itself against municipal interference in those matters, but we have no doubt that state action in regard to both canals and to roads would be welcomed by the business community.' [109]

Campbell-Bannerman, having first intercepted Brunner's schemes in the guise of 'social purchase', and dismissed them as 'vague and wild', admitted that a canal network

would be an immense blessing, but it could (I presume) only be done by the State, which would be a *very* new departure, and would mean ultimately the taking-over of the railways, and therefore a couple of millions in government employment. And the first effect would be to scare every railway shareholder in the country ... Our opponents would raise the cry of a new plunder, and all the quiet people who live on railway dividends would vote against us. [110]

To which Herbert Gladstone agreed, but pointed out that government intervention might be necessary to improve the canals' viability; McLaren, Kitson and Furness were, after all, he said, 'practical men'. Gladstone suggested a Royal Commission (and one was established upon the canals in 1906).

Much of the Liberal reluctance to commit themselves before 1905 can be attributed to Campbell-Bannerman's own influence. In resist-

[109] CBP, Add. Mss 41242, 6 May 1904, ff. 1–7. The eight Liberals were: J. T. Brunner, Sir William Holland (cotton), Sir Francis Evans (finance), Sir Charles Furness (shipbuilding), D. A. Thomas (coal), Sir Charles McLaren (railways), Sir James Kitson (iron and steel), Sir Michael Foster (surgeon and ex Liberal Unionist).

[110] Campbell-Bannerman to Gladstone, 2 January 1905, MGP, Add. Mss 45988.

ing Liberal Imperialism, he stood firm upon the virtues of traditional Liberalism. He rejected Rosebery's call for ' a clean slate ' at Chesterfield as ' a mere rechauffé of Mr. Sydney Webb '. While the Liberal League was active in the country, he could, perhaps, do little, but it was not until mid-1903 that he began to refer in detail to the problem of poverty. On 3 June, he referred to 12 million people ' underfed and on the verge of starvation ', citing the discoveries of Booth and Rowntree. On 10 June, he referred to a submerged third, rather than a tenth.[111] However, on 24 June, Gladstone thought it necessary to ask if it were not time ' that you should take stock and on general lines indicate the course which should be taken? ' He was, he said, frequently asked for guidance, and he accordingly suggested an array of topics.[112]

Nothing happened very quickly. In 1904, on 19 October, the Social Democratic Federation (S.D.F.) wrote an open letter to Campbell-Bannerman asking for the Liberal policy on the state-feeding of schoolchildren, the payment of members and election expenses. Campbell-Bannerman promised a reply in the course of his speeches, but at Norwich on 27 October, and at Edinburgh on 7 November, in what purported to be statements of Liberal policy, he failed to mention either topic.[113] The S.D.F. was moved to ask for something more than abstract principles of freedom, and on 30 November, Campbell-Bannerman, in the course of a speech at Newport, said: ' if there is a mass of poverty in this country co-existing with our ever-increasing collective wealth, we believe that much of it is preventable ', and he promised ' a better distribution of wealth and a fairer apportionment of taxation '. His biographer, J. A. Spender, claimed that ' C.B. ' was well aware that free trade had to mean something more than the freedom of industry, but the evidence does suggest that Campbell-Bannerman was content to speak to and for those elements within the party with which he was familiar, rather than meet the Progressive demand for a social programme.

It was not until the winter of 1904-5 that Gladstone was able to establish ' small and confidential ' committees to examine the feeding of schoolchildren, education, the unemployed, and the province of the local government board – Poor-Law, housing and sanitation.[114] In this winter, the plight of the unemployed became acute,

---

111 Spender, *Campbell-Bannerman*, p. 120.
112 24 June 1903, CBP, Add. Mss 41216.
113 *The Times*, 19 and 27 October, 7 November 1904.
114 Gladstone to Campbell-Bannerman, 10 December 1904, CBP, Add. Mss 41217.

and the Conservatives through Long and G. Balfour were driven to establish the first permanent machinery to deal with the problem.[115] *The Daily News* and Masterman raised £12,000 to relieve the distress in West Ham, but it was now evident that voluntary help and charity could not meet the problem alone, and Campbell-Bannerman, for one, found himself in a quandary. On 5 December, he ' had the Unemployed on hand at Manchester and did not know what the mischief to say '. Gladstone, who believed ' a new departure ' was called for, submitted a memorandum advocating relief through the provision of national works under central organisation for which the state would be responsible. On 20 December, Campbell-Bannerman spoke on the issue of the unemployed at Limehouse in a major policy speech with 14 Liberal M.P.s on his platform, including Samuel, Macnamara, Broadhurst, Cremer, Bamford Slack, Sir William Robson, Fletcher Moulton, Sir William Holland and Sir Walter Foster. He went as far in Gladstone's direction as he ' thought judicious '. He supported relief-works, provided these were justified as profitable and ' reproductive ' in themselves, and were not solely to manufacture work. He suggested establishing public utility works, paying fair wages and operating at prices which would not damage private enterprise. He recommended the further equalisation of rates in London, the abolition of Poor-Law disfranchisement, and the formation of a strong Labour Department at either the Home Office or the Board of Trade. He remained sceptical regarding the provision of national funds to enable local authorities to provide work for the unemployed in exceptional periods of distress at trade union wages.[116]

If this was an advance in official thinking, the reception of the memorandum in the inner sanctum was altogether more instructive. Bryce, although agreeing to ' reproductive ' works, and to the provision of work at periods of slack demand for labour, thought ' it would be prudent for us to prevent it being supposed that we recognised any duty on the part of the State to provide work ' – ' a doctrine which would cause general alarm, or lest we should appear to make promises which in office we could not redeem.' [117] Spencer thought the memorandum ' very good, and in many ways most cogent in its reasoning '. Yet while relief could not be left solely to local

---

115 See following Chapter.
116 *The Times*, 21 December 1904.
117 Bryce to Campbell-Bannerman, 19 December 1904, CBP, Add. Mss 41211; Bryce to Gladstone, 14 December 1904, HGP, Add. Mss 46019.

authorities, the difficulties in the way of national undertakings were great: 'What are the relief works to be? Where are they to be placed? How are the unemployed to be brought to them? How are we to prevent the inrushing of destitute to places where relief is given?'[118] It raised related issues of land and rating reform. Fowler was 'totally opposed to national workshops. That would be at once to start competition with existing industries, and would involve a heavy loss to the State.'[119] To which Gladstone sought to show that the demoralisation of 'genuine workmen in thousands' through charity, called for government responsibility for seeing that relief-works were available locally, even if it did not provide them itself. Sinclair thought the present distress was exceptional, and new machinery therefore unnecessary. He was content to rely upon administration through the existing Poor-Law. He stressed the expense 'and works dragging on for years ... I think we should be very careful. Let this Government splutter in it themselves.'[120] Morley was the most distant, simply remarking 'I'm more than content to be one of the unemployed myself', and apparently making no comment upon the actual proposals at all.[121]

At least two members, however, were more forthcoming. Asquith agreed to the urgency of the issue, and to the admission of national responsibility. He supported public works of utility, although he thought Gladstone indecisive; for example, if expensive plant was to be employed, it could not be allowed to lie idle. Personally, he favoured 'a well-thought-out scheme of afforestation'.[122] Sydney Buxton supported Long's Unemployed Bill, particularly the provision of work through the responsibility of the public authority in question.[123]

Liberal speeches in 1905 contained a plethora of progressive sentiments, although few positive commitments. Consequently, when the party was about to assume office, there were grounds for believing it to be 'in a profoundly unsatisfactory condition'.[124] Campbell-Bannerman had spoken of organising the home labour market, of dealing 'vigorously with vested interests', undertaking housing,

[118] Spencer to Campbell-Bannerman, 16 December 1904, CBP, Add. Mss 41229.
[119] Fowler to Campbell-Bannerman, 26 December 1904, CBP, Add. Mss 41214.
[120] Sinclair to Campbell-Bannerman, 30 January 1905, CBP, Add. Mss 41230.
[121] Morley to Campbell-Bannerman, 5 and 24 January 1905, CBP, Add. Mss 41223.
[122] Asquith to Campbell-Bannerman, 1 January 1905, CBP, Add. Mss 41210.
[123] Buxton to Campbell-Bannerman, 16 January 1905, CBP, Add. Mss 41238.
[124] Haldane, *Autobiography*, pp. 158-9.

rating and land reforms, as well as the reform of the law of combination. ' While we are a practical party ', he said, ' dealing with
plain matters of policy, and anxious to avoid high-flying theories of
policy and distant and somewhat nebulous ideals, yet we must have
those ideals.' [125]

The primary cause of victory in 1906 certainly lay within the
traditional areas of policy, economical administration and fiscal
reform, public control of education and the licensing question. The
traditional areas of support, non-conformity, Wales, Scotland, rallied
to the party. The emotive cry of free trade and cheap food as an
economic doctrine of international and external significance rather
than domestic and internal, gave the Liberals a powerful, if negative,
rallying point. Over two-thirds of Liberal candidates pledged
assistance for the aged, reform of trade union law, the taxation of
land values and (often unspecified) action over unemployment. They
all stressed that Home Rule was not a current issue (10 per cent of
Liberal candidates were opposed to it altogether),[126] and this in conjunction with pledges carefully given upon retrenchment and a
peaceful foreign policy endowed the party with a most welcome air
of respectability.

With victory came a ' whiff of Naseby '; W. T. Stead confidently
envisaged the New Jerusalem, and his five principles perhaps better
summarised the mood and outlook of the post-1900 Liberal party
than any statement of intent.[127] *The Liberal Magazine* having asked,
before the election, whether the electorate was prepared to support
a government with a record of mismanagement, extravagance,
Chinese labour, errors in education and licensing, commented after
the election: ' This question, so emphatically answered in the negative, is the question upon which, on the negative side, the election
turned.' But the magazine also suggested that the Liberal and
Labour parties would be combined in a judicious blend of social progress and a careful defence of Liberal principles,[128] and with this
mixture of old cries happily remembered and new ones hopefully
brandished, the Liberals entered office.

[125] *Report and Proceedings of the 27th Annual Conference of the N.L.F.*, May 1905.
[126] A. K. Russell, ' The General Election of 1906 ', unpublished Oxford D.Phil.
thesis (Nuffield, 1963).
[127] *Review of Reviews*, February 1906. The five were: International Brotherhood,
Religious Reunion, Humanity and Citizenship of Women, The Condition of the
People, The Inspiration of Life.
[128] *Liberal Magazine*, February 1906, p. 14.

5

The Liberals in Office 1906-9

IN PARLIAMENT

While Liberals generally were agreed upon the negative character of the causes, if not the implications of their victory, in the new parliament Masterman for one was 'surprised and delighted' at 'the real demand for large measures of social reform ... found throughout the whole of the great Radical majority'. Massingham too considered Radicalism 'the most powerful force in the party', and while Radicals and Labour remained united, he foresaw a difficulty for the government in keeping pace with the impatient spirit of its supporters.[1] Chiozza Money thought the Liberals could boast of more avowed collectivists than the L.R.C.,[2] a fact which received a certain grudging admission amongst Labour. Graham Wallas named over a score of Liberals of whom he had high hopes, and pleaded for an efficient use of the parliamentary majority, for a proper consideration of legislative priorities to avoid congestion, a plea in which he was supported by Keir Hardie.[3] Snowden also considered that 'among the new Liberal members there are quite a considerable number of earnest young men who are more in sympathy with the Labour and socialist movement than they are with the Whiggism which is so largely represented in the Government', and he hinted at an alliance with the 'socialistic Liberals.'[4] Gladstone's own analysis of the majority was in more sober tones: 'The most striking thing ... is the preponderance of the Centre Liberals. There is no sign of any violent forward movement in opinion. In other words, apart from the extreme group of Labour men, the party as a whole seems ... more homogeneous than in 1885 or 92.' He could only discern two Whigs, David Davies in Montgomeryshire, whom both parties had invited to stand, and Eddy Tenant in Salisbury. He added: 'There are some excellent young enthusiastics like Masterman. The dangerous element does not amount to a dozen.'[5]

---

[1] *The Speaker*, 24 February 1906.
[2] Chiozza Money, 'Liberalism, Socialism and the Master of Elibank', *Independent Review*, 11 (1906) No. 37.
[3] *The Speaker*, 27 January and 3 March 1906.
[4] *The Daily News*, 20 January 1906.
[5] Gladstone to Campbell-Bannerman, 21 January 1906, CBP, Add. Mss 41217.

Events were to prove his estimate mistaken. Meanwhile, the Radical element, regrouping through the medium of Dilke, was estimated by him at not less than 50 (although this presumably was an estimate based on Dilke's own, more traditional, criterion of a Radical). In February, the Advanced Group set up a committee of three (Fred Hall, Alden and M. Levy) to consider new applicants for membership.[6] The 24 Lib-labs decided to form a 'Trade-Union Labour Group', and Shackleton and Clynes intimated that the Labour party would act as a pressure-group.[7] A Radical group was formed on foreign affairs, and an unofficial group under Sir Charles MacLaren was established to consider women's suffrage. The Welsh Liberals and the Liberationists set up their own committees, while a meeting of some 60 non-conformists decided to appoint a Committee of Ten to watch and promote their own interests.[8]

If the problem of the sections was not so acute as in 1892, still it was an important factor. Education and licensing were imperative concessions to non-conformity in the same way that trade disputes and the pensions were priorities for Labour. While a number of the more articulate traditional Radicals had gone (Lawson, Stansfeld, Stanhope, Caine), their causes lived on; Leif Jones and A. J. Sherwell advocating temperance; Murray Macdonald, now the champion of reducing arms expenditure, Wedgwood, Billson and Whitley, extreme land reformers, D. A. Thomas still insistent upon Welsh disestablishment. But the 1906 intake had lain a new emphasis upon the numbers of Social Radicals – the 'New Liberals' and 'Social Politics' were the most important elements of Radicalism,[9] including therein not only intellectual and academic groups, but the 'model' employers, Brunner, Mond and W. H. Lever, Weetman Pearson, Sir John Barker and Theodore Taylor. Arthur Markham, a Midlands' coalowner, had built the first model village for miners at Woodlands, had made a study of economics from Smith to Marx and believed firmly in 'the human rights of labour'.[10] Of J. A. Baker, an engineer who held East Finsbury from 1906 to 1918 with full Labour support, it was said: 'he had a vision of co-operative public action doing for the community as a whole what no individual or group of individuals could do.'[11]

[6] *The Times*, 15 February 1906. [7] *The Daily News*, 23 January 1906.
[8] *The Daily News*, 15 February 1906. [9] Cf. *The Speaker*, 3 March 1906.
[10] V. Markham, *Friendship's Harvest* (1956) p. 7.
[11] Baker, *J. A. Baker*, pp. 71-2.

By April 1906, *The Economist* was remarking on the lack of cohesion amongst the Liberal majority, 'the party means to impose its wishes upon the Cabinet', but there was always a section which, in response to a new demand from (for example) Labour, 'wants to go one better than the Government'. The Ministry were never quite certain of where their support was coming from: 'Is there any solid body of supporters on whose votes (they) can rely irrespective of the use which (they) propose to make of those votes? That is not at all an easy question to answer.'[12]

By January 1907, Masterman was recording fissures in the previous unanimity,[13] and by mid-1907, *The Nation* was lamenting the emergence of sectional politics – temperance, education, land and pensions. Masterman saw the majority more as a mob than a disciplined phalanx: 'it desires above all things action', and it was baffled by procedural checks. Weetman Pearson found the House 'a weary business', Alfred Mond too was frustrated by the delays and considered himself therefore a very different type of Liberal to Asquith. To a democratic purist like Belloc the preponderance of the executive was intolerable. Sir George Kekewich blamed the government for not acting speedily enough, so making it difficult for Liberals to justify themselves in their constituencies. The government, he wrote, were 'parliamentarians of the old school', and were perhaps insensitive to the changing variations of Liberalism amongst their supporters.[14] Parliamentary discipline was always a problem, for quite apart from businessmen like Mond, Lever and Thomas who could only afford half their time for politics, there were those like Markham who 'never took a party whip or attended a party meeting',[15] and others whose place in the Liberal party was purely transitory. Major Renton, for example, voted with the Unionists after 1907, and he and Carlyon Bellairs both stood as Unionists in 1910.[16] The individualism of Harold Cox caused him to stand as an Independent Unionist for Cambridge University in 1911, and both he and the coalowner, Clifford Cory, opposed the bulk of the Liberal social programme before 1909, while J. Bertram and Samuel Whitbread did not stand again as Liberals because of their opposition to the Licensing Bill.

---

12 *The Economist*, 21 April 1906.
13 C. F. G. Masterman, '12 Months of Parliament', *Independent Review*, January 1907.
14 Sir G. Kekewich, *The Education Department and After* (1920) pp. 263–5.
15 Markham, *Friendship's Harvest*, p. 15.
16 See N. Blewett, 'The British General Elections of 1910', D.Phil. thesis (Oxford, 1967) pp. 368–9.

A division between the Liberal Cabinet and the views of their back-benchers was implicit in their separate views of their parliamentary function. To Snowden, for example, victory signified ' a new conception of the use of politics. The Labour party stands pledged to make the condition of the people its political work.' [17] The Radicals looked forward especially to a reversal of executive control of the Commons, to more effective debate, and to gaining a reasonable share in the moulding of ministerial measures.[18] The Cabinet, however, did not share the same sense of urgency, and seemed more content to enjoy the prospect of seven years of power.[19] Crewe recorded ' the leisurely and methodical existence ' of the Cabinet.[20] Haldane spoke of a want of system, of Cabinets more akin to meetings of delegates: ' in those days, we lived as a Government too much from hand to mouth, dependent for our achievements on the initiative, not of the body as a whole, but of individual members ',[21] a view which reflected not only Liberal inadequacy, but also the greater autonomy then attaching to individual departments and to ministers in the creation of policy, and the resultant scope given to reformers and senior civil servants within the departments themselves. While the government was reasonably energetic, it was ' not sufficiently representative of the new spirit which it ought to have represented ', and the Conservatives, wrote Haldane, missed an important chance of capitalising on divisions within the Liberal party.

Haldane pictured a party and a programme impelled by a series of challenges, emerging either from within the departments as administrative necessities made their presence felt, or from the ideas and demands of the back-benchers, Labour and Liberal alike. As a party assuming power after ten years in opposition, the Liberals faced the problem of relating these challenges firstly to their own conception of government, i.e. to that conception of individualism (see Chapter 1) which was instrumental in determining their view of what

[17] *The Daily News*, 20 January 1906.
[18] H. W. Massingham, ' The Revival of Parliament ', *Contemporary Review*, March 1906.
[19] Cf. Asquith at the N.L.C., 12 June 1908, ' there is plenty of time before us ', *Liberal Magazine*, July 1908, p. 178.
[20] J. Pope-Hennessy, *Lord Crewe* (1955) p. 66.
[21] Haldane, *Autobiography*, pp. 217–18. Also Crewe to Ripon, 22 January 1907. In 1907, there had been no Cabinet before the first week in February, Campbell-Bannerman was in Scotland, Asquith in Italy. This was ' unfortunate ' and liable ' to lead to last year's confusion '. RP, Add. Mss 43552.

legislation was either desirable or practicable, and secondly to their own scale of priorities. Campbell-Bannerman, for example, could scarcely be blamed for initially concentrating upon the issue of the Transvaal constitution, while Haldane's army reforms possibly appealed more directly to the interests of many M.P.s than elaborate schemes of social reform. Given the Cabinet's admitted lack of any conceptual framework within which to shape and order legislation, it is hardly surprising that they appeared open to pressure from well-informed sources, and aloof from, rather than committed to, social reforms with which they claimed to sympathise. The Cabinet also suffered from the after-effects of previous party divisions; tensions still existed between the Liberal Imperialists and the descendants of the pro-Boers, Morley for one continued to think in these terms.[22] Although personal differences, such as the Rosebery-Harcourt clash, do not appear to have been so significant, great differences in temperament existed; the more staid members of the Cabinet were fearful of outbursts from Lloyd George, and Churchill, after reaching Cabinet rank, laboured under considerable distrust.[23] By and large, however, this was a more gifted Cabinet than that of 1892, it was not saddled with the mill-stone of Home Rule, it faced a weaker opposition, and it possessed a far greater sense of political security.

TOWARDS A SOCIAL POLICY

The immediate concern of the Cabinet was to strike a balance between the demands before them, and committees were established in December 1905 on education and unemployment. By January, the government regarded themselves as committed to a trade disputes bill and to workmen's compensation, and Campbell-Bannerman thought that:

if we have two sops for Labour, we ought to have some other bill . . . of general interest to balance them. Otherwise . . . will not colour be given to the assertion which seems to be their (i.e. Conservative) main weapon now, that we are in the hands and at the mercy of Labour (which = Socialism).[24]

---

[22] S. McKenna, *Reginald McKenna 1863-1943, a Memoir* (1948) pp. 54-5.

[23] E.g. Ripon to Campbell-Bannerman, 26 November 1906, for criticism of Lloyd George, RP, Add. Mss 43518, and Gladstone to Samuel, 6 June 1911, on Churchill, HSP, A/29.

[24] Campbell-Bannerman to Asquith, 21 January 1906, AP, Vol. 10.

The King's speech included accordingly, a major education bill, a plural voting bill, a measure for the further equalisation of London rates and an Irish cottage bill. The government further agreed to establish a small select committee at the end of February to consider ways of improving the efficiency of the House.

On 22 February, the Labour party introduced their trade disputes bill which sought to confer upon the unions complete immunity for their funds in respect of industrial action. Amongst the Liberal lawyers (Walton, Robson, Asquith, Haldane) this was thought ' too violent a proposition ',[25] and ' with some doubt ', Walton introduced for the government, on 28 March, a bill which followed the views of the Royal Commission [26] and proposed, by defining the law of agency, to leave trade union funds liable for only such actions as were committed with the prior sanction of a special executive committee of the union which would take responsibility for all actions likely to involve contact with the employers. The bill proposed to legalise peaceful picketing, but to outlaw intimidation. The unions, Walton emphasised, must possess a sense of responsibility; ' do not let us create a privilege for the proletariat, and give a sort of benefit of clergy to Trade Unions '.[27]

Shackleton condemned the bill as inadequate, and was supported by four Liberals, Brace, Norman, Llewellyn Williams, and Ivor Guest, who pointed out that it was not so much a matter of equality in the eyes of the law as effective equality in bargaining, which involved issues of policy. This being so, the Cabinet could not shelter behind ' legal intricacies ', but had to throw their weight positively on the side of the unions if they wished to have any effect. On the second reading of the Labour Bill,[28] Hudson emphasised that it was grossly unfair that employers, within their respective associations, and in individual dealings with the men, could proceed in private (and no court was going to require them to produce their letters), whereas the unions would be exposed continually to the

---

[25] Haldane, *Autobiography*, p. 212.

[26] *Report of the Royal Commission on Trade Disputes* (1906) Cd. 2825, LVI. The Report opposed the reversal of Taff Vale: ' That vast and powerful institutions should be permanently licensed to apply the funds they possess to do wrong to others, and by that wrong inflict upon them damage . . . and yet not be liable to make redress out of those funds would be a state of things opposed to the very idea of law and order and justice.'

[27] Parl. Deb., 4th Series, Vol. 154, C1307, 28 March 1906.

[28] Before which Shackleton had already obtained from Campbell-Bannerman a promise of support (Clegg, Fox and Thompson, *British Trade Unions*, p. 394).

public light in the courts.[29] Four more Liberals supported him, and
T. W. Dobson explained that nine-tenths of the Liberals were
' steeped to the lips ' in pledges in support of the Labour Bill [30];
Campbell-Bannerman thereupon promised that if this bill passed, the
differences between the two would be ironed out in Committee. On
25 April, Robson explained that the government based its *volte-face*
in now accepting the Labour Bill on the logical grounds that either
the unions had to become fully incorporated bodies, and receive the
privileges as well as the obligations of their position, or else they
received a status only, and their activities would be founded upon
mutual consent. If incorporation was granted, then the unions could
legally proceed against workmen who refused to obey strike-calls,
and against employers who attempted to foment breaches of contract
between workmen and their union. This position the government
now regarded as too extreme.[31] The Conservatives protested that this
was a direct encouragement to new irresponsibility in the labour
market, and refused to accept that the privileges now granted to the
unions were in any sense rights.

The second major labour measure of 1906 was the Workmen's
Compensation Act, which proposed to extend the Act of 1897 to
another six millions, chiefly transport workers, seamen and fisher-
men. As originally introduced, this bill excluded domestic servants,
shop assistants, certain classes of clerks, and those employers with
less than five employees. Certain industrial diseases (anthrax, poison-
ing from arsenic, lead, mercury or phosphorus) were scheduled for
compensation and the maximum rate was fixed at 50 per cent of the
injured worker's weekly earnings. The exclusion of the small
employers and the shop assistants led to a strong demand from
Liberals for compulsory state insurance (especially from Dilke, T.
Taylor, McArthur and Alfred Mond) as being the only means by
which all workers could receive equal protection, and the cost be
shared proportionately amongst the employers. Dilke and Mond
both drew attention to continental systems of invalidity insurance,
whereby the principle of liability was a universal one, and was
backed by state-enforced guarantees of payment to the worker.[32]
Gladstone, however, indicated that the government had not yet got
as far as this principle.

29 Parl. Deb., 4th Series, Vol. 155, C21, 30 March 1906.
30 *Ibid.* C45.
31 *Ibid.* C1486–99 (25 April 1906).
32 Parl. Deb., 4th Series, Vol. 154, C914; Vol. 155, C523, 529; Vol. 166, C1003.

With the exception of attempts by the shipowners of both sides to get seamen excluded from the provisions of the bill, the amendments were favourable, although in Committee the bill underwent considerable change. On report it now included the small employers, and Sydney Buxton had to promise favourable consideration for a scheme whereby this group could insure themselves through the medium of the Post Office, in order to forestall yet another Liberal amendment for compulsory insurance.[33] Three days had been substituted for seven as the minimum injury qualification period, 'against the advice of the Government', and although Gladstone managed to reinstate seven he had to make technical concessions to do so. The long-standing Labour desire to delete the doctrine of contributory negligence now received Radical support, especially from Markham, and Gladstone had to agree that the employer would be liable for compensation if the misconduct of the worker were to result either in his own death or in permanent disablement.[34]

Labour also made a new effort to exclude contracting out from the bill. The government had already agreed to guarantee a workman the minimum scale of compensation even if he had contracted out, but Ward and Wardle claimed this did not go far enough; it did not prevent a workman's dismissal for refusing to accept a voluntary scheme, and Mond thought the 'practical experience' of Labour was superior to 'the theoretical arguments of the Treasury bench'.[35] In the ensuing division 33 Liberals supported Labour, and the Radicals, through Masterman, gained a further concession in that the Schedule of Industrial Diseases was certainly to be increased the following year. Finally, they persuaded the government to include domestic servants within the bill,[36] and defeated a government attempt to allow old or infirm workers to contract individually with an employer for a lower rate of compensation in order to secure employment.[37]

Radical pressure was likewise evident behind the Labour Bill for the feeding of schoolchildren, and it may well have been decisive in ensuring the bill's passage for, despite previous debate, Morant had recorded that Birrell's mind was 'practically a blank on the subject'.[38] Because it was strongly supported, the government thought it wise to allow it an autumn passage,[39] and although it lost its com-

---

[33] *Ibid*. Vol. 166, C325, 334, 29 November 1906.   [34] *Ibid*. C307.
[35] *Ibid*. C818.   [36] *Ibid*. C1057.
[37] *Ibid*. C1241.   [38] Gilbert, *National Insurance*, p. 110.
[39] Campbell-Bannerman to Edward VII (copy), 31 October 1906, CBP, Add. Mss 52512.

pulsory nature, it did allow local education authorities the option of
a ½d rate in order to 'take such steps as they think fit for the
provision of meals '.

Although it was a comparatively short session (156 days), and
despite the loss of the Education Bill, the Plural Voting Bill and a
Land Bill in the Lords, 1906 ranked as a successful session. As such,
it encouraged expectations which 1907 failed to satisfy; only three
small social measures passed (a probation Act, the inclusion of
laundries under the 1901 Factory Act, and the inauguration of
Schools Medical Inspection, which clearly owed as much to administrative pressure as to Liberal initiative). On 3 June, Campbell-
Bannerman refused an autumn session, and indicated that a Housing Bill and the Miners' Eight-Hours Bill could expect discussion
only. The session was mortgaged to a series of land bills which
suffered severely in the Lords.

In 1907, the parliamentary committee of the T.U.C. listed eight
reforms which they regarded as essential,[40] and on three of the most
important, the Liberals were clearly prevaricating. The Miners' Bill
had been introduced in 1906 by a group of Labour and Radicals, but
Gladstone had chosen to set up a committee under Russell Rea to
investigate the economic effects of an eight-hour day in the mines,
and did not introduce a government bill until 1 August 1907, only
to withdraw it on 21 August. With regard to unemployment (see
below), the Cabinet had met increasing criticism for their dilatoriness, and over pensions, Asquith's early warnings that he did not
possess the money to grant them, were repeated to a deputation in
November 1906. In 1907, Hardie moved an amendment to the
Address regretting the omission of pensions, and Lever introduced a
bill to give 5s per week to all over 65 which passed its second reading
by 232 votes to 19. In March, the annual business meeting of the
General Committee of the N.L.F. passed a resolution in favour of
old-age pensions as a matter of urgency, and in the 1907 budget
Asquith indicated that he had tentatively set aside £1·5 million
towards the cost of a scheme.

Increasingly through 1907 the government, both in parliament and
in the country, saw the euphoria of 1906 dissolving. In 1907 the

---

40 B. Roberts, *The Trades Union Congress 1868-1921* (1958) p. 206. The eight
were: miners' eight-hour day and a general hours reduction, old age pensions,
unemployment relief, compulsory state insurance, land nationalisation, Poor-Law
reform, legal limits to systematic overtime, working-class housing.

pensions issue, with unemployment, constituted the critical test of the government's sincerity upon reform. The pensions campaign in the country was a contributory factor in the loss of two seats to the Labour party in July, Pete Curran gaining Sir C. M. Palmer's seat in Jarrow and Victor Grayson winning Colne Valley.[41] The Cabinet were under further pressure from their own back-benchers whose attitude towards the grant of pensions differed markedly from the considerations of practicability and cost which predominated in the Cabinet. W. H. Lever, for example, introducing a pensions bill in 1907, emphasised that thrift was of no use as a principle in itself; the power of the state was quite legitimately employed to secure an admitted good beyond the reach of individuals.[42] The Liberal-Radicals were prepared to support Labour in holding that if such a good were admitted, then practical considerations, such as cost, became secondary.

The advent of pensions in 1908 certainly owed as much to administrative pressures for reform and to electoral exigencies as to any Cabinet commitment to reform,[43] but it might still be a mistake to hold that the Liberal party uniformly followed the lead of the Cabinet or that the party was itself agreed upon the scale and the nature of the reform. Individualists like Cox and Cory opposed the reform, and the speeches of Lloyd George in particular revealed a desire to conciliate the moral objections of the individualist school to the bill's effects upon the individual's character with the views of the Radicals. The Poor-Law disqualification clause, according to Lloyd George, was not a test of character but a test of industry, and the government denied any intention of disavowing a responsibility for paupers because of their personal failings. Rather these would be dealt with when cost and the reform of the Poor-Law permitted.[44] Nevertheless, the Labour attempt to delete the principle of the sliding scale from the bill was supported by 40 Liberals in the minority of 118.[45]

[41] Stead, *Coming Men on Coming Questions*, p. 233.
[42] Parl. Deb., 4th Series, Vol. 174, C472, 10 May 1907.
[43] See Gilbert, *National Insurance*, and D. Collins, ' The Introduction of Old Age Pensions in Great Britain ', *Historical Journal*, VIII (1965) No. 2.
[44] Parl. Deb., 4th Series, Vol. 190, C564, 15 June 1908.
[45] House of Commons Division Lists, No. 133, 1908. The Liberal Act finally gave 5s per week to those whose income was not more than 8s per week (or £21 p.a.), while a reduced pension was claimable up to an income of approximately 13s per week (or £31 10s p.a.). Gilbert, *National Insurance*, pp. 223–4.

UNEMPLOYMENT

The context for the unemployment debates after 1906 had been established by the Conservatives' Unemployed Workmen's Act of 1905. The Conservative response to rising levels of unemployment after 1900 provided, in fact, ample evidence of the growing urgency of this issue. The Labour Bureaux (London) Act of 1902 represented the first official measure on behalf of the unemployed. By September 1903, 16 bureaux were open in London, although six were soon closed because the reaction of local employers was discouraging. The particular lack of employment in London caused the L.C.C. to establish a committee under John Burns which, on 3 April 1903, reported in favour of the provision of relief works by municipal authorities and a national relief-works programme, the abolition of Poor-Law disfranchisement and the establishment of ' a more complete industrial organisation throughout the country '.[46] This was followed by the report of a Mansion House executive committee, a body which included Canons Barnett and Scott-Holland, W. Beveridge, J. W. Benn, Steadman and Bamford Slack, in favour of providing colony relief-works both as a test of willingness to work, and as a means of relief. The report instanced the examples of Hadleigh Bay (Salvation Army), and Hollesley Bay (Poplar Guardians). In 1903 and 1904, Mansion House appeals were launched, and in 1904 Walter Long proposed that joint committees be established in the metropolitan boroughs, composed of representatives from the boroughs, the local guardians and the charities under a central body of co-opted members. These committees were to receive applications for work and to distinguish those who might be tided-over a temporary period of distress, from those who would be dependent upon the Poor-Law. Long initially contemplated drawing upon the rates for finance but his Conservative successor at the L.G.B., G. W. Balfour, relied wholly upon voluntary funds.[47]

The 1905 Act gave statutory form to this structure and extended it to the rest of the country, establishing Distress Committees in every borough with a population of over 50,000. The Committees were given absolute power to enquire into the circumstances of any man seeking relief, whether he was of good character, thrifty, and ' had not from any source sufficient means to maintain himself and his dependants ', nor had received poor relief (other than medical relief)

[46] Beveridge Collection on Unemployment, Vol. 9, No. 5.
[47] *Ibid*. Vol. 8, Nos. 1 and 2.

in the previous 12 months. If the Committee was satisfied, it could assist the man to emigrate or seek other work in England and Wales by advancing him travel money; it could itself contribute towards the cost of temporary work, providing this was in the nature of a public utility, was effectively supervised and paid a substantial portion of its own cost. Farm and labour colonies were now given power to buy or lease land, and the central body in London, with the consent of the L.G.B., could borrow upon the same terms as local authorities. The Committees were given power to establish their own local labour exchanges.[48]

This was the structure which the Liberals inherited and adopted. In April 1906, the Cabinet indicated that they did not envisage any new departure upon policy for the unemployed, and while waiting for the report of the Royal Commission upon the Poor Laws (also appointed in 1905), they would continue to operate the system of Distress Committees.[49] On 23 May 1906, Campbell-Bannerman refused a separate department for the unemployed within a Ministry of Labour. On 30 May, Barnes requested that the power to enable local authorities to pay wages out of public funds be reinserted in the 1905 Bill, and suggested specific schemes of land reclamation and reafforestation. Tudor Walters, a Liberal, asserted that the government would have to set aside ' sound economic doctrines,' and find the money from the national exchequer to repair the neglect of former years. Hardie asked for the provision of £1 million for the local authorities to conduct experiments in unemployment relief. It was not until 19 July, however, that the government agreed to provide a sum of £200,000 to enable local authorities to finance farm and labour colonies and emigration, although Burns remained altogether sterile in this realm of ideas. He opposed the renewal of the 1905 Act itself, and regarded Labour claims for a policy of relief-works as sapping self-reliance, aggravating the irregularity of work, and as being liable to check the flow of labour. Artificial work which was ' state-aided, charity-fed, tax-founded or rate-subsidised ... would only be a form of public benevolence (and) would divert the right money in the wrong way to wasteful ends with demoralising results '.[50] In July, Labour received considerable support from the

---

[48] *Statutory Rules and Orders*, No. 1071, 10 October 1905 (G. W. Balfour) Copy, Beveridge Coll., Vol. 1.

[49] Parl. Deb., 4th Series, Vol. 155, C1364, 11 April 1906.

[50] *Ibid*. Vol. 161, C426, 19 July 1906.

Radicals; Masterman and G. H. Roberts thought the grant too small, Vivian thought that unless the Committees paid union wages the basic problem of lack of purchasing power would remain, while Percy Alden blamed the inequality of wealth and the unequal distribution of population.[51]

The government's early reluctance to enter the field of unemployment established the pattern of challenge and response which characterised the life of this parliament. This reluctance may have been due to both Burns' stubborn ignorance and to the unwillingness of Cabinet to interfere in individual departmental affairs. On 29 January 1906, Ripon had suggested to Burns that a meeting of the labour committee of the Cabinet would be necessary as a bill upon the unemployed ' would have to be brought in in the coming session ',[52] but there were no signs that any consistent pressure was brought to bear on Burns to jog him into action. The Government had already set up a Royal Commission on Canals and a Committee on Coastal Erosion, both of which were expected to provide proposals for work upon the land, and Burns further promised an English equivalent of the Irish Labourers' Cottages Act, which had provided over £4 million for housing and allotments.

The Distress Committees themselves were evidently unable to cope with the rising waves of applications. From the Report upon the working of the 29 committees in London and 89 in the provinces for the winter of 1906-7, the relief bodies received 87,000 applications (20 per cent less than in 1905-6), of which just over 60,000 were dealt with.[53] But in 1907 and 1908, Russell Wakefield, as chairman of the central body in London, was reporting that ' it is impossible to deal adequately with unemployment by local authorities and (we are) therefore of opinion that in future legislation the question should be dealt with nationally '. Succeeding reports stressed that temporary works were useless as a remedy for permanent unemployment as the same men were simply returning year after year. The colonies were being swamped with casuals and unemployables, the work was failing to attract the ' best type ' of unemployed, few trade unionists came within the ambit of the Act, and there was generally an insufficiency of work available. Emigration and colonies, while the

---

[51] For further details, see K. D. Brown, ' The Labour Party and the Unemployment Question ', *Historical Journal*, XIV (1971) No. 3, pp. 599-616.

[52] JBP, Add. Mss 46299.

[53] W. H. Beveridge in *The Sociological Review*, January 1908.

best methods, were proving too expensive, and the measure was only nibbling at the numbers involved.[54]

In March 1907, Burns blamed any failure to solve the unemployment problem upon the Distress Committees, and threatened to resign rather than instigate relief works,[55] but his obduracy was by now enraging organised Labour. The L.R.C. had originally welcomed the 1905 Act as a move towards the admission of national responsibility while simultaneously deploring the inquisitorial character of the Act, ' every line of it has C.O.S. stamped across its face '. Labour demanded the provision of work for the genuinely unemployed, and in July 1907, the party introduced its ' right to work ' bill for the first time. Basically, the bill sought to register the unemployed by means of the local authorities whose duty it would be to provide work. There was to be a central unemployment committee which would provide the missing initiative in finding work, and would co-ordinate its activities at local level by means of special commissioners. Funds were to come from the rates and parliamentary grants.[56]

Labour and Radical criticism together had some effect and the King's speech for 1908 indicated a new Liberal emphasis upon domestic reform; pensions, the miners' bill, working-class housing and a children's bill being included. Ramsay MacDonald, however, moved an amendment regretting the government's failure to act positively, in providing for the unemployed, work ' of actual and substantial utility ', and for the failure to help the District Committees to dovetail their work into the general municipal work existing in their area.[57] Labour now received support from a section of the Conservatives and Irish Nationalists, and, despite speeches from Masterman, Macnamara and Alden in favour of the government, 29 Liberals voted for the motion, which was only defeated by 195 votes to 146.[58]

On 13 March, the ' right to work ' bill appeared again, sponsored now by a Liberal, Whitwell Wilson, who did, however, make the point that the bill was not moved ' as a vote of censure upon Governments, whether past or present. Many of us who support this second reading voted for the government in a somewhat critical division on

[54] *Reports from Distress Committees*, copies, Beveridge Coll., Vols. 4, 5 and 14.
[55] Parl. Deb., 4th Series, Vol. 171, C1880, 27 March 1907.
[56] *Ibid.* Vol. 177, C1446, 9 July 1907.
[57] Parl. Deb., 4th Series, Vol. 183, C247, 30 January 1908.
[58] H.C. Division Lists, No. 2 (1908).

the Address.'[59] The Bill was lost by 241 votes to 95, but this minority included 54 Liberals.[60]

Evidently, a division was emerging, over unemployment, between ' Progressive ' opinion, and the general opinion of the Cabinet. Asquith thought the ' right to work ' bill involved ' the complete and ultimate control by the state of the full machinery of production '.[61] This was a panacea, and would not of itself solve a many-sided problem like unemployment, whose roots were so largely economic. This did not mean, however, that the state should not interfere. The state ' must co-ordinate and supplement the ineffectual private and communal efforts ', although intervention of this kind had to be judged on practical rather than *a priori* grounds. He was only prepared to admit the responsibility of the state in specific cases, whereas Whitwell Wilson's emphasis was wider, and relied upon the admission of state responsibility in 1905 for the grounds on which to base a national state-initiated policy of relief. The Progressives wished to know why, if the government were prepared as in their land bills of 1907 to grant security of tenure to the agricultural labourer, could not the townsman receive the same security in the form of an assurance of continuous work? Respect for the individual surely indicated concern for his material welfare as much as concern for the strength of his character. Ramsay MacDonald indicated that every trade union in the country had ' unanimously and emphatically declared . . . in favour of (this) principle . . . They had come to the conclusion, and every economist (with the exception of those who stood for lost causes . . .), and every social investigator . . . had laid down the dictum that modern industry demanded a surplusage of labour in order to carry on.'

If this was the case, surely some provision should be made to deal with it?[62]

This division in social policy represented firstly a divergence in political priorities; for example, should the government await the report of the Royal Commission on the Poor-Law before acting? Could the government find time and money to act at once? Few challenged the desirability of action and Morley, who did believe that

59 Parl. Deb., 4th Series, Vol. 186, C10, 13 March 1908. Wilson pointed out that the bill had been drafted by the T.U.C., the G.F.T.U. and the L.R.C., and had been placed first upon the lists of measures for which the Committee of Advanced Radicals had balloted at the beginning of the session.

60 H.C. Division Lists, No. 41 (1908).

61 Parl. Deb., 4th Series, Vol. 186, C85, 13 March 1908.

62 *Ibid*. C20.

little could be done, was probably the exception.[63] There were those in the Cabinet, like Campbell-Bannerman, Fowler and (until 1907), Bryce, who were averse to regarding the state as directly responsible for the provision of work, and who were inclined to follow the lead of land reformers, Sinclair, Loreburn, Carrington and Crewe, in looking for a solution solely to the land.[64] Their attitude, while removed from semi-socialistic demands made by the 'advanced' reformers, was nevertheless empirical. Like McKenna and Asquith, the Cabinet, certainly before 1908, were 'practical social reformers', whose governing limitations were certainly those of cost and problems of administration, rather than any principled fear of the effect such policies might have upon character, worth and individual effort.

IDEAS AT ISSUE

It would be easy, in the light of the evidence, to assume that Liberal hesitancy to act in the face of Progressive demands amounted to a continuing unwillingness to countenance new ideas, especially where these involved a collectivist emphasis. Yet this would be to miss the very significant change which had taken place in the nature of the issues and the substance of the legislation.

The Liberals displayed no undue reluctance to legislate within the social field, their major concern arising where regulatory legislation in turn involved interventionist legislation in the sphere of wages and hours.[65] Neither did they display any noticeable reluctance to invoke the authority of the central government in implementing solutions for social problems. The Workmen's Compensation and Scottish Lands Acts of 1907 might both be adduced as examples, and so might the Children Act of 1908 which established a local inspectorate concerned with the prevention of cruelty to children, set up reformatory schools for persons aged between 12 and 16, and industrial schools where the child offender was in need of care and protection. The Act established separate juvenile courts for young offenders, banned imprisonment for the under-16s, laid down more liberal methods for proceedings against young offenders, and further included provisions for excluding children from the bars of licensed premises and for the compulsory cleansing of verminous children.

---

[63] Cf. R. Churchill, *Winston Churchill* (Vol. 2) *Young Statesman 1900–1914* (1967) p. 242.

[64] See Chapter 6.   [65] See Chapter 7.

The Act clearly stood within the mainstream of nineteenth-century social legislation: social responsibility, as a principle, had been clearly established, but this principle could not pass into the wider principle of collective responsibility until the nature of the state's relationship with individuals in particular, their respective rights, duties and obligations towards one another, and with economic affairs in general, the nature of the qualifications to be imposed upon property-rights, had both been more sharply delineated. Collectivism as such involved an economic dimension which was new to late Victorian politics.

The debate regarding the state's relationship with the individual still rested in large part upon the criterion of how the individual was supposed to behave, the degree of moral responsibility he was expected to assume for improving his own character. The emphasis upon the relative worth of the individual did not die away with the advent of social empiricism and the categorising of degrees of unemployability, but in fact lived on within the new categories. There was, for example, an evident willingness to utilise the powers of the state to help the 'worthy' poor to better themselves, but there was greater reluctance to hold that it was a function of the state to reform, train and otherwise improve the mass of 'unworthy' poor i.e. the unemployables.

No group of reformers attempted, in fact, to remove the moral considerations associated with individualism altogether from their recommendations on policy. The 'right to work' bill was hostile to the loafer and Ramsay MacDonald 'hoped it would not again be said that the Labour party had any sympathy with the loafer and shirker of work who tried to batten and fatten on public funds'.[66] Beatrice Webb equally demonstrated a profound concern for character, and therefore opposed the unconditionality of insurance payments in 1911 for 'the state gets nothing for its money in the way of conduct'.[67] The Webbs' policy on unemployment made a clear distinction between treatment that was morally, and treatment that was socially, necessary. For Sidney Webb, the core of the problem was the existence of a class of unemployables, without the resources to tide them over a period of unemployment, and for whom moral and physical deterioration was an accomplished fact. Such men, he suggested, 'should be given, without stigma of pauperism...full main-

---

[66] Parl. Deb., 4th Series, Vol. 177, C1446.

[67] W. Beveridge, *Power and Influence* (1953) p. 85.

tenance in return for training' which would be both physical and mental. Training and 'remedial drill' would of itself serve as a deterrent. A Ministry of Labour should be established to co-ordinate the activities of a system of labour exchanges, with the responsibility of regulating the demand for labour, if possible by linking supply and demand through the medium of the exchanges. Attached to the exchanges would be a series of 'graduated training establishments', which included five grades varying from a 'first-class reserve' on constant call for employment, with industrial training for the 'second class' to increase their 'physical and mental efficiency', to intensive training for the unemployables in farm colonies, and penal settlements for the incorrigible. This structure would replace the Distress Committees, and attendance at the prescribed establishment would be necessary for the provision of relief which would be in the form of board and lodging and not wages.[68]

Liberals could certainly be found who attached a great deal of weight to the issue of moral worth. Harold Cox objected to state pensions as involving a permanent subsidy to the poor, thereby removing any incentive for them to improve their own position.[69] References to the virtues of self-reliance were relatively common and the Lib-labs, Maddison and Vivian, used such arguments against the 'right to work' bill, but within the context of their speeches, their individualism took the form of a defence of what they conceived to be the essential interest of trade unionism: would the bill diminish the working class's incentive to join and to look to the unions to defend their interests? If Labour came to rely upon the state and forsook its own organisations in the search for work, would it always receive the same guarantee of protection?[70] Individualism of this type was always more likely to be conditioned by the ends in mind than by any absolute belief in the virtues of individual activity. If the question was asked: 'are such virtues not only necessary but sufficient for securing the individual's own good?', the answer was increasingly seen to lie in the negative.

Care must also be taken to preserve a due sense of perspective upon

---

[68] Sidney Webb's Evidence on Unemployment to the Royal Commission on the Poor-Laws, 3 and 4 February 1908, Cd. 5068, XLIX (1910). Webb also suggested the control of contracts by all public bodies, the encouragement of private regularisation schemes (e.g. in the docks) and reclamation schemes.

[69] Parl. Deb., 4th Series, Vol. 190, C612.

[70] *Ibid.* Vol. 186, C28, 36–48 (13 March 1908). (Webb also considered that union schemes for unemployment benefit might be strengthened through the receipt of a national grant-in-aid equal to one-half of the union's scale of payment.)

the issues involved. The moral argument, for example, cannot be truly abstracted from the circumstances which gave it force. An investigation into the problem of vagrancy in 1906 found the problem to have reached serious proportions in large urban areas. The report recommended much tighter control, for all casual wards to be placed under police control and for all shelters and lodging-houses to be licensed. The vagrant was to be henceforth dealt with outside the existing framework of the Poor-Law, possibly in labour colonies run by county councils.[71]

The majority of Liberals did differ in emphasis from the type of individualism associated with (e.g.) the Charity Organisation Society or their opponents. The view of *The Spectator* was that 'for the major part of unemployment what is wanted is a moral, not an economic, remedy ',[72] although such a view had been discarded by *The Times* by 1910.[73] The Liberals denied the overdrawn distinction between the individual's true good and governmental action, placing proportionately more emphasis upon environmental reforms, and the co-ordination of social agencies through the state as the happy medium betwen the extremes of individualism and collectivism. As such, they stressed the state's impartial responsibility for the community's good, reading into this responsibility the Whiggish belief that all legislative principles and goals were alike subject to the needs of the balanced society and the balanced constitution :

To protect the interests of all cannot be accomplished by espousing the cause of one or other divisions in society . . . to preserve due equilibrium amongst all parties, securing justice to each in the pursuit of its particular object, forms the principal part of governmental intervention.[74]

The Liberal party had also moved some way from the circle of advisers, administrative and intellectual experts, who do seem to have played so important a rôle in policy formation in these years. The most significant instance here is that of W. H. Beveridge, who held the view that moral distinctions might be justified upon political grounds. He thought it foolish to abolish Poor-Law disfranchisement for this would give 'the undeserving unemployed' too great an electoral control over any public relief agency through which they

[71] *Report of the Departmental Committee on Vagrancy*, Cd. 2852, CIII (1) (1906).
[72] *The Spectator*, 18 January 1908.
[73] Cf. *The Times*, 19 June 1910.
[74] P. Dougan, ' Where Nationalisation Fails ', *Westminster Review*, January 1909.

might benefit. Disfranchisement was aimed at men who were ' not citizens in fact and should not be so in right '.[75]

It would be as well to bear this in mind when considering Beveridge's study of unemployment for it illustrates how even when economic causes had been isolated and diagnosed, moral implications lingered. In that he considered unemployment to stem from a basic disequilibrium between the supply of and demand for labour, the problem was ' insoluble by any mere expenditure of public money. It represents not a want to be satisfied but a disease to be eradicated.'[76] Hence his emphasis fell upon the creation of adjustive machinery, such as labour exchanges, to link supply and demand in the labour market, encouraging a greater degree of regularity in the work of certain industries, and removing from the market and retraining those who were palpably incapable of earning a continuous livelihood. Any large-scale policy of relief-works, he opposed as costly, likely to interfere with private enterprise, and interfering also with his criterion of labour mobility; ' to set up a reservoir of labour at the public cost is simply to perpetuate industrial disorganisation '.[77] His emphasis was entirely orthodox, relief-works being justifiable on grounds of improving efficiency, not for any redistributive character they might have. If their cost was met from money that would otherwise have been spent in Poor-Law grants, then private industry would not be unduly affected, but in the event of financing relief works from taxation the presumption was that taxes would contract private employment in much the same degree as public employment expanded, in so far as the sum of money set aside for capital investment to generate work, as well as the sum of money set aside for actual wage payment, would certainly be reduced.

Beveridge advocated the policy of staggering public contracts according to the demand for labour, but he opposed the ' right to work ' bill for ' to give the individual a state guarantee against unemployment is . . . undoubtedly to condone inferiority and to weaken the incentive to industry '. There was nothing fundamentally new in his proposals; he was concerned to defend the distinction ' between industry and relief, between the man who by his labour is adding to the wealth of the community and the man who is being supported . . . by the citizens '.[78]

[75] Toynbee Record, March 1905.
[76] W. H. Beveridge, Unemployment : A Problem of Industry (1909) p. ix.
[77] Ibid. p. 196.
[78] Ibid. pp. 232–3.

The point of his argument was quite different to that of either Webb or J. A. Hobson, both of whom were in the process of escaping from the determinism implied in lingering notions of the wage-fund and the ' fixed stock of capital ' notion, as well as from a dominant individualism. Webb in particular condemned the view that any increase in the aggregate demand for labour was impossible without a corresponding increase in the availability of capital. He stressed the importance of industrial expectations and the provision of money-credit as equally significant in affecting expansion and the demand for labour. He further condemned the orthodox view that the cost of any government scheme to promote industry and the market economy, having to be met through taxes or loans, could not increase net employment. This was a fallacy (he said) based upon the assumption that private funds automatically went into productive resources, whereas much of them went into the consumption of luxuries, and any decrease in such consumption did not by any means involve an equivalent decrease in the volume of employment. Webb was, in effect, making a familiar radical attack upon unnecessary, wasteful and non-productive expenditure, but the point was now that the government could make more useful (i.e. productive) employment of such money than private individuals.[79]

This point was more explicitly developed by Hobson in his under-consumptionist approach to the problem of low wages, which stressed the importance of stimulating the demand for goods, the redistribution of income and a reassessment of the place of capital as a factor within the productive process.[80] Radicals and progressives in general had adopted an under-consumptionist standpoint in debate (although their formulations were sometimes curious and their meaning obscure),[81] but their position, especially in regard to unemployment, was complicated in that Hobson had little to say upon governmental activity within the labour market and indeed, he opposed any undue reliance upon a programme of public works. His interpretation of the function of government as an investor differed little from that of

---

[79] S. Webb's Evidence to the Royal Commission, Cd. 5068, XLIX, 1910.

[80] J. A. Hobson, ' Do Foreign Investments Benefit the Working Classes? ', Financial Review of Reviews, March 1909: ' The notion that the volume of employment is determined by the volume of capital, in the sense that every increase in the supply of capital compels a corresponding increase of employment, is a barren survival of the exploded wage-fund theory.'

[81] For examples of under-consumption: Parl. Deb., 4th Series, Vol. 158, C450 (H. Vivian); Vol. 183, C247 (Ramsay MacDonald); also Vol. 169, C125 (Leif Jones), for a qualification of the orthodox emphasis upon capital.

orthodox economists. He too saw government and private industry as potential competitors for a given supply of loanable funds and believed in the higher efficiency of private industry. He was prepared to allow the government to redirect identifiable surplus funds to productive uses outside the scope of private industry. But he was only prepared to see the state redirect (by means of progressive taxation and redistributive social policies such as pensions) those surplus funds [82] which would otherwise finance excessive and unnecessary production, towards ' solid works of permanent and fructifying improvement, such as railways, harbours, land reclamation . . . (which) produce continuously an output of useful services '.[83] In contradistinction, the orthodox school saw any identifiable surplus of loanable funds as indicative of an absence of investment opportunities which the government could not eradicate, because private industry was not only the best judge of investment situations, but could perform any given work more efficiently than the government.[84]

Hobson was opposed to any interference in the distribution of capital resources, for the system could manage this most efficiently for itself. All relief works were to be on a purely short-term basis, to be justified in terms of maintaining the interrelated demand for goods, and to be financed out of current taxation rather than by borrowing.[85] Extensive public-works programmes, even of a utility nature, were likely to tilt the industrial balance towards overproduction, for without any notion of the multiplier or feedback relationships, Hobson was unable to envisage any productive activity generating more than an equivalent expansion in consumptive capacity. Such programmes were to be justified in terms of either improving the supply of services for private industry or the efficiency of the labour supply.

Although he denied that the volume of employment depended directly upon the volume of capital, his idea of an industrial balance further implied that in a depression nothing could be done to stimulate productive industry until consumers' demand for goods had already shown signs of recovery. Such a recovery might be encouraged through a careful policy of redistribution, but there was nothing to justify action by the state to create a separate demand for labour. Hobson warned especially against the ' artificial creation ' of

---

[82] See Chapter 4.

[83] J. A. Hobson, *An Economic Interpretation of Investment* (1911) p. 23.

[84] Cf. A. C. Pigou, *Economic Science in Relation to Practice* (1908) p. 28.

[85] Hobson, *Economic Interpretation of Investment*, pp. 19ff.

purchasing power, the level of which had ideally to bear a direct relationship to productive capacity. If purchasing power exceeded productive capacity, inflation was forecast with rising prices and falling real incomes. Hence he rejected the creation of credit on a large scale,[86] which only went to demonstrate his view that the principal justification for state intervention in the labour market was in terms of promoting efficiency and in making necessary, but minor, adjustments to the basic mechanism of supply and demand. Collectivism, as a scheme for the state control and direction of economic affairs, had no economic foundations; the price-mechanism was the final arbiter of social relationships. Masterman, for example, declared himself willing to support proposals for the state organisation of industry, ' but in the name of all that was sane in socialism, they were not going to start national industries out of unemployed labour – labour which had been squeezed outside the ordinary demand '.[87]

Hence the Radical demand for ' organising the labour market ', which, seemingly, was a demand for the state to undertake an economic initiative in the positive creation of work, was in fact a heavily qualified demand. Moreover, while his criticisms of the results of economic orthodoxy were basically the same as those of Labour, the Radical was much closer, intellectually, practically and politically to that economic tradition he was criticising, and he found it accordingly much harder than Labour to shift the premises of the economic debate, and to ignore the evidence of the ' economic realities ' to which his orthodox opponents constantly returned. When the Radical was convinced of the need for a positive initiative by the state, it was usually because his awareness of the broad social and ethical factors involved outweighed his respect for the economic realities. While Hobsonian welfare economics provided real grounds for believing in the practicality of ideals at odds with those currently prevailing, it did not give the Radical intellectual licence to make common cause with the theory and claims of socialism.

The Radical was really more sympathetic to a policy of empirical investigation and treatment by the legislative creation of new machinery with which to adjust the prevailing shortcomings of the market economy. This was to offer, to the collectivist demand, a

[86] J. A. Hobson, ' The War Loan as a Means of Economy ', *Nineteenth Century And After*, September 1915.

[87] Parl. Deb., 4th Series, Vol. 183, C259, 30 January 1908.

structural and remedial alternative, and this was a source of the gulf which persisted between Radicalism and Labour.

The inability of the Radical Liberal to discover a fully coherent alternative to both the claims of economic orthodoxy and those of socialism, left Liberalism itself in a particularly awkward position now that the burden of the issues it confronted after 1908 was so largely economic in nature, and now that it needed especially a convincing justification for its actions where these departed from the path of orthodoxy.

By 1908, the Liberals had effectively brought the legislative trend of the previous century towards the greater admission of social responsibility to a logical close; henceforth, their principal legislative efforts were directed to solving what might be termed the economic problem in politics. This is to distinguish between first, reforms in which the primary emphasis was of a regulatory nature, where the problem lay in eliminating certain ' weaknesses ' by the provision of a service (e.g. reforms in education, health, safety, housing, in the condition of defenceless minorities, the old, the children and the feeble-minded), and where the limiting factors were those of cost, practicability, and the prevailing conceptions of political responsibility; and secondly, those reforms where the principal limiting factor was of an economic nature, involving the nature of the state's duty and ability to impose discriminatory restraints upon the movements and opportunities of individuals and their property within a hitherto free economy.[88] Of course, all social problems must contain economic factors of some kind, but a change in emphasis takes place when the primary objection becomes not that a reform is too costly, is sectional in incidence or benefit, will undermine personal responsibility, etc., but rather that a certain reform *must* rebound, in the long run, to the economic disadvantage of the entire society.

Social reform, in the later nineteenth century, took place upon the logical expansion of the premises of an individualistic, utilitarian norm which effectively governed legislative activity. In its broadest sense, the argument for social reform was grounded in the claim that ' the good of all ' was the paramount consideration. Since the 1880s and the findings of Booth in London, since Rowntree's distinctions between primary and secondary poverty, since the realisation of the

---

[88] It is worth noting that Hobson's advocacy of the nationalisation of ' routine ' industries was based primarily upon ' social ' grounds (the work was repetitive and monotonous), and it was to be the state's responsibility to introduce non-economic criteria into the work.

periodic insecurity of the working-class household in the early times of parenthood and in old age, and since the link was established between old age and pauperism, the existence of a social problem as such was irrefutable. With regard to this problem, action could be seen to lie within a social field where the appeal to the social good was readily supportable by both empirical evidence and the precedents of the nineteenth-century health and factory Acts. Now, from a primary concern with environmental problems, reformers had begun to grapple with the core of the problem of poverty, and that core primarily involved the elimination of insecurity. It was at this point that the premises of the debate shifted, and entered more immediately into the province of the dismal science. Here, the state's bargaining responsibility for ensuring minimum conditions of existence throughout society did *not* automatically transform itself into responsibility for ensuring economic minima in employment and industry – low wages, sweating and unemployment involved new and more complicated considerations.

Reform which now took as its broad end the elimination of poverty and insecurity, incorporated an abiding emphasis not only upon new social machinery, but upon new ideals, especially those of social and economic equality, which involved an immediate breach with the economic assumptions underpinning later Victorian society. This society had very definite views upon the economic functions, abilities and usefulness of the various classes, and had a definite idea too of the type of personal responsibilities and relationships which should prevail if a satisfactory rate of progress and improvement was to be obtained. These views, euphemistically subsumed within respect for the balanced society and the balanced constitution, were decidedly on the side of paternalism, rank and hierarchy, and this social order in turn rested upon a belief in its necessary relationship to the prevailing economic order. When unemployment (for example) raised the question of direct state intervention in the process of distribution within the market economy, this raised the spectre of the state moving beyond the simple regulation of the social and industrial environment to specify both the conditions upon which industry should operate and the manner in which human effort might be called forth and rewarded; the state, in effect, was claiming to be an arbiter in a process hitherto regarded as self-sufficient. The argument hinged upon whether the state could directly improve the efficiency of the labour market and secure a greater utilisation of resources; here it was far more difficult to claim an empirical justification when the problem was itself so diverse, expert opinion was divided and largely hostile, and when, due to the very nature of the labour market, state intervention could rarely be neutral but had to be on one side or the other; in this context, the attempt to reinterpret the goal of a balanced society was called in question by those who placed an orthodox emphasis upon the primary necessities of capital and production, and who were fearful that to change the economic order would produce unwelcome changes in the social order.

In this context, the concept of the ' minimum ', or ' the carefully constructed bottom to the state ', first gained credence amongst the Liberals as a solution to the dilemma of an admitted responsibility opposed to an economic barrier. The idea of creating a floor to the market economy was inherently an attractive one, promising as it did to conceive of reform as contributory to the continued efficiency of the market economy, while succouring those unfortunates who fell through the sometimes rotten floorboards with money drawn from the ' non-necessary ' or non-productive elements within the economy. A measure of responsibility would be imposed by the state upon society at large, while hopefully, it would become apparent to those interests which were either paying for the machinery of the minimum or benefiting from its provisions, that their joint interests could be better served by their own recognition of their interdependence within the productive process. The ' minimum ', as an exercise in social and economic policy, was in reality an exercise in distributive justice, not only in re-establishing proper and objective links between incentive, effort, and reward, between rights and obligations, but in attempting to guarantee social progress in terms of the individual's rational and equal opportunity to realise his own good.

The emergence of the ' minimum ' suggests that some Liberals did have a concept of the type of society they wished to see emerge, and in countering criticisms that Liberal legislation, overall, did not positively embody such a concept (at least not before 1909–10), one has to remember that the concept, like the demand for a programmatic commitment to policy, was quite new. In that the idea of such a concept and such a policy involved problems of social theory as well as problems of the scale of governmental activity, it constituted a response to a changing political experience, the implications of which were further instrumental in transforming the idea of a party from an organisation solely concerned with operating the machine of government upon a specific and limited basis, into an organisation sharing a continuous responsibility for eliciting, and then attaining, all those goals in which an individual might legitimately conceive his interest to lie.

To proceed from the criterion of an empirical norm of legislative activity to criteria drawn from the ever-widening interpretations of a government's responsibility was a process which placed a strain upon both the institutions of government and upon the traditional assumptions regarding their working,[89] and this was a further point of origin in the difference between Liberals and Labour. The Liberal emphasis upon electoral and parliamentary reform reflected not only their belief that they suffered some disadvantage compared with the Conservatives, but also the belief that the ideal of the balanced constitution demanded efficient and economical administration, in which each arm of government (legislative, executive and judicial), performed an identifiable and complementary function, and where the twin bastions of separation of powers and rule of law preserved the individual from arbitrary (and discretionary), powers of government, and gave to him the defensive shield of constitutionalism, or ' due process of law ', by which he might refer any act of government to impartial judgement.

The Liberal (and especially the Radical), in admitting governmental action to define and enforce widening conceptions of social responsibility upon an individual in the disposition of his own property and resources, considered it legitimate to invoke the (democratic) authority of the government to secure the (majority) social interest. The Liberal did not concede, however, that to invoke the authority of government (or more widely, the power of the state) was tantamount to declaring in favour of a collectivist society, in which permanent control of conditions of work, employment and social relationships in general, was to be incumbent upon the state. Acting within the framework of his constitutional values, the Liberal was concerned to see that by invoking continuously the power of the state to subserve the requirements of the principle of social responsibility, however beneficial that principle might be in itself, he ran the risk of elevating the authority of any government beyond the point at which the legal control and enforcement of a measure of equality

---

[89] Cf. Sir C. Ilbert, *Legislative Methods and Forms* (1901) pp. 212–13: ' (Since 1832) the building up piecemeal of an administrative machine of great complexity, which stands in constant need of repair, renewal, reconstruction and adaptation to new requirements as the plant of a modern factory.'

between government and individuals became inadequate; i.e. social responsibility as an umbrella concept, and social equality, social justice, as the various spokes of the umbrella, might, if translated immediately and without forethought into political practice, prove capable of upsetting the existing values and virtues of political responsibility upon which all progress might, in part, be seen to depend.

The vestigial influence of Whigs and lawyers within the Liberal party no doubt provided strong support for this somewhat legalistic approach. The Radical wing in particular does seem to have been torn between its desire for controlled and efficient government responsive to clear demands, and its eagerness for government to assume both the responsibility for directing the course of social development, and the rôle of mediator in ensuring a balance between the respective interests of sociey and the individual. Their apparent compromise involving the limitation of functions but the admission of a wide responsibility, seemed insufficient to Labour and naïve to the constitutionalists.

REACTION AND RESPONSE

By the summer of 1907 the seeming slowness of the government's legislative timetable had induced some disillusionment amongst the Radical ranks. Masterman was now describing the Radicals as predominantly loyal and middle aged, and acting as much from a fear of socialism in their constituencies and anger at the House of Lords as from any more constructive influence.[90] The party remained particularly sensitive to the political threat of Labour. The initial loss of Cockermouth in August 1906 to the Conservatives, due to the intervention of a Labour candidate, Smillie, had sparked off a heated debate within the party. The Master of Elibank made a strong attack upon socialism. Asquith declared he was against ' going woolgathering with the Socialists ', and Haldane promised Liberal opposition to any ' abstract propositions ' imported into the House of Commons by Keir Hardie. Electoral defeats in 1907, coupled with the loss of a major part of their programme, turned the Liberals once more upon ' the dominant political fact of the day ', the House of Lords.[91] So anxious were Liberals to distinguish themselves from ' the Socialist dragon ', that they were prepared to despatch too,

[90] *The Nation*, 24 August 1907.
[91] According to Campbell-Bannerman, 5 October 1907.

schemes of social reconstruction,[92] and the situation was well expressed by Hobson, who saw, in terms of an historical crisis, the 'advanced guard' of the Social Radicals struggling to shift the Liberal centre.

This 'centre' is, alike in sympathy and in formal policy, more advanced than it has ever been before. But upon the critical issues of social reform it lacks passion and principle, and is continually disposed to enervating compromise. In Parliament, it consists largely of well-to-do men whose social policy is weakened by fears of high taxation and of encroachments upon private profitable enterprise; in the country, this same large class, well but not vigorously disposed towards social reforms, stands halting in opinion, fearful of the Socialistic movement, not because of any definite individualism or abstract theory of the limits of the state, but because certain phrases and spectres have got upon their nerves.[93]

Similar sentiments were expressed by Hobhouse: 'within the Liberal party there is a real and deep division between the men who are for developing and expanding the radical tradition, and those who regard Liberalism as the more enlightened method of maintaining the existing social order'.[94]

In 1906 and 1907, Liberalism was being forced onto the defensive by the emerging force of Labour. The Labour victories in Jarrow and Colne Valley in July 1907 were followed by the by-election at West Hull on 28 November where the Liberal majority fell from over 2,000 in 1906 to 241 largely because a Labour candidate, standing for the first time, gained 4,512 votes. But in 1907, Conservatism too began to recover, almost certainly based on the growing middle-class opposition to the tenor of Liberal policies. By the beginning of 1908, there was said to be 20 Conservative vans touring the country campaigning against Liberalism and confounding it with socialism.[95] On 17 January 1908, a Liberal majority in mid-Devon of over 1,300 was turned into a minority of 559 by a Liberal Unionist. On 24 March, at Peckham, a Liberal majority of nearly 2,400 was turned into a Conservative majority of 2,494, possibly reflecting the strength of the campaign against the Licensing and Miners' Eight-Hours

[92] E.g. Sir W. Robson: Socialism involved ' a great scheme of social reconstruction just as difficult as any scheme of reconstruction based upon the Sermon on the Mount '.

[93] *The Nation*, 12 October 1907.

[94] L. T. Hobhouse, ' The Prospects of Liberalism ', *Contemporary Review*, March 1908.

[95] *Liberal Magazine*, January 1908.

Bills. In April 1908 the Liberal majority in Dewsbury fell by nearly 2,500 and Winston Churchill was beaten in Manchester. In May, the Liberal majority in East Wolverhampton fell from 2,665 to 8, and despite Churchill's victory in Dundee the adverse trend continued, the Liberals suffering another heavy defeat in Pudsey on 20 June, and losing Haggerston in August.

Between 1906 and 1910, the Liberals were certainly aware of a rising tide of resentment amongst the middle classes. J. A. Spender thought such people ' resented having to pay for the insurance of their servants' (under the 1906 Workmen's Compensation Act), and certainly disliked the prospect of rising taxation. Masterman wrote of the 1906 election that it was ' quite true to say that the vote . . . was not in any degree a vote for revolutionary change . . . the Liberals then obtained assistance from quite a number of middle-class supporters who had swung round to them, for the first time in many years, from the Conservative ranks '.[96] In 1908, he thought the Liberal hold upon the middle class was still considerable, although the professional classes were being lost and the Liberals were now relying more heavily upon solid artisan support.[97] In 1909, however, he remarked upon the suburbs swarming to the polling-booths to vote against a truculent proletariat. The middle-class elector, he agreed, was ' growing tired of the plaint of the unemployed and the insistent crying of the poor '.[98] A constant theme amongst political commentators of the time was the growing antipathy of the middle towards the working classes, the lack of serious thought amongst the former for arguments upon social reform, their insistence upon maintaining a proper social differentiation between themselves and the working class by insisting upon habits and characteristics of dress, manners and style of life, and the general opposition of those who paid income-tax (i.e. those earning above £160 p.a.) to rises in the rate of taxation.[99]

Such themes formed the principal complaint amongst the plethora of right-wing organisations active after 1906 which, although claiming to be non-political were evidently anti-Liberal. The Middle-Class Defence Organisation claimed some 70 committees by July

[96] C. F. G. Masterman, ' Liberalism and Labour ', *Nineteenth Century*, November 1906.

[97] C. F. G. Masterman, ' Politics in Transition ', *Nineteenth Century*, January 1908.

[98] C. F. G. Masterman, *The Condition of England* (1909).

[99] E.g. J. A. Spender, ' At the Crossways ', *Contemporary Review*, August 1907; R. G. Davis, ' The Middle-Class and Social Progress ', *Westminster Review*, 174.

1906, and their manifesto expressed strong opposition to the ' extravagance of local bodies ', and continued : ' we want to abolish the absurd pampering of paupers at the expense of struggling shopkeepers . . . Above all, we want a revision of the income tax system '.[100] This organisation opposed the Trade Disputes Act, the ' unfair ' extension of Workmen's Compensation, and the principle of income-tax differentiation introduced in 1907 (see Chapter 6). The Income-Tax Reduction Society also disliked Liberal financial tendencies, and with Sir William Bull (one of the leaders of the London Municipal Society) and Sir Guileford Molesorth, a couple of archetypal Conservatives, campaigned vigorously against Liberal social legislation.[101] The British Constitution Asociation concerned itself with the perils of socialism, and their views were reflected in the writings of St Loe Strachey in *The Spectator*.[102] Finally, there was the Anti-Socialist League which merged with the Industrial Freedom League in 1909.[103]

The strongest manifestation of middle-class feelings was sparked off in July 1906 by a series of articles in *The Tribune*[104] (nominally a Liberal newspaper and owned by Franklin Thomasson) by George Sims entitled ' The Bitter Cry of the Middle Classes '. These constituted almost the last trumpet-call of orthodox nineteenth-century individualism. ' Millions of public money are spent annually, to the grave injury of the ratepayer, in endeavouring to combat the great natural law of the survival of the fittest.' This was a hit at Labour demands for unemployment relief to be made compulsory on the rates. Sims condemned ' gorgeous altruistic schemes with the ratepayers' money '. He upheld the protests of those ' who are compelled to pay heavily to keep thriftless people's children in . . . luxury '. The responsibilities of citizenship did not mean that one man had to support two families, and he envisaged the prospect of a large section of the middle class being reduced permanently to a lower station in life. ' The great black-coated brigade ', the clerks and the shop-assistants, had been ignored by Labour. ' The threatened classes must organize ' or be ' crushed under the heel of a relentless and unreasoning majority '. Socialistic influence must be destroyed in all local councils; the middle class, as the class of employers, ' cannot be rated

100 *The Tribune*, 30 July 1906.
101 *The Times*, 16 April 1907.
102 Cf. St Loe Strachey, ' The Perils of Socialism ', *National Review*, August 1907.
103 *The Times*, 11 January 1911.
104 *The Tribune*, 17, 19, 21, 24, 26, 28 July 1907.

and taxed out of existence' without the labour market suffering accordingly. The fact that the Liberals refused to reduce the income-tax below 1s. was 'commercially a disaster in itself'.

The Tribune articles brought forth literally scores of letters discussing the theme of the plight of the middle-classes; the vast majority of those printed in *The Tribune* supported Sims, but the most detailed and the most eloquent was printed in *The Fortnightly Review* and signed by seven middle-class professional men. These emphasised the falling standard of living enjoyed by the middle-classes and contrasted it with the favourable treatment the working-class was receiving, thanks to its gaining 'the servile respect of the governing powers'.[105]

Amidst this uncertain electoral backcloth, the Radical challenge to the Cabinet over social policy was underpinned in the summer of 1907 by the growing furore over the cost of armaments and the issue of where the money was to come from to pay for social reform. On 4 November 1907, a memorandum signed by 136 Liberals was presented to Campbell-Bannerman by Sir John Brunner and Murray Macdonald asking for some reduction in the current arms bill, which, they claimed, was endangering the country's financial resources and using money badly needed in the domestic field.[106] In December, the demand that naval estimates be held at their existing level seemed likely to provoke Cabinet resignations and party feeling was high. On 7 February 1908, Murray Macdonald's amendment to the address on the estimates was postponed by mutual agreement, for Whiteley, the Liberal chief whip, finding that the Conservatives intended to support the Liberal dissidents, foresaw the government emerging in a minority of 100.[107] When the motion was finally moved on 2 March, it was comprehensively lost (320–73), but 57 Liberals did vote against the government.[108]

1907 saw some transition from the more traditional concerns of Liberalism (including therein the debts to non-conformity upon education and licensing) to a stronger commitment to a social policy. On 24 June 1907, Campbell-Bannerman introduced his resolution into the Commons proposing that full effect be given to the will of the elected chamber within a single session. This was both a gesture to traditional radicalism and an essential step towards establishing

[105] 'The Burden of the Middle-Classes', *Fortnightly Review*, 1 August 1906.
[106] Memo dated 4 November 1907. CBP, Add. Mss 41240.
[107] *Journals and Letters of Viscount Esher* (ed. M. V. Brett) 2 (1934) pp. 268, 280–3.
[108] *House of Commons Division Lists*, No. 29, 1908.

control over the legislative timetable, for not only had the Lords'
obstruction plagued the Liberals sorely in 1906–7, but Whiteley had
already informed Campbell-Bannerman that he was 'gravely concerned at the prospect of public business'; the Liberals had promised
too many bills, licensing would prove 'a hornet's nest', and he
therefore suggested a more deliberate approach to reform.[109] With
this Campbell-Bannerman agreed, and accordingly, the session was
shortened and a reform of the standing committee structure
introduced.

Certain members of the Cabinet were now in contact with progressive sources, notably the Fabians; Grey and McKenna in 1907,
Churchill and Masterman in 1908,[110] and, in 1907, a Cabinet committee was set up upon the Poor-Law. Haldane further submitted a
memorandum to Asquith in September 1907, suggesting four Poor-
Law categories that could be used as a basis for reform: the sick and
infirm; 'persons capable of maintaining themselves but unable to
work'; 'those capable of working who will not work', and children.[111] While this memorandum was an admission that men were
out of work through no fault of their own, it still ignored the progressive claim that there were many men not only unable to work,
but unable either to maintain themselves. Haldane gave no apparent
recognition that any fundamental policy change was necessary; for
his second category, he suggested strictly temporary relief and help
towards re-employment, while for the third, he advocated detention
colonies.

By March 1908, the Liberals were seen to be in search of 'a new
constructive policy', and *The Spectator* for one was looking to the
speeches of Lloyd George and Churchill for clues, forecasting that
the party was looking for more control over industry.[112] In 1906,
Churchill had spoken of the 'tendency of civilization . . . towards the
multiplication of the collective functions of society', and at the
beginning of 1908 he produced an article announcing Liberal support for the policy of the 'national minimum', 'social machinery'
and labour exchanges.[113] The evident tendency of his thoughts was
illustrated in the collection of speeches published in 1909.

[109] Whiteley to Campbell-Bannerman, 1 March 1907, CBP, Add. Mss 41231.
[110] B. B. Gilbert, *Evolution of National Insurance*, pp. 250–1; Beveridge, *Power
and Influence*, ch. 2.
[111] Copy in the Asquith papers, Vol. 74, dated 13 September 1907.
[112] *The Spectator*, 14 March 1908 ('The New Liberalism').
[113] *The Nation*, 7 March 1908 ('The Untrodden Field in Politics').

There is a growing feeling (he said), which I entirely share, against allowing those services which are in the nature of monopolies to pass into private hands, a feeling in favour of intercepting the unearned increment of income . . . I am of opinion that the State should increasingly assume the position of the reserve employer of labour. I am very sorry we have not got the railways of this country in our hands.

Defining his own Liberal philosophy, he said :

I do not want to see impaired the vigour of competition, but we can do much to mitigate the consequences of failure. We want to draw a line below which we will not allow persons to live and labour . . . we decline to allow free competition to run downward . . . (we want) to spread a net over the abyss.[114]

This was in line with the ideas of Social Radicalism, stressing responsibility, the state as a balancing agent, enforcing and creating social minima. In the Dundee election of May 1908, consequent upon his own elevation to the Cabinet, he drew clear distinctions between socialism and Liberalism,[115] and made it evident that while he was no apostle of collectivism, he was appealing to Labour on the grounds of Liberal willingness to use the state to redress the balance of society in their favour.

The commitment to social reform, as a priority in the Liberal programme, may be dated from the spring of 1908. In April, Masterman was appointed Under-Secretary at the Local Government Board (L.G.B.), with an understanding that some internal reform would occur here.[116] The government also made the Miners' Eight-Hours Bill and Pensions two priorities. These steps were no doubt a response to several factors, rising unpopularity in the country, Labour criticisms, the exhaustion of more traditional issues and the rapid emergence of Lloyd George and Churchill. However, the fact is still significant that the Liberals chose to opt for an advanced social policy despite, by now, clear signs that their opponents were assured of considerable support in their criticisms. This course may reflect, in fact, a Liberal reading of just where their electoral support lay (i.e. working class rather than middle class), and it may reflect too the

[114] W. S. Churchill, *Liberalism and the Social Problem* (1909) pp. 80, 82.
[115] *Ibid*. p. 155: ' Socialism would kill enterprise; Liberalism would rescue enterprise from the trammels of privilege and preference. Socialism assails the preeminence of the individual . . . exalts the rule. Liberalism exalts the man. Socialism attacks capital; Liberalism attacks monopoly.'
[116] L. Masterman, *C. F. G. Masterman* (1939) p. 105.

strength of a uniform pressure from within the parliamentary party in favour of such reform. After 1908, the consistent theme emerges of a Liberal leadership constructively experimenting with social legislation under the continual impetus of a section of their own back-benchers. The energy amongst the reformers at Cabinet level is paralleled by the energy of their supporters within the party, although this became more apparent after 1911 with the impact of the Miners' Minimum Wage Bill and Land Reform.

Meanwhile, Churchill in August warned the Cabinet that unemployment had reached 7.2 per cent of registered trade unionists, and the trade outlook was serious. By October, unemployment had reached 8.9 per cent and 'a period of exceptional distress' had begun.[117] To Labour requests that local authorities be given the power to levy a penny rate to pay adequate wages to persons employed on relief works, Burns replied that to concede the principle of paying wages out of the rates would be an unwelcome precedent for the 'right to work' bill.[118] The optimistic accounts of the situation produced by Burns clashed with those of Churchill, and although at first Asquith inclined to Burns' view,[119] a Cabinet committee was established in October on unemployment, nominally to supersede Burns.[120] On 21 October, and again on 15 December, Asquith promised definitely that the government were going to deal 'with the permanent causes and conditions of unemployment'. On 1 October, at Swansea, Lloyd George spoke of a comprehensive programme to combat the social evils of the aged, the infirm, the weak and the unemployed. Since the early summer, loans sanctioned by the Local Government Board for 'works of public utility' (mainly sewerage, waterworks, street improvements) had exceeded £700,000. The year's ship-building programme had been accelerated in order to boost the demand for labour. The L.G.B. regulations governing the kind of work provided by local authorities and distress committees, and the eligibility of applicants for relief, had both been relaxed, and the Cabinet now authorised an immediate increase in the grant (under the 1905 act) towards the provision of relief work, first to £300,000 and later to £400,000.[121] These measures elicited a

[117] Cab. 37/94, No. 107, 8 August 1908; Cab. 37/95, No. 123, 10 October 1908.
[118] Cab. 37/95, No. 125, 17 October 1908.
[119] Asquith to King Edward VII, 20 October 1908, AP, Vol. 5.
[120] Masterman, *C. F. G. Masterman*, p. 110. It included Lewis Harcourt, Lloyd George, Churchill, Buxton, Burns, McKenna, Gladstone.
[121] Asquith to Edward VII, 20 October 1908, AP, Vol. 5.

motion from Alden congratulating the government on recognising ' the national importance of the problem of unemployment ',[122] and although Keir Hardie thereupon moved an amendment regretting the inadequacy of their proposals, he attracted the support of only 13 Liberals.

The concern for the permanent causes of unemployment was expressed by Churchill. On 10 October at Dundee, he asserted the government's responsibility to provide the social organisation necessary to counteract industrial fluctuations, and identified three basic industrial faults: first the lack of either any central organisation of industry or of any concerted control of either ordinary government work or extraordinary relief-works. He suggested allocating to a department the responsibility for ' increasing temporarily and artificially the demand for labour during a period of temporary and artificial contraction ' i.e. the provision of averaging machinery within the labour market. Secondly the increasing pool of casual labour, the ' tap-root of under-employment ', caused by the tendency of many trades to create their own reserves of labour to meet periods of increased demand, such reserves simply being left to fend for themselves in depressions. Thirdly the exploitation of boys' labour to do men's work at boy's wages, the boys being later turned adrift without any training or skill.[123]

These three conditions were fatal alike to individuals' hopes of security and society's desire for stability. The three formed the justification for unemployment insurance, which, with labour exchanges, was presented to the Cabinet on 11 December 1908, as the means to mitigate the irregularities of the labour market.[124] To Asquith, Churchill suggested ' a tremendous policy of social organisation ', a programme of large designs to include (apart from insurance), national infirmity insurance (being developed by Lloyd George), special expansive state industries (afforestation), a modernised Poor-Law, railway amalgamation under state control, and compulsory

---

[122] Parl. Deb., 4th Series, Vol. 194, C1631, 26 October 1908.

[123] W. S. Churchill, *Liberalism and the Social Problem*, pp. 199f.

[124] Cab. 37/96, No. 159, 11 December 1908. This scheme proposed to include three million men in the building, engineering, and ship-building trades, on a contributory basis: 2d from the worker, 1d from the employer, 1d from the state (per week). Weekly benefits were to be 7s 6d for the first five weeks, 6s for the second five weeks, and 5s for the last five weeks. It envisaged encouraging insurance in other trades by a subsidy to those associations and societies paying unemployment benefits. For the administrative history of the National Insurance Bill, Gilbert, *Evolution of National Insurance*, pp. 265–88.

education until 17. The aim he claimed, was to ' thrust a big slice of Bismarckian tissue over the whole underside of our industrial system '.[125]

The reference to Bismarck was in keeping with the increasing knowledge of German insurance schemes, common to both Churchill and Lloyd George, who was also recorded to be moving in search of a more democratic policy during the winter of 1908-9,[126] although his emphasis was falling more upon land and finance. These two ministers apparently agreed at the end of 1908 to take insurance, health and unemployment, as one whole in 1910, and meanwhile to go ahead with labour exchanges as a first instalment. The preparation of the 1909 budget, however, was absorbing a great deal of time at the beginning of the year, and already there were foreshadowed Cabinet divisions which emerged more clearly with the budget.[127] Masterman considered resignation because of the absence of any departmental reform under Burns. On April 26 (1909), a Cabinet committee was established to examine insurance, and the following day Churchill was writing to his wife : ' My Unemployment Insurance plan encountered much opposition from that old ruffian Burns and that little goose Runciman, and I could not get any decision yesterday from the Cabinet. Asquith is however quite firm about it.' [128]

Meanwhile, in February 1909, the Royal Commission on the Poor-Laws finally reported. The Majority Report declared that ' something in our social organisation is seriously wrong ', and remarked upon the continuing high level of pauperism, the incidence of relief amongst the old, the cost of out-relief, and the fact that improvements in public health and education had not of themselves materially reduced the extent of the social problem.

Both Reports agreed on the necessity of replacing the old Poor-Law by a new concept of ' public assistance ', and on the abolition of

[125] To Asquith, 29 December 1908, AP, Vol. 11.

[126] Churchill had been pressing the merits of the German scheme since the beginning of 1905 (R. Churchill, *W. S. Churchill*, p. 301). Lloyd George had visited Germany in August 1908, to study the German scheme (Gilbert, *Evolution of National Insurance*, p. 291) while a trade union deputation had reported favourably upon German state insurance schemes in November 1908 (pp. 255-6). Also W. Beveridge (*Power and Influence*, ch. 2) for background history of labour exchanges. L. Masterman, *C. F. G. Masterman*, p. 112. Also R. Churchill, *W. S. Churchill*, p. 301.

[127] L. Masterman, *C. F. G. Masterman*, p. 112.

[128] R. Churchill, *W. S. Churchill*, p. 308.

the union areas and the general work-house, together with the devolution of their previous functions to a new administrative structure. The Majority recommended the establishment of a new Public Assistance Authority as a statutory committee of the County or County Borough Council, to be responsible for administration of relief, half of whose members would be co-opted for their own experience, and half being *ex officio* members of the Council. Local Public Assistance Committees would deal with the investigation and supervision of specific cases; their area of administration would firstly be the old union area, which would become synonymous with the rural or urban district. These Committees would also contain *ex officio* members of the local authorities, and would work closely with Voluntary (i.e. private) Aid Committees, where such existed. 'Assistance' in this context included medical and home assistance (i.e. out-relief), a strong emphasis being placed upon the control of excessive expenditure by the L.G.B., the ability of the local authorities to refuse relief on grounds of personal worthlessness, and on their ability to transfer such persons to training institutions.

The Minority Report placed more stress upon the classification and specialised treatment of the existing multifarious Poor-Law categories. They favoured devolving the separate classes, the children, the sick, the mentally defective, to separate committees which either did exist or might be set up. For example, the Poor-Law Medical Service might be handed over to the Public Health Authorities, and new committees to deal with the mentally defective should be set up. Where the Majority thought the existing responsibility of the L.G.B. over the Public Assistance Committees should remain, the Minority considered the Poor-Law division of the L.G.B. should be disbanded amongst the separate departments who were responsible for education, health, etc. (with a separate Ministry of Labour and a Ministry of Health envisaged). Only by developing such a consistent, and functional, allocation of responsibilities did the Minority think it possible to obtain full control over and adequate treatment of the separate categories.[129]

For the government, neither the Majority nor the Minority report could 'be accepted without qualification', and Asquith felt that on the question of whether or not to abolish the Poor-Law '*in totum*', the balance lay 'slightly but distinctly' in favour of continuing a

---

[129] *A Summary of the Majority and Minority Reports of the Royal Commission on the Poor Laws*, Cd. 4499 (1909), xxxvii.

distinct Poor-Law administration.[130] In regard to policy, he accepted the need to proceed by means of a social classification involving the removal of specific categories from the Poor-Law to new Public Assistance Authorities, although he was not clear about the form and scope of such authorities. While accepting that their administrative area should be the county or county borough, he inclined to the Majority opinion that any authority should be a statutory committee of the elected council. Amongst the categories to be transferred he listed the mentally defective, the sick (who were to be transferred to a unified state medical service), and vagrants (who were to be segregated in detention colonies under the responsibility of the Home Office). Seemingly, for all other classes of the destitute there was to be one authority controlling the administration of public assistance (i.e. relief), and this was to stand in place of the 1905 Distress Committees, the Guardians, and the voluntary organisations.[131]

Both Reports dealt with unemployment as one problem, although the major one, within the general context of social problems. Both envisaged a system of labour exchanges, both stressed the regularisation of the demand for labour and the control of the casuals, both favoured a system of unemployment insurance on the basis of extending and strengthening the benefits paid by trade unions and friendly societies (although the Majority Report did not feel able to recommend any specific scheme). The Majority did not think it necessary to establish a separate Ministry of Labour, and they did not support the Minority over state support in return for training. The Majority favoured helping the ' better class of workmen ', largely by voluntary means, leaving the necessitous workers to be assisted at public expense by the Public Assistance Authorities. The guiding principles of treatment, the Majority felt, should be co-operation amongst the various authorities, and discrimination to ensure the correct treatment, with restoration of the worker to an independent life in mind. Home assistance and daily work in ' an institution ' would be provided for the temporarily unemployed; for those requiring longer maintenance, partial assistance and more training; and discipline and

---

130 Cab. 37/97, No. 20, 12 February 1909 (H. H. Asquith); Cab. 37/98, No. 40, 10 March 1909 (H. H. Asquith).

131 In a further memo circulated to the Cabinet in June 1909, Asquith appeared less certain of legislating for the specific categories. In particular, he was doubtful whether there was a case for creating a new Public Assistance Authority if so many functions were to be hived off.

detention for the unemployables. This scheme was similar in outline to Sidney Webb's, but differed by denying an equivalent responsibility to the state, and by taking as the criterion of treatment, the personal welfare of the individual (which was to be judged for him on moralistic grounds), rather than the welfare of society (in which the criterion became how best to fit the individual into a social framework). Both reports stressed training for the young, continuation schools for the provision of skills, and the provision of works of a public utility nature, although the Majority were careful to emphasise that such works should be for a strictly limited, transitional period.

The Minority, on the other hand, felt that the government might take advantage of the under-employment of capital which was implied by the under-employment of labour. They therefore suggested that out of the £150 million expended annually by national and local authorities on works and schemes, it would be possible to earmark at least £4 million a year which might be directed to influencing the fluctuating demand for labour. Such a sum would not necessarily be spent, year by year, as a matter of course, but might be thought of as part of a programme of expenditure, totalling perhaps £40 million in all over ten years. The money could finance works before unemployment became acute e.g. before the unemployment index reached 4 per cent. The works themselves would be purely an adjustment of planned investment, and would not, in any sense, be artificial. They would stimulate demand through ordinary trade sources, and would not be swamped with unemployables, as was the fate of work provided under the 1905 Act. Finally, wages would be paid strictly on the basis of the work done i.e. upon an ordinary commercial footing.

Here, Asquith fell in line with the analysis of cause, which was largely uniform in both reports and followed the views of Beveridge. Hence the recognition of permanent, cyclical, seasonal and casual fluctuations in the demand for labour, and the need to adjust supply and demand through labour exchanges, together formed the foundations of a policy which looked to eliminate the sources of casual and unskilled labour entering the market; to train, educate or treat the existing pool of casuals, and to attempt to regularise the demand for labour. Asquith's emphasis again inclined to the Majority report whose three guiding principles of treatment (co-operation, discrimination and restoration), involved no very novel break with established procedures. He was opposed to the more far-reaching policies proposed by the Minority Report [132]; to a fully-fledged Ministry of Labour; to extending the functions of the labour exchanges to include an actual responsibility for the provision of work; to insisting upon a requirement of work before any treatment was given, and to the suggestion that the state embark upon a £40 million programme of investment.

Asquith's emphasis was in contrast to that of the Radical wing of the party. On 19 May, E. Pickersgill moved to call attention to the recommendations of the Minority Report regarding unemployment, mentioning as worth considering both trade union based insurance and the ten-year public works programme.[133] Percy Alden thought the government should subsidise all those existing organisations which provided unemployment benefits, and Ramsay MacDonald asked that the state finance ' new industries ' which would create a new labour market and a new source of consumers. This would ' create a new economic demand ' and ' widen the basis of employment '.[134] Amid mounting criticism of the government's views, Churchill rose to give a definite announcement of an unemployment insurance scheme, with a compulsory and contributory basis, initially to include the building, ship-building, and engineering trades. This was to be the corollary of attempts to minimise casual labour and irregular employment, and the attempt to underpin wages in certain sweated trades by means of wages boards.[135] He also announced a three-fold division of the functions of the Board of Trade. In future, one section was to deal with wages, conciliation and arbitration, and the wages boards; a second was to supervise special enquiries and statistical information; while the third was to look after the exchanges and insurance, watch the labour market, the demand for labour, the distribution of government contracts, municipal work and public utility schemes. His announcement was welcomed by Henderson, on behalf of Labour, as leading towards the principle of the ' right to work ', and Pickersgill responded by not pressing his division to a vote.

A previous speech from Churchill in February, replying to a critical amendment to the Address on the government's policies for

---

132 Cf. Cab. 37/97, No. 20, p. 35: ' If the state imposes the duty to work, either in open industry or a Training establishment, it must sooner or later be driven to recognise a duty to provide work, and so recognise the right to work.'
133 Parl. Deb., 5th Series, Vol. 5, C484, 19 May 1909.
134 *Ibid*. C497.
135 *Ibid*. C507 (see also Chapter 7).

social organisation, had also met some of the Radical demands. 'I do feel most strongly (he said) that there ought to be in the machinery of the State something which corresponds to the governor of an engine, which does to some extent regulate the speed of the machinery.' On this occasion, however, 31 Liberals voted against the government.[136]

There was, indeed, in 1909, very little to separate Labour from the Liberal-Radical wing. On 10 March the two groups were combined to press the government to widen the interpretation of the Fair Wage Clause in government contracts, and Buxton agreed to extend the clause to subcontracting, and to base fair wages explicitly upon trade union rates.[137] On the day following Lloyd George's budget speech of 29 April, the 'right to work' bill appeared again, in a slightly more stringent form and won, as before, considerable support from Liberals. W. P. Beale seemed to express their opinion when he said that although the Bill was both financially and administratively haphazard, it was still 'too pressing to be thrown aside, as long as there is a germ for development into a practical shape'. 53 Liberals voted for the Bill, out of 115 in favour.[138]

Liberals also expressed criticism of the delay the government had shown in not proceeding earlier with either labour exchanges or wages boards. The latter had, in fact, appeared under Radical auspices in every session since 1906, and Liberal frustration with Burns was fully equal to that of Labour. Liberals too were keen to remind the government that labour exchanges, being only organisational remedies, were of little use in meeting the basic defects of the market economy. Something more Radical was needed, for it was recognised that individualism in the economic order meant unemployment. If the government were prepared to admit a general responsibility for social conditions, would they also admit a direct responsibility to enforce upon individuals the obligation to conform to those conditions?[139] Specifically, would the government enforce upon employers the obligation to recognise non-economic criteria in determining issues of pay, employment and production? Could, in fact, the government enforce upon an industry the responsibility for looking after any labour surplus it might create? How far might

---

[136] *Ibid.* Vol. 1, C191, 16 February 1909; H.C. Division Lists, No. 2, 1909.
[137] Parl. Deb., 5th Series, Vol. 2, C416, 10 March 1909.
[138] *Ibid.* C674. H.C. Division Lists, No. 80, 1909.
[139] Parl. Deb., 5th Series, Vol. 5, C492, 19 May 1909 (Alden), and Vol. 6, C1013 (Chiozza Money). Also Vol. 1, C157, 16 February 1909.

one section of the community be held to account and penalised for the creation of un-social conditions, such as the exploitation of boys' or women's labour? These questions now focused upon the real point at issue: how far would the government extend the concept of the 'minimum', and would they insist upon the primacy of social goals (and the public interest) over and above the purely economic laws? This issue emerged into the open after 1910, when the test question for the Liberals as reformers changed from their treatment of unemployment to the demand for a minimum wage.

THE RADICALS IN PARLIAMENT

The Liberal Radicals were not themselves demanding a new economic structure, believing instead that the social good could be best achieved through increasing the efficiency of the competitive system and subjecting it to a definitive set of humanistic and welfare-oriented goals. Political economy was to be reduced from the master science of wealth production to one amongst an interdependent series of social disciplines. Production would be for use and not for profit, and it would be stimulated by the need and the choice of the consumer. 'The extent of production obviously depends ... on the power to consume. The power is deliberately limited by the producers in order that they might obtain as great a control as possible over prices and wages in the interests of profit.'[140] In this context, the concept of welfare was, perhaps, less the product of an explicitly collectivist emphasis upon the regulation and control of the environment by the state, but owed more to the emergence of 'the new economics', the importance of consumption, the allowance for non-economic costs in production, the concern with social utility, ideas which Labour believed in almost instinctively and which Hobson, Hobhouse and the parliamentary Radicals tried to explain more self-consciously.

The emergence of an 'extreme Radical' wing was recognised amongst contemporaries,[141] and would go some way towards explaining the Conservative emphasis upon the near-identity between the New Liberalism and socialism. Towards the end of 1908 and 1909, it was the Liberal Radicals who were setting the pace in parliament, rather than Labour. This was evident in the debates upon unemploy-

---

[140] Parl. Deb., 5th Series, Vol. 6, C1014 (Chiozza Money), and Vol. 4, C672 (Robert Harcourt).
[141] Cf. Elibank papers, Mss 8802, f. 38.

ment, and in regard to the growing vehemence of the land reformers, the demand for a radical taxation policy, and in the debate upon armaments. At the time of the 1909 Navy scare, it was the Radicals who led criticisms of the government in March, and despite the government's compromise (i.e. to build four dreadnoughts then and retain an option for four more later), forced a division on March 17 upon the naval estimates in which 36 Liberals voted against the government. In July, when the government decided to proceed with the four further dreadnoughts, 42 Liberals voted against the supplementary estimates.[142]

An examination of twelve divisions in the four sessions 1906–9,[143] which might be said to raise points of principle with regard to policy and which the government opposed, reveals a somewhat confused picture. The Radical bloc clearly did not form a cohesive pressure-group in the same way that the Labour party members did. Equally, the Radical record on advanced issues was not so uniform and consistent as to lead one to say that to all effective purposes, Labour and the Radicals were one. Clearly, they were not, and Radicalism was no doubt torn between the desire to demonstrate their sincerity for the progressive cause, and their desire to differentiate themselves sufficiently from the L.R.C. These factors being so, the best index of Radical strength is the number of Liberals attracted into the lobbies on specific issues, rather than the number of hard-core Radicals alone.

Those Liberals voting against the government in five or more divisions numbered 26 in all, 15 of whom opposed the government in exactly five divisions. On the wider issue of how far Liberals were prepared to record votes in sympathy with Labour demands, support was more extensive. Over 70 Liberals cast votes for at least one of the two 'right to work' bills, and on each occasion the Bill went to a division, the Liberal contingent was the largest in its favour.[144] Some

---

[142] H.C. Division Lists, No. 35, 1909 (lost 322–83) and No. 367, 1909 (lost 280–98).

[143] As follows: 1906 – No. 458, to remove contracting-out clause from the compensation bill. 1907 – No. 38, to reduce the hours of railwaymen, and No. 455, to reduce hours of work in laundries. 1908 – No. 2, amendment to the Address on unemployment, No. 29, to reduce military estimates, No. 41, 'right to work' bill, and No. 133, to omit the sliding-scale from the pensions bill, and No. 292, Hardie's amendment to Alden's motion on unemployment. 1909 – No. 2, amendment to the Address on unemployment, Nos. 35 and 367 on the naval estimates, and No. 80, 'right to work' bill.

[144] The 15 were: Percy Alden; Timothy Davies; A. E. Dunn; H. Fullerton; W. Johnson; E. H. Lamb; R. C. Lehmann; Murray Macdonald; H. F. Luttrell; C. Fenwick; F. Hall; J. Wadsworth; T. Richards; J. Wilson; A. Richardson.

Liberals, such as Atherley-Jones and Beale voted against the government only on these Bills, while a much larger group (Jacoby, Keke-wich, Yoxall, Whitwell Wilson, Masterman,[145] Sir John Bethell, Sir H. J. S. Cotton, W. H. Dickinson, Hamar Greenwood, Leif Jones, Charles Roberts and J. A. Baker) voted against the government on these two occasions, but did not vote against the government on more than three or four occasions. In fact, when issues arose involving principles of either government responsibility for the unemployed, or of economic intervention by the state, the 26 Radicals received fairly substantial support from those whose overall voting record was much more regular. Finally, there was a further group of known Labour sympathisers who did not support the 'right to work' bill, and whose voting deviations came solely from questions of hours limitations, or the handling of unemployment and naval estimates; this group included people like Channing, R. L. Everett, George Toulmin, A. B. Markham and Henry Vivian.

The three divisions on military estimates are included here as providing a further indication of the Radical profile; the Social Radicals, especially the leading score, all reoccurred at least once in the three divisions. However, the three are also useful in indicating a further muster of Radical opinion which was not prepared to defy the government on Labour questions, and which hints at the continuance of a strong traditional Radical element within the party. This included Sir John Brunner and J. E. Ellis who voted in all three divisions for the reduction of the estimates while Thomas Lough, Sir John Barlow, J. F. L. Brunner and Sir W. Brampton-Gurdon, all voted in two of the three.

Voting on six occasions against the Government: J. Rowlands, H. C. Lea, J. Williams, A. H. Scott.

On seven occasions: Felix Cobbold, W. Abraham, F. H. Rutherford.

On eight occasions: W. P. Byles, Chiozza Money, E. H. Pickersgill.

On nine occasions: G. J. Cooper.

Only seven had sat in parliament before 1906; apart from the nine Lib-labs, they were all professional men, or writers. A. H. Scott was a provisions merchant, but had been secretary to the Bolton Shop Assistants.

The Lib-labs have been included with the Liberals for this purpose, although the miners were nominally members of the Labour party during the last three divisions in 1909. Generally, the Lib-labs were not amongst the most radical advocates, and apart from the nine listed above, only one other voted on as many as four occasions against the government. For whatever reason, it is interesting that both Burt and Fenwick, neither of whom could be classified as Labour, voted for the 1909 'right to work' bill.

145 As a member of the government after April 1908, Masterman voted against the second 'right to work' bill.

In sum, this suggests that Liberal back-benchers were exposed to some conflict between their duty to support the government, and their wish to uphold new principles of governmental responsibilities which were beginning to harden. This would be in keeping with an impression of Liberal voting habits, which is one of considerable fluidity. Some 160 Liberals did record a vote against the government, and although 55 only voted once, and a further 33 only twice, against the government, all of these divisions possessed more or less direct implications for policy.[146] The overall impression is of an advanced Social Radical section, rarely less than 25 strong in any division, and drawing on a further body of support which in itself (including the Lib-labs), may well have exceeded 40. Behind this group ranged a somewhat larger number of Radicals who were prepared to lend support, in the manner of traditional Radicalism, to causes of which they approved, and who wished to preserve an air of independence in dealing with what they saw as principles.

It would be difficult to prove that the government were directly influenced by the existence of this Radical wing, although it is worth remarking that the measures which the government did adopt bore an immediate resemblance to the demands being made in parliament (in debate as well as in the presentation of private members' bills), for pensions, wages boards, and land legislation; certainly the government's official unemployment policy, by the end of 1909, incorporated most of the specific demands made in the previous four years.[147] Perhaps the most interesting bill in this context (apart from the 1909 budget) was the Development and Road Improvement Bill, for which provision was made in the budget. This bill proposed to allow

---

[146] Amongst this section were the future ministers, Illingworth, J. A. Simon and J. M. Robertson (who voted three times against the government).

[147] Herbert Samuel explained the government's unemployment policy to the Northern Liberal Federation at Durham (*Manchester Guardian*, 25 January 1910). After rejecting the Right to Work Bill as a palliative, and rejecting the limitation of hours as restricting output, he listed four preventive measures, aimed at reducing the numbers of the unskilled:

(a) technical education and compulsory continuation schools;
(b) the development of the land;
(c) the maintenance of industrial peace by (e.g.) conciliation boards;
(d) encouragement to industries affected by recurring depression to work short-time rather than dismissing their men;

and three remedial measures:

(a) penal farm colonies for the unemployed;
(b) labour exchanges and insurance;
(c) 'large national works of a productive kind', the development of canals, in accord with the principle of regulating the demand for labour.

the Treasury to make free grants and lands to a Development Commission for the purpose of developing forestry, agriculture, rural industry, rural transport, harbours, canals and fisheries. It was, in effect, taking up both the demand for works of a public utility nature and the previous claims made by Sir John Brunner for a specific policy of internal development.[148] It was an example of the Liberal willingness to legislate in fields where no administrative or economic complications were evident, and while the precise content of Liberal policy owed a great deal to the ability of the administrators in overcoming these complications, still the ideas and actions of the parliamentary party was of some significance in creating the context within which policy was considered.

[148] The Royal Commission to enquire into Canals and Inland Navigations (Cd. 4979, xii) reported, in 1910, in favour of an extensive state programme to improve the canal system, to subsidise and take over existing companies. Buxton, however, received the scheme cautiously and, on behalf of the Board of Trade, favoured state subventions and guarantees to be made available indirectly through the Development Commission. (Cab. 37/106, No. 45, P.R.O. May 1911.) The Cabinet do not seem to have taken a definite decision on the issue and, apparently, it faded out of sight in the pressure of events.

6

Taxation, the Land, and the Budgets of 1909 and 1914

The high peak of this Liberal government was the budget of 1909, but it would be a mistake to view the budget solely within the context of the post-1906 administration, determined first by the urgent necessity of raising money for social reform, and secondly, by traditional Liberal antipathies towards landowners. The budget certainly reflected such factors, but the form and nature of its provisions were only made possible by previous and significant changes in the Liberal attitude towards the purpose of taxation itself, and further, by the growing preoccupation of a section of Liberal Radicalism with land reform and land taxes as a remedy for unemployment and industrial ills. For a large section of the Liberal party, social organisation did mean land reform. The two debates, over the purpose of taxation and the nature of a land policy, are instructive in providing both an example of the passage of radical ideas into the Liberal party and their expression in policy, and an insight into the real nature of Conservative opposition to the New Liberalism. The two debates, in effect, provide an indication of the continuity of Liberal thinking and the development of Liberal policy throughout the period, indicating that the course of events after 1906 did owe much to the lessons of previous years.

THE DEBATE UPON TAXATION

Orthodoxy, within a financial context, stemmed from the nineteenth-century tradition of peace, retrenchment and reform. Ideally, a government's expenditure would be limited in scope and economical in design, concerned with the financing of those activities the individual was unable either to afford or to provide for himself. The principles of taxation had remained the same from Adam Smith to John Stuart Mill, and Mill remained the authority in 1892. Taxes should be levied in proportion to revenue, in regard to both their certainty in raising revenue and to their convenience; they should have as little effect as possible upon private activities.[1] With a few small exceptions

---

[1] Mill, *Principles*, p. 804.

Mill favoured proportionate rather than progressive (or graduated) taxation, and, with the possible exception of the taxation of economic rent, he refused to admit that taxation might be used expressly to redress inequalities of wealth. That, he said, would be ' to relieve the prodigal at the expense of the prudent ', and furthermore, to tax large accumulated incomes would be to ' tax industry and economy ', and might penalise savings and weaken ' the springs of industry '. Neither were taxes to be levied on capital resources to meet the necessities of current expenditure, for this would be to divert productive funds in private hands to probably unproductive public usage. Any tax which struck at production struck at the future source of revenue, and any government thereby unable to finance normal expenditure out of the current revenues, risked competing with private industry for a limited supply of funds, so driving up interest rates against both itself (and industry), consequently increasing the burden of repayment.[2]

The field for taxation was therefore sharply circumscribed by the prevailing nature of economic and political individualism: thrift and savings, incentive and enterprise, industry and production, these were primary goals in themselves; taxation was specific and controllable, in the same way as were a government's responsibilities and actions. Leaders of both parties accepted willingly that a government's chief financial responsibility was to maintain the conditions of financial stability i.e. to ensure that market conditions encouraged a steady supply of funds for investment and for the provision of credit.

And yet there were, by the 1880s, suggestions of a rift between the parties over taxation. The Radical Programme declared in 1885 that ' the taxation of the future ought to take the character of insurance, or of investments for the general welfare ', while *The Quarterly Review* insisted in 1888: ' A tax, the amount of which is not replaced by exertion or economy, is a distinct deduction from the wealth of a country unless it is, what few taxes can ever be, laid out in a productive manner '.[3] The National Liberal Federation, after declaring in favour of taxing groundrents and mineral royalties, from 1888 supported the simplification of the existing death-duties, and the introduction of a low but progressive scale of duties. The Liberal willingness to turn to the direct taxation of both wealth and

2 *Ibid*. pp. 821f.
3 *Quarterly Review*, 166 (1888) No. 331.

income, increasingly contrasted with the Conservative preference for indirect taxation as the main source of revenue; and to the nineteenth-century debate over the level of expenditure was added the more modern debate as to how the money was to be raised, and what attention was to be paid to the source and the nature of the income. If expenditure still involved the familiar argument for retrenchment, the debate upon taxation now involved issues of principle which sharply divided the pre-1914 parties.

Bernard Mallet noted from the late 1880s the growing contemporary preoccupation with both the ability (i.e. capacity) of the taxpayer to bear taxation, and with the growth of more refined ideas of equity.[4] The first breach in the orthodox tradition came with the reform of the death-duties, a question which had, in Sir William Harcourt and Sydney Buxton, two strong proponents in the 1892 government.[5] It was Buxton's book in 1890 which set forth a fairly detailed case for the reform, arguing that death-duties were not a tax upon capital in the sense of a tax upon industry, because personal wealth was only accumulated income, and would only be indirectly available for productive investment. Moreover, the revenue from death-duties would allow other taxes to be repealed, which was a valid justification on Peelite and Gladstonian grounds.[6] The 1894 Budget proposed to merge the existing plethora of legacy, estate and succession duties, into one graduated estate duty which would be levied upon the aggregate value of both real and personal property changing hands over the owner's death. The scale of payment rose from 1 per cent on property worth £500 or under, to 5 per cent on property worth between £25,000 and £50,000, and ultimately to 8 per cent on property worth over £1 million.

In the Commons, Harcourt justified his measure on grounds of financial rectitude (i.e. he was not borrowing, which was a greater crime than increasing taxation), and in terms of administrative reform. Of the death-duties he said: ' they have never been established upon any general principles, and they present an extraordinary specimen of tussellated legislation '. He then proceeded to adopt arguments hitherto more common amongst land nationalisers. In

---

[4] B. Mallet, *British Budgets 1887–1913* (1913) pp. viii–ix.

[5] For further details on this point, see the author's article ' The Impact of Financial Policy on English Party Politics Before 1914 ', *Historical Journal*, xv (1) March 1972.

[6] S. Buxton and G. S. Barnes, *A Handbook to the Death-Duties* (1890).

future, when property changed hands upon death, the state's claim was to be established prior to that of the beneficiaries:

The title of the State to a share in the accumulated property of the deceased is an anterior title to that of the interest to be taken by those who are to share it . . . Nature gives a man no power over his earthly goods beyond the term of his life. [The power to make future provision] was a pure creation of the law, and the State has the right to prescribe the conditions and limitations under which that power shall be exercised.[7]

While the Liberal party and the majority of the Cabinet were in agreement with the budget, Harcourt found one opponent in Rosebery who doubted the wisdom of the redistributive effects of the budget, as well as its political wisdom. Too much, however, must not be made of this budget, for the Liberals had only adopted a very mild rate of progression and anyway , discussion still moved ' entirely in a context of contemplated rates which made any effect on the distribution of income appear negligible '.[8] The main identification between the social good and the redistribution of income by means of direct, progressive scales had yet to come, and although Harcourt had, in fact, toyed with introducing a graduated income-tax, the emphasis had barely begun to shift from indirect to direct taxes.

Yet a gap had undoubtedly begun to open between the parties. First, there was the inherent incompatibility of the Whiggish notion of the balance of classes and equality of sacrifice from taxation proportionately levied, and the idea of graduated taxation and ability to pay. Secondly, the Conservatives did not admit that taxation involved other than an equal responsibility upon all classes; they refused to believe that one class could be taxed for the benefit of another,[9] while this was a principle to which the Liberals, especially in connection with the ideas of ' betterment ' and ' social values ' accruing to the land were now moving.

Beneath the party-political level, the idea of income redistribution began to emerge with Henry George's popularisation of the economic rent of land as a surplus, ' non-necessary ', element in distribution. From the classical inheritance of Ricardo and Mill, economic rent

---

[7] Parl. Deb., 4th Series, Vol. 23, C485–90, 16 April 1894.

[8] F. A. Hayek, *The Constitution of Liberty* (1959) pp. 309–10.

[9] Cf. W. Lecky, *Democracy and Liberty* (1896) Vol. 1, p. 347: ' Highly graduated taxation realises most completely the supreme danger of democracy, creating a state of things in which one class imposes on another burdens which it is not asked to share, and impels the state into vast schemes of extravagance under the belief that the whole costs will be thrown upon others.'

had been particularly associated with the market for land, in which a rising (social) demand curve pressing upon a vertical supply curve, forced up the price of land and provided the landowner with a surplus that was both unearned and gained at the expense of the community. From the idea of economic rent existing as part of the income of a privileged landowning class which might be taxed without diminishing the supply of land, sprang the Radical-Liberal demand for appropriation of rent, either through nationalisation or the single-tax, and the diversion of the social value of the land to the community. The argument was taken a step further by J. A. Hobson and by Sidney Webb who both perceived that the case of land was analogous to the ability of any productive factor in a monopolistic situation to extort a reward greater than its true economic worth as measured by its equilibrium market-price.

For Webb and the socialists, as for Hobson and the growth of Social Radicalism associated with the Hobsonian emphasis upon under-consumption, it was only a short step to link economic rent and social value with the unearned increment of production. Both denoted the power of a privileged (capitalist) class, to provide itself with incomes which were both 'unjust' in that they were obtained through the exploitation of economically weaker classes, and uneconomic in that they laid an extra and unnecessary burden upon cost (i.e. the productive services of the capitalist class in general had been over-valued). From this line of argument, two conclusions followed: first that wherever it could be shown that a productive factor enjoyed a monopolistic situation within the market and was using its power to distort the free movement of resources, it was permissible to intervene to redress the imbalance of economic advantage, either directly by state control or indirectly by taxing the unearned element of that factor's income, and redistributing it by means of some form of social relief. Secondly, this argument led to the realisation that the existence of monopoly power within the market implied that the existing distribution of income within society need not necessarily be the most ' useful ' (i.e. productive), and that it might be possible to use redistribution as a means towards the more efficient utilisation of productive resources.

The explicit development of the latter point owed much to Hobsonian theory which first believed that an endemic tendency to over-production stemmed from the over-saving of a small high-income class, and secondly, believed that the product of industry could be basically divided into costs and surplus; such a division in particular isolated the unproductive surplus in distribution, and postulated that such a surplus was a return to the favoured (i.e. monopoly) position of the high-income class, who either diverted the surplus (through savings) back to the production of more goods which it was beyond the capacity of the market to absorb, or squandered it on luxury, frivolous, and above all, unproductive means. The diversion of this surplus, by taxation, to more productive uses (i.e. to raising the income of those classes whose propensity to save was negligible) would certainly stimulate the demand for the basic necessities, and so widen the basis of employment, and it would go some way to redressing the existing imbalance between production and consumption.

It should be noted that the case for a measure of redistribution was not at this stage (between 1895 and 1905) phrased in terms of social justice alone i.e. it was not an argument which said simply that some people received too much and others too little money. The initial purpose of redistribution was to improve and expand the market for production; hence graduated taxation, when it eventually arrived in 1914, did not owe its original impetus to social welfare theory. As the realisation dawned after 1906 that policies of social reform were going to prove more expensive than had been estimated, it became evident that only direct taxation could pay for them, and it became necessary to justify graduation as the most equitable method of finance as well as the most efficient. When this stage was reached, the Conservatives concentrated on showing that once, within the principles of taxation, the criterion of the self-sufficient individual was replaced by the ambiguous goal of social equality, the prospect of steepening graduated scales, far from becoming a stimulus to production, became instead a millstone guilty of all the disincentive effects forecast by Mill.

Of course, demands for social reform (e.g. old-age pensions) had always involved a measure of social justice – the principle was inherent within the concept of social responsibility – and it is necessary to emphasise again the substantive difference involved in the interpretation of this concept at a purely regulative or administrative level, and the interpretation that called for government intervention in the sphere of the individual's private financial and property rights; when, for example, the government was called upon to distinguish between the sources of an individual's income, and began too to query the hitherto, absolute right to enjoy and utilise one's property as one liked [10]; when, in fact, the government began to move from the passive regulation of the individual's private affairs to positive intervention within the individual's utilisation of his own resources. Throughout the host of related issues that characterise this period – the compulsory acquisition of land, taxation specifically directed against a class or group, state intervention in the sphere of wages and hours, the concept of public ownership itself – the critical issue was the struggle between private rights and the public or social good in the particular context of socio-economic development.

There were no precedents for the public acquisition of social values on the scale envisaged by the growing group of Liberal land reformers, and there were certainly none for the discrimination, through income differentiation, against unearned rather than earned incomes. What was being claimed was that income 'unearned' by the individual was therefore earned by society, by virtue of its own growth and expenditure upon the environment, and that such income might be appropriated as 'social income'. This claim 'had two important reactions upon the theory and policy of taxation'. It designated an income, hitherto regarded and protected as private property, as having an absolute 'ability to bear' taxation, in that such income, being part of the unproductive surplus of distribution, could be taxed without impairing any industrial incentive. Secondly, such income, being socially earned and 'belonging by right to society', must necessarily be expended for purposes of social welfare, for (and this was significant in implying the strength of the orthodox commitments amongst even the Liberal Radical group), 'the idea that public expenditure involved a sacrifice of individual property must be kept at a minimum'. The state would stand in the same relationship to this social income as the individual stood to his own consumption pattern:

Then will devolve on (the State) the duty of taking as much of the public income as it can secure and of expanding it most economically for the public welfare. Such a state ... will no longer say, 'what is the least revenue which is needed to fulfil the functions imposed upon me?' but 'what is the largest amount of useful work which I can do with the income that belongs to me?'.[11]

---

[10] This distinction begins to assume a direct political significance after 1885 when Chamberlain first popularised the 'ransom' doctrine.
[11] J. A. Hobson, 'The Taxation of Unearned Income' (1908) *Transactions of the Political and Economic Circle of the National Liberal Club*, Vol. 3.

While these views were evolving upon one side of the political spectrum, upon the other a restatement of financial orthodoxy was taking place – including herein the Liberal *Economist* which had proved very critical of the Liberal administration of 1892–5 for its extension of state powers which it condemned as ' a costly luxury '.[12] *The Quarterly Review* continued to deny that direct or progressive taxation was either just, or suitable for democracies. The Conservative Chancellors of the Exchequer after 1895, Hicks-Beach, Ritchie and Austen Chamberlain, based themselves upon a strict theoretical basis of retrenchment – which was unfortunately for them marred by the episode of the Boer war. Even with the strongest inducements for financial experiment they refused to innovate, beyond flirtations with the corn and coal taxes, and they were moreover exposed to sharp public criticism when the standard rate of income-tax touched 1s 3d (for a year). Numerous letters appeared in *The Standard* from outraged Conservative supporters; half-a-dozen variously signed ' middle-class ' withdrawing their support from the party, and blaming as usual ' the petted working-man ' for the cause of the trouble. Indeed, at this point, the Liberal emphasis upon reform and economy may well have gained them votes.[13]

The war, however, underlined the Conservative view of the income-tax as the first financial reserve, a tax to be kept solely for emergencies. In peace, the first priority for the chancellor was to lower this tax as speedily as possible. Ritchie, for example, in 1903, in finding himself with a surplus had ' no doubt that the great bulk of a remission ought to go to the payers of income-tax ', and considered that ' it was in the interests of the country that the income-tax should be brought to a lower level as quickly as possible '. This view was specifically in accord with the Conservative acceptance of a ' broad base for taxation ' whereby a number of taxes would rest lightly on a number of points. Mr Ritchie ' remembered years ago that the principle of taxation in this country was that direct taxation should only be half of indirect taxation, but as years had gone on that proportion had been reversed '. Neither he nor his audience were disposed to view the change favourably.[14]

Where the Liberals emphasised ability to pay, the Conservatives, expounding equality of sacrifice, emphasised the principle of pay-

12 *The Economist*, 25 May 1895.
13 Cf. *The Standard*, 24 March 1903.
14 Mr Ritchie's address to the City, 17 July 1903; copy in the Lloyd George papers C/14/1/1 (Ritchie lowered the income-tax by 4d to 11d).

ment in accordance with the benefits received; i.e. if any class was disposed to ask the state to provide certain, special benefits, then they were to contribute if not the whole cost, at least such a proportion of the cost as the scale of the benefits demanded. The Conservatives quoted Mill in support of this principle: ' A peculiar tax on the income of any class, not balanced by taxes on other classes, is a violation of justice and amounts to a partial confiscation.' [15]

It seems fair to suggest that at least by 1900, each party had become identified with a dominant concern for a particular element within distribution, the Liberals with wages and the Conservatives with capital. The Conservatives were concerned to expand the definition of and hence the return due to capital, stressing the rewards due to ability, management and enterprise as well as stressing the necessity for safeguarding capital in its various manifestations (property, interest, etc.) as the fount of the productive process. The Conservatives interpreted ' reproductive ' expenditure in much narrower terms than the Liberals. The Conservatives had been reluctant to countenance increased expenditure upon education in general and technical education in particular; they saw intangible expenses, the administrative expenses of government and money spent on social services as justifiable only in terms of their indirect services to private production. The government-financed promotion of a socio-economic end such as the provision of relief-works for the unemployed could only have a short-term transitional justification, for in the longer term it must represent a conflict with resources for the private sector:

Taxation always reduces the spending power of the tax-payer by the amount he contributes to the State; although expended by the Government in employing Labour ... it yet reduces the consumption of commodities by those from whom the tax is taken, and to that extent their power of creating a demand for Labour is contracted.[16]

As the government was under a strong obligation to limit its current expenditure to accord with current revenue, and as it was uneconomical for a government to burden its successors with the repayment of its own debt, government borrowing was only justifiable if there was an identifiable surplus of funds in the market, or if speculative capital was moving abroad, or if there was an emergency. All loans were, however, a necessary evil for:

[15] Mill, *Principles*, p. 824.
[16] G. Armitage-Smith, *The Principles and Methods of Taxation* (1906) p. 13.

The very same causes which go to make an individual poor impoverish a nation. An individual whose debts are heavy will find that his credit is low unless his income is so much greater than his expenditure that he can afford to devote a considerable sum every year to paying-off his debtors.[17]

And in the case of a nation, the surplus of revenue over expenditure had to be achieved in a time of normal trade, and not through (e.g.) the artificially high level of taxation possible in a boom. The repayment of debt ensured that a government would be able, in an emergency, to raise new loans at reasonable rates of interest, and this constituted the second financial reserve.

It was the creation of a huge new debt by the cost of the Boer war which so perturbed orthodox financial opinion between 1900 and 1905. Since 1875, each budget had set aside a fixed sum for payment of the interest on past debt, and allocated a sum towards a sinking-fund for the gradual redemption of the principal.[18] Between 1901 and 1904, the operations of the sinking-fund were suspended, and a principal, or dead-weight debt, rose from approximately £640 million to £800 million. Orthodoxy demanded as an imperative principal of finance that this debt be reduced, that proper principles of economy be re-established, government expenditure reduced, and the flexibility of the two financial reserves, the income-tax and the power to raise cheap loans at short notice, preserved. It is almost certainly the case that the vehemence of the Conservative attack upon Liberal social and financial policies after 1906 was due to the fact that the Liberals had appeared to adopt the orthodox case for retrenchment before 1906 and to have reneged upon their commitment when in office. However, while the Liberals did indeed before 1905 make much of the rise in debt ' dissipating ' the ' patient savings ' of two generations, and stressed the sanctity of economy and the sinking-fund, their basic criticism was that the increases in direct taxation were proportionately far too small for the burden of debt involved. Furthermore, their emphasis upon retrenchment was couched in

17 F. W. Hirst, *National Credit and the Sinking Fund* (1905).
18 One aspect of this process of debt-reduction which caused confusion, especially to the Labour party after 1906, was the distinction between the *realised* surplus of the past financial year, which *by law* went into the sinking-fund to pay off interest on the debt, and the *estimated* surplus of the coming financial year. In 1907, Asquith had to point out that he had no choice in the allocation of a realised surplus, and it could not therefore be devoted to old age pensions.

terms of redirecting government expenditure from wasteful to more productive ends.[19]

Before the Liberals came to office, F. W. Hirst begged Campbell-Bannerman to realise 'the vast sums destroyed and wasted during the last ten years, and the results; borrowed credit, less enterprise in business and manufactures, reduced home demand and therefore reduced output to meet it, reductions in wages, increase of pauperism and unemployment'.[20] He accordingly demanded retrenchment, in which he was supported by Sir Robert Giffen, who further favoured a low income-tax and the postponement of further graduation.[21] On the progressive side, Chiozza Money's book [22] outlined a detailed case for a fully-graduated taxation system, while Brougham Villiers declared Labour stood for 'fruitful constructive expenditure' and considered a policy of state finance for national assets to be a supplement to a traditional policy of debt-reduction. Keir Hardie, meanwhile contrasted the heroic days of the 1880s with the more prosaic hopes of the present: 'It is budgets, and not barricades, which chiefly interest practical Socialists. "Taxation to extinction of unearned incomes" has taken the place of "death to the capitalist classes." '

In 1905, a departmental committee on income-tax had revealed the existence of widespread evasion,[24] and in 1906 a select committee reported in favour of graduation by the extension of the existing system of abatements. It also supported the principle of a super-tax, income differentiation, and the compulsory personal declaration by each individual of his total net income in respect of which tax was due.[25] All were staunchly opposed by the Conservatives and all became law within four years.

In 1906, however, Asquith was ' not wedded or even engaged to

---

[19] E.g. S. Buxton, *The War, Its Cost, Finance and Legacies* (1903); Sir W. Harcourt, ' National Finance ', *Liberal Magazine*, May 1901.

[20] 19 December 1905, CBP, Add. Mss 41238.

[21] R. Giffen, ' The Prospects of Liberal Finance ', *Nineteenth Century*, May 1906.

[22] *Riches and Poverty* (1905).

[23] K. Hardie, ' A Labour Budget ', *Financial Review of Reviews*, April 1906; also P. Snowden, *The Socialist's Budget* (1907). It is interesting that the suggested rates of the socialists, which seemed utterly ludicrous in 1906, were quite within sight in both income-tax and death-duties by 1914. For details, see ' The Impact of Financial Policy on English Party Politics Before 1914 '.

[24] *Report of the Departmental Committee on the Income-Tax*, Cd. 2575, Parl. papers (1905) Vol. XLIV.

[25] *Report of the Select Committee on the Income Tax*, November 1906, Parl. papers, Vol. IX.

the super-tax ' and still believed full graduation to be impracticable.[26] His first budget in 1906 was unremarkable except for the state grant of £200,000 towards the 1905 Unemployed Workmen's Act, but in 1907 he introduced the principle of differentiation. Henceforth, the full rate of income-tax, then 1s in the pound, would apply to all un-earned income up to £2,000, earned incomes would meanwhile pay at 9d in the pound, while existing abatements would be reckoned from earned incomes only. It was this budget which introduced compulsory returns for all classes of taxable income, and also estab-lished compulsory returns from employers giving details of their employees' wages and salaries.

1907 also marked a change in the traditional Liberal view of retrenchment. Whereas *The Economist* attacked the government for having ' utterly failed to make substantial reductions in the level of expenditure ' and for ' maintaining war-taxes in time of peace ',[27] Asquith stressed that there could be ' no permanent distribution of revenue of a substantial character '. With regard to future financial policy, he said:

The country has reached a stage in which, whether we look merely at its fiscal or at its social exigencies, we cannot afford to drift along the stream and treat each year's finance as if it were self-contained. The Chancellor ought to budget, not for one year, but for several years.[28]

The government was under ' an immediate obligation of re-instating and improving national credit ', but Asquith admitted an equal obligation to social reform, to ' giving vitality to human personality ' through providing finance for school-meals and old-age pensions. The income-tax must be regarded as ' a permanent and integral part of the financial system '.

This idea of financial continuity was new, and both it and its corollary, the financial obligation to provide for an expanding level of social policy, were challenged strongly by the Conservatives from within their annual amendment ' that the basis of taxation should be broadened in order that the anomalies and hardships inseparable from the present high rate of particular taxes may be diminished '.

Asquith's speech evidently owed its inspiration to a Treasury memorandum circulated in February 1907, which said:

[26] Sir E. Hamilton papers, Asquith to Hamilton, 20 March 1907 (Add. Mss 48612) and 18 February 1906 (Add. Mss 48683).

[27] F. W. Hirst, *The National Budget* (1907).

[28] Parl. Deb., 4th Series, Vol. 172, C1186, 18 April 1907.

The present Government have recognised the pressing need for social reforms which must entail heavy additional expenditure. No one now expects that reductions of existing expenditure will provide the necessary means. A good deal has been done, and more perhaps may be possible in the way of reduction of Army or Navy votes. But the automatic growth of the civil services, and the constant extension of their scope, are only too likely to absorb the bulk of these savings. The time has gone by when it was possible to look to indirect taxes ... to supply the want of funds. The country refuses any longer to drink itself out of its financial straits. Unless the whole system of our taxation is to be recast, the solution must be found in the increase of direct taxation.[29]

The memorandum went on to say that the only feasible remedy lay in a super-tax on large incomes, starting at a moderate rate, but providing the precedent for future increases. It recommended a tax of 3d in the pound on all incomes between £5,000 and £20,000, and 6d on all higher incomes. The estimated yield was put at £1·75 million: 'It is the existence of so much income in the shape of incomes far above the average level that makes the incidence of a uniform rate of tax inequitable, and calls for redress by means of a supertax.'

This was followed in March 1907 by a memo from Chiozza Money demonstrating that in terms of total taxation, the lower classes paid an effective rate of taxation of 1s 3d in the pound, while the rich paid only at 1s 7d. The next 14 months witnessed the government's inability, despite pressure, to effect any sizeable reduction in the military estimates, and the launching of the pension scheme which, even with its age limit of 70 and its pauper disqualifications, was estimated to cost £6·5 million in a full year.

On 8 August 1908, Haldane submitted a report to Asquith in which he identified the two crucial problems facing them as Poor-Law and financial reform. 'As to the first ... we know what we want, and the question is how to guide Burns into doing it'; as to the second, Haldane saw a great opportunity:

We have not *stumbled* into the introduction of an old age pension system, nor into the increase of the proportion which direct bears to indirect taxation. These two changes are reforms which the True Spirit has called for as definitely as it called for electoral reform in 1832.

After reviewing the changes in the distribution of wealth, Haldane continued:

[29] Cab. 37/87, No. 22, 26 February 1907.

We should boldly take our stand on the facts and proclaim a policy of taking, mainly by direct taxation, such toll from the increase and growth of this wealth as will enable us to provide for (1) the increasing cost of social reform (2) national defence (3) a margin in aid of the sinking fund. The more boldly such a proposition is put the more attractive I think, will it prove. It will commend itself to many timid people as a bulwark against the nationalisation of wealth.[30]

He accordingly suggested a Cabinet committee under Asquith – ' no-one else is competent to handle the matter ' – but seemingly the rising concern with the unemployed in the winter of 1908–9 submerged the suggestion.

By the Budget of 1908 Conservatives were uncomfortably aware of the trend of rising expenditure. They complained of ' a want of elasticity in the existing taxes ', and accused the Liberals of undermining the reserve function of the income-tax and of expanding national liabilities without making adequate financial provisions. Gladstonian finance had vanished and:

The present Government are acting on an entirely different principle. They are not merely extending liabilities beyond the provision that they made this year, but they are encouraging hopes and expectations which subsequent parliaments will be expected to fulfill, and which must themselves involve an increase of the very liabilities for which the Government are at present failing to provide.[31]

There was some truth in this accusation, for the old-age pensions scheme had apparently been set up without any actuarial consideration of the impact of changes in future demographic patterns.[32] Liberal finance had acted as a malaise throughout society. In 1908, there was fear of financial institutions ' trading on credit far beyond limits of reason ':

If this is typical of the constant habit of financial institutions, the national danger is appalling. The habit of economy, or lack of it, if spread among the individuals of the nation affects the stability of that nation which is but a collection of individuals.[33]

Speaking for the City, Giffen thought direct taxes were wasting ' our national resources '. Conservatives like Sir Frederick Banbury

---

30 Haldane to Asquith, 8 August 1908, copy, AP, Vol. 11 (original emphasis).
31 Parl. Deb., 4th Series, Vol. 193, C665, 25 July 1908 (A. Chamberlain).
32 H. Bunbury (ed.), *Lloyd George's Ambulance Wagon* (1957) p. 71.
33 J. S. Sterling to R. Giffen, 5 March 1908, Giffen papers.

thought the high rates of taxation and rising government expenditure were driving capital abroad, so creating the serious unemployment of 1908–9. The leading authority on public finance (Professor Bastable) was, however, reassured that all was well in that the Liberals had managed in three years to redeem some £41 million of debt.

THE DEBATE UPON THE LAND

The demand for land taxes was an integral part of changing ideas about taxation, and the radicalisation of the Liberal party was accompanied by a growing demand for a Radical land policy, which, it was hoped, would contribute a solution to the problems of an industrial society.

Policy towards the land had always marked a point of difference between Liberals and Conservatives. The Liberal antipathy to privileged 'landlordism' and to a semi-feudal system of land tenure was in strong contrast to the Conservative respect for land as the basis of all property rights. In 1881 the Irish Land Act, giving the tenant some security over his rent and tenure, was interpreted by Conservatism as undermining the doctrine that 'a man could do what he wills with his own'. The 1881 Act was regarded by both Lecky and Hobson as the precedent for the Liberal introduction of later and more far-reaching social and financial doctrines, while the Radical emphasis in the 1880s upon the need to stress the obligations, rather than the rights of property, was a forerunner of the later development of ideas of social responsibility.

Property, especially landed property, for the Liberals, was seen within the context of securing the overall good of the community. The overall good, in regard to the land, had a double significance. First, there were the social and legal implications, the Liberals did not want proprietary rights in land to extend so far as to allow the individual a right of absolute possession, a right which the individual might set against the state's desire to interfere with and regulate his own private affairs. Hence the frequent Liberal attempt to claim that all ownership in land was held, as a trust, of the state, and all rights involved reciprocal duties. Secondly, there were the economic implications, for the problem of securing the overall good involved the most efficient utilisation of a society's resources. As the land was the original primary resource of the nation, in and from which all natural resources were obtained, the state was justified in assuming an overall and positive responsibility for ensuring these resources were made available, upon utilitarian principles, to serve the greatest good of the greatest number. In the late nineteenth century, the only means by which the state could positively intervene within the sphere of personal activities was through taxation, and with the notion of taxing economic rent came the related idea that taxation was more than a necessary evil, and might be used itself to penalise a certain activity and to enforce a specific responsibility upon a group (or class). Hence, the character of the Liberal land policies was determined not only by their traditional social attitudes towards the land, but also by their changing conceptions of the state's rôle as a positive agent in national development.

With Henry George's emphasis upon the taxation of economic rent (i.e. the single-tax), the argument for making the income from the land the chief, if not the only source, of the community's revenue, received a stimulus.[34] The idea emerged that landlords were receiving an element, or an increment, of income that was unearned. As the value of land increased automatically with the growth of the community and the improvement of the environment, so landlords received a bonus income. Therefore, they might contribute a special sum towards the community's own expenses. This was the reasoning behind the Liberal policy for the taxation of groundrents, and the Radical and Progressive idea of a betterment levy.

The Conservatives on the other hand, argued that rent from the land was only a moderate interest-payment asked by the owner of his tenant on the amount of money invested in the land, i.e. rent was simply a return upon a capital asset, and as such, should take into account the money invested in improving the land over some considerable time. They stressed the cost of an estate's upkeep, rates and taxes, new cottages and repairs, contributions to local schools and sanitation. Their case was strengthened in that the income of many landed estates in the 1880s was falling, and the capital value of the land, decreasing. The idea that landowners were to be subjected to a 'social' tax of hazy dimensions based upon arbitrary calculations as to value, appalled them. They could again cite Mill to advantage,[35] and in answer to the claim that the economic rent of land was peculiarly fitted to bear taxation, they fell back upon the orthodox interpretation of property as inherently part of the community's stock

---

34 J. A. Hobson, ' The Influence of Henry George ', *Fortnightly Review*, 1 December 1897.

35 Mill, *Principles*, p. 824 (cited p. 197 above).

of capital. Any tax upon either property or capital was likely to divert resources from their most efficient private usage to potentially wasteful public usage. ' No property can be safe when the general security that protects all is lost ... the unearned increment is absurd, for what article of trade –apart from manufactures – is enhanced in price or value save by some neighbouring market? ' [36]

In the 1890s, Liberal parliamentary opinion inclined to bodies like the Land Law Reform Association (whose committee of 31 included in 1898, 28 Liberal M.P.s, past and present), rather than the Land Nationalisation Society. Although bodies like the London progressives had adopted the full taxation of site values by 1892, the bulk of the Liberals still favoured taxing groundrents alone. After 1900, however, the plight of the rural areas, well-publicised by Progressives,[37] growing statistical evidence of agricultural depression,[38] and increasing interest in land-based remedies for unemployment, brought new interest in the land as a political issue. The issue was in turn underlined by growing demands for rating reform, which were upheld by the Royal Commission on local taxation. The Commission declared in favour of a more uniform criterion of valuation, and felt the situation to be particularly acute in urban areas, where the rating burden often fell heavily upon businesses, and where poor areas were without the rateable resources to provide much-needed reforms. Furthermore, the Minority Report produced a cautious recommendation for a separate site value rate.[39]

As the argument for the taxation of site values developed, the idea of social justice came to form an integral part. If a landowner was intending to sell his land for its real (i.e. highest) use-value, then he should also (it was argued), be assessed for taxation upon that value, and not upon the present use-value, which might be purely nominal. The valuation of a site was to be upon the basis of the price that a willing seller might obtain in the market, and by then placing a tax upon the intrinsic value of the land, at the same time including all vacant land and making a separate valuation of buildings and

[36] *Quarterly Review*, 166 (1888) (' Landed Incomes and Landed Estates ').

[37] C. F. G. Masterman, *Heart of the Empire* (1901), and Masterman (ed.), *To Colonise England* (1907); also R. Haggard, *Rural England*, 2 Vols. (1901).

[38] *Report of the Inquiry into the Decline in the Agricultural Population in Great Britain 1881–1906*, Cd. 3273, xcvi, 1906.

[39] *Royal Commission on Local Taxation and Financial Administration* (1901) Cd. 638, xxiv. Also A. H. H. Matthews, *50 Years of Agricultural Politics* (A History of the Central Chamber of Agriculture, 1865–1915) (1915) p. 129 for local complaints regarding national burdens upon the rates.

improvements, it was hoped that the primary incidence of local taxation at least could be shifted away from property and improvements as such, and onto the landowner himself. This policy, it was thought, would encourage improvements, and divert more land onto the market as the speculator's motives for holding it were discouraged. The existing owner-occupier would benefit through the broadening of the basis of assessment (i.e. the inclusion of vacant land), and through having such improvements as he made to his property rated only indirectly (i.e. in so far as they improved the value of the site). The existing tenant would benefit by being able to improve his property without facing a demand from his landlord for increased rent to pay the higher rate-bill. In particular, it was hoped that business tenants, holding under a terminable leasehold, would benefit through having their rents reassessed (upon termination) upon the site-value alone, and not upon a rateable value due in part to their own business success.[40]

After 1900, the land was increasingly brought forward as the core of a constructive policy for which Liberalism was seeking in its defence of free trade.[41] Campbell-Bannerman received several memoranda explaining the expected advantages of land reform, including the taxation of land values, and in 1905 and 1906 his speeches encouraged hopes that a land policy would form part of the New Liberalism. In 1904, for example, Massingham felt that the land question would fulfil the need of 'a great question' which would 'fire men's imaginations'.[42] In 1902, the United Committee for the Taxation of Land values had been formed, and for three years, 1902–4, private bills for the rating of land values were introduced in the Commons by either T. J. Macnamara or C. P. Trevelyan. The Trade Union Congress in 1905 also attacked the land monopoly, while a national conference of rating authorities agreed to petition for a bill for the separate assessment and rating of land values.[43]

Undoubtedly, for many Liberals, land reform was a panacea. Some Liberals, for example John Orr, laid the blame for industrial problems like unemployment solely at the door of the land monopoly.[44] Much

---

[40] *The Progressive Review*, March 1897.
[41] E.g. C. P. Trevelyan to Campbell-Bannerman, 5 October 1903, CBP, Add. Mss 41232; also J. Dundas White, *Economic Ideals* (1903).
[42] H. W. Massingham, 'The Need for a Radical Party', *Contemporary Review*, January 1904.
[43] *The Times*, 23 November 1905.
[44] J. Orr, *Unemployment : Its Causes and their Removal* (1908).

Liberal thinking was clearly more optimistic than informed about the revenue that taxing site-values would produce. Franklin Thomasson guessed at a figure of £200 million, otherwise figures were few.[45] The Liberal land nationaliser also had an awkward task in explaining why full nationalisation of the means of production was unacceptable. To a socialist, it was impossible to control landlordism without controlling all aspects of capitalism,[46] while to Liberal nationalisers or single-taxers, the means of production were essentially two-fold, land and labour were primary resources, and the opportunity (and duty) to earn a living, and the right of access to the land, were complementary principles which the state was expected to uphold. Industrial wealth in the form of plant, investment in production, and property itself, were the products of labour, and every man had a just right of property in what he had created. Land was the one exception which had been created by no man. This argument, however, failed to meet the case of the individual worker within industry, who had laboured and who had at least shared in the creation of a final product. Where the Socialist claimed that this man must receive either a greater control over, or a greater share in the process of distribution, the Liberal seemed merely concerned with providing an alternative source of work, so reducing the competition in one sector and assuming that wage-rates would then rise.

This was, perhaps, the last occasion on which the good old cry of 'Back To The Land' could be proffered as a possible solution to urban problems. For despite the growth of the cities in the late nineteenth century, town and country were still two entities distinct enough to encourage the belief that reform did not have to be a complete reform of the existing competitive system, but might only be a matter of a redistribution of resources (especially manpower), a reattaining of some previous equilibrium. It was only some 30 years since the onset of agricultural depression, and many Liberals were at the most second-generation men to whom the appeal of a strong agricultural sector was quite natural. Land reformers made much of their intention to restore the primary industry of the country i.e. agriculture, and they believed that a large part of the answer to irregular employment and a rootless urban labour force was to offer

[45] F. Thomasson, ' Land Nationalisation ', *Westminster Review*, 154 (1900).
[46] Cf. preface by Snowden to J. C. Wedgwood, *Henry George for Socialists* (1908); also Hobson's criticisms of extreme land reformers, who identified only one element of rent, or monopoly power, within the market.

to as many men as possible the prospect of a secure, stable and independent livelihood in the country.

Men who fitted into the above pattern, especially single-taxers like Josiah Wedgwood, often accepted a very orthodox interpretation of production and distribution. Wedgwood, for example, was a believer in a residual theory of distribution, with the landlord as the favoured 'last receiver'. He believed in a semi-deterministic view of a wage-fund; all he was trying to do was to provide labour with a means of escaping the inevitable rigidities of their position within the industrial labour market, and to discover a new source of revenue for reforming specific social problems.[47] In this sense, the single-taxers themselves had no long-term solution.

Yet a more positive view did exist which accepted the impossibility of reversing the trend to industrialism, and accepted also that the multiplication of owners on small quantities of land was no more than a palliative. Indeed, within this school (to which it is hard to attach a label, but which was nearest to the land nationalisers) by 1906 or thereabouts, the emphasis had shifted away from the outright owner-ship of land by individuals, to the idea of holding land on the basis of a practical but not unconditional freehold; this idea being the outcome of the concept of land being held of the state.[48] This second group looked for a basic redirection of resources, not indirectly through taxation, but positively through the action of the state or public agency. Aneurin Williams suggested that if all land were under public supervision, then it would become an easy matter to instigate forestry and reclamation schemes, and to develop housing and roads, while the public ownership of land on the edges of expand-ing towns would allow for town and country planning on garden city lines.[49]

Such a view further incorporated an Hobsonian belief in the necessity of developing alternative sources of employment, which would thereby function as markets and as further sources of con-sumptive power.[50] The evident failure of the agricultural sector to provide a market for the goods industry produced, because of the low wages of the agricultural labourers, paralleled the trade union

[47] Cf. J. C. Wedgwood, 'The Principle of Land Value Taxation', *Economic Journal*, 22 (1912) p. 388, and Dundas White, *Economic Ideals*.

[48] Cf. C. F. G. Masterman, *To Colonise England*, p. xxl.

[49] A. Williams, *Unemployment and Land Nationalisation* (1909).

[50] See e.g. Trevelyan to Campbell-Bannerman, 5 October 1903, CBP, Add. Mss 41232.

inclination to see unemployment as the outcome of a basic failure of demand in certain very low-income groups. Hence this view put great store in government-promoted and financed industries which would be both reproductive and non-competitive with private industry.[51]

Contemporaries themselves distinguished between three categories of land-value taxation advocates. First, those who simply wanted to make all land accessible, and to divert some of its proceeds into public hands, but had no intention of ending private property. This was more or less the view of the Land Law Reform Association. Secondly, the single-taxers like Wedgwood who wanted to tax all private landlords out of existence. Thirdly, the land nationalisers, who wanted to abolish all private property in land, and who favoured site-value taxation because it was a means of arriving at a fair basis upon which the actual transfer of the land to public ownership might be safely (and profitably) effected. The nationalisers thought it impossible to tax private landlords out of existence, pointing out that such taxation, if intended to first break up the big estates, must also increase the number of landowners, and hence the opposition to further taxation would also increase. In parliament from 1906 to 1910, the land reformers were largely united to get a valuation bill, this being essential to all three groups, but after 1910 the groups were again separated to complicate Lloyd George's land campaign.

It was some indication of the new Radical influence within the Liberal party after 1906 that the Land Nationalisation Society could claim nearly 130 M.P.s to be their supporters.[52] When J. H. Whitley formed a Land Values Parliamentary Campaign Committee, 280 M.P.s joined before Easter 1906.[53] The Land Values Group were certainly one of the most active pressure-groups in the House, presenting a draft bill for site valuation before Easter 1906, and introducing

---

[51] Runciman told Brunner that it would be unwise to rely purely on the rating of site-values, favouring Brunner's scheme for developing the canals instead (Copy HGP, Add. Mss 46062, 16 December 1904).

[52] *21st Annual Report of the L.N.S.*, April 1908. The precise figures for the strength of the three land groupings is hard to ascertain, but J. C. Wedgwood later recorded that there were only a few single-taxers in the Commons before 1910, namely, Dundas White, Charles Price, Arthur Dewar, Morrell, Trevelyan, Ure and himself. Hence the nationalisers and the L.L.R.A. would appear to have been dominant. (J. C. Wedgwood, *Memoirs of a Fighting Life* (1940) p. 67.)

[53] P. W. Raffan, *The Policy of the Land Values Group in the House of Commons*, 25 November 1912, *Transactions of the Political and Economic Circle of the N.L.C.*, Vol. 4.

their annual 'tax and buy' bill in every session before 1909.[54] In
October 1906, Campbell-Bannerman promised 'active attention' to
the demand for a tax upon urban site-values,[55] while in December
1906, and in June 1907 (provoked by the loss of three land reform acts
in the Lords) the Land Values Group presented massively-supported
memoranda in favour of site taxation.[56] At the beginning of 1908,
the Group further launched a national campaign which coincided
with the Land Club movement, over 30 clubs being founded to
reinvigorate agriculture and rural life, which were banded together
in March 1909 to form the Land Club League.[57] Finally, in 1908, the
King's speech included for the first time the promise of land valuation for England, and on 12 May, Asquith gave a definite promise
that a valuation bill would be produced by the L.G.B. for a separate
assessment of sites and buildings. The continued failure of this bill
to appear led to a third memorandum being presented on 24 November 1908, reminding Asquith of his promise, with 250 signatures
attached, setting forth four principles, and urging all Liberal associations to pass resolutions urging action upon the government.[58]

The government were also under pressure from the Central
Chamber of Agriculture which had been demanding since 1906 a
national readjustment of the methods of rating assessment and valuation. They, however, wanted a valuation based on 'the net annual
value of the land' (i.e. a valuation on present use alone), and a shedding of such local responsibilities as roads and education to the
Exchequer. They gained from Asquith on 20 March 1908 an
admission that the present incidence of rates was unjust, and to the
1908 budget 23 members put down amendments regretting the
absence of any aid for local taxation. The Chamber, while nominally
a non-party body, relied principally upon Conservative spokesmen,
but they did gain some support from Liberal back-benchers. On

---

[54] A. Williams, *Unemployment and Land Nationalisation*; the Bill proposed that
landowners, in the process of a valuation, should themselves declare the
unimproved capital value of their land, whereupon the local authorities could
either tax that value or buy the land at that value.

[55] *The Times*, 8 October 1906.

[56] Raffan, *Land Values Group*.

[57] *The Times*, 12 January, 22 February 1909.

[58] Raffan, *Land Values Group*. (When the *Nation* tried to withdraw from this
pressure for land reform, the *Westminster Review* (May 1907, p. 589) insisted
the Liberals were 'pledged to the hilt'.) Also *Manchester Guardian*, 19 August
1908, for the four principles: separate valuation of sites and buildings, relief
for improvements, full site-value rating.

18 February 1908, two Liberals, A. F. Hedges and F. E. Rogers, instituted a debate on local taxation, and after extensive lobbying for the readjustment of taxes in the winter of 1908–9, on 25 February 1909, Hedges, Rogers and a third Liberal, E. H. Lamb, voted against the government over rating reform.[59]

THE BUDGET

The combination of this pressure for rating and taxation reform was of some significance in providing for the two leading reformers in the Cabinet, Lloyd George and Churchill, a political common denominator in which to absorb the series of pressing demands to which the party was exposed in the winter of 1908–9: unemployment and the ' right to work ', rising military estimates and the demand for more productive expenditure. Both Lloyd George and Churchill were believers in the rôle of land policies within a framework of social reform, and Lloyd George as a Welshman was especially hostile to the ' land monopoly '. He was, however, in something of a dilemma for he had already posed as the champion of economy in the face of demands for money from both McKenna and Haldane, and one of his first acts as chancellor had been to remind the Cabinet that they were collectively pledged to the reduction of expenditure, and ' sections of our own supporters will attack ' unless the commitment was honoured.[60]

At the beginning of 1909, Lloyd George circulated to the Cabinet descriptions of American and Australian methods of land taxation. By March, he had decided upon the separate valuation of site-values and buildings, and in order that this might be accepted as constitutionally a part of the Finance Bill, he intended to attach two clauses for the taxation of vacant land valued below £50 per acre, and for the taxation of mining royalties and ground rents. This he estimated would bring in half a million pounds in the next financial year.[61] Out of the proposal to tax vacant land sprang the increment and development duties, and the land clauses as finally announced included a 20 per cent tax on the incremental value of land accruing

---

[59] Matthews, *Agricultural Politics*, pp. 132, 141–3. The local authorities met 61 per cent of the cost of police forces, 48 per cent of education, 91 per cent of the Poor-Law, and 86 per cent of highways. *The Times*, 26 February 1909, criticised ' doctrinaires ' who imposed new burdens upon local government without meeting any part of the responsibilities of finance.

[60] Cab. 37/93, No. 62, 19 May 1908.

[61] Cab. 37/98, No. 44, 13 March 1909.

from the date of valuation (30 April 1909) to the date of sale, a tax of a half-penny in the pound on the capital value of undeveloped land (agricultural land being exempt), a 10 per cent reversion duty placed upon any benefit accruing to a lessor from the redetermination of a lease. While to meet an estimated deficit of £16 million, Lloyd George raised the tax on unearned incomes from 1s to 1s 2d, increased the death-duties to a maximum of 15 per cent (from 8 per cent) on estates worth over £1 million, imposed a super-tax of 6d in the pound on incomes over £5,000, imposed a petrol tax, raised the duties on spirits and tobacco, and raised both stamp and licence duties. Finally, all incomes below £500 were henceforth to receive a children's allowance of £10 for every child under 16 in addition to the existing abatements.

Among the Liberals, the budget did not pass without criticism. In the preliminary Cabinet discussions, A. O. Murray opposed the reversion duty, the petrol tax, the concession to the 'brats', and forecast trouble over the evasion of super-tax.[62] He and Runciman thought Lloyd George had put the estimated yield of the new taxation too low, and Runciman thought the increased revenue for 1910–11 would be sufficient to meet the new liabilities without the raid on the Sinking Fund (see below). Runciman wanted to drop one of the direct taxes at least, and thought Lloyd George was angling instead to be in a position to drop one of the indirect taxes when he came under pressure.[63] Lewis Harcourt forecast the budget would mean 'the triumph of Tariff Reform'.[64] Burns thought it 'the most kaleidoscopic budget ever planned' and wrote of a Cabinet on 1 April: 'Lloyd George piano, deftly fighting for his view; nearly all against him for good and sound reasons. His deficit only £700,000 as against his prediction of 5 or 6 millions. His estimate of trade for year just as wrong. He is very much out of his depth.'[65]

Within the parliamentary party, feeling was equally divided. Haldane evidently had to preside over a critical meeting of over 200 M.P.s and reported that six M.P.s attended with resignations in their pockets, but differences were smoothed over.[66] It was rumoured that

---

[62] AP, Vol. 22, Memo. by Murray, 7 April 1909. The super-tax, although it did not affect incomes which were (gross) below £5,000, was levied on the amount by which incomes over £5,000 exceeded £3,000.

[63] Note from Murray to Runciman, Runciman papers (General Correspondence) undated.

[64] *Ibid.* Cabinet Note from L. Harcourt, 24 March 1909.

[65] JBP, Add. Mss 46326 (Diary), 1 April and 28 April 1909.

[66] Haldane papers, Mss 5981, f. 258.

nearly 100 Liberals were 'irreconcilably opposed' to the half-penny development duty, although only seven, seemingly, voted against the duty and only eight voted against the increment value duty.[67] It was apparent that the provisions about the land taxes had 'never been thought out, and were obscurely and awkwardly expressed'.[68] Orthodox Liberals were highly antagonistic; A. E. Pease dated the beginning of 'neo-Liberalism' from 1909, and Sir Walter Runciman, chairman of the Northern Liberal Federation, wished to resign his position as soon as he heard of the 'destructive character' of the budget. He too believed in unemployment resulting from 'a lack of funds that have been exhausted by taxes'.[69] In marked contrast, *The Daily News* thought the budget rested on 'the principle of taxing surpluses and luxuries' and considered there was no danger of it interfering with 'the productive operations of capital'.[70] The budget was explained by J. M. Robertson as encouraging production through the development of natural resources, especially via the medium of the development commission. Sound taxation, he thought, meant a great deal more than mere revenue-raising.[71]

On the Conservative side, *The Times* thought that 'the doctrine of social ransom has never been carried quite so far'.[72] Sir Robert Giffen thought 'it continues to aggravate the vice of swelling direct taxation' which was 'altogether excessive and dangerous' in that it was diminishing the savings of the principal class of investors. 'All graduation is an interference with individual right which it is one of the main functions of the state to support.'[73] Sir William Bull saw the budget as a 'social weapon'. The Conservatives bitterly opposed the taxation of land as a discrimination against one class of property, and attacked the principle of 'differentiating between the sources from which the wealth of the individual is derived', which they declared was socialistic: 'the fundamental right of individual ownership was at stake'.[74] The Central Chamber of Agriculture opposed the increment value duty because, they said, to tax any recovery in

---

[67] Note via Runciman to Asquith from A. O. Murray, n.d., Runciman papers. H.C. Division Lists, Nos. 400 and 413, 1909.

[68] Sir C. Ilbert to Bryce, 3 August 1909, Bryce papers (uncatalogued).

[69] Sir W. Runciman, *Before The Mast And After* (1924) p. 281.

[70] *Daily News*, 1 May 1909.

[71] J. M. Robertson, *The Great Budget* (1910).

[72] *The Times*, 30 April 1909.

[73] R. Giffen, 'The Budget', *Quarterly Review*, 211 (1909) No. 420.

[74] *The Land Union Journal*, 1 (1911) (H. Cox, 'The Broad Case Against the Land Taxes').

the value of agricultural land, after the value had declined for 40 years, would be unjust.[75] Conservatives generally opposed a dated valuation as a concept fictitious and harmful, producing uncertainty and arbitrary decisions, and being above all, costly. They denied that it was possible to distinguish social value adequately from the values due to individual effort – especially in the case of agriculture. They instanced the case of builders, who would legitimately expect their work to increase the value of land.[76] So far as this was a direct tax upon the landowner, it was yet another increase in his costs which might possibly be met by a further decline in the money he was willing to invest in the land. Hence there might be an uncertain market for land which would accentuate the already low prices, and discourage further improvement.[77]

The government did admit the validity of some of these criticisms. In June, it was agreed that no increment duty should be charged upon agricultural land in respect of increases in value due either to improvements in or to expenditure upon the land. By July, the Cabinet had accepted a 5 per cent tax on mineral royalties, which represented a withdrawal from their previous intention to tax all 'ungotten minerals'. The whole cost of valuation was now to be borne by the state instead of the owner, and provision was allowed for right of appeal from the decisions of the valuation referees. In September, the owners of agricultural land were allowed to claim a 25 per cent deduction (instead of the previous 12 per cent) against income-tax in respect of the cost of improvements on their land, including buildings and cottages. This latter concession was estimated to cost £50,000, 'and its effect is calculated to be to leave the owners of agricultural land better off as regards the total taxation exacted from them (overall) than they were before the present budget'. In October, the total cost of the concessions in the passage of the budget was estimated at £1,325,000.[78] Finally, the Liberals had come under the strongest

---

[75] Matthews, *Agricultural Politics*, pp. 145–6.

[76] Lloyd George promised that builders would receive special consideration, but in 1911–12, several test-cases were fought which seemed to undermine the value of his promise.

[77] There is reason to believe that the budget did increase uncertainty within the land market: F. M. L. Thompson, *English Landed Society in the Nineteenth Century* (1963) pp. 318–20, and *30th Annual Report of the L.N.S.*

[78] Asquith to King Edward VII, 23 June, 30 July, 18 September, 21 October 1909, AP, Vol. 5.

pressure from orthodox financial opinion to abstain from a recasting of the functions of the sinking-fund.[79]

In the Commons, a Liberal, E. A. Ridsdale, criticised the budget by criticising the analogy of a war upon poverty: 'This idea of taxing people in order to build up a fund to promote their prosperity seems to me ... to be absurd and dangerous.' He claimed that 'the great bulk of the Liberal party ... dislike the extraordinary increase in the taxation of capital', and held that to increase direct taxation, especially on higher incomes, was to reduce the fund of capital which one generation might pass on to the next, and discriminated against the one class whose savings provided the essential source of productive capital upon which all industry depended.[80]

A former Liberal, J. A. Clyde, argued against the prevailing Liberal conception of property and social right, particularly as expressed in the speeches of Lloyd George and Winston Churchill. To discriminate against certain kinds of property upon the theory that some was 'earned' more than another, and that there existed various gradations of property-rights, was both 'socialistic and fallacious'.

This idea of social value is new. The idea that you can deal not fairly, not equally, but exceptionally with one kind of property because it has a social value is new, and the novelty in it is the attributing a less degree of sanctity, a less degree of right and justice and fair treatment to one kind of property than to another.[81]

The replies from various Liberal back-benchers dwelt upon the principle of ability to pay. D. Maclean believed, with Adam Smith, that

The subjects of every state ought to contribute to the support of the Government as nearly as possible in proportion to their respective abilities, that is, in proportion to the revenue which they enjoy under the protection of the state.[82]

Maclean was careful to stress that by 'proportionate' he meant 'progressive'. George Harwood rejected the idea that a tax upon the rich was a tax upon industry:

[79] For details, see 'The Impact of Financial Policy on English Party Politics before 1914'.
[80] Parl. Deb., 5th Series, Vol. 12, C1715–19, 2 November 1909.
[81] Ibid. C1760–4 (2 November 1909).
[82] Ibid. C1720–2.

The whole country must be regarded as one. The capital fund of the country, whether it goes to capital, or to pay wages or for food, is all one common fund, and we do not diminish it in the least by passing a portion of it to one class of the population rather than to another class.[83]

As long as the money remained within the country and 'goes for the purchase of commodities, there will therefore be employment of labour'. This amounted to a somewhat broader conception of the place of capital within the productive process, and was an implicit denial of that view which saw capital as representing a stock of vital wealth in the hands of a social group whose further security constituted the first object of the state's protection.

J. A. Simon (i.e. the later Lord Simon), also used a form of under-consumptionism to justify taxation falling on a rich man's surplus income, which would not thereby affect his normal or basic demand for goods; whereas any change in the incidence of taxation in favour of the poor, who had only one 'necessary' fund with which to support themselves, would at once allow them to raise their level of consumption; i.e. the extra demand for goods resulting from an effective increase in a labourer's wages, would more than compensate for any fall in demand resulting from an equivalent decrease in a rich man's income, due to the rich man's higher propensity to save, or possibly to his inclination to fritter away his income.[84]

THE LAND CAMPAIGN

By 1909, the notion of social reform was giving way to the wider goal of social reconstruction, in which the rôle of the state was seen as a positive agent in ensuring not only the principle of equality of opportunity amongst individuals, but also the productive utilisation of society's resources in the interests of the great majority of individuals. Given the admitted responsibility of the state to ensure that social and economic minima in wages, housing and living conditions existed on a scale adequate to give some meaning to the idea of 'equality of opportunity', the Liberal problem was to locate some sphere of action within the market economy wherein they could set their progressive principles to work without directly affronting the representatives of economic orthodoxy. The case for state intervention had to be established beyond doubt, the party had to be basically

[83] *Ibid.* C1734-6.
[84] *Ibid.* C1734-6.

united, the Radicals placated and the electoral prospects good. Land reform was an obvious choice, embracing as it did traditional Liberal sympathies, as well as more modern ideas for rural reconstruction and development in the context of relieving some of the ills of an industrial society.

In 1909, the various land reformers had achieved their immediate objective of a national valuation and this, rather than the land clauses themselves, gained their immediate support. Both then and later, Wedgwood, for the single-taxers, made it clear that they opposed the increment value duty as this could still be included in the final selling price of land,[85] so foreshadowing a running conflict with Lloyd George before 1914.

The Land Nationalisation Society raised a special election fund in January 1910, and after the two elections, were still able to claim 98 supporters in the Commons.[86] By now, the balance within the Parliamentary Land Values Group as a whole had apparently tilted towards the single-taxers, who included the Group's Chairman, C. E. Price, and such leading speakers as P. W. Raffan, Sir A. Spicer, Wedgwood, Francis Neilson and Dundas White. On 3 August 1910, the Group submitted a memorandum which represented a significant advance on their previous proposals, in that they now asked for two taxes, for a national tax on full site-value and for power to be given to the local authorities for them to adopt also, full site-value as the uniform standard of rating (instead of the annual letting value of the land and its buildings). The proceeds of the national land tax were to go in relief of rates, to finance the abolition of the food taxes, and to provide a national fund out of which newly-allocated, fully national services should be met, education, poor relief, roads, police and asylums.

This was a significant change in emphasis, for previously, valuation had been advocated within the context of local finance – a national tax upon the land was something new, with distinct echoes of Henry George. A policy shift was further suggested by the view of the Land Values Group that valuation, not expected to be completed before 1915, would take far too long. In a memorandum submitted on 18 May 1911, and signed by 174 M.P.s, they called for the expediting of the valuation. By 1912, they had moved a stage further, and were suggesting that valuation should omit a separate assessment

[85] J. Wedgwood, *Memoirs of a Fighting Life* (1940) p. 68.
[86] *30th Annual Report of the L.N.S.*, 1911.

of buildings and improvements, and be simply a valuation of the whole land value, which might then be capitalised for purposes of taxation. On 24 April 1912, Francis Neilson introduced a land values rating bill which adopted full site-value as its basis, and on 12 July, the Land Values Group agreed to adopt the previous text of their memorial as a statement of basic policy. In effect, they had moved on from the taxation of incremental land values, the basis of the previous compromise between the sections, to the taxation of the land itself. This was a move away from policies of development, public owner-ship and positive intervention, towards a reliance upon taxation alone as the instrument of reform. The emphasis and the trend is very shadowy between 1910 and 1912, but it does seem that the main par-liamentary view of land reform had moved away from the policies foreshadowed in 1909 with the Development Commission. Wedg-wood's statement of the Group's policy described it as more than a financial reform i.e. a social and economic reform, lessening the rate-burden on productive enterprise, increasing the availability of land for settlement and encouraging the development of agriculture and of land-based industries; yet it was surely doubtful if land taxation would achieve such ends by itself.[87] Herein lay the seed of the emerging quarrel between the single-taxers and the nationalisers.

During 1911, with the passage of the Parliament Bill and the insurance measures, with Ireland and Welsh disestablishment firmly placed on the time-table, there was little time to contemplate large land programmes. A Departmental Committee on local taxation was established in 1911 to review financial progress since 1901, and on 13 December 1911, Lloyd George did give a hint that valuation might be extended on the two-fold scale envisaged by the Land Values Group.[88] Meanwhile the Group received increasing support in the country. On 7 October 1911 the General Council of the Scottish Liberal Association backed their policy, including a call for the speeding-up of valuation. On 10 May 1912 the General Council of the N.L.F. did likewise. On 31 May E. G. Hemmerde succeeded Sir George White in north-west Norfolk, and on 13 July R. L. Outh-waite won Hanley from Labour on the death of Enoch Edwards. Both were strong advocates of a single-tax and both campaigns were won ostensibly on the land issue.[89] An informant stressed to Lloyd

---

[87] J. C. Wedgwood, ' The Principle of Land Value Taxation ', *Economic Journal*, 22 (1912) p. 388.

[88] Raffan, *Land Values Group*.   [89] *The Nation*, 20 July 1912.

George that a real land campaign would draw the wind from Labour sails:

I pleaded with Ramsay MacDonald, Keir Hardie and Snowden to join in our (land) propaganda. They admitted it was the economic bedrock of reform, but could not identify themselves with it for fear of losing their independent position and bringing grist to the Liberal mill.[90]

The style of the land campaigners was, however, arousing opposition, A. C. Murray writing in his diary:

This group is running for all it is worth an extreme land policy, which in effect, although they deny it, amounts to a single tax on land values. The members of the group are becoming more arrogant every day, one of them having the audacity to say that there was no place in the Liberal Party for anyone who did not accept their policy.

He recorded the moderates' dislike of a ' raging, tearing campaign ', and forecast the loss of many of the party's ' best supporters if such a campaign is allowed to mature '. He further remarked upon Lloyd George's isolation in the Cabinet, ' he is making a mistake if he thinks he can run a land campaign single-handed '.[91]

In the country and from the Conservatives, Liberal financial and land polities met increasing criticism. ' The better-class Liberal is ... sick and tired of Lloyd Georgian finance and the " people's budget " is beginning to be felt '.[92] The Conservatives argued that the Liberals were directly responsible for the falling price of government securities while their policy of placing direct taxation upon capital assets coupled to their dallying with the idea of the minimum wage was affecting industrial confidence and driving capital out of the country.[93] The argument for broadening the basis of taxation now became part of the general argument for tariff reform, and for financing social reform without imposing a drain on home resources.

In June 1912 the Land Enquiry was launched by Lloyd George, and quickly confirmed the findings of the 1907 agricultural census regarding low wages, long hours and poor housing.[94] Housing and

---

[90] Llewellyn Davies to Lloyd George, 4 August 1912, LGP, C/9/3/10.

[91] A. C. Murray papers, Mss 8814, 19 and 22 July 1912.

[92] W. Long to Bonar Law, 8 March 1912, Bonar Law papers, 26/1/76.

[93] *Morning Post*, 9 February 1912.

[94] For full details on the following see the author's essay: ' The Land Campaign: Lloyd George as a Social Reformer, 1909–1914 ' in A. J. P. Taylor (ed.), *Lloyd George : Twelve Essays* (1971).

wages emerged as the two main targets for reform, with the Liberals, through Runciman, considering a state housing programme for rural areas, and, through the medium of Lloyd George, a minimum living wage for agricultural labourers. The principal administrative agency which was to handle these ideas, and questions of security of tenure for the tenant farmer, compensation for improvements, etc. was the idea of a Land Commission which was proposed by Haldane in July 1913.

While debate proceeded in the Cabinet as to the functions and powers of this commission, in the country the land succeeded the Insurance Bill as the primary political issue. There was mounting agitation in the country for the idea of an agricultural minimum wage, aided and abetted by the Labour party. The Conservative leadership was evidently split over the degree and kind of reform to support, toying themselves with the idea of extending wages boards to the rural areas, an idea which the leadership rejected in late 1913. Meanwhile, the agricultural interests were becoming vocal in their dislike of the implications of a single-tax policy, which Liberal Radicals seemed to be favouring increasingly by 1913. Agriculturalists were perturbed as to how the full site-value of their land was being calculated, a point which also worried Liberals like A. C. Murray and Lord Eversley. It was, in fact, becoming evident that two Radical views of land reform were in conflict. For the single-taxers, Outhwaite and Wedgwood held to a residual theory of distribution, with the landlord as the favoured 'last receiver'. They favoured appropriating the rent-fund by taxation, assuming that this would free resources and provide money for national services. For the nationalisers, Chiozza Money and Masterman disputed that land was the one natural source of wealth. Taxation of unproductive funds (i.e. the unearned increment of rent) was a necessary but not a sufficient policy for development.[95]

By late 1913, with Churchill's demand for new naval construction, and new educational commitments, it was clear the estimated deficit for 1914–15 would be a large one. Lloyd George was also under pressure to introduce a measure of rating reform. Clearly, a further financial initiative was probable, a fact which made Lloyd George more vulnerable to single-tax pressure. The single-taxers had already threatened Lloyd George that their support for a land campaign was conditional upon the adoption of full site-value for

[95] *Ibid.* pp. 55–6.

both national and local taxation.[96] In August 1913 Charles Price renewed this threat, and the single-taxers further wrecked an attempt by Lloyd George to make some concessions to agriculture by defining more closely the procedure for valuation.[97] Until this moment the Cabinet had scarcely considered site-value taxation.

In October 1913, the first report of the Land Enquiry was released upon rural conditions. It found that over 60 per cent of ordinary agricultural labourers received less than 18s a week, 20–30,000 received less than 16s, and accordingly recommended a living wage to be enforced by 'some form' of wages tribunal. It also recommended a state housing initiative to help provide the 120,000 new cottages which were needed, and a land court to which farmers could appeal against excessive wage awards, and over questions of tenure.

On 11 October Lloyd George officially opened the Land Campaign at Bedford, although as he was unable to announce specific policies, these not having yet been finalised by the Cabinet, his speech lost something in impact. On 18 October the Cabinet met and agreed upon the form of their land proposals, and these Lloyd George announced at Swindon on 22 October. The government proposed a new Ministry of Lands and Forests, which would supersede the Ministry of Agriculture, assume all responsibility for Land Valuation, matters of the sale and transfer of land, small-holdings, land purchase, and the development of land-based industries. Through land commissioners, it would supervise and provide rights of appeal for all questions of fair rents, tenure, and the securing of a physical minimum wage to landowners, farmers and labourers. The commissioners would be empowered to authorise loans for housing and development schemes, and when the new Domesday Book of land-values was ready in 1915, it would form the basis for the commissioners in their power of land acquisition. He emphasised that they would, in all such matters act judicially, and that their functions would rest as much in conciliation as in the exercise of their legal authority. The government adopted the figure of 120,000 as the number of cottages required, and apart from the scheme to establish commissioners, their proposals followed those of the Land Enquiry fairly closely.[98] The proposals had an enthusiastic reception; some

---

[96] 25 June 1913, LGP, C/9/4/62.   [97] 'The Land Campaign', p. 57.

[98] *Daily News*, 23 October 1913. (Lloyd George committed the Liberals to the principle of the living wage, to be based on considerations of efficient work as well as on physical sustenance, and to a national housing campaign.) (LGP, C/2/3/37. Memo. to Asquith, 8 November 1913.)

farmers even found the guarantee of security of tenure ' too good to be true '. The policies were transmitted over the country by Lloyd George, Runciman and Samuel; Lloyd George emphasising to the chief whip, Illingworth, the electoral advantages that were to be gained.[99] By December, Rowntree was training some 80 men as lecturers to spread the policies, at a private cost of £800, and these were joined by a voluntary force of 150. On 9 December, at the National Liberal Club, Asquith endorsed the campaign, particularly the proposals for a physical minimum wage, and the compulsory acquisition of land by public authorities in anticipation of its development. His audience was composed of delegates from the local Liberal Federations of England and Wales, and here they elected an executive, the Central Land and Housing Council, which was to have overall charge of the campaign.

In his speeches, Lloyd George had attacked the rating system, but had announced no proposals, and the single-taxers therefore maintained their pressure. On 13 October, the Committee for the Taxation of Land Values held a conference at Cardiff, where they again adopted a resolution in favour of the principle of taxing land values.[100] In November, both Trevelyan and Outhwaite pressed Lloyd George to grant a national land-values tax in return for their help in the campaign.[101] On 30 October, Lloyd George asked Sir Matthew Nathan, the Chairman of the Board of Inland Revenue, for the complete valuation figures on two or three towns, in order that he might present to the Cabinet the possible revenue-gains obtainable from transferring a portion of the rating burden to site-values. In the towns, however, the valuation was behind schedule.[102] On 18 November, Lloyd George reported to the Cabinet that the increased expenditure by the Departments for 1914–15 was estimated at £10 million, of which only £6.5 million could be raised without new taxation, and the case for rating reform became imperative when it was seen how much of this expenditure, on roads and education especially, would require complementary local expenditure.[103] In a Cabinet paper of 13 December 1913, Lloyd George accepted that

[99] LGP, C/4/17/3, 24 October 1913.

[100] *The Times*, 14 October 1911.

[101] LGP, C/1/2/32.

[102] LGP, C/6/6/1. By December 5 1913, no town with a rateable value of over £1 million had yet been completely valued.

[103] Cab. 37/117, No. 90, December 1913. Note on the ' Necessity for Increased Financial Aid to the Local Education Authorities, 1914–15 '.

land reform should include a measure of rating reform, and he admitted the case for national aid for national services. A scheme for a local rate on site-values had now been prepared by the Inland Revenue, although it was still tentative; 60 per cent of the valuation having been completed, many of the most complicated areas (town-centres), remained. The scheme suggested that a rate of 1d in the £ on all site-values would produce an additional £9·5 million on local revenue; if agricultural land was rated at a half-penny in the £, this sum would drop to £8·9 million, but the scheme was justified not only on the grounds of revenue, but also in terms of encouraging the better utilisation of resources. On 17 December P. W. Raffan asked for a definite commitment to both the rating and the national taxation of site-values. On 1 January 1914, Lloyd George wrote him an open letter in which he assured the taxers that the government was even then considering the most appropriate methods:

You may depend upon it that the Government definitely intend to utilise the valuation, which they are putting through at great expense, for the purpose of compelling the owners of the sites which are not now bearing their share of local taxation, to contribute on the basis of the real value of their property.[104]

The land nationalisers, however, felt that the government were in danger of making too many concessions, and of forgetting the real purpose of development. Rowntree was anxious that the land campaign should not become a mere vendetta against landowners,[105] while Heath, the secretary to the Land Enquiry Committee, told Lloyd George that 'a large section of the Liberal party who are in favour of nationalisation are really disappointed with the land proposals'.[106] Lloyd George, however, and his supporters had already launched into extensive speaking tours of England and Wales, and the Chancellor had further proposed to Asquith a national survey of slum housing, with grants-in-aid to urban authorities being conditional upon their acting upon the problems exposed. He now envisaged the extension of the Trade Boards Act (1909) to urban areas to enable the many poor to afford a commercial rent, as well as the rating of vacant and undeveloped land.[107]

The Land Enquiry's Report upon urban conditions was not published until April 1914, and its emphasis fell again upon housing and wages. It should be, it said, a statutory duty upon all local authorities to provide adequate housing accommodation for their working-class population, and to this end, each authority should embark upon an immediate survey of its own housing situation preparatory to submitting a scheme of development to the Local Government Board. Although their terms of reference excluded the direct investigation of wages, the Report still felt it imperative to call upon the government to ' take means to secure that within a short and defined period a minimum wage shall be fixed for all low-paid wage earners '.[108] The Report accepted the full case for rating reform, and thought that all future increases in local expenditure, chargeable to the rates, should be met by a site-value rate. Furthermore, part of the existing expenditure should be met by a penny rate on capital site-value, and authorities should have the option of increasing the proportion of their expenditure to be financed locally in this way, with the one proviso that new burdens should be placed on agricultural land. Further relief in the form of grants-in-aid up to £5 million should be provided from the Imperial Exchequer.

This Report and the Departmental Minority Report (below) were acclaimed by the Land Values Group as the admission of their case, although in the statement they issued, they insisted that their minimum condition of support was still the national land value-tax. However, the influence of the land nationalisers was also present, for this statement regretted that the case for rating site-values had been couched in terms of administrative practicability and financial necessity :

What the Reports lack is a frank avowal that the new system, in applying public values to public purposes, is in itself right and necessary as a matter of social justice. Nor is there any clear statement to be found as to the liberating effect of the change in opening up opportunities for labour and thereby enabling it to secure its fair reward.[109]

THE 1914 BUDGET

From the beginning of 1914, Lloyd George had begun to draw the threads of his campaign together in preparation for his budget. To the Commons on 12 February, he promised that the government

---

[108] *Report of the Land Enquiry Committee*, Vol. 2, pp. 209–10.
[109] *Recommendations for the Taxation of Land Values Explained and Criticised.* By the Land Values Group (1914).

would submit rating reform proposals. In March the Departmental Committee on Local Taxation reported. The Majority group of seven agreed that state relief for semi-national services was overdue, especially for education and the Poor-Law; it agreed with ministerial supervision of local expenditure, and rejected the rating of site-values. The Minority group of six favoured a local site-value tax, and thought that half of all future increases in local expenditure should be met by a rate on site-values, while relief should also be given on all improvements by reducing the charge levied on the present basis of rateable value, and making good the deficiency by another extra-ordinary rate on site-values.[110]

When the budget was finally presented on 4 May, it did not contain a national land tax, but the rating of site-values was included. Lloyd George told Cabinet that

> While there is no intention of transferring the whole burden of the rates from the composite subject to the site, taxation of site-values must henceforth constitute an integral part of the system of local taxation.[111]

He explained to the Commons that of all the objects listed in 1909, only local taxation reform remained. As regards the valuation:

> The vast majority of the hereditaments of this country have already been surveyed and inspected, all the necessary information with regard to them has been collected, and boundaries have been ascertained for the first time. The annual values and the total values have been assessed, and in urban sites the value of the improvements has been ascertained.[112]

All that remained was to ascertain the value of agricultural improvements, and then he proposed to adapt this national valuation to local use in order that the rating of site-values might be introduced. This would establish a uniform (and national) criterion by which full site-value might be assessed by the taxation authorities. It would also establish what improvements were to be included in this full site-value, and on which improvements, and at what rate, rating-relief might be granted. (Lloyd George in fact suggested that the relief might be equivalent to a shilling rate on improvements, as they had been valued in the national survey.) He adopted the Report's suggestions that all such relief should be at the expense of extra levies

110 *Report of the Departmental Committee on Local Taxation*, Cd. 7316 (1914) xl.
111 LGP, C/12/4.
112 Parl. Deb., 5th Series, Vol. 62, C69, 4 May 1914.

on site-values; in this way it was hoped that the rating burden would always be placed directly upon the owners of land.

He further announced extensive increases in Imperial grants-in-aid to the local authorities. Henceforth, grants-in-aid would constitute the only central–local financial link, for all assigned revenues, the local taxation account, and the Agricultural Rates Relief Act, were to be abolished. The grants-in-aid were to be assessed on a percentage basis, but they would not be granted as of right but were instead liable to two conditions: they would be related to the efficiency of the service provided by the local authorities, and to the authorities' own views of their responsibilities; they would be distributed proportionally, taking into account those areas most in need of assistance, and where the services to be provided constituted a heavy burden in relation to the rateable value. The grants to police forces and for the upkeep of main roads were to be raised to at least half their total cost. The educational grant was to be raised by up to £4 million, and was to be distributed primarily according to need; this included further state provision for school-meals services, grants for open-air schools for tuberculosis victims, schools for the deformed, and for the training of specialist teachers. Further grants included new provisions for sanitoria, maternity centres and ancillary health services under the 1911 insurance bill. The total cost in a full financial year was estimated at £11 million (including the cost of the local valuation scheme).

Not the least of the budget's interest lay in its proposals for further increases in direct taxation. The year 1914 saw the introduction of a graduated income-tax on earned incomes rising to 1s 4d in the pound on earned incomes over £2,500. The upper rate on unearned incomes also became 1s 4d. The overall limit of the super-tax was lowered from £5,000 to £3,000, and all incomes over £3,000 would now pay on their excess over £2,500. The new rate would be 5d on the first £500, 7d on the next £1,000, increasing at 2d per £1,000 until all incomes over £9,000 paid at 1s 4d in the pound, at which point the maximum tax on such incomes would be 2s 8d in the pound. To the death duties, 1 per cent was added to all estates worth over £60,000, while for those over £250,000 in value, the scale steepened to impose a maximum of 20 per cent (previously 15 per cent) on estates worth over £1 million. Finally, the income-tax relief in respect to children was doubled from £10 to £20 for each child under 16.

Radicalism welcomed the budget enthusiastically, rejecting the notion that heavy direct taxation injured trade by pointing to trade prosperity after 1910. They asserted the state's responsibility for basing the taxation system upon principles of social justice.[113] Productive expenditure, emanating from the state, was a necessary condition for the further development of society. Haldane believed the adoption of this principle marked a fundamental change in English party politics. ' You could not have had this budget ten years ago ', he told the National Liberal Club, where he outlined five stages in Liberal social purposes. A child had first to be born healthy, hence maternity centres and child care; while at school it had to be cared for in body and in mind, it had to receive help in choosing a career and in obtaining the most suitable training for employment. He forecast the raising of the school leaving age, the provision of continuation schools, and looked forward to a separate Ministry of Health.[114]

In their opposition to the budget, the Conservatives reiterated their previous arguments. Especially, they claimed, the ability of the country to bear taxation and expenditure upon this scale was due only to the favourable trading balance Britain had enjoyed since 1910; when trade declined and depression returned the country would lack the financial flexibility to meet the crisis because the liabilities entered into by the Liberals in respect of social reform represented a commitment which would expand over time; hence it would be impossible to reduce either taxation or the scale of government activity. Already, by 1913, the orthodox reaction to government intervention in industrial affairs and to the implications of Lloyd George's willingness to abuse the sanctity of the sinking-fund and to evade the maxim that all normal expenditure must be met from current revenue and not by borrowing, was producing the highly restrictionist interpretation of government's economic functions later denoted as the ' Treasury view '. The first coherent explanation of this view seems to have been Ralph Hawtrey's *Good and Bad Trade* published in 1913.

The Conservatives were supported in their views by elements within the Liberal party. Sir Richard Holt, a prominent Liberal industrialist, disliked the fact that each social reform was costing a great deal more than was forecast: ' In my opinion, national expenditure has increased more rapidly than national wealth and income.' [115]

[113] Cf. L. G. Chiozza Money, ' Our £200 million Budget ', *Contemporary Review*, April 1914.
[114] R. B. Haldane, *The Inwardness of the Budget* (1914).
[115] Parl. Deb., 5th Series, Vol. 63, C1593, 22 June 1914.

There was again a suggestion of Lloyd George in opposition to the moderate or orthodox opinion in the Cabinet. He wrote to Samuel over the possibility of a budget leak, disturbed that such a leak ' gravely imperils our chances of getting this plan through the Cabinet '.[116]

The major difficulties, however, arose once again from the combination of a lack of clear legislative intention, and pressure upon the parliamentary timetable. Although Samuel had begun drafting the Rating Bill well before the budget, by 29 June the Cabinet had still not decided whether the criterion for site-value was to be based upon the present use-value alone, or whether the final valuation was to include some estimate of capital-value. If the latter was adopted, it would necessarily have to include the value of some improvements, and also have some regard to market price, or optimum use-value, and for agricultural land in particular, this would undoubtedly represent an increase in its rateable value. On the other hand, if capital-value were ignored altogether, the main purpose of valuation i.e. to provide a basis of measurement from which to gauge future (incremental) increases in rateable value, would be defeated, for present use value was a purely relative standard of measurement. (The value of agricultural land, for example, would vary according to a particular crop produced and/or the state of the market.) [117]

While the Cabinet struggled with this problem, the parliamentary timetable reached saturation point. On 29 April, E. S. Montagu warned Lloyd George that legislative prospects were bleak. The Liberals were then dealing with Bills for Home Rule, Welsh disestablishment and plural voting. An education bill, the budget and now Samuel's ' elaborate Rating reform ' which promised to be ' a long and arduous business ', were in the offing.[118] The impasse was aggravated by the formation of a liberal ' cave ' of about 40 members led by Sir John Jardine which opposed the new grants-in-aid because they felt that the scheme for the reform of local government finance should properly be considered within a separate bill.[119] On 22 June the Speaker ruled that part of the Finance Bill relating to the grants was, indeed, out of order.

On June 23, the Cabinet accordingly decided that the Finance Bill should be divided into two parts. First, they would proceed with

116 Copy LGP, C/7/9/4, 25 April 1914.
117 Cab. 37/120, No. 77, 29 June 1914. The Rating Bill (Samuel).
118 LGP, C/1/1/16.
119 *The Times*, 18 June 1914.

necessary taxation, and forgo pressing for the full extent of the graduated scales,[120] meanwhile abandoning the grants for the present session, with the exceptions of grants to insurance and education; secondly, in the later part of the session, they would deal with the principles on which future grants were to be allocated, and with a Revenue Bill, which would provide the basis for the division of rates between land values and improvements. On 26 June, however, in the second reading of the Finance Bill, the government majority fell from a nominal 94 to 38. 35 out of 37 Labour M.P.s abstained, and one Liberal, Sir Luke White, voted against the Cabinet's decision to delay the local reforms.[121]

Possibly this hinted at a certain loss of confidence within the party, for on 14 July the Cabinet further agreed that the present session should be terminated as soon as the Finance Bill and Home Rule had been dealt with. At the end of November there would be a new session to dispose of the Revenue Bill, and accompanying legislation – presumably education and housing.[122] The Cabinet were by now resigned to the fact that the Ministry of Lands could not be established that year. The Board of Agriculture had been working on the transfer of powers and on the creation of the Judicial Commissioners since January, but by June several practical details were still outstanding e.g. the hours of work for agricultural labourers, especially half-holidays, whether the Board of Agriculture should build cottages for townsmen who wished to settle in the country, and whether trade boards or commissioners should fix the wages in the country districts.[123] It was intended that a Cabinet committee be established to deal with these. The government were also committed to begin their housing programme that year, and on 8 July, Runciman and Samuel introduced a measure which would have given the Board of Agriculture power to acquire land and make provision for working-class dwellings in agricultural districts – including the power to loan money to authorised utility and building societies.[124]

Lloyd George's parliamentary preoccupations were, as he told Rowntree, diverting his attention from the campaign in the country.

---

[120] The last increase (2d) in the graduated scale on earned incomes and the last 1d increase on unearned incomes were dispensed with.

[121] *The Times*, 26 June 1914.

[122] Asquith to George V, 14 July 1914. AP, Vol. 7.

[123] LGP, C/1/1/18.

[124] *Liberal Magazine*, August 1914, p. 250. The Bill set aside £3 million for this purpose.

On 12 May Rowntree sent him a list of seven points which needed clearer exposition; these included the machinery necessary to establish a minimum wage, the extent of the minimum wage in towns, the agricultural labourers' half-holiday and hours of labour, when the housing campaign was going to start, and rating reform.[125] On 25 May Rowntree asked: ' whether you want us to slow down or hurry up? At present we are counting on a 1915 election and organising accordingly '. On 28 May he told Lloyd George that ' the first series of meetings covering the whole country will be practically completed by the end of July '.[126] On the same day Lloyd George received a highly favourable account of progress from the secretary of the Central Land and Housing Council:

Speaking of the country as a whole I may say without any exception the Government's proposals are arousing unprecedented enthusiasm in the rural constituencies ... The people will stand for an hour or more in drenching rain or piercing wind to hear the proposals explained. For the first time in the history of modern Liberalism, farmers who do not support the Liberals are attending Liberal meetings to get information ... the complete success of the rural campaign is assured.[127]

In the urban areas of the north-east, the Eastern Counties, Lancashire, Devon and Cornwall, the campaign was going ' fairly well ', ' but for the rest of the country the campaign in the boroughs has been disappointing ... Public attention has been so occupied with gun-running, army revolts ... that it has been difficult to arouse interest on Land and Housing.' If, he suggested, Lloyd George were to say publicly that ' the principle of the Trade Boards Act will be extended to include all low-paid workers, it would place our urban campaign on an entirely different level '. So far, he reported, there had been very little opposition from any quarter.

This picture was confirmed exactly by the reports from the Regional Liberal Associations. In the Midlands, the labourers were ' pathetically keen ', but in the towns the proposals, more complicated and directed to much more diverse audiences, continued to hang fire. The crucial point seemed to be to what extent the government would commit themselves to the extension of the minimum wage, and this was undecided in June, when attention was focused thereon

[125] LGP, C/2/4/18.
[126] LGP, C/2/4.
[127] *Ibid*.

upon Ireland.[128] On 12 June Lloyd George told Runciman that Asquith was 'highly gratified' at the progress of the campaign, but the decision upon the living wage had not been taken by the end of June.

The land campaign and the 1914 Budget were the evident corollaries of the 1909 Budget and the insurance legislation. The emphasis upon land reform has to be seen within the context of a search for an unemployment policy, in which three elements were distinct: the recovery of the long-lost rural–urban balance, the prevention of the accumulation of unemployables in the cities (for without these two factors, unemployment insurance for a limited, organised sector of the labour market would be but a drop in the ocean), and the growing concern for establishing minimum wages and a maximum hourly working day. These elements were in turn linked to a land campaign as an expression of the Radical principle 'that the owner of land has not the right to do, uncontrolled, as he will with his own'.[129] This principle was now capable of a broader expression in that it was the owner of *property* who was now to be constrained by the community. This was the progressive message in 1914: 'the relative character of the right of property ... has no privilege which forbids control by the community ... There is no legitimate claim which property can make against what appears to be the welfare of the state.'[130] And this principle was being read into Liberal industrial legislation as a consideration greater than economic criteria.

The land campaign, especially the movement for site-value taxation, had roots in both traditional and in more modern Social Radicalism. The school of single-taxers were nearest to the traditional radical dislike of an undue reliance upon the state, either in the direct invocation of state powers, or in the establishment of public administrative machinery. They retained a strong belief in individual freedom, a belief in the virtue of financial retrenchment, an acceptance of orthodox economic views regarding the inevitable limitations of the worker's position, and a dislike of hampering industry, which were the hall-marks of the Radicalism of Bradlaugh, Labouchere or Lawson. The single-tax seemed to offer to them a plausible alternative to socialism and the drift to high direct taxation.

On the other hand, the land nationalisers, after 1906 at least, refused to treat the landowner as the scapegoat for modern industrial

128 *Ibid*.   129 Cf. H. Samuel, *Urban Land Housing Reform* (1914).
130 *Property : Its Rights and Duties* (1914). Preface by Bishop Gore.

problems. The scope of their policy extended on the one hand to incorporate the movement for town-planning, municipal improvement, housing and transit, each with a need for extensive public acquisition of land; and on the other, to the progressive concern for the provision of publicly-operated industries, state farms, afforestation, as a partial answer to unemployment. Nationalisers like Chiozza Money, Masterman or Clem Edwards were willing, within the context of development, to support the nationalisation of railways and canals, and they were prepared to support a state initiative rather than to blithely hope that improvement would follow from fiscal reform. They were not hypnotised by rising expenditure, and they were prepared to support state loans to municipalities and private societies, so long as the expenditure was itself 'reproductive', providing employment, raising wages, allowing of increased consumption, or increasing the demand for necessities. Their view might fairly be that of George Harwood: 'Politics mean more than the struggle of the individual. They mean the development of the nation, and they mean that development cannot be maintained by the principle of individualism.' [131]

The dilemma of Lloyd George lay in his attempt to strike a compromise between these two groups; hence a site-value rate but not a land tax; development of the land and the towns, but not outright nationalisation, merely extended facilities for purchase. While always prepared to exploit anti-landlord sentiment, his policy was yet on a different level to his speeches. His acceptance of development in 1909, his willingness to budget for expanding social commitments and to increase direct taxation to do this, seems to indicate that he did not view land taxation simply as a welcome source of further revenue, or as a means of shedding a direct social responsibility on behalf of the state in favour of a fiscal palliative. His acceptance of the principle of the 'living wage' at once placed him far closer to Chiozza Money than to Wedgwood, and indeed, the Cabinet's willingness to accept this principle, at least in the counties, demonstrated some advance since their vacillations in 1912 (see below). Equally, their willingness to accept wide responsibilities on behalf of the state in housing, in the arbitration of contractual relations between landlord and tenant, and in the proposed establishment of a powerful Ministry of Lands, indicated a considerable change in the nature of Liberal political individualism.

[131] Parl. Deb., 5th Series, Vol. 12, C1736, 2 November 1909.

As a policy for the ills of industrial society the land campaign was no doubt an anachronism, although it certainly did not appear as such in 1914. What is significant, however, is the degree to which the campaign and the budget gave further expression to the principles of public welfare and social justice associated with the 'new Liberalism' of the Social Radicals. In this context, one might argue strongly for the principles upon which the campaign was based, for the imposition of social responsibility upon property owners, for a greater measure of fiscal equality and taxation according to one's capacity to pay, and for the greater responsibility of the state to eliminate gross income inequalities and to undertake a measure of redistribution itself. There were several strands in the emergence of radical and progressive thought before 1914, Hobsonian welfare economics, the ethical idealism of the Guild Socialists, the sociology of Leonard Hobhouse, and Graham Wallas' conception of *The Great Society*, but all were agreed that social and ethical goals should form the guiding criteria in future, conscious, development. Unable, however, to agree on the precise nature of their challenge to the existing economic order, they united in support of a financial policy which seemed to all to be a step in the requisite direction:

A new cry is needed to express the newer doctrines – that the cry for reform precedes finance and does not follow it, that the wise state is that which raises wisely and expends wisely the largest percentage of the national income.[132]

And much of what they desired had already come to pass. In this period, the maximum rates of direct taxation had risen from 9d to 2s 8d in respect of earned income and the super-tax, and from 8 per cent to 20 per cent in respect of death duties. The scale of normal governmental expenditure had risen by a third; the 1914 Budget was the first to project a national outlay in excess of £200 million. Between 1888 and 1913, expenditure upon the 'social services', health, education, pensions and insurance (but not poor law) had risen from £5 million to £33 million, and there was 'an almost inevitable prospect of increasing growth'. Rising expenditure and rising taxation together represented 'a revolution in public sentiment and political thought'. By 1914, the proportion of revenue obtained from direct taxation had reached 60 per cent, having risen from 44

132 R. Jones, *Our Taxes As They Are And As They Ought To Be*, Fabian pamphlet No. 152 (1913).

per cent in 1888. Mallet recorded that 'opinion is, of course, sharply divided as to whether the rates of direct taxation are dangerously high or not', although he considered that views such as those of Giffen would now be regarded as extreme.[133] There still remained a strong demand that expenditure upon direct benefits for the poor should entail some minimum (direct) contribution from them in return, but the principle of ability to pay had gained a more or less conclusive victory over the old, proportional concept of equality of sacrifice. This in itself marked a recognition of the validity of principles of social justice, for from the principle of equity expressed in financial terms was to come the wider commitment to social equality.

[133] B. Mallet, *British Budgets 1886-1913* (1913) p. 455. Also H. H. Asquith, *National Finances and the Finances of 1914-15* (1914). (Giffen had held that 'on the whole an equal amount of indirect taxation causes perhaps only the half or the third of the privation and suffering entailed by an equal amount of direct taxation'.)

7

The Liberals in Office 1910-14

In 1910, contemporaries were agreed that a point of no return had been reached, and from 1910 it was indeed possible to claim that ' a displacement both of ideas and political power had started '.[1] The budget crystallised the latent divisions between the two major parties. In 1909, J. A. Hobson attributed growing Conservative intransigence to their fears that social reform, financed by the taxation of the unearned increment in the form of heavy direct taxation upon high incomes and property, was to become a continuous Liberal policy rather than a series of isolated acts. With the prospect of an extensive, and expensive, insurance programme ahead of them if they failed to overthrow the Liberals, the Conservatives had little to lose by risking all on fighting the budget.[2] This may have been a shrewd analysis, for J. S. Sandars informed Balfour that Lloyd George was reputedly planning the nationalisation of the railways as well as land nationalisation; accordingly, he suggested the Conservatives fight all the way under the banner ' a vote for the budget is a vote for socialism. It would go through the country '.[3]

The crux of the Conservative case lay in their refusal to accept that policies of income redistribution and the state redirection of resources to weak or deprived sectors of the community was, as a primary goal, compatible with the continued functional efficiency of the productive process. For Liberalism, the further provision of social reform and the efficacy and viability of free trade as the basis for progressive politics, were entwined within the fate of the budget.[4] For Conservatives, although tariff reform occupied the first place in their programme, the core of their appeal rested in the 88 pages their handbook devoted to socialism: opposition to rising direct taxation (and expenditure), to the taxation of a class for a class, opposition to the whole concept of a taxable surplus, to schemes of ' social reconstruction ' and to the public management of an individual's property and

---

1 Markham, *Friendship's Harvest*, p. 19.
2 J. A. Hobson, *The Crisis of Liberalism* (1909) Preface.
3 J. S. Sandars to A. J. Balfour, 21 September 1909, A. J. Balfour papers, Add. Mss 49766.
4 See C. F. G. Masterman, ' How it Strikes a Contemporary ', *The Nation*, 8 January 1910.

affairs.[5] The Conservatives accused the Liberals of sectionalism in respect of their domestic programme and of separatism in regard to Ireland. The Liberals in their turn appealed to organised Labour to reject a Conservative party whose handbook revealed a reliance upon a branch of negative individualism.

There was, within these two elections, an appeal to class, in the sense of an appeal to social prejudice and economic self-interest, which was largely new. *The Nation* referred to the scorn amongst Conservatives for the humble status of certain Liberal candidates, and condemned the outlook of the peers, ' who are so profoundly immersed in the conviction that politics is their business . . . they assume the nation will admire their violence '.[6] No one pretended now that social reform was ' non-party ', and justifiable on the grounds of enlightened self-interest; social reform was labour politics and neutrality was at a premium. The Liberals regarded their own eroded majority as evidence of their failure to command the same middle-class support they had gained in 1906. Lewis Harcourt ' found all over the country that all Lloyd George's speeches and Winston's earlier ones . . . had done us much harm even with advanced men of the lower middle-class . . . and probably account for the heavy losses in the south '.[7] Herbert Samuel reported in similar fashion:

The debâcle in the Home Counties and in so many agricultural divisions is lamentable. It is the abiding problem of Liberal statesmanship to rouse the enthusiasm of the working-classes without frightening the middle-classes. It can be done but it has not been done this time.[8]

The Conservatives saw the final outcome as fresh proof of the inherent tendency in a democracy for electoral victory to go to the highest bidder, and this gave new point to their accusations of irresponsibility.

The Liberals suffered most heavily in England (in Scotland and Wales, the Liberals and Labour together held 88 out of 100 seats), but the Conservatives notably failed to make significant recoveries in either Lancashire or London; in the latter, the Liberals, after December 1910, still held 31 seats as against 39 in 1906. The most marked Conservative advance did come in the suburban areas of

---

[5] *The Case Against Radicalism* (1909).
[6] *The Nation*, 15 January 1910 (Who started the Class-War?).
[7] To Asquith, 26 January 1910, AP, Vol. 12.
[8] To Gladstone, 22 January 1910, HGP, Add. Mss 45992.

south-east England where the Liberal breakthrough in 1906, when the party won 39 out of a possible 75 seats, was almost completely eliminated. Overall, the Liberal and Labour strength stood at 314, as against a Conservative strength of 272 (i.e. after December 1910).

The bald statement of figures, however, must not obscure the particulars of the composition of the governing coalition. Not only were there the 40 members of the L.R.C. to reckon with, there were too the 84 Irish Nationalists. During 1910, the Irish had extracted a promise from the Liberals to deal with the Lords' veto in return for Irish support upon the budget.[9] This bargain, within the finely-balanced electoral context, re-opened the issue of Home Rule. This, in turn, drew threats from Welsh non-conformity, supported by Welsh M.P.s, to withdraw support from the Liberal party unless they were assured of equal treatment with the Irish, which re-opened the issue of disestablishment, now interpreted as ' a point of honour '.[10] Elsewhere, Liberalism was under pressure from the suffragettes to live up to its principles, while the circumstances of 1910 had given fresh strength to those Liberals who argued for the importance of electoral reform. Between 1910 and 1914, it was the resurrection of the more traditional issues which proved most capable of arousing bitter party strife, but these were still fought out as set battles within a wider campaign where the significance of victory rested with the control of social policy, and all that such control implied within the fields of taxation, the land, the growth of government and the nature of the principle of social responsibility.

Given the growing scale of the party conflict, it was all the more infuriating to the Conservatives that the new ideas they were combating seemed to exist solely at Westminster amongst a relatively small group of Radicals whose links with the constituencies were tenuous. The reduction in Liberal numbers after December 1910 involved once again some considerable change in the composition of the party. Several prominent Radicals had been eliminated. G. J. Cooper (Bermondsey), H. C. Lea (St Pancras), Felix Cobbold (Ipswich), V. H. Rutherford (Brentford), A. H. Scott (Ashton), A. E. Dunn (Camborne), H. Fullerton (Egremont), R. C. Lehmann (Market Harboro'), and H. C. F. Luttrell (Tavistock) were all beaten. Indeed, out of the 25 Radicals noted previously (allowing for the passage of five miners to the Labour party), only ten were still sitting as

[9] T. P. O'Connor to Asquith, 10 February 1910, AP, Vol. 5.
[10] J. A. Spender, *Life, Journalism and Politics* (1927) Vol. 2, p. 1. See also *The Times*, 6 and 8 March and 10 April 1911.

Liberals in 1911, and one of these, Pickersgill, retired in July 1911.[11] Other casualties included Whitwell Wilson, G. P. Gooch, A. E. Hazel, E. G. Lamb and T. B. Silcock. The Radical element, however, was still significant. The three Liberal Fabians (Money, Alden, Randell), were joined by a fourth, H. G. Chancellor; the leading land reformers were still in the House, so were Radicals like Leif Jones and A. J. Sherwell, 'overseas' Radicals such as Phillip Morrell and Ponsonby, while the bulk of the Liberal writers, publishers, etc. remained, Dalziel, W. H. Dickinson, George Toulmin, J. H. Yoxall, F. G. Kellaway, C. H. Roberts and G. P. Collins. Amongst the new entrants were Arnold Rowntree and Noel Buxton. Possibly there was more uneasiness within the Liberal party after 1909 than a mere perusal of the division lists might imply. The rate of turnover amongst Liberal M.P.s was high, some 70 retiring, of whom nearly half were reckoned to be either disgruntled or out of sympathy with the trend of Social Radicalism. Apart from Bellairs, Renton, Cox, and the brewers, Bertram and Whitbread, there were at least half-a-dozen cases of Whiggish M.P.s quarrelling with their more advanced constituent supporters, and recorded remarks indicated further dissatisfaction at Westminster.[12]

BACKGROUND TO THE INDUSTRIAL ISSUE, 1906–9

Dissatisfaction was especially present amongst those businessmen who feared the twin repercussions of Liberal financial and industrial policies. By 1910, the inherent conflict between the directives of the New Liberalism and the premises of orthodox economics had emerged far enough for it to become a most significant criterion in determining political allegiance.

If the previous rigidity of the wage-fund had gone and if marginalism was gradually replacing residual theories, the orthodox emphasis still remained upon the economic model of perfect competition, upon the efficacy of supply and demand schedules, upon stocks and funds of wealth, and upon, in fact, a logical but highly

---

[11] The ten included Rowlands, J. Wilson and Fenwick.

[12] See N. Blewett, 'The General Elections of 1910', Oxford D.Phil. 1967 (since published) pp. 369–72. The Whigs included F. W. Chance in Carlisle, Lord Wodehouse in Mid-Norfolk, Lord Dalmeny in Midlothian, while R. W. Perks (Louth) and E. A. Ridsdale (Brighton) disliked the budget. A further group of Liberals, including Sir Charles Furness, specifically disliked the land clauses. Fitzmaurice told Bryce in 1909 (p. 59) that the Commons 'was never so full of financial cranks as it is now'.

static analysis of the economic process. Pigou, for example, accepted that there was an aggregate wage-fund directly related in size to the amount of investment in the business sector, which was in turn related to business confidence and to the existence of reserves of capital (two essential components of the 'security of capital' argument), for business to draw upon. In that real income was determined by the level of productive capacity, and as both were considered fixed in the short-term, wage-rises could only properly be based upon an increase in the workers' productive capacity, and not upon social or humanitarian grounds, for the latter could only result in the same amount of money being shared amongst fewer people.[13]

Orthodox strictures were specifically opposed to the minimum wage. Wage-rates should follow a flexible movement in accordance with fluctuations in the relative demand for labour (Pigou himself favoured the sliding-scale). A fixed minimum would be a distortion of the wage–output ratio, and the only resort an employer would have if he were forced to pay a minimum wage would be to refuse to pay anyone not worth that wage. The hire of an inefficient workman would be 'to diminish the fund, elastic only within limits, out of which Labour is remunerated'.[14] A 'Yorkshire Liberal' further criticised J. A. Hobson for failing 'to perceive that once a wage is conceded beyond the economic value of the labour as a moral right...you cannot stop at any particular figure but give away the whole case against socialism'.[15] A minimum wage would represent a fixed charge upon an employer and would reduce his flexibility in the face of (foreign) competition. Consequently, it would become more difficult to maintain the rate of production, and there would be less wealth available for distribution. Such views further made a distinction between the wage-earning classes and the propertied classes, implying that as wages and employment could only be expanded on the basis of increased output, so Labour occupied a secondary place to the prime consideration of boosting confidence and credit. Pigou refused to emphasise the redistribution of income as a means of increasing total demand, believing instead that it was more important to encourage the most 'productive' demand; i.e. the real future for

[13] A. C. Pigou, *Unemployment* (1913) ch. 8, p. 112. Also *The Times*, 11 August 1910: 'There is a limit to all experiments, inexorably fixed by the nature of things. Definite quantities of capital and labour together produce a definite quantity of wealth, and no more can be made of it by any ingenuity.'

[14] *The Times*, 12 March 1912.

[15] *The Nation*, 20 February 1908.

Labour lay in allowing other classes to make the crucial decisions affecting investment and production, for Labour did not possess the requisite knowledge, which only came from the possession of high levels of income.[16] These views were the more important now that the trade unions had committed themselves to the ' right to work ' and the minimum wage. After 1910, Labour's actions in raising wage-rates was held by orthodox opinion to be a direct cause of both British competitive difficulties overseas, and at home, of the failure to absorb the unemployed. In modern parlance, the unions were the most heinous of cost-pushers; in 1913, *The Spectator* could assert that ' Trade-Unions raise the dignity but not the remuneration of labour '.[17]

While the Liberal party possessed a school of Radicals who challenged the dictates of orthodoxy, it also possessed after 1910 a still considerable group of businessmen who, not unnaturally, inclined towards orthodoxy. This group, however, might be divided into two. First, there were the heavy industrialists, like Furness and Kitson, and eminent financiers such as Sir A. Williamson, S. M. Samuel (brother of Herbert Samuel), or Sir C. D. Rose, whose opinions seem to have been closely akin to those previously ascribed to D. A. Thomas and Weetman Pearson, but were removed from the complete ' freedom of production ' school upon their right, represented by Lords Wemyss and Fitzwilliam, or Sir William Lewis. From these, they differed in their sense of the harmonies of production, the interdependence of capital and labour, their willingness to recognise organised trade unionism, and in their belief in schemes of co-partnership and profit-sharing.[18]

Furness, for example, stressed the three fundamental factors in the productive process – capital, labour and enterprise. Each was entitled to a fair reward for its services, but ' the superiority of the wages of ability must be accepted as an axiom of our economics '.[19] He condemned ' ca'canny ', and trade union policies which militated against the differentials due to skill, and condemned any policy of setting ' an inflexible standard wage in each country '. He gave a warning, in the same way that Sir William Rathbone had warned 30 years before, that international competition must threaten Britain's com-

---

[16] Pigou, *Unemployment*, pp. 173f. Also H. Stanley Jevons, ' The Causes of Unemployment ', *Contemporary Review*, May and July 1909.

[17] *Spectator*, 15 March 1913.

[18] Cf. Sir C. Furness, *Industrial Peace and Industrial Efficiency* (1908).

[19] *Ibid*. p. 8. Also *The Times*, 3 February 1908.

mercial supremacy – Britain should rely on ability, and encouragements to ingenuity and productive efficiency amongst her workers.

As a Liberal, Furness possessed a more positive view of the responsibility of the state to assist trade,[20] and whereas D. C. M. Platt found that the debate as to whether governments should assist traders by influence and by diplomacy abroad inclined largely to a laissez-faire conclusion up to 1914,[21] Furness regularly wrote to *The Times* to urge government assistance for traders abroad through the consular services, through trade treaties, and at home through the promotion of scientific research, technical and business education, and by the appointment of a Minister of Commerce.[22]

The second Liberal business school was that of the paternalists, who included those like the Cadburys and Rowntrees who conceived of business in the Quaker conception of a trust undertaken, and those like the Brunners, Alfred Mond and Arthur Markham who saw business management as a responsibility imposed. In part, the difference between the two schools was a matter of interpretation. The paternalists considered the personal welfare of their workers to be a consideration of management inseparable from the most efficient utilisation of labour,[23] and saw labour relations as more than simply the buying and selling of a commodity called labour. Where the concern of a Furness might be to improve the efficiency of his workforce by devices such as the scientific division of labour, the introduction of machinery, the breakdown of restrictions, and devices to speed output (such as the premium bonus system), paternalism aimed at devising a beneficial policy affecting the worker at all levels and stages of his life, such that he would be irretrievably drawn to the firm. Both schools approximated, if not to a theory, at least to a consistent method of approach to industrial relations i.e. enlightened production or social duty. The pre-war years were a testing time for both approaches, and increasing intransigence in the labour market involved a gradual process of polarisation being imposed upon the two.

Prior to 1910, Liberal industrial legislation, although small in quantity, had been of importance in foreshadowing this later process. After 1906, it was soon clear that some industrialists did fear

---

[20] Cf. Sir C. Furness, *The American Invasion* (1902).
[21] D. C. M. Platt, *Finance, Trade and Politics in British Foreign Policy 1815–1914* (1968) pp. xviii, xxxiv.
[22] *The Times*, 27 October 1908; 3 November 1909; 8 February 1910; 14 March 1911.
[23] Cf. E. Cadbury, *Experiments in Industrial Organisation* (1911).

socialistic pressure upon Liberal policies. August 1906 found Furness complaining to Ripon that the government were giving way unduly to Socialism. He resented the I.L.P.'s antagonistic attitude towards employers and their contempt for the doctrine of interdependence between capital and labour. His was in part a plea for the Liberal 'balance of society' view, but it had implications for government intervention (on one side or the other) in the labour market.[24] In 1907 the Workmen's Compensation Act, applying to seamen, dissatisfied two prominent Liberal shipowners, Russell Rea in parliament, and Sir Walter Runciman outside. New socialist activity in the summer of 1907 caused Joseph Walton to write anxiously to Campbell-Bannerman of the activity of the I.L.P., ' a great impact is being made ', and he accurately forecast the switch among the miners to the Labour party. He offered to contribute £100 to a special fund to be established to counteract ' Socialist misrepresentation and fallacies '.

The year 1908 saw the eventual appearance of the Miners' Eight-Hours Bill (Gladstone having set up a Departmental Committee under Russell Rea in July 1906, to investigate the economic effects of an eight-hour day upon production, wages, employment, and the export trade). The Committee reported the average working week underground to be a fraction under 50 hours, and forecast a reduction in hours worked of some 10 per cent (although for hewers only 6 per cent), and an estimated drop in the annual output of coal by 26 million tons. The introduction of machinery and a multiple shift system would partly mitigate lost production, and the rise in coal-costs would not necessarily be serious.[25] The main argument ranged over whether the resultant fall in output (which nobody challenged) would lead either to a fall in wages or to an increase in prices. Gladstone, who had declared at one stage that he had ' had to figure in Parliament [since 1906] as the only critic of the proposal ', now discovered opposition to have grown. Amongst the Liberals, Lupton thought the bill would reduce output by a fifth, Clifford Cory, a coal-owner, was completely opposed (as were Sir Walter Runciman and

---

[24] CBP, Add. Mss 41225, Ripon to Campbell-Bannerman, 9 September 1906 (Ripon quoting Furness): ' The Liberal party aim at legislating for the WHOLE people, and not for a class. We do not seek to upset the entire social order, but rather to so adjust the balance as to promote the well-being of the people as a whole, the stable prosperity of our country, and a righteous national attitude towards the other peoples of the world.'

[25] *Final Report of the Departmental Committee on the Miners' Eight-Hour Day*, Part 1 (1907) Cd. 3505, xv.

A. E. Pease), while large coal-consumers like Kitson and Furness were worried about the possible increase in their costs. Upon the Liberal side, the arguments against were almost exclusively economic, but the Conservatives did indulge more in individualistic arguments against intervention.[26]

In February 1908, Gladstone introduced a bill to secure an average working day of eight hours from bank to bank with one winding time included, which was to come into force on 1 January 1909. By June he admitted that he had come under considerable pressure, not only from the Coal Consumers' League, who were forecasting increased prices of up to 2s per ton, but from numerous deputations of managers and owners.[27] Accordingly, Gladstone now proposed that the bill incorporate a transitional period to allow a basic working day of eight hours with time added on for both winding times. This, it was thought, would cut by half the actual drop in hours worked, and was supported both by Enoch Edwards and, on behalf of the owners, by Ratcliffe Ellis. It would operate for a five-year period when the original bill would come into operation.

The Bill was supported by both Arthur Markham and Sir Charles Maclaren, both with coal interests in the Midlands, but Russell Rea, although declaring his support in principle, now declared himself fearful as to the repercussions in British industry following cost increases. In December, to a wrecking amendment moved by the Conservative Viscount Castlereagh, ten Liberals voted in support.[28]

This measure was the apparent reason for Alfred Pease detailing to Herbert Samuel his profound dissatisfaction with Liberal domestic policy (although he also disliked old-age pensions); he felt the government were sacrificing ' the principles and traditions ' with which Liberals like himself had always been identified:

The idea that the State can take from one class and give to other classes and take the place of individual enterprise is a very corrupting one, and goes to the root of human relationships. At present we are reaching a

---

[26] For example: Parl. Deb., 4th Series, Vol. 190, C1394–5, 22 June 1908 (Lyttleton): ' I say in principle the interference of Parliament ought to be jealously restricted to (the powerless, weak and unorganised).'

[27] Cf. RP, Add. Mss 43518, Ripon to Asquith (copy) 19 March 1908: ' The coal-owners are obviously trying to alarm the consumers . . . I strongly deprecate any signs of weakness on the second reading.' (Asquith, ' entirely agreed '. 19 March 1908.)

[28] H.C. Division lists, No. 439, 1908. The ten were: Sir C. Cory, H. Cox, Sir C. Furness, J. M. Paulton, R. Armitage, C. W. Bellairs, J. A. Bright, D. Davies, A. Lupton, E. A. Ridsdale.

condition when the bulk of the population are being taught that though those above them in the social scale have learnt that they must exercise self-restraint, prudence, thrift . . . in order to succeed in life . . . they may marry when they like, have as many children as they like, shall have their families provided with food, education, with work, with free this, that and the other, the right to have employment, the right to have a certain wage, the right to have their hours of work state-fixed, and the right to have pensions from the State. Beyond this then is the divorce of common interests that results from all this interference with social life.[29]

By 1907, the Home Office was examining the proposal to establish wages-boards in certain sweated industries. In 1907, before he (as Governor-General) went to South Africa, Gladstone recommended that the government commit itself to the principle of the minimum wage in such industries, and assent to the second reading of George Toulmin's bill to establish trade boards for that purpose. Neither Gladstone's suggestion nor a similar report in 1908 from the Committee on Home Work were, however, taken up. Not until Churchill visualised wages-boards as an element in the central organisation of industry was a bill drafted – and by the Board of Trade. Briefly, it provided for the establishment of trade boards in four sweated industries, possessing the power to establish district committees which might fix a minimum wage on the basis of a minimum time-wage.[30] Although Churchill himself saw the Boards as ' a centre of information ' and hoped they would ' become the foci of organisation ', it seems fair to say that the government's hesitancy in this instance was indicative of their uncertainty in intervening too directly in the industrial field. By way of comparison, mention might be made of the Coal Mines (Safety) Bill of 1911 which drew upon the Report of a Royal Commission on the Mines set up in 1907 and which found evidence of widespread negligence in the observance and enforcement of safety regulations. The government showed considerable alacrity in promoting this bill of 123 clauses which imposed new and considerable responsibilities upon owners and management in the fields of health, safety and the prevention of accidents, and increased the factory inspectorate allotted to the newly-formed Mines Department of the Home Office to enforce them. It was, perhaps, significant that where a thorough case for legislation could be adduced on

---

[29] HSP, A/155 (iii), A. Pease to Samuel, 14 and 19 August 1908.
[30] The four trades included 200,000 workers, of whom 140,000 were women and girls. In 1913, the Act was extended to a further five trades (170,000 further workers).

such social (and expirical) grounds as these, and where a precedent for legislation so clearly existed, the Liberals displayed a greater willingness to challenge established views. By 1912, this act too was being accused of saddling coal-owners with yet another increase in costs.[31]

LABOUR AND THE INDUSTRIAL ISSUE

While precedents were established in the sphere of industrial regulation, trade union opposition to the existing market economy grew in coherency, and also in bitterness. Wages were fast declining as a proportion of total income. Whereas in 1900, wages had formed 41·3 per cent of total income, by 1913 they had fallen to 36·2 per cent. In 1909–11, real wages were less than 90 per cent of the levels attained in 1899–1900.[32] Only in textiles had wages, in money terms, shown any appreciable tendency to rise. In coal-mining, wages had appreciably fallen.[33] Meanwhile, wholesale prices, which had been falling in the 1890s, were rising steadily after 1906, and wage-earners, who spent some 70 per cent of their income on necessities, food and clothing, clearly stood to lose the most from these relative price movements.[34] While wages remained relatively static, so did hours – the average working week remained between 55 and 60 hours for most trades. Once again, however, it was unemployment, touching 8 per cent in 1908 and 1909 which the trade unions ' persist in putting forward . . . as the most important problem that can be considered '. First, because it put a strain upon their funds; from 1896 to 1906 the unions had distributed 21 per cent of their total income in unemployment benefit, and between 1900 and 1910 such benefits amounted to £4 million. Secondly, because unemployment was affecting the skilled virtually as much as the unskilled, although it was the latter who most caught

---

[31] R. S. Churchill, *W. S. Churchill*, Vol. 2, pp. 423–4. The 1911 Shops Bill might also be adduced as an example of the extensive nature of Liberal social legislation. Originally this bill contained provisions for a weekly half-holiday for shop assistants, limits to hours and overtime enforceable by government inspectors, Sunday closing clauses and provision for seating, ventilation, sanitation and reasonable meal-times for the assistants. But so much opposition ensued that Churchill could only secure the general passage of the weekly half-holiday and a general upper limit of 60 hours per week, but with inadequate enforcement.

[32] Figures from S. Pollard, *An Economic History of Great Britain 1914–50* (1962) pp. 24–5.

[33] *Thirteenth Annual Abstract of Labour Statistics of the U.K. 1907–1908*, Cd. 5041, cx, p. 58.

[34] *Fifteenth Annual Abstract* (Cd. 6228, cvii) p. 138.

the eye.[35] Thirdly, the remedy was seen to lie increasingly in the field of state expenditure and 'construction', and amongst all trade unionists, whether Labour or Liberal, the uniformity of view was apparent. In 1906, the T.U.C. had declared to its members that ' we must no longer be content to fight for a living wage, which is measured by the iron-bound law of supply and demand. We want something even beyond. The demand should be for a higher standard of living.' [36]

The T.U.C. was blaming unemployment upon the unchecked spread of machinery, and on unnecessary overtime working. Aggressive capital, in its drive towards cheaper production, had proved itself unmindful of a worker's (physical) minimum requirements. The unions disliked the growing number of Employers' Associations [37]; specific unions, such as the engineers, distrusted the spread of piecework, the speeding-up of work, and the introduction of machinery. The evidence to the Poor-Law Commission submitted by the T.U.C. Parliamentary Committee contained all these points. In his statement, W. C. Steadman said:

Goods are produced for profit irrespective of demand, the consequence being that there is, at points, over-production, which in turn leads to confusion and displacement. This evil is intensified by the increased introduction of labour-saving machinery, without adequate reduction of hours of labour or increased remuneration of the workers. Moreover, as an effect of this new machinery, youths at lower rates of wages are substituted for skilled craftsmen, thus decreasing the economic efficiency of labour, and consequently the area of employment.[38]

The statement further blamed unemployment upon an absence of proper training, the absence of regularisation schemes, the discharge of young men at an early age, systematic overtime in many trades, and rural depopulation. The effects were a loss of spending power due to poverty, physical and moral deterioration. Remedial proposals should be directed towards stabilising the demand for labour, improving its productive efficiency, and hence its wages and spending capacity.

[35] Parl. Deb., 5th Series, Vol. 4, C640, 30 April 1909 (Hodge) and W. Beveridge, *Unemployment*, p. 21. Also Cab. 37/96, No. 143, 3 November 1908.

[36] *The Times*, 4 September 1906.

[37] By 1907, there were 72 national associations of employers, and 698 local trade associations in England and Wales.

[38] *Royal Commission on the Poor Laws, Minutes of Evidence*, 1910, Cd. 5066, XLVIII, p. 241.

As to the nature of the proposals, however, two views here obtained. One saw the basic problem of unemployment as resulting from the unequal distribution of wealth. In aggregate, sufficient wealth was being created for everyone, therefore, ' the creation of more employment is not absolutely necessary as a means of solving the problem '.[39] A greater equalisation of the existing wealth produced, bolstering the spending capacity of the poor, would go far towards creating a more stable demand for commodities, and hence for labour. Cyclical fluctuations could then be met by short-time instead of dismissals, and by maintaining a system of reproductive, public works in reserve.

The second view put a greater emphasis upon state expenditure, in order to add to the productive resources of the country. It saw unemployment as the inevitable offshoot of the existing competitive system – a structural defect within a capitalist organisation which could not be remedied purely by redistribution alone. Clynes, for example, doubted the efficacy of insurance payments in this context. ' It would be far better to use your money so that [a] man by his work should make wealth than that you should pay him to remain idle. You are driven into these measures of mere relief by the force of circumstances.' [40]

' The shortage of employment should be made up by state intervention ', and both Clynes and O'Grady inclined to such schemes as the Development Commission for the permanent involvement of the state in industrial expansion.

This type of division was a familiar one within the period. (It was to occur again in the argument between the single-taxers and the land nationalisers over the extent of development schemes.) The distinction was between those who favoured the redistribution of existing wealth and those who looked to the state for assistance in the positive creation of more wealth. It is hard to associate any group (in particular, either socialists or trade unionists) with one view or the other. Often, it seemed, an inclination towards reconstruction, where the state either took over, or actually created new industries, such as afforestation, depended on one's relative proximity to, and awareness of, orthodox economic arguments. Hence practical trade unionism which had been involved with the ' primacy of capital ' and the

---

[39] Ibid. p. 276 (evidence given by J. Ward in respect of the Report on Unemployment submitted by the Labour party).

[40] Parl. Deb., 5th Series, Vol. 21, C597, 10 February 1911.

'importance of production' arguments, might be inclined to doubt an explicitly socialistic emphasis upon the virtues of nationalisation, but from their own experience of low wages and their knowledge of under-consumptionism, the redistribution of income by means of a progressive taxation system would have seemed a more plausible alternative to prevailing economic determinisms.

In a real sense, the choice confronting the trade unions paralleled the dilemma of the Social Radicals – how to achieve the broadest enactment of a minimum throughout society without offending against the economic dictates governing society's progress. There was a similarity between trade unionism, concerned with eliminating immediate problems affecting its members in their search for economic security, and Liberal-Radical willingness to extend state responsibilities upon empirical and utilitarian grounds. Unions and Radicals alike found themselves in a dilemma in that their principal theoreticians, Sidney Webb and J. A. Hobson, while fully acknowledging the demand for economic equality and social justice, required unions and Radicals in their turn to acknowledge that all reform depended upon their ability to increase the efficiency of the capitalistic system. By 1906, it is possible to claim that any argument which took as its premise, 'produce more to get more', was suspect to Radicals and to the unions; to the Radicals, because they opposed the waste and inhumanity within modern society, and to the unions because they now feared the implications of any 'production-style' argument. Hence, at the particular point in time at which the principal social evils were winning recognition as economic in character, the two remedies which claimed to be the specific economic means to reform were both in doubt. Private, capitalistic production for profit because it involved too great a social cost, and public, state-organised production for use because (again at that stage of time) it completely lacked any coherent or generally creditable explanation of its own proposals. Hence trade unionists and Radicals were prepared to place their greater emphasis upon what seemed to them to be the more attainable views of Webb and Hobson, in which the demand for social minima – for safety, in health, education and housing, and at work, the demand for minimum levels of income, the creation of social safety-nets – became the overriding goal, a goal which private producers saw as economically unjustifiable, and which socialism treated as a palliative.

OSBORNE — A CATALYST

While the conditions of Labour deteriorated, certain unions had experienced further trouble in the courts. In South Wales, the Miners' Federation by 1905 faced a bill of over £57,000, having lost a court action against their employers' claim for compensation in respect to production lost through miners' 'stop-days'. In the West Riding, labour relations were embittered between 1902 and 1905 by a series of court cases of which the Denaby Main case was probably the best known.[41] In Northumberland and Durham, socialist activity amongst the miners in the aftermath of the 1903 Barnard Castle by-election steadily weakened the standing of the Lib-lab leadership. In particular, the socialists were able to use the lever of declining wages and the case for the minimum against the sliding-scale and the Burt-Wilson argument for industrial harmony.[42] There can be little doubt that legal and economic insecurity were powerful factors contributing to political decisions of some significance; the South Wales miners' support for affiliation with Labour in 1906, the affiliation of Northumberland in 1907 and Durham in 1908 to the M.F.G.B., and the majority amongst the M.F.G.B. in 1908 for affiliating to the Labour party.

A combination of economic insecurity and a new sense of political strength after 1906 may also have provoked the initial stirrings of labour unrest. In 1906, for example, the A.S.R.S. drew up a national programme for England and Wales demanding a standard eight-hour day for all railwaymen, overtime at time-and-a-quarter, and adequate provision for rest-days. Following the refusal of the companies either to recognise or to negotiate with the union, a ballot amongst the A.S.R.S. revealed a majority of 9 to 1 in favour of a strike, whereupon Lloyd George intervened, in 1907, to establish new negotiating machinery which, in effect, delayed the strike for four years.[43]

The only major strike in 1907 was amongst the Belfast dockers under Larkin, but the period of industrial peace was abruptly ended

---

[41] Cf. F. Bealey and H. Pelling, *Labour and Politics 1900–1906* (1958) pp. 223–9.

[42] R. G. Gregory, *The Miners in Politics in England and Wales 1906–1914*, Oxford D.Phil. thesis (1963) pp. 68–9 (since published).

[43] This machinery consisted of a central board for each railway elected from the local or sectional boards which in turn incorporated representatives of all grades. All boards were based on the principle of equal representation between employers and employees. Disputes were to be referred upwards, and ultimately, if either party requested it, to independent arbitration.

in 1908 when 897 disputes were recorded. The G.F.T.U., which between 1899 and 1907 had spent only £35,500 on strike benefits, now spent £137,000 in this one year.[44] 1909, despite two long strikes among the engineers and the shipwrights on the north-east coast, showed some deceleration in the strike-rate, although a national coal strike was only narrowly averted when Smillie and the M.F.G.B. backed the Scottish miners in their refusal to accept a cut in wages. The dominant impression, however, remained one of uncertainty.

In these circumstances, the Osborne decision restraining the use of railway union funds for political purposes, came as an added aggravation at a critical moment. Through the efforts of the Anti-Socialist Union, the decision was speedily extended to a series of unions; by 22 August 1910 13 unions had been restrained by injunctions from directly financing any political activity, and 16 Labour M.P.s were affected.[45] A joint board from the G.F.T.U., the T.U.C., and the Labour party issued a statement claiming that:

The decision denies the right of Trade Unions to carry out their nominal statutory purposes of ' regulating the relations between employers and employed ' in so far as modern conditions of industry and the highly organised state of capital render Parliamentary action necessary for this purpose.[46]

Labour claimed that the payment of M.P.s would solve only a part of the problem for in the immediate future it was not national, but local Labour politics that would suffer. As Ramsay MacDonald pointed out, an injunction debarred a union from giving aid to local trades councils and to Labour members of town councils. Trade-union branches would have to withdraw from education, Poor-Law, housing and other reformist committees (except in a voluntary capacity); even union-financed deputations were debarred, and the Parliamentary Committee of the T.U.C. was itself in an ambiguous position. While it was admittedly true that trade unionists were under a compulsion to contribute towards the payment of a Labour member, they nevertheless benefited from any advance that trade union and political labour were together able to secure. MacDonald demanded that the government give an undertaking to bring in a bill for the payment of M.P.s, or else Labour would vote against the

44 *The Times*, 5 February 1909.
45 *The Times*, 22 August 1910.
46 *The Times*, 23 August 1910.

budget.[47] On 10 November 1910, a special conference of the three main Labour bodies decided that the repeal of Osborne should be a test question for all candidates at the coming election. In the Commons on 18 November, Asquith promised the payment of M.P.s 'next year', although this did not satisfy the Labour M.P.s who clamoured for their 'civil rights'. On 5 October, however, the chief whip, Elibank (A. O. Murray), had already informed Lloyd George that MacDonald had agreed 'to an understanding, after the passage of payment of M.P.s ... that he and his friends should give general support to the Insurance bill '.[48]

In October 1910 members of the Cabinet circulated their views in a series of memoranda. J. A. Pease and Haldane thought any legislation should take the form of allowing the trade unions to specifically establish a political fund to which any unionist who wished to do so might contribute (i.e. contract-in). Samuel and Sydney Buxton, on the other hand, thought the unions were the proper bodies to organise independent labour representation, and to find such funds as were needed. These two accordingly favoured contracting-out. Loreburn and Carrington both visualised the solution in terms of payment to members (the others had considered this an ancillary solution only), while Runciman was opposed to any reversal of the Osborne judgement. He thought the number of trade unionists opposed to a political levy 'form undoubtedly a large majority, and so far as they are concerned, the reversal of the judgement means coercion and taxation, which they are very likely to resent at the polling-booth '. He believed a struggle with socialism in the constituencies to be inevitable, and considered it foolish to give the socialists command of a ready income of £100,000 a year. He advocated a policy of 'standing up to the Socialists ',[49] and was not without support in the Cabinet, for Asquith wrote to him: 'There is, as you say, some danger of our weaker-kneed brethren giving thoughtless pledges in regard to the Osborne judgement ' before the government had announced its policy.[50] Possibly Asquith was mindful of a resolution which had reached him from the Scottish Liberal Association expressing a desire ' that

---

[47] Memo from Ramsay MacDonald (n.d.) in LGP, C/5/11/1A. *The Times*, 11 November 1910. For the fullest account, W. Gwyn, *Democracy and the Cost of Politics* (1962) ch. 7, Gregory, *The Miners in Politics*, Appendix 1.

[48] LGP, C/6/5/5.

[49] All memoranda are within Cab. 37/103.

[50] Runciman papers (General Correspondence), 25 September 1910.

the Government will uphold the law as defined in the Osborne judgement, so as to safeguard the political liberties of Trade Unionists '.[51]

Liberal opinion certainly opposed the element of compulsion involved in the Labour party's pledge to uphold the party constitution and policy, and accordingly welcomed the modification of the Labour constitution in 1911.[52] The Trade Union Bill, first introduced in May 1911 and eventually passed in 1913, defined a union as an industrial body and allowed it the right to carry out any industrial activity for which its rules gave it authorisation. Specific political objects which needed a separate political fund to finance them now required both the assent of the majority of the union's members (by ballot), and the authorisation of its new rules by the Chief Registrar of Friendly Societies. Labour, in general, disliked the bill,[53] while the Conservatives sought rather to criticise the immunity conferred in 1906 upon trade unions. They opposed union money being used to finance socialist propaganda, and in 1912, they tried to insert a clause which would have made a union liable for any libel it might commit in its corporate capacity in the course of a political action, and for which its political funds (although not the general benefit funds) would be liable.[54]

Within the Labour movement, opinion varied as to the extent of opposition to the political levy, and, in fact, opinion may well have been more evenly divided than was indicated by the overwhelming defeat Osborne's supporters received at the 1910 T.U.C.[55] A more useful division might be made between the economic views which Osborne expressed and those of the majority of the trade union movement. Osborne may have struck a responsive chord amongst trade unionists when he asked that the movement concern itself with ' purely Trade Union work ', but his ideas of just what that work was

---

[51] AP, Vol. 23(b).

[52] E.g. Rufus Isaacs, Parl. Deb., 5th Series, Vol. 26, C921, 30 May 1911.

[53] Cf. Clynes: ' There is the foolish impression that this Bill was offered to us by the Liberal Government. The reverse is the case. This Act represents the most we could abstract from them.' (Roberts, *A History of the T.U.C.*, p. 258.) But Brace thought the bill ' worth having ', and he recorded his ' appreciation of the services rendered to the Labour Party . . . by the Attorney-General '. (Parl. Deb., 5th Series, Vol. 47, C1726, 27 January 1913.)

[54] *Ibid*. Vol. 47, C1092, 27 January 1913.

[55] An anti-Osborne resolution was carried by 1·7 million votes to 13,000 (*The Times*, 16 September 1910) but when the unions balloted in 1914 over the adoption of political action and political levies, up to 16 January 1914, 25 ballots had taken place, 473,880 men had voted in favour of adoption, and 323,613 against. (*The Times*, 20 February 1914.)

were clearly outdated. Broadly, he believed in the older Lib-lab conception of industrial harmony, in combining wholeheartedly in the production of wealth. He opposed the idea of the minimum wage and believed the 'right to work' to be impracticable because it implied a divorce between the provision of work and the incentive to work.[56] The British Labour Party which was founded by A. E. Beck to expound these principles, and which claimed 200,000 affiliated members in 1911, proved an abject failure;[57] Lib-labism was evidently not the creed of the new generation of trade unionists. E. R. Pease, for example, produced a Fabian pamphlet which rejected 'harmony' through profit-sharing or co-partnership schemes as, in essence, a palliative founded on 'the permanent continuance of the antithesis between employer and employed'. Such schemes (and he instanced that of Furness) were simply an employer's device to solve the problem of industrial relations in his own interest and upon his own premises. They hindered industrial combination, split up trades into privileged sectors, too rarely gave the employees any participation in management, often required them to buy shares out of their wages and so prevented increases in production being reflected in rises in real earnings, and finally, forbade industrial action upon a scale wide enough to raise standards of work and pay within a whole industry.[58] And trade union emphasis after 1910 fell increasingly on organisation and amalgamation, the industry-wide agreement and national programmes to strengthen class and economic ties. This was not merely the prerogative of the advocates of direct industrial action, it was also the message of the Webb's *Industrial Democracy*, the proper defence of the normal day and the standard rate, the policy of the national minimum and the collective raising of the margin.[59]

TOWARDS THE MINIMUM

1910 was itself a year of continual pressure upon the government and their domestic programme receded into the background. In February a group of Radicals led by Belloc, Pickersgill, Wedgwood,

[56] W. V. Osborne, *Sane Trade Unionism* (1913) pp. 168–72.

[57] *The Times*, 20 February 1911. The party intended ' to secure direct parliamentary representation, not in antagonism to capital, but as a joint partner with capital, demanding equal right and equal voice '.

[58] E. R. Pease, *Profit-Sharing and Co-partnership : A Fraud and a Failure ?*, Fabian Pamphlet No. 170 (1911).

[59] This was re-expressed by J. H. Greenwood in 1911, *The Theory and Practice of Trade Unionism*, Fabian Socialist Series No. 9.

Pirie, Spicer, Martin and Hemmerde, were pressing the Cabinet to
deal stringently with the Lords, but the Cabinet were divided and
Asquith's authority evidently suffered.[60] Both Radicals and Labour
were awaiting the National Insurance Bill, and the political initiative
lay with the Conservative party which, under Bonar Law, re-
emphasised tariff reform. In 1911, the only two significant Radical
revolts came over Murray MacDonald's motion to reduce the military,
and G. H. Roberts' motion to reduce the naval estimates, when 37
and 27 Liberals respectively voted in support.[61] John Burns, however,
in a debate upon Poor-Law administration managed to provoke a
small group of Radicals into rebellion by referring to the Majority
Report as ' somewhat archaic ' and to the Minority Report as ' somewhat obsolete '. He argued instead in favour of general mixed workhouses under Boards of Guardians.[62]

Insurance had been long in the making,[63] and as with pensions in
1908 and the land clauses in 1909, was evidently difficult to cast into
legislative form. It was originally intended that unemployment
insurance should be brought forward in 1910 but circumstances
prevented this, and health and unemployment were jointly presented
in 1911. Some jealousy was apparent between the two exponents,
Churchill and Lloyd George, the latter accusing the former of pur-
loining his ideas in 1908, and of confining ' his labours ... to deliver-
ing an elaborate speech in the House of Commons '. Lloyd George
was contemptuous of the Unemployment Bill as drafted by the Board
of Trade, ' a hopeless indefensible muddle ', and this evidently
prompted him to ask for complete and overall control of the insurance
programme in the Commons.[64] In the event, and despite the unpopularity of its compulsory contributions amongst trade unionists, despite
the criticism of Belloc and Cecil Chesterton that the measure would
undermine the independence of the working class, and despite the
Webbs' opposition to the unconditionality of unemployment benefits,
the unemployment provisions received a relatively quiet acceptance
in the Commons, evidence perhaps of how much opinion had been
prepared by the debates of 1906-9. Labour and Radical opinion saw
the entire bill, but especially the unemployment provisions, as
a further recognition of state responsibility for modern industrial

[60] A. C. Murray, *Master and Brother* (life of Elibank) (1945) pp. 39f.
[61] H.C. Division Lists, Nos. 70 and 71 (1911).
[62] Parl. Deb., 5th Series, Vol. 24, C2035, 27 April 1911.
[63] See Gilbert, *The Evolution of National Insurance*, pp. 268f.
[64] Lloyd George to Elibank, 17 April 1911, Elibank papers, Mss 8802.

conditions – Sydney Buxton voicing the idea that the employer should contribute something to the expenses of the trade in which he was interested. The bill was 'a humane investment', a practical recognition of the interdependence of modern industry.[65] It demonstrated the advance in opinion: 'if the bill had been introduced ten years ago it would not have found . . . a single supporter from either of the front benches'. In part, however, it was a choice between partially satisfactory legislation and none at all, a point well expressed by Ramsay MacDonald:

I am afraid this is a type of bill of which in the years to come we are to have a good many examples. We are going to have large measures of social reform abounding in clauses and rich in detail, and it will become more and more difficult for any group of men in this House to say that as a whole they accept a bill.[66]

Health insurance aroused much more opposition, the Conservatives giving a certain amount of organised direction to the campaigns variously waged by the friendly societies, insurance companies and the doctors to modify the bill. The Conservatives were, in fact, so successful in whipping-up opposition to the compulsory principle within the bill that by-election results showed a strong anti-Liberal reaction and Asquith confessed that 'no doubt the Insurance Bill is (to say the least) not an electioneering asset'.[67] The Conservatives even managed to link the workman's fourpenny contributions under the Act to the grant in 1911 of £400 salaries to M.P.s, in a highly slanderous attack upon Lloyd George.[68] Bonar Law announced early in 1912 that the Conservatives would repeal National Health Insurance, and only retracted this under pressure from Austen Chamberlain's supporters.[69] Walter Long described the Insurance Act as 'vital' to the Conservative recovery of 1912; in particular, he wrote: 'Lloyd George had lost popularity with the business Liberal' and was moving too fast for him.[70] Conservatives referred to the opinions of Sir Charles Macara, the leading Lancashire cotton magnate, a Liberal and a strong free-trader, that the effect of the unemployment 'tax' upon the cotton trade 'would be far worse than

[65] Parl. Deb., 5th Series, Vol. 26, C281, 24 May 1911.
[66] Ibid. Vol. 32, C1433, 3 December 1911.
[67] Gilbert, The Evolution of National Insurance, p. 396.
[68] Cf. Liberal Magazine, March 1912, p. 100.
[69] Gilbert, The Evolution of National Insurance, p. 397.
[70] Long to Bonar Law, 8 March 1912, Bonar Law papers 26/1/76.

anything tariff reformers proposed or are ever likely to propose ', and any increase in the cost of production would undermine ' the slender margin ' on which British cotton supremacy depended.[71]

There would seem to be little doubt that the Conservatives were able to capitalise to a large extent on both the Insurance Bill and upon payment of members, the latter measure arousing a great deal of controversy amongst the constituencies, and a surprising amount of opposition amongst local Liberal notables. Bonar Law was strongly in favour of abolishing the payment of members.[72] This being so, it seems unlikely that the Liberals obtained any short-term benefit from either of these two measures, or indeed, from the Parliament Bill which also took so much time and energy in 1911. By 1911-12, the Liberals were fighting upon two distinct fronts, against a Conservative opposition that found increasing electoral fuel in attacking Liberal legislation from orthodox premises, and against the growing intransigence of both labour demands in general, and the particular demands made by powerful unions, the suffragettes and the land reformers. Amidst this complexity of issues it was scarcely surprising that the Cabinet was showing considerable signs of strain. Lloyd George was ill in 1911, Grey and Runciman were reportedly exhausted, Asquith's authority was continually questioned, usually unsuccessfully, and the parliamentary machine was no longer running so smoothly.[73] In sum, Liberalism was itself under strain in both parliament and the country, and the escalation of Labour unrest prevented any respite. Social unrest, in general, convinced the Conservatives of the importance of their regaining power, and gave added spite to the parliamentary conflict.

The Times had noted in 1910 that ' the working-classes are possessed with the notion of a *minimum wage* '.[74] The T.U.C. had been turning to this notion since 1908; in 1909 they asked for a 30s minimum for adult government workers in London, and in March 1910, Ramsay MacDonald moved for public employers to provide conditions of service equal to those of the best private employers. Haldane was most conciliatory, and Buxton suggested that a committee then sitting under Sir George Askwith (head of the Board of

---

[71] Parl. Deb., 5th Series, Vol. 32, C1495-6, 3 December 1911.

[72] See Long to Bonar Law, 30 June 1914, Bonar Law papers, 33/1/1, and Bonar Law to Cockerell, 26 July 1913, 33/5/47.

[73] See A. C. Murray's Diary, Mss 8814 for 29 November 1911. Also Haldane MSS 5923, f. 7.

[74] *The Times*, 11 August 1910.

Trade's labour conciliation machinery) to examine wages in public employment be empowered to deal with all matters regarding fair wages, a suggestion which satisfied Labour.[75]

The first debate upon the 30s general minimum wage took place on the 26 April 1911, but only Chiozza Money gave Thorne, for Labour, support in his emphasis upon the decline in working-class purchasing power due to higher rents and rising prices. For the government, H. J. Tennant favoured the 'free play of economic forces to settle the rate of wages', and thought to legislate for the minimum would be 'in defiance of economic law'. The Conservatives took a highly deterministic view of the minimum e.g. Lord Hugh Cecil: 'it is perfectly evident that less than a living wage cannot be paid', for a labourer would always receive just what he was worth, as measured by his equilibrium market price.[76]

This debate was marked by a speech from Steel-Maitland which shed some light upon contemporary views to government intervention. Having pointed out that a general minimum would confound skill differentials, raise costs, and pay attention neither to the varying cost of a labourer's subsistence, nor to the special circumstances of the old, boys and inefficient labour, he declared he had no objection in principle to the legal regulation of wages if it was based in 'real business' foundations.[77] To Thorne he said:

We both of us have given up the old theory that the State should no longer interfere in any way with industry at all. That has been relegated to the rubbish basket. But one thing equally necessary is when you have got the whole of the complex phenomena of modern life, if you are going to give up the old policy of non-interference, you have got to analyse the conditions and inquire into the difficulties, and if this scheme is to affirm a principle you have got to show that you have realised those difficulties and that you are ready to meet them.

The issue of the minimum found its fullest outlet in the mines where discontent was rife, seemingly fostered in the north-east by the introduction of the eight-hours act and the consequent change from a double to a treble shift system, and in South Wales, by another adverse legal decision in 1907 which declared that payments to hewers as 'consideration money' for work in abnormal places were *ex gratia* and had no legal foundation. In South Wales, where seams were poor, and miners working in abnormal places were under

[75] Parl. Deb., 5th Series, Vol. 14, C1340, 8 March 1910.
[76] *Ibid.* Vol. 34, C109, 15 February 1912.   [77] *Ibid.* Vol. 24, C1096.

pressure to cut enough coal to secure a reasonable living wage, the accumulated bitterness erupted in the Cambrian Combine strike, which began in September 1910 and was prolonged, ultimately without the support of the M.F.G.B., until August 1911 – a strike which marked the final passing of Lib-labism as a political and economic reality in South Wales. In October 1910, the annual conference of the M.F.G.B. made the living wage for abnormal areas a national question, but the owners, despite two joint conferences in September and December 1911, continued to stand upon the principle of 'a fair day's work for a fair day's wage'. At their annual conference in 1911, the M.F.G.B. demanded a minimum wage based upon the district average rate, and threatened a strike if the owners refused to treat. The December conference having proved unavailing, a strike ballot in January 1912 revealed a majority of 4 to 1 in favour of a strike. The M.F.G.B. settled on the principle of 5s a day for adult workers and 2s a day for boys, with specific rates to be negotiated within the districts. Upon this point, the coal-owners were themselves split – the owners in Wales, Scotland, Northumberland and Durham alone standing out against the ' 5 and 2 '.[78] On 29 February 1912, on the eve of the projected strike, Asquith called both sides to the Foreign Office where he accepted the need for ensuring that the miners, ' with adequate safeguards ', earned ' a reasonable minimum wage ', and proposed district conferences with government arbitration to reach a solution.[79] The miners, however, would only accept the offer if the schedules [80] they had drawn up were recognised as a national basis for negotiations. Despite 60 per cent of the coal-owners being in favour, those from Wales, Scotland and the north-east refused, and a strike ensued.

D. A. Thomas, on behalf of the Welsh owners, attributed the strike to political causes, to ' the dominance of Socialist and Syndicalist doctrines ' amongst the miners, a reference to the *Miners Next Step*. Lord Joicey from Northumberland explained that the owners could not afford higher wages. Wages already took from 60–70 per cent of every £1 of income; only 6s–8s were left to cover capital

[78] R. P. Arnot, *The Miners – Years of Struggle* (1948) pp. 57–80.
[79] *Daily News*, 4 March 1912. Asquith's promise to the effect that ' we shall not allow the standing-out of a minority of coal-owners to interfere ' with an acceptable national settlement, was later interpreted as a pledge to secure the 5 and 2, and was a factor in the miners' later accusations of betrayal.
[80] The Schedules were a set of wage-rates related to the circumstances of each coalfield which treated the ' 5 and 2 ' as the norm and did in fact drop below it in a few cases, such as the Forest of Dean.

charges and depreciation; profits he estimated at 5 per cent.[81] C. B. Crawshaw wrote to Runciman:

The men's demands in our case would mean an addition to the cost (of wages per week ?) of between £8,000 and £9,000, that is, providing that the same quantity of coal is got per man as is got today, which would not be. The tonnage would go down very considerably, and consequently the standing charges would be enormously increased.[82]

L. E. Pilkington, of the Haydock Collieries in Lancashire, forecast a drop in the Company's dividend from 5¼ per cent to ½ per cent if the minimum were granted. The owners in particular hoped that Grey, Runciman and McKenna would be strong enough to prevent Asquith giving way to Lloyd George.[83] Labour emphasised that the ' 5 and 2 ' represented ' rock-bottom rates ', and W. E. Harvey claimed 100,000 miners were receiving less than 5s a day. The first fortnight in March was occupied with attempts to get the government to incorporate either the ' 5 and 2 ' or the schedules within their bill, and Radical opinion supported Labour. *The Daily News* and *The Manchester Guardian* both urged the government to include some figures in their bill, and give a real basis to the living wage.[84] The government's original draft did, in fact, contain a penal provision against employers who paid less than the ' 5 and 2 ', but this was felt to be ' one-sided ' and was dropped.[85]

The party, however, did contain opposing views. A. C. Murray recorded that there were ' strong objections amongst our moderate and business Liberals ' to the insertion of the ' 5 and 2 ' in any bill, and talked of ' a strong feeling against giving way on this point '. C. E. Hobhouse persuaded A. C. Murray to get as many Liberals as possible who took similar views to sign a letter to Asquith expressing their opposition to legislation for the ' 5 and 2 '. Such a letter was, apparently, sent, and according to A. C. Murray, referring to 26

---

[81] *The Times*, 1 March 1912.

[82] Runciman papers (Mines) 18 March 1912. Crawshaw was a colliery owner and the representative of the West Yorkshire coal-owners' association.

[83] Crawshaw to Runciman, 11 March 1912 (*ibid.*). *The Yorkshire Post*, 18 March 1912 quoted Lloyd George as saying that if the Welsh coal-owners refused to get coal, it would be for the government to go in and get it themselves.

[84] *Daily News*, 23 March 1912: ' The Bill itself must be made acceptable to the miners, the modesty of whose demands at this stage is beyond question.' *Manchester Guardian*, 23 March 1912: ' If we admit legislation we have a sufficient case for the adoption of this particular minimum.' Any omission of the ' 5 and 2 ' would ' stultify their own bill ' (25 March).

[85] AP, Vol. 6, Asquith to George V (copy), 20 March 1912.

March, the final day of deliberations upon the miners' minimum wage bill ' proved very useful at this morning's Cabinet '.[86]

The bill which Asquith introduced ' with great reluctance ' on 19 March established district wages-boards to fix minimum rates subject to local conditions, which were to have regard to the regularity and efficiency of the work done. They were to settle the general minimum rate and the general district rules and would have power to subdivide or amalgamate their districts, and to vary rates and rules. They would have equal representation between employers and employees, and an independent Chairman with a casting vote. Asquith was, he said, ' asking Parliament here to make a legislative declaration of the principle of a statutory minimum wage ',

it is presented to Parliament as a provisional and ... experimental measure to meet a special emergency in regard to a particular class of workers working under peculiar conditions in one great industry. It does not purport to lay down any general principles. It is quite possible for anybody to support this bill who holds, as I hold, that it is very undesirable for Parliament to fix wages. It is quite possible also for anyone to support this bill who holds, as I believe many I see sitting there (indicating the Labour benches) hold, that anything in the nature of compulsory arbitration is unnecessary.[87]

For the Conservatives, Bonar Law expressed distrust of the measure, but could offer no alternative solution, beyond a tentative approach to compulsory arbitration. Lord Robert Cecil mentioned co-partnership, otherwise the Conservatives retailed tales of syndicalism and forecast the closing of pits. For Labour, Ramsay MacDonald ' regretted ' the bill, but thought there should have been figures included, and Enoch Edwards ' resented ' government interference. Amongst the Liberals, Sir C. Cory accused the government of acting prematurely, and Asquith of ' inciting ' the miners by telling them that he considered their case ' in every way justified '. Sir Alfred Mond preferred an early warning system of arbitration. Sir Edward Grey thought that ' a door has been opened with regard to the minimum wage which cannot be closed again '. Henceforth, he said, the struggle would not be for the principle of the minimum, but over the right of the state to investigate the conditions of a dispute in order to decide what was just and reasonable.[88]

[86] A. C. Murray Mss 8814, pp. 70–3.
[87] Parl. Deb., 5th Series, Vol. 35, C1732, 19 March 1912.
[88] Ibid. and 21 March, C2097.

On 21 March, the Cabinet, with Grey, Haldane, Runciman and McKenna in alliance, decided against including any figures in the bill, but Lloyd George was absent from this meeting, and the next afternoon he lobbied in favour of the '5 and 2' and persuaded Asquith to call another Cabinet. The original decision stood, however, largely on the necessity of preserving local flexibility in negotiations.[89] The same afternoon, with the bill in committee, a Labour amendment to insert the '5 and 2' won Radical support from P. W. Raffan, Whittaker, Leif Jones and Atherley-Jones, before being withdrawn. A further amendment to insert a full schedule of rates into the bill was defeated by 367 votes to 55, but 17 Liberals voted in the minority.[90] A third amendment to prevent the subdivision of districts found 32 Liberals in support out of 65.[91]

On 25 March, the government made another prolonged attempt to get the owners to accept the '5 and 2', but were unsuccessful, and without the owners' full support the government would not insert the figures as they still had no assurance that the men would then return to work, although Whitwell Wilson reported in *The Daily News* that 'there seem to have been ministers prepared to take the risk'.[92] Also on 25 March, the Radicals held a meeting under Sir J. H. Dalziel, which produced a deputation to Asquith led by Mond, Leif Jones, Rowntree and Chiozza Money to ask for the '5 and 2'.[93] On 26 March William Brace's amendment for these figures went to a division and was beaten by 326 to 83, but the minority included 47 Liberals, and 'the whips kept tight hold on every safe member'.[94] To another amendment by Brace requiring that in settling a minimum rate, a district wages-board should not fix a rate of wages below the average daily rate of the class of workman concerned, the government were again dependent on Irish and Conservative support. The amendment was lost by 271 to 101, but 64 Liberals voted against the government.[95]

[89] Asquith to George V (copy), 22 March 1912, AP, Vol. 6 and Runciman papers, Cabinet Note dated 21 March 1912.

[90] H.C. Division Lists, No. 49, 1912.

[91] H.C. Division Lists, No. 51, 1912 (Labour claimed that to subdivide the districts would weaken the bargaining power of the M.F.G.B.).

[92] *Daily News*, 26 March 1912. *Manchester Guardian*, 26 March 1912 reported that to insert the '5 and 2' would mean the resignation of at least two 'important' ministers.

[93] *Daily News*, 26 March 1912.

[94] *Daily News*, 27 March 1912. H.C. Division Lists, No. 56, 1912.

[95] H.C. Division Lists, No. 57, 1912.

The bill did produce a settlement to the dispute, most men being back at work by mid-April, but the government in the event gained little credit. Complaints afterwards continued from the miners that the ' 5 and 2 ' principle was being neglected by the district boards, and these were endorsed by the miners' conference in 1912. Asquith showed no disposition to intervene further.[96] While some Labour leaders had disliked intervention at the time, the employers later blamed the government for giving encouragement to inflated wage demands, and for allowing the miners' national programme to override local difficulties. ' If you were not our M.P.,' wrote Crawshaw to Runciman, ' I would not vote Liberal at the next election. I consider Asquith and others have been frightfully weak.' [97] The bill provoked a new outcry against the uneconomic living or minimum wage, and added to the demand for steps to be taken to curb the power which combination placed in the hands of irresponsible men.[98] The Shipowners' Parliamentary Committee expressed ' grave alarm ' at the injury done to collective bargaining, and forecast an unwelcome rise in costs and prices.[99] That there was some substance in the fears of the effect of this precedent upon other industries appeared from *The Railway Review*: ' To realise the full meaning of the miners' strike, and to prepare ourselves for such changes in our theory and practice of economic doctrine as it implies, ought to be our first duties ',[100] while the bill found support amongst the Radicals: ' The minimum wage bill embodies the boldest assertion of the right of society to regulate the wage-bargain that has been made in modern England '.[101]

The Nation and *The Railway Review* both agreed that this was the ' clearest challenge ' to the commodity view of labour. The bill demonstrated again the degree to which the Radicals were prepared to support legislative intervention in industry, and it raised, as Grey had intimated, the entire issue of the government's responsibility for ensuring and preserving industrial peace.

THE STATE AND INDUSTRY

The issue now was two-fold; not only the extent of any intervention (for there were few after 1910 who disputed the need), but the matter

---

[96] Arnot, *The Miners*, pp. 119–20.   [97] Runciman papers (Mines), 2 April 1912.
[98] Cf. J. Macaulay, *Effects of Trade Disputes* (Newport, 1912).
[99] Runciman papers (Mines), N. M. Farrer to Asquith (copy), 21 March 1912.
[100] *Railway Review*, 15 March 1912.   [101] *The Nation*, 23 March 1912.

of on what ground and on whose terms should intervention be based i.e. to maintain trade or to secure for the men a minimum wage? In the event, the Liberals relied on the formula, 'for the good of the community', which rarely satisfied either side.

Industrial conciliation had been based upon the principle of the joint board, which could impose an obligation to collective bargaining upon employers from without, by providing the services of an independent arbitrator. Following the government's interventions in the coal strike of 1893 and the boot and shoe stoppage of 1895, the Conservatives had passed the Industrial Conciliation Act of 1896, in which power was given to the Board of Trade, upon the application of both parties to a dispute, to appoint either an Arbitrator or a Court of Arbitration. The Board might also, upon the application of either party, appoint a single conciliator, and without any application at all, might appoint an investigator, or promote, upon its own initiative, Boards of Conciliation. Certain trades, such as mining, and the railways after 1907, had their own scheme of arbitration, and in 1908 the Board of Trade, seeking to remove the suspicion which attached to single arbitrators, made provision for a type of Industrial Court consisting of three (variable) members chosen by the disputants from three permanent panels of workers, employers, and neutral persons. By 1911, however, this latter scheme had only been invoked some 20 times, and overall, the number of disputes settled through the conciliation machinery had risen little in ten years, from 708 in 1901 to 1,087 in 1910.[102]

Amongst Labour, strikes and unrest after 1910 were attributed both to specific causes, rising prices, rents, and to more general long-term factors.[103] The strikes were hailed in historical terms as the culmination of working-class solidarity, the rejection of economic orthodoxy and of always being the buffer between profit-margins and fluctuating prices. As the strikes were now in a time of prosperity, so they were strikes from a growing position of strength, and in the capability for sympathetic action which the men exhibited, their concern with the issue of non-unionist labour, the issue of management rights, and the increasing identification by the trade unions of their own

---

[102] *Fifteenth Annual Abstract*, p. 156.

[103] J. R. MacDonald, *The Social Unrest* (1913) p. 53. In 1901–10 there was an aggregate loss of income by wage-earners of £100,000 a week. Not until 1912 did the total wage-bill paid out by industry exceed that paid in 1900. Also M. S. Reeves, *Round About a Pound a Week* (1913); A. L. Bowley, *Livelihood and Poverty* (1912).

problems with the greater problems of society, there was perhaps a real basis of truth in these claims. Certainly amongst the younger men and the new leadership, the impact of new ideas, and of education in general, marked a complete rejection of Lib-lab theories of harmony and capital–labour interdependence. ' Higher moral demands and a quickening appreciation of social idealism have been contemporary with increased poverty and a loss of confidence in the justice of the social order.' [104] The ' New Trades Unionism ' after 1910 showed a strong preference for extending the traditional emphasis upon voluntary collective bargaining from district to national level. In 1910 those covered by national collective agreements numbered 2·4 million, and by 1913, 3 million. The T.U.C. evidently feared that any move towards compulsory or obligatory arbitration might weaken the spread of collective bargaining, and with it the power of trade unions to alter industrial conditions. After 1906, the T.U.C. regularly defeated ' hardy annual ' motions favouring the introduction of compulsory arbitration. In 1911, the T.U.C. opposed a bill promoted by Crooks, Henderson, Barnes and Fenwick to enforce a 30-day period of notice before a strike could take place, although this bill was trying to improve the existing voluntary system by compelling negotiation before a strike. In 1912, Ramsay MacDonald's bill, seeking to give voluntary agreements between masters and men in the Port of London a legal basis, received equally little Labour support, although MacDonald too disbelieved in the suitability of legal intervention in the labour market and favoured wages-boards only for unorganised labour.

This distrust of state machinery was puzzling to Liberal Radicals. ' The steady refusal of the bulk of the socialists in this country to consider seriously state compulsory arbitration, or any public interference with the liberty of private war between capital and labour in the several trades, is a curious commentary upon their conception of socialism.' [105] The reason partially involved organised labour's growing distrust for any machinery whose justification sprang from othodox premises. Snowden, who did favour compulsory arbitration, seemed to regard state wage awards as a means of overcoming the obstinacy of employers, and of overcoming their economic determinism. ' A thing that is morally right can never be economically

---

[104] MacDonald, *Social Unrest*, p. 57. Also E. H. Phelps-Brown, *The Growth of British Industrial Relations* (1960) p. 313.

[105] *The Nation*, 28 September 1912.

wrong ',[106] he wrote of the miners' strike in 1912, which was exactly the point at issue between the progressive and the orthodox.

The argument for the incorporation of trade unions and the legal enforceability of collective agreements was only an undercurrent within this period, being recommended in passing by the Majority Report of the 1894 Labour Commission, and whose logical implications were mentioned by Sir William Robson in 1906 as an argument *against* incorporation. As business discontent developed after 1910 with the labour unrest, so the argument grew for enforcing full responsibility for their actions upon the unions, for example, by the legal attachment of their funds (a remedy rejected by the Industrial Council, see below).

The widespread striking in 1910 amongst the transport workers, seamen and dockers, the repetition in 1911, the sporadic outbursts of violence culminating in a national railway strike in August 1911, provoked a strong demand amongst employers for some limitation of union freedom, either by the repeal of the Trade Disputes Act or by a measure of compulsory arbitration. Sir James Joicey referred to the Disputes Act as 'a legalised form of intimidation ',[107] while in October 1911, a group of Conservatives, Banbury, Bathurst, Cripps, Craik and Rawlinson, introduced a bill for the repeal of the Act.[108] Previously, employers had been apt to encourage conciliation and arbitration only when a specific item, such as wages, was at stake, and where an arbitrator might be given specific criteria on which to base his decision. After 1910, however, the very intangibility of the issues, the vexed questions of picketing, the employment of non-unionist labour, and the implied threat to the prerogatives of management, brought a demand for certainty in the negotiation and enforcement of decisions made.[109] The apparent inability of the Labour leadership to control their followers was especially galling, and caused frequent allegations of sinister socialist or syndicalist influences.

---

[106] *Daily News*, 5 March 1912.
[107] *The Times*, 1 June 1912.
[108] See also *Report of the Unionist Social Reform Committee on Industrial Unrest* (1914) introduction by F. E. Smith, and R. V. Sires, 'Labour Unrest in England 1910–1914 ', *Journal of Economic History*, September 1955.
[109] The threat to management, and its implications, was probably as fundamental as the challenge from the minimum wage: e.g. *The Report of the Royal Commission of the Railway Conciliation Scheme of 1907* (1911, Cd. 5922, xxix, paragraph 52) stated: ' We think that with their great responsibilities the (Railway) Companies cannot and should not be expected to permit any intervention between them and their own men on the subjects of discipline and management.'

In the summer of 1911, Sir Charles Macara proposed a scheme for an Industrial Court for the settlement of labour disputes. The scheme involved the creation of a new department under a permanent, non-political chairman, with an advisory body drawn from employers and employees in the most prominent positions in the staple industries of the country. In any dispute seriously affecting these industries, the advisory body could recommend that the dispute be referred to a special impartial tribunal to be established by the department, whose decision, however, would not be binding. The intention of the procedure was to provide a period for the debate and publication of grievances, which, it was hoped, would prevent industry-wide strikes, and the resultant industrial and public inconvenience.[110] The scheme was widely supported amongst businessmen, and also by a group of nine Labour M.P.s, including Barnes, Bowerman, Macdonald, Henderson, Hodge, Hudson, and Clynes.[111]

In July 1911, Sir G. Askwith prepared a memorandum for the Cabinet on the labour unrest, which contrasted the decline in real wages with the rising returns to capital since 1897, and placed a great deal of blame upon ' the publicity of private luxury '. He remarked on the spread of sympathetic strike action, ' the rapidity and success of [this] movement amongst the transport workers, and the readiness with which the better-organised trades, such as miners and railwaymen, show a disposition to give support '.

Askwith also attributed unrest to the growth of propagandist influences, and to a lack of economic security, inducing ' the unorganized men, who are worst off and have least to lose ', to move with ' unexpected spontaneity and unanimity '. He too sought to place the upheavals in perspective:

It looks as though we are in the presence of one of those periodic upheavals in the labour world such as occurred in 1833–34, and from time to time since that date, each succeeding occurrence showing a marked advance in organisation on the part of the workers and the necessity for a corresponding change in tactics on the part of employers.

He stressed the effect of a ' transitional period ' – the decline of the moderating influence of Lib-labism and the rise of new ideas as to organisation and industrial action:

[110] Sir C. W. Macara, ' The Proposed Industrial Court for the Settlement of Labour Disputes ', *Financial Review of Reviews*, October 1911.
[111] A List of Supporters exists in the Asquith papers, Vol. 92, f. 173.

The Victorian theories as to Capital and Labour have become obsolete, but no settled body of doctrine has taken their place. There is therefore a disposition to try to see things from the point of view of the workman, and to wonder not that he is discontented, but that he has remained patient so long.[112]

The events of August prodded the Cabinet towards action. In a debate on labour disputes on 16 August, Austen Chamberlain demanded protection for the individual and for the community's lawful business. He condemned the ' civil war ' in Liverpool, and asked that the government consider the possibilities of arbitration.[113] Ramsay MacDonald in turn wished that the government would take a less stilted attitude towards the issue of law and order, and the passage of a House of Commons resolution requesting that the employers agree to negotiate in the national railway strike was a further indication of whither opinion was tending.

Sydney Buxton now submitted in a memorandum that the dominant feeling was that industrial disputes could no longer be left solely to the two parties concerned. There was a need for machinery which would operate swiftly and automatically to forestall strikes, and he drew attention to the practice of New Zealand, where there was an obligation upon both sides to refer a dispute to an industrial tribunal which had the power to make a binding award, and to Canada, which required the examination of a dispute before a stoppage took place. Circumstances in the U.K., which favoured ' elasticity of machinery ', were he felt, very different, and compulsory arbitration would be too great an abrogation of the system of ' arbitral awards ... resting solely on moral sanctions '. He rejected Macara's idea on the grounds that it would be inadvisable to set up an independent tribunal outside of political control which might well prove inflexible, while if there were any grounds for one side to doubt its impartiality, there would again have to be provision for the Board of Trade to intervene.

Buxton admitted that the political significance attached to the Board of Trade itself was a handicap, and he suggested the delegation of the Board's responsibility for action in any particular case to an Industrial Commissioner, who would be responsible to, but not under the immediate control of the Board. He would in fact, work within an industrial office at the Board, with the help of an advisory

112 Cab. 37/107, No. 70, 25 July 1911.
113 Parl. Deb., 5th Series, Vol. 29, C1948.

council. Buxton further proposed to appoint 24 Industrial Commissioners, 12 from each side of industry, under the chairmanship of the Industrial Commissioner. Although the latter would be a permanent official, and would assume the responsibility for the working of the Board's conciliation machinery, the 24 would be unpaid, and would assist only in an advisory capacity.[114]

The scheme was put, most cautiously, to representatives of the masters and the workmen, and this Industrial Council was established in October, along with a separate Industrial Department under Sir George Askwith. In an introductory speech, Asquith himself was careful to point out that the Council was 'not a panacea for trade difficulties', but 'should have the greatest possible elasticity of action'.

The Council will not interfere with the freedom of action of the employers or the employed. But what we do believe is that, if the Council obtains and retains the confidence of the country, it will come more and more to be considered the proper, the right, and the natural course in the case of a dispute.[115]

The scheme had a mixed reception – the Council had attracted the support of leading employers and of moderate Labour men like Henderson, Bowerman, Wilkie, and the Lib-lab Burt, but it was denounced by others, such as Thorne, who saw it as an attempt to gag the militants.[116] Meanwhile in the same month, Asquith received a memorial from the Employers' Parliamentary Council signed by 65 associations of employers blaming the Trade Disputes Act of 1906 for the unrest, and asking for the restraint of picketing, for sympathetic strikes to be declared illegal, and for the repeal of the 1906 Act.[117] Asquith refused to grant a committee of enquiry, but on 30 November a report from a Special Commission of the London Chamber of Commerce also asked for the repeal of the 1906 Act, the effective maintenance of law and order, and full protection for those willing to work. Such representations continued into 1912. On 12

---

[114] Cab. 37/107, No. 98, 9 August 1911.

[115] *Liberal Magazine*, November 1911, p. 665.

[116] The opinion of some employers was also sceptical (G. Askwith, *Industrial Problems and Disputes* (1920) p. 180) but the government did persuade some powerful industrialists to sit on the Council. These included Sir Hugh Bell (iron and steel), Sir G. H. Claughton (railways), J. H. C. Crockett (boot and shoe), T. L. Devitt (shipping), Alex Siemens (engineering), Ratcliffe-Ellis (coal), Macara (cotton).

[117] From a parliamentary question on 30 October 1911 (Vol. 30, C529).

March the Association of the Chambers of Commerce asked for a government enquiry into the Trade Disputes Act and into picketing.[118] In June (and coinciding with the Transport Workers' strike in the Port of London) the Association sent a deputation to Asquith to ask for four points to be considered: the financial responsibility of unions, the prevention of intimidation, compulsory arbitration, and schemes for co-partnership and profit-sharing. Asquith, who was known to have been much annoyed by the unsuccessful intervention of no less than five Cabinet ministers in the Port of London dispute, and the resultant bad publicity,[119] tried hard to strike a conciliatory note:

I entirely subscribe to the view ... that it is extremely undesirable that a Government as a Government should concern itself in industrial disputes. It is not and it ought not to become a part of the function of any Government that those who are responsible for administering affairs ... should be expected, as it were, to assume the part of conciliators or arbitrators for the nation at large.[120]

A government should adopt ' a normal attitude of complete detachment and impartiality ', unless ' the general interest of the community ' was imperilled.

Asquith's own predilection for avoiding continual intervention found support from Buxton who pointed out that although the public would probably support stringent action to preserve industrial peace, any move by the government to bring in compulsory arbitration would provide Labour with good grounds for demanding that the state ensure for them a proper wage and minimum working conditions. The power to strike remained essential for the men, and he was of the opinion that the wage-claims were usually justified, and even more might, no doubt, be justly claimed.[121] Both Buxton and Sir George Askwith urged that the men's current successes were coming from the very spontaneity of their actions, and from the failure of the employers to appreciate the force and the determination of the men's position.

In April 1912 the government established a small Cabinet Committee including Lloyd George, Haldane, Beauchamp, Buxton and Mackinnon Wood to enquire into the possibility of improving indus-

118 C. Watney and J. A. Little, *Industrial Warfare* (1912) pp. 287–8.
119 G. Askwith, *Industrial Problems and Disputes*, p. 231.
120 *Liberal Magazine*, July 1912, p. 350.
121 Cab. 37/110, No. 62, April 1912.

trial relations. The evidence they heard confirmed the view that the trouble, although stemming from economic insecurity, was being aggravated by the accumulation of smaller issues involving privation and injustice. There was still no agreement on a solution, the only common element being a demand for a greater initiative from the Board of Trade.[122] The government's chief advisers, Mitchell and Askwith, were both disinclined to favour any show of force by the government, although Askwith was now coming to believe in the feasibility of following the Canadian example of ' prior warning '.[123] The Cabinet, however, could come to no agreement. In the Port of London strike, Lloyd George and Haldane ' inclined to favour ' legislation, ' either to make the rates of wages recognised in representative agreements compulsory in regard to all persons employed in the port ', ' or to give power to the Port Authority to fix a scale of wages from time to time '. Asquith, for one, disagreed, recording that there was ' a considerable diversity of opinion ' in the Cabinet which subsequently decided that there was no case for legislation.[124]

Instead, it was decided to send Askwith to Canada to investigate Canadian conciliation machinery, and meanwhile, on 14 July, to ask the Industrial Council to investigate two questions; first, what was the best method of securing the due fulfilment of industrial agreements and, secondly, how far, and in what manner, industrial agreements made between representative bodies of employers and of workmen should be enforced throughout a particular trade or district?

While the Cabinet was debating these issues, Radical opinion inclined again towards the minimum wage. In a debate upon the address in February 1912 16 Radicals voted for Ramsay MacDonald's motion for a minimum,[125] and there was within this debate a three-fold clash amongst Liberals, between the advocates of co-partnership, land-reformers (notably single-taxers) and under-consumptionists – it being the latter who were most in favour of the minimum. This was followed by the divisions over the Miners' Bill, and by Radical opposition to the attitude of Lord Devonport, chairman of the Port of London Authority, and the shipping employers in June and July. On

---

[122] Evidence to the Cabinet Committee on Industrial Unrest, 24 April and 1 May 1912, copy, LGP, C/21/1/12.

[123] Cab. 37/110, No. 63, April 1912.

[124] AP, Vol. 6, Asquith to George V (copy), 12 June 1912. Lloyd George and Samuel favoured legislative action (LGP, C/7/9/2).

[125] H.C. Division Lists, No. 1, 1912.

23 July 1912 a Labour motion calling for government intervention in the Port of London drew support in the lobby from 21 Liberals.[126] This pattern recurred within the much disputed Railways (No. 2) Bill, introduced on 4 December 1912, to allow the railway companies to increase their rates to recoup themselves for increased labour costs resulting from the 1911 settlement. To a Labour amendment to introduce a minimum wage of 21s a week for all railway servants, 48 Liberals voted in support,[127] Munro-Ferguson for one declaring that he was 'much more in sympathy with the proposal to raise the scale of pay of any low-paid labour than I was in favour of the minimum wage in the case of miners'. He even went so far as to say, 'I believe we shall have to fix a minimum wage in the towns at something like 25s '.[128]

Such statements may well have played a part in shaping the Cabinet's views upon the minimum wage in the land campaign. Certainly, it was the prospect of Lloyd George's land campaign which, in 1913, drew the sting from Radical criticisms of the government's handling of the industrial situation. The number of Radicals supporting the minimum wage on 13 March 1913 fell again to 16,[129] and the only further revolts came in February 1914 when first 19 and then 20 Liberals joined with Labour in criticising the introduction of martial law in South Africa, due to labour unrest, and the government's handling of the labour unrest in Dublin.[130]

The movement of advanced, and specifically Social Radical, opinion in the year of 1912 may be judged best from a memorandum submitted by an influential group of Liberals to the Cabinet Committee. The Group launched an unofficial enquiry of their own into three related questions – the minimum wage, 'the further organisation and development of the industrial resources of the country', and the relief of the trading classes from some of the burdens pressing upon them. Those questions, the Group believed, were 'necessary

---

[126] H.C. Division Lists, No. 157, 1912.

[127] H.C. Division Lists, No. 599, 1912–13.

[128] Parl. Deb., 5th Series, Vol. 48, C817–8, 11 February 1913.

[129] H.C. Division Lists, No. 4, 1913.

[130] H.C. Division Lists, Nos. 2 and 7, 1914. Allowance must be made for the fact that from July 1912 to August 1914, there was no major strike in England. 1913 saw an extensive minimum wage demand in the Midlands, and the Transport Workers' strike in Dublin. Unemployment fell to 2·1 per cent in 1913 amongst trade unionists. There had also been a fall in weekly hours, and in the first nine months of 1913, a marked upward tendency in wages and a slight fall in the wholesale price level. Cab. 37/118, No. 19.

parts of a Liberal and democratic policy, aiming first at the relief of conditions plainly intolerable to a civilised community, and secondly, at the raising of the standard of national efficiency '. They hoped that what had been done already in the way of wages boards and the Coal Mines Act would be a precedent for the railways and the transport industries, and would thereby ' impose upon the Government direct and special responsibilities both for large bodies of workers and for traders, and also for the efficient conduct of vital public services '. They asked for the acceptance of ' the general principle of a living wage for every worker ', and for the extension of the wages boards to agriculture, for the nationalisation of the railways, and their treatment as ' national highways ', for agricultural development and land reform (including a site-values tax).[131]

By December 1912 Askwith had given a definite recommendation in favour of the Canadian Industrial Disputes Act,[132] but the government did not act, partly because the Industrial Council's Report was not yet ready. When it did appear in July 1913 it expressed a faith in the existing voluntary machinery, in collective bargaining relying upon the ' strong moral obligation ' felt by both sides to preserve agreements, and, despite recording that a considerable number of witnesses favoured monetary guarantees or penalties as a method of enforcement, the Report considered such schemes to be impracticable. However, it did recommend that the conciliation machinery could be improved if it inculcated as a matter of course ' some independent determining authority ' with the power to decide points of interpretation and with the means of ' arriving at finality '. The Council recorded widespread support for a ' cooling-off ' period, possibly, they suggested, of 30 days from the notification of the grievance to the stoppage of work. They did note that motives on either side of industry varied with regard to such suggestions, the employers wishing simply to limit the strike weapon, especially the sympathetic strike, the unions wishing to limit the employment of ' blackleg

---

[131] *Labour Unrest and Liberal Social Policy*, 20 May 1912 (Confidential), copy, LGP, C/21/1/17. Signed by H. W. Massingham, J. Rowntree, J. A. Hobson, L. T. Hobhouse, P. Alden, B. S. Rowntree, E. R. Cross, A. S. Rowntree.

[132] Cab. 37/113, No. 137, 31 December 1912, Report on the Industrial Disputes Act of Canada (1907). The Act applied only to the staple industries (mining, rail, shipping). The government required that any dispute had to be submitted to a Board of Arbitration, with a view to arriving at a settlement before a strike or a lock-out could occur. If either party took industrial action while the Board was still sitting, they were liable to be sued for damages by the other party.

labour'. Hence it was agreed that neither side should give aid to persons in breach of an agreement.

Regarding the spread of agreements, majority opinion amongst both witnesses and Council favoured making an agreement as wide as possible, but agreements were better based upon the facts of organisation and collective bargaining, than upon the principle of legal enforceability. They suggested that agreements made between the majority of employers and employees in a trade or district might be extended by their asking the Board of Trade for an independent enquiry as a preparatory step to such an extension. The Board might appoint, for example, the Industrial Council itself to supervise the conditions and the spread of collective agreements. There was, finally, every motive for this spread, for it was where sections of a trade remained outside an agreement, particularly if that section indulged in competitive practices, that instability and uncertainty of economic conditions provoked one side or the other to break an agreement.[133]

The Report's interest lay also in the fact that 13 out of 14 employers sitting on the Council signed separate memoranda requesting an enquiry into the Trade Disputes Act – a fact stressed by the Association of Chambers of Commerce in January 1914 when they again asked Asquith for a formal judicial enquiry into the Act's working.[134] 1913 saw continual agitation by Macara's 'non-party' Employers' Parliamentary Association for the 'material amendment of the Insurance Act'.[135] In his Presidential Address in January 1913 Macara claimed that 'leaders of industry are realising more every day the imperative necessity for protecting industrial interests against hastily-conceived or ill-considered legislation'.[136] In April he condemned the Insurance Act as 'the thin end of a wedge which threatens to make serious inroads into the profits of employers, which everybody knows in normal times run upon fine margins'. 'There is a great objection to the taxation of industrial employers exclusively as such.'[137] In September, another organisation, the U.K. Employers' Defence Union, was formed. It also claimed to be non-political, but was pledged to maintain the rights of the individual employer and

[133] *Report of the Enquiry into Industrial Agreements*, Cd. 6952 (1913) xxviii.
[134] *The Times*, 17 January 1914.
[135] *The Times*, 20 December 1911, for the origins of the Association (which was a body distinct from the Employers' Parliamentary Council).
[136] *The Employers' Parliamentary Association – First Annual Meeting*.
[137] *The Times*, 28 April 1913.

employee against intimidation and threats. This union aimed at the creation of a fund of £50 million for its purposes, and at its formation, it already had two guarantees worth £50,000 each.[138]

By 1914 the Liberal Land Campaign and the decline in the number of strikes were together diverting attention from the industrial scene. Although criticism of the government continued, the impulse behind the demand for Compulsory Arbitration had been largely removed.[139] Buxton intimated that he was considering a bill on Industrial Disputes ' next session ' (i.e. in 1915), but ' even if (compulsory) legislation were so forced through, the passive or active resistance it would meet with would make it practically inoperative and ineffective '. Buxton apparently intended to act upon the Industrial Council's Report in favour of the extension of agreements under the auspices of the Board of Trade, and in regard to conciliation, he intended to introduce the cooling-off period favoured by the Council (and by Askwith) with possible powers for the Board of Trade, upon the Canadian lines, to conduct an authoritative investigation of the dispute before any stoppage could take place.[140] The T.U.C. in 1913 had, in fact, rejected suggestions for the use of penalties and/or the legal enforceability of agreements, but in 1914 all the signs were that any further industrial unrest would have pushed the Liberals into legislation, and such unrest was indeed forecast for the autumn of that year.[141] In January 1914 the railwaymen, now reorganised in the National Union of Railwaymen, demanded full union recognition, a 48-hour week and a 5s rise for all grades. J. H. Thomas, acting with the implicit support of the miners and the transport workers within the newly-formed ' Triple Alliance ' threatened a general strike as from 1 November 1914. This was a clear warning to the Cabinet, which had already told the Royal Commission on the Railways not to concern itself with conditions of employment and work. Tillett meanwhile warned Lloyd George that without some conciliation machinery in London's docks, violence was likely.

IN RETROSPECT

Enough evidence is available to suggest that far from the Liberal concern for social politics slackening after 1911 through their pre-

138 *The Times*, 3 October and 25 September 1913.
139 Smith, *Unionist Policy*, preface.
140 Cab. 37/118, No. 14, 23 January 1914.
141 Roberts, *The T.U.C.*, p. 268.

occupation with Home Rule and Welsh disestablishment, the opposite may have been the case i.e. the traditional issues were simply debts which had to be honoured while social and industrial reform remained the major theme. A fair assessment must also recognise Liberal legislative difficulties. They were called upon to provide time for at least four unlooked-for measures, the miners' minimum, the Railways (No. 2) Bill, and bills for the reversal of the Osborne and Gibson Bowles judgements.[142] In 1912, they were called upon to find time for the Scottish Land Act that had failed in 1907, for women's suffrage, and for their own Plural Voting Bill. Each possessed its claimants, and mention might also be made of the growing time needed for foreign affairs, the navy and the estimates. The Mental Deficiency Bill, introduced in May 1912, met systematic obstruction from Josiah Wedgwood and did not become law until August 1913.[143] Finally, much of 1913 was mortgaged to the issue of land reform, while 1912–13 witnessed the struggle to translate the Insurance Act into reality, necessitating an Insurance Amendment Act in 1913.

The government after 1910 had advanced considerably in establishing precedents for direct intervention within industry, and the idea of wages boards and a minimum wage, begun in 1909 and extended in 1912, was confirmed in the land campaign of 1913–14. The appeal to the social or community interest permitted the government to invoke its latent powers to enforce settlements within the industrial sphere. The need for such intervention was now widely admitted – the Conservatives had become too deeply involved in the debate upon Arbitration not to be aware of the empirical justification at least.[144] All intervention was necessarily tentative, for it was, after all, only 20 years since Rosebery's initial intervention in the coal strike of 1893, and the Liberals were not only reluctant to assume a central responsibility for economic and industrial affairs, but feared too to

---

[142] In 1913, Gibson Bowles gained a court decision that it was illegal to collect income-tax solely on the strength of a Commons resolution.

[143] Wedgwood protested against the ' compulsory segregation of the unfit ' at the discretion of the local authorities, whereby a County Council committee was given the power to certify and to detain the mentally ill, including children, without the parents' consent; there was to be no right of appeal against a doctor's decision. Wedgwood allied himself with extreme Conservative individualists, Banbury, Bull and Robert Cecil, in opposing the Bill. (Parl. Deb., 5th Series, Vol. 41, C703, 19 July 1912.)

[144] *Report of the Unionist Social Reform Committee*, p. 5, ' It is uncontestably the right and duty of statesmanship to supervise and control the conditions of employment in the interests of the State as a whole '.

give any indication of partiality. At all stages between 1910 and 1914, the Cabinet was in the invidious position of relating uncertain theory to confused and increasingly dogmatic practices, without having either a clear body of precedent or an established body of opinion upon which to rely. They were dubious of creating machinery which implied a continuous commitment and desire to intervene, and in this they were removed from their Radical wing. The Cabinet, in interpreting the traditional virtues of a balanced society and responsible government, preferred the analogy of an umpire, one who gave decisions when appealed to, to that of a referee, one whose discretionary authority obligated him to continual action. This theory of industrial harmony certainly declined as the union movement had greater cause to question a productive process and a social order dominated by the emphasis upon capital. There can be little doubt that the Labour rejection of co-partnership, the trade union encroachment on territory which the 'harmony' concept had long reserved for management alone, and union policies for the restriction of hours and overtime, were interpreted as in the nature of a threat to the system's continuance by all those entrepreneurs who inclined to the 'self-evident' view within orthodox economics.[145] Similarly, paternalists, who also found themselves attacked as sappers of the power of organised labour, were discovering that they had miscalculated the gulfs appearing between capital and labour after 1910. Neither the operation of social responsibility within the national labour market nor the example of social duty within the single firm proved capable of bridging the gulfs of experience between one side of industry and the other.

The advocates of industrial harmony and the paternalists both attacked the unions for their sectionalism and for mistaking their function. There was an evident sense of disappointment amongst Social Radicals and reformers that trade unionism had appeared so negative in regard to policy, demanding social reforms and new rights for labour with which Radicalism fully acquiesced, but apparently failing to make any contribution itself towards their attainment. *The Nation* could not discover 'any large, insistent public policy' amongst the T.U.C. programmes.[146] Charles Booth thought 'Trade Union policy has been too narrow; aimed too

---

exclusively at amount and method of remuneration '. Trade unionism had done ' nothing for the creation and little if anything for the
wider distribution of wealth; it has rarely aimed at increasing the
efficiency of Labour '.[147] By 1914, even the Webbs seemed to think
that trade unionism was failing in its wider services to ' the well-
ordered Democratic State '. At some date between 1910 and 1914, the
Webbs wrote: ' Trade Unionism must be judged, not by its results
in improving the position of a particular section of workmen, but by
its results in permanently raising the efficiency of the nation as a
whole.' [148]

Yet Booth was only partly right, for union horizons were
admittedly widening, and *The Nation* could applaud that ' the collective labour employed in a factory . . . is beginning to demand a
status, a vested interest in the conduct of the business, in the shape
of a stable tenure of employment upon reasonable terms of pay '.[149]
The Times had admitted that nationalisation was ' not a chimerical
proposal ', and the N.U.R. in 1914 declared that nationalisation must
secure for railwaymen ' their full political and social rights '. The
proposal, it seemed, was on the verge of practical politics. When the
Railway Nationalisation Society was formed in 1907, Clem Edwards
was president and over a score of Liberal M.P.s were positively in
favour.[150] The unions formulated demands for both railway and
mines' nationalisation after 1910 (this being an emphasis distinct from
the socialists' abiding commitment) which were opposed by the
Cabinet on economic grounds. Sydney Buxton did not see how the
government could assume a responsibility for closing down unprofit-
able mines, thereby creating unemployment, nor how new mines
would attract the necessary risk capital without continuing to pay
high dividends.[151] Asquith thought railway nationalisation would
produce two conflicting demands: for lower fares and rates, and
from the employees for higher pay and shorter hours; the state was
not the proper body to make such a choice.[152] There was, however,
a keen appreciation of the implications of the contemporary course
of events. Radicals like Charles Buxton were increasingly worried
over the potential irresponsibility of big business, and Lord Farrer

---

[147] C. Booth, *Industrial Unrest and Trade Union Policy* (1913) p. 5.
[148] Webb Trade Union Collection (L.S.E.) Coll. E, Section B, xi, f. 35.
[149] *The Nation*, 31 January 1914.
[150] *Financial Review of Reviews*, November 1907.
[151] Cab. 37/110, No. 62.
[152] AP, Vol. 89, Minutes of a Trade Union Deputation, 12 February 1914.

in 1910 considered that the pressing question of the future would involve the government's relations with 'enormous concentrations of capital'.

The real question is why did Radicalism within the Liberal party, and trade unionism, apparently differing little in essentials, display so hesitant a face to one another before 1914? In part, the answer might lie within the Radicals' growing pre-occupation with land reform as a panacea for industrial ills, and in part with the recurring difference between a purely empirical affinity with the need for reform and the more urgent motivation which sprang from personal experience. The answer might also be seen to lie within the conflicting interpretations of the minimum. Whereas the unions desired above all economic security, and where Labour as a whole demanded that legislative regulation be carried over into the sphere of hours and wages and the provision of work, the Liberals and Radicals baulked. The Radicals had indeed voted for the minimum wage as a first charge upon industry, but from their arguments, they were voting both for the principle and for the under-consumptionist criticism of low wages, rather than for any specific figure. The Radicals, in common with the entire Liberal party, still believed in the basic factors of supply and demand governing prices and costs within a competitive economy. They were more closely aware of the financial limitations upon social progress, and they stressed that 'constructive social reform' was a function of the real increase in national wealth.[153] No reform involving expenditure was justified unless it could be shown to lead either to the further creation of wealth, or to the more productive utilisation of existing wealth. In the final analysis, social reforms and social goals could not stand by themselves, and the trade union's apparent inability to satisfy the criteria of efficiency and industrial harmony demanded of them as the precondition to all reform made Radical support a conditional affair. The Radicals disbelieved in the full logic of private production, but they refused to accept that any change in the formal organisation of industry (i.e. nationalisation) could change the economic principles upon which it functioned.[154]

At the point where Radicalism faltered in social reform, the claims

---

[153] Cf. S. Rowntree, *The Effect of Minimum Wage Legislation upon British Industry. Financial Review of Reviews*, July 1914. ' There is a . . . definite limit beyond which wages cannot be raised without throwing many workers out of employment.'

[154] *The Nation*, 25 October 1913. *The Reality of Social Progress*.

of labour (in part a function of their very different experience) for economic reform, carried them towards nationalisation as the only fundamental alternative to the competitive economy, whose fluctuations and weaknesses they had increasing cause to distrust. Labour, involved with a growing measure of social idealism, wished to exert a complete, conscious control over the economic processes of society. Radicalism, doubting whether this could ever be achieved, opted instead for a form of Social Democracy with the emphasis upon the equal participation of all in the conscious pursuit of some intangible goal, loosely termed the just society.

Finally, the Radical challenge to the government was of slightly larger proportions than between 1906 and 1910, bearing in mind the loss of miners and the fall in the size of the party. Out of 15 divisions [155] which might be said to raise points of principle and which the government opposed, 30 Liberals voted against the government in five or more divisions.[156] At least 60 voted for the minimum wage, either in a debate upon the address, for the ' 5 and 2 ', or for the railways' 21s minimum. Once more, the ability of the arms debates to call out a further group of Radicals was evident. In all, 107 Liberals recorded at least one vote against the government [157] (and it is worth noting here that among the land reformers, only three, de Forest, Raffan and Wedgwood displayed considerable independence over labour questions). The existence of this group of 30 does go some way to bear out *The Nation*'s claim that ' Advanced Liberalism ' differed little in essentials from Labour, and also, that ' young men with brains and a conscience ' still preferred to call themselves Radicals.[158]

---

[155] I.e. the 13 Divisions mentioned, plus the division on unemployment policy, 10 February 1911 (Division No. 1), and the division on the Railways (No. 2) Bill, 30 January 1913 (Division No. 566).

[156] Voting against the government on five occasions: W. H. Dickinson, J. D. Hope, L. A. Atherly-Jones, D. Mason, J. D. Miller, A. B. Markham, J. H. Yoxall.

On six occasions: J. S. Dawes, E. W. Davies, de Forest, E. R. Jones, J. M. Hogge, P. Morrell, F. G. Kellaway, P. W. Raffan.

On seven occasions: J. H. Dalziel, J. Martin, L. G. Chiozza Money, J. Rowlands, H. A. Watt, J. Wilson.

On eight occasions: W. P. Byles, J. H. Edwards, C. Fenwick, R. Lambert, J. H. Whitehouse.

On nine occasions: P. Alden, H. J. Glanville, E. T. John.

On ten occasions: J. C. Wedgood.

(This takes no account of Wedgwood's revolt over the Mental Deficiency Bill.)

[157] 49 voted against only twice, many of these voting only against the increased arms estimates e.g. R. D. Holt, T. Lough, J. F. L. Brunner, A. J. Sherwell, J. M. Robertson.

[158] *The Nation*, 18 April 1914.

This was a probable reference to men such as J. D. Millar and J. D. Hope who entered parliament in 1911, J. M. Hogge in 1912 and Tom Wing in 1913. Once again, the Radical occupational pattern displayed a ' non-business ' weighting,[159] and one might suspect that by this time Radical conceptions of social justice were becoming removed from the outlook of many businessmen. After 1910, the business element within the party dropped further and the Liberals retained relatively few industrialists – the sons of Sir Charles Palmer, Furness, Weetman Pearson, Sir John Brunner, Russell Rea and his son, three members of the McLaren family and three coal-owners, Cory, Markham and Joseph Walton. Apart from a small band of ship-owners (R. D. Holt, the Reas and Runciman) the largest single business group was in textiles, none of whom were especially well-known. The Liberals, in fact, by 1914, did not at all give the impression of being a ' capitalist party '; rather, their diversification both within their ranks and in ideas give them a singularly un-homogeneous appearance, hardly typical of the powers which clashed within Edwardian England.

---

[159] E. T. John was the managing director of a smelting company, Glanville was a mill furnisher, Wedgwood a potter and Markham a coal owner, the remainder were an assortment of lawyers, journalists and writers.

8

Towards a Conclusion

By 1914, the social problem and its ramifications, concern for poverty and social inequality, for welfare and economic insecurity, had come to form a significant test issue in modern British politics. As such, it was fast becoming the touchstone of political allegiance and of party alignments.

The significant relationship between the nineteenth century's theory of society and its political practice, loosely referred to as individualism, was an inadequate explanation of the Liberal party's own interpretation of and reaction to the social problem. Individualism was only one of the constraints at work limiting the Liberal party's acceptance of a fuller central responsibility for social reform. More importance should be attributed to the economic theory of society, to the prevailing orthodox interpretation of the necessary and proper relations obtaining between the factors of production, and to political theory itself, particularly where this included a reliance upon the Whig tradition of careful, practical and deliberate government. In this dual context, there were areas where legislation might be deemed quite irrelevant, unable to alter the economic facts (or laws) and there were still further areas, twilight zones, where social responsibility for the minimum conditions of life met economic determinism, where the actual drafting of legislation and the subsequent embodiment of an act into administrative machinery was a supremely formidable exercise; formidable not only in so far as the mechanics of the operation were concerned, but also in the probable antagonism such legislation might be expected to produce. Individualism, if it is to be given any meaning at all with regard to the Liberal party, has either to be interpreted in one of the two ways outlined above, or it has to be seen as denoting a commitment to preserve the ' individual basis ' of society, which further involved a belief in civil freedoms, in constitutional maxims and liberties (such as the rule of law), as well as in maintaining that the individual's good was no longer in itself a sufficient criterion of either social progress or society's good.

The Liberals rejected mechanistic theories of society in favour of the ideal of a balanced and harmonious society. The Liberal Radicals rejected any overt emphasis upon historical determinism; indeed, their struggle was against all determinisms, and to replace one brand of economic determinism by another was anathema to them. J. A. Spender made this point long afterwards when he wrote of the pre-war Liberals' rejection of class-war as 'repulsive', and of their sense of gradualism in the face of the necessities and complexities of social organisation: 'Those who condemn (he wrote) the economic "unfreedom" of the working class and wish to grant them an easier way of living ignore the elementary facts of social organisation that are essential to allow anyone a living'.[1] Social discipline and self-restraint were basic needs of any society, and in any society every 'free' man existed in some economic relationship to another, in so far as he had to buy the skills and services of others. Organisation was basic, and the pursuit of economic freedom without regard to the values and liberties which social organisation and stability together provided, was simply to substitute one criterion of progress for another without a proper attempt to combine the two. Spender emphasised that the existence of the public order and the opportunity for continuous politics were preconditions for any kind of freedom, and could on no account be compromised for the sake of a utopia.

Yet before 1914, it did appear that Liberalism was incapable of reconciling the demands and expectations it had unleashed with regard to reform in general, with the traditional virtues of a hierarchical society. This much the Conservatives believed. Balfour looked 'with much misgiving upon the general loosening of the ordinary ties of social obligation'. He feared the effects of violence, manifested in the activities of suffragettes and syndicalists alike, upon the 'orderly basis of society'.[2] The Conservatives both assumed a highly orthodox interpretation of economic limitations and the rôle of government, and deliberately acted as the spokesmen of powerful and essential interests 'harassed' by the Liberals.[3] The Conservatives sought to retain the operation of government upon the limited and practical plane of the nineteenth century. When the ambiguity of the utilitarian equation regarding the reciprocal obligations of individual and government was exposed, the Conservatives sought to maintain the balance of the equation in favour of the individual. The Conservatives accused the Liberals of both political and financial irresponsibility, of taxing a single (and productive) class at confisca-

---

[1] J. A. Spender, *Men and Things* (1937) pp. 69–70.
[2] A. J. Balfour to Bonar Law (copy), 23 September 1923, Balfour papers, Add. Mss 49693.
[3] F. E. Smith, *The Unionist Party and Other Essays* (1913) p. 14.

tory rates for the benefit of a labouring class whose true interests lay more in the stimulus of constructive human motives, self-interest, self-help and incentive.[4] The Liberals, they claimed, were confusing social justice with state charity, and were invoking a false balancing agent in society in their reliance upon the state, for in the long run the only truly constructive society was a society founded on individual effort:

I have a fanatical belief in individual freedom. I believe it is a vital thing for this country, and I believe it is the cornerstone upon which our prosperity and our existence are built, and . . . I believe that the civic qualities of self-control, self-reliance and self-respect depend upon individual liberty and the freedom and independence of the people of this country.[5]

The Conservatives re-emphasised their accusation of irresponsibility: against the payment of members, the over-loaded legislative time-tables, and against the growth of the civil service. The Conservatives sought to redress the balance of attention in favour of all who saw themselves as forgotten and penalised by Liberal social programmes.

A large section of opinion is unmistakably weary of the incessant legislation of the last few years. Social Reform legislation . . . has only resulted in additional Labour unrest. Men . . . now see that there can be no finality in it, that it means ever-progressive transference of wealth from those who have worked and saved to those who, whether from misfortune or from fault, have no claim but their poverty to the charity of the state. Such a system of legislation, apart from the moral corruption it entails, must ultimately . . . sap the sources of our wealth and make general that poverty which is now exceptional.[6]

Such criticisms did not go unheeded amongst Liberals, especially in the country. Quite apart from the dissatisfaction amongst the party over specific measures such as the 1908 Licensing Bill and the 1909 Budget, there was discontent amongst the constituencies at the growing familiarity of the party with progressive and labour politics, expressed in the discontent of Whigs like A. E. Pease at the party's ' neo-Liberalism '; there was too a rising current of dissatisfaction with Liberal financial and industrial policies amongst the party's

---

[4] Cf. H. Cecil, *Conservatism* (1912).
[5] Parl. Deb., 5th Series, Vol. 26, C1477, 24 May 1911. (Lord Robert Cecil attacking compulsory contributions in the Insurance Bill.)
[6] H. Cox, ' Contemporary Politics ', *Quarterly Review*, 216 (1912) p. 235.

business wing: D. A. Thomas, Lord Joicey, Furness, Macara, Holt, Cory and Devonport (Hudson Kearley). 1910 saw another ' dribble of local notables away from the party ',[7] while the number of individual malcontents grew after 1911. Lord Eversley opposed the single-taxers, Sir E. Beauchamp opposed Welsh disestablishment, Cory and Agar-Robartes voted against the Home Rule Bill, while Horatio Bottomley and Hilaire Belloc were both classed as Independents by 1912. A small section of the party were associated with the ' Personal Rights Association ' which, under its president, Franklin Thomasson, opposed Trade Boards, the Insurance and Shops Acts. Three Liberal M.P.s were vice-presidents, W. S. B. MacLaren, Lupton and Wedgwood, while the opinions of its magazine, *The Individualist*, were not dissimilar to those of the British Constitutional Association.[8]

Such indications of internal fragmentation throws the avowedly Radical section of the party into greater prominence as a relatively coherent and potentially significant body for influencing legislation. Their voting strength, measured, for example, in the 1912 minimum wage divisions, was not inconsiderable, but here too it would be unwise to impute either a single commitment or a single motivation to progressives in general. For one thing, important differences in premises and in emphasis remained; the land campaign demonstrated the gap between the single-taxers and their anti-collectivist tenets in favour of fiscal reform, and the exponents of a state-led developmental strategy who were broadly associated with Hobsonian underconsumptionist ideas. Secondly, and of more long-term significance, the Radical element seems to have had little organised or institutional strength either in the constituencies, at the N.L.F., or in parliament itself. One may wonder if the particular motivation which drove so many of them to succeed, was, to some extent, a chance combination which gave to the Liberal party a peculiarly idealistic tenor (and also an intellectual content) at a most propitious moment. It is possible that in terms of further recruitment, of control over constituency machines and of financial support, the Radical element was without the means of self-perpetuation within a distinctive Liberal party. Many of them, elected from south-eastern county constituencies in 1906, were antipathetic to the beliefs of their predominantly middle-class electorates, while others, elected from inner

---

[7] N. Blewett, *The General Elections of 1910*, p. 371; also P. F. Clarke, *Lancashire and the New Liberalism*, pp. 226f, 245f, 293f.

[8] Cf. *The Individualist*, Nos. 314, 315 (1911).

urban areas, needed working-class support which was only available to them in so far as no more viable candidate then existed. In this context, Radical candidatures may well have fulfilled a particular need of newly-politicised, working-class electorates before a distinct Labour machine emerged.[9]

The growing influence of the Radicals within the parliamentary party, and the weakening of the party's links with its 'powerful men' in the country, threw an increasing strain upon the party's electoral organisation. Although the Liberals were, financially, still able to compete successfully with the Conservatives in 1910,[10] between 1910 and 1914, the Liberals lost considerable ground to the Tories, losing 15 seats to them and gaining only one.[11] Admittedly, the Liberals suffered from a run of electorally damaging acts and actions, insurance, suffragettes, Marconi and Home Rule, but neither the Parliament Act nor the initial impact of the Land Campaign did anything to reverse the losing trend; the Conservatives gained 4 seats in 1912, 3 in 1913, and a further 4 in the first five months of 1914. Neither was the trend isolated in any one part of the country, the Conservatives winning in Midlothian, and in London, Manchester and the south-west.[12]

This trend once more focused attention upon the organisational weakness of Liberalism, despite further reforms in 1908 and 1910.[13] Cecil Beck, a Liberal organiser, attributed the Tory success ' *entirely* to machinery. They have absolutely no case to lay before the country.' He admired their ' steady work in the constituencies at all times '. The Liberals lacked ' co-ordination and planning ', despite the chief whips ' who work themselves to death ', and he thought there ought to be some further devolution to a chief organiser outside parliament.

---

[9] Elibank was reputedly more favourable to the man of parts than to the man of wealth (Blewett, p. 415).

[10] *Ibid*. ch. 10.

[11] Conservatives also gained two from Labour.

[12] Cf. M. Kinnear, *The British Voter : An Atlas and Survey Since 1885* (1968) p. 72 for an analysis of the effects of the 1918 Redistribution Act in three areas in which the Liberals were exhibiting serious weaknesses between 1910 and 1914 (E. Lancashire, E. London and Mid-Scotland) and the suggestion that Liberal inability to meet Conservative and Labour challenges in these three marginal areas exposed them to immediate and heavy loss in 1918 following redistribution. The Liberals also stood to lose from rural depopulation in the south and west (p. 70).

[13] See P. F. Clarke, *Lancashire and the New Liberalism*, chs. 8 and 9.

The Tories possess a by-election team as well trained as a good football team. They are used to working together, each with his accustomed job, each with the experience of 20 or 30 by-elections behind him . . .

This team know exactly what particular ' cry ' has proved effective in previous similar contests, know exactly what the Liberal moves are likely to be and have their counter-moves ready.

Our own good men are wasted by local incompetence and lack of decent machinery, while just now there is a slight rot in the party.

Local Liberals were often unwilling to accept the help of outside (ancillary) bodies, candidates were often chosen by chance and there was too much friction at grass-roots level.[14] Beck asked Masterman to bring the matter urgently before the Cabinet, which led to the projected creation of a new post of senior organiser under the chief whip, to which Wedgwood Benn was apparently to be appointed.[15]

Beck said enough to suggest that the theme of inadequate local foundations had remained appropriate throughout the period, that the Liberals had, in fact, failed to create the political foundations necessary to maintain a modern parliamentary party in a time of a growing electorate and widening party commitments. After 1886, there is good reason to believe that the caucus failed to attract popular enthusiasm in numbers sufficient to maintain that particular machine as a credible political instrument. The emphasis was switching to systematic canvassing, registration, the continual nursing of constituencies, and this called for both volunteers and money, which the Liberals found difficult to supply. Neither was the caucus a suitable machine for resolving increasingly vital differences of social and economic interest. Basically, the caucus existed to deliver a vote where opinion was either sufficiently homogeneous or deferential enough to be relatively uncritical of the use to which the vote was put. Widening horizons amongst the lower classes, accompanied by growing hostility amongst the middle class, increasing divisions between the two major parties, and the emergence of a distinct Labour vote coupled to a new brand of political criticism, together demanded a much more positive rôle from party organisation. Perhaps the lingering remnants of Whiggism in the party prevented it from entering into new and closer ties with the electorate. A dislike of programmes, commitments, sectional policies, was only justifiable

---

[14] Beck to Masterman, 20 May 1914 (Beck was a member of the Executive of the Home Counties Liberal Federation), LGP, C/5/15/5.
[15] LGP, C/6/11/15 (Lloyd George to Asquith (copy) 5 June 1914).

if it knew (like the Conservatives) that it could rely upon some size-able and secure basis of support. Perhaps the Liberal party was inherently incapable of transforming its amalgam of interests and idealists into a disciplined phalanx capable of effective competition on national terms.

However, Radicalism did prove instrumental in holding Labour at bay. Whereas Labour parliamentary strength had risen to 42 after December 1910, this figure had declined to 37 by mid-1914.[16] By 1912, it was clear that the electoral entente with the Liberals had broken down, with interesting implications for both sides. In Barnard Castle, local Liberals wished to oppose Henderson, but matters were complicated because the most likely local candidate, a member of the Pease family, had Conservative leanings.[17] In July 1912 R. L. Outh-waite's victory in the previous Labour seat of Hanley caused sharp recriminations. In Bradford, the local Trades Council determined to oppose Sir William Priestley, and in January 1913, Henderson sug-gested that a new committee on Scottish electoral organisation be established in view of Liberal intransigence.[18] Labour organisation, however, was still little-developed, and consequently the party was unable to mount an effective challenge to the Liberals. W. J. Davis, the secretary to the T.U.C.'s Parliamentary Committee, admitted that in encouraging three-cornered fights the Labour party were only hurting themselves, while Snowden thought at least five-sixths of Labour M.P.s depended upon the political quiescence of the other parties; in three-cornered fights 'not half-a-dozen' of them would be returned (Snowden saw a solution in proportional representa-tion).[19]

Considerable significance attached to the electoral intentions of the miners, this being one area where the Liberal party stood to lose heavily from the decline of the traditional policy of accommodation in the coalfields, miners probably constituting 10 per cent or more of the electorate in over 70 constituencies in England and Wales, and over 30 per cent in 35 divisions.[20] On the occasion of the 1912 national

---

16 Cf. Gregory, *The Miners and Politics*, pp. 48–9. Labour lost two seats to the Conservatives, Hanley to the Liberals, two miners withdrew from the party, a third refused to join, and the party won one electoral seat.

17 *The Times*, 22 August 1912.

18 *The Times*, 20 September 1912; 30 January 1913.

19 *The Times*, 29 January 1913. Also P. Snowden, *Autobiography*, Vol. 1 (1934) p. 319, for a pessimistic assessment of Labour's pre-war prospects, and Cole, *British Working-Class Politics 1832–1914* (1941) pp. 201–34 *passim*.

20 Gregory, *The Miners and Politics*, p. 11.

strike, a spokesman for the Miners' Federation remarked that there were 64 seats held by the Liberals 'by the goodwill' of the Miners' Federation, and there were by then signs that Liberals were forfeiting that goodwill, either by their associations with unpopular coalowners, or through the friction between local Liberalism and militant leaders on the coalfields.[21]

By 1914 the Liberal party's reliance upon a marked geographical pattern of support was becoming a weakness rather than a strength, as fragile constituency associations strove to reconcile the varying interests of the party's supporters, old and new. Especially in those areas where Liberal roots were strongest, Yorkshire, the north-east, Wales and Scotland, the conflict between the established industrial supporters of Liberalism and a sizeable working-class electorate was at its greatest. In such areas, the prevailing tenor of Liberalism remained anchored to its traditional roots, with little room for compromise between the style and experience of Gladstonian Liberalism and the new social politics. In such areas, the Liberal party apparently failed to bridge the growing sense of difference between classes, and its failure was revealed in its inability to hold support amongst a new generation of voters: J. M. Hogge wrote to Lloyd George on the loss of Leith Burghs in 1914:

The older generation of Scotsmen have been bred in Radicalism, but there is growing up a large industrial element, the component parts of which are for practical purposes unknown to the official party. This section of the electorate is disposed to use the vote not so much for principles as for individual purposes. Like the publican, these men have arrived at the idea of 'our trade, our politics', and whoever will meet them on this idea will get their votes. As the contest showed, the Labour party are prepared to go a long way to meet such people.[22]

A similar tale could be told of South Wales, and the impending alienation of the miners' vote,[23] while the Liberals' apparent failure to establish efficient organisations in the larger urban areas, of which London was the prime example, left them very vulnerable to the extension of Labour organisation.

---

[21] *The Times*, 21 March 1912.
[22] LGP, C/10/3/29. Also D. W. Urwin, 'Scottish Conservatism', *Political Studies*, June 1966, for the expansion of the Conservative base.
[23] Morgan, *Wales in British Politics*, pp. 243–4, 248–9; Gregory, *The Miners and Politics*, p. 595.

The Liberals had not followed the Conservative example of linking national to local politics, and after 1910 it was evidently unlikely
that the Liberal party could recoup any losses in its own traditional
areas of support by attacking Tory strongholds, the south in general
or the Home Counties in particular. Liberal organisation was
dependent upon the resources and voluntary efforts of a distinctly
limited band of supporters, and in a few of their safe areas, the north-
east and South Wales, for example, there did not seem to be any
replacements emerging for the earlier generation of industrialists who
were now growing disenchanted with Liberal policies.[24] The lack of
central control, the fact that Scotland and Wales behaved often as
completely autonomous bodies, the failure of the Liberals to evolve
a chief organiser of comparable status to the Conservative chief agent,
and the failure of the N.L.F. to maintain a close watch over the
strength of its own associations, do together suggest that Liberalism
in the country may have had something of the character of a hollow
shell.

This being so, the fortunes and future direction of Liberalism as
an organised political force lay, to a large extent, in the hands of
Radicalism in parliament. Yet this body too lacked any abiding
discipline or homogeneity of opinions and ideas. This may further
be inferred from the diverse paths they followed after war broke out.
The largest contingent was composed of those who had migrated to
Labour by 1918, some via the Union of Democratic Control (C. P.
Trevelyan, Outhwaite, Wedgwood, Ponsonby, Morel, Joseph
King),[25] and others from more various motives of their own, E. G.
Hemmerde, E. T. John, C. R. Buxton, F. Martin, Wedgwood Benn
and S. Arnold. Others wandered in search of a party, Percy Alden
moved to Labour and back to the Liberals, J. A. Baker was reportedly
'heart-broken' in 1918, J. M. Hogge became a Liberal Independent
but later returned to the Lloyd George Liberals. Few Radicals, however, remained with Lloyd George, Ryland Adkins, Markham,
Dalziel, Macnamara and Tudor Walters, and fewer still with
Asquith, J. M. Robertson and Leif Jones.[26] Certainly the war and its

---

24 One sign of Liberal strength was the growth of the Young Liberal movement,
begun in 1903 and numbering 540 branches by 1912. W. B. Forster Bovill, *The
League of Young Liberals* (1912); C. F. G. Masterman, *Youth and Liberalism*
(1911).

25 Cf. R. Dowse, ' The Entry of the Liberals into the Labour Party, 1910–1920 ',
Yorkshire Bulletin of Social and Economic Research, November 1961.

26 See T. Wilson, *The Downfall of the Liberal Party 1914–1935* (1966).

attendant issues of conscription and national self-determination wrecked Liberal-Radicalism as a coherent voting bloc on social issues, although Trevelyan later wrote that ' even without the war it is more than doubtful whether the mass of Radical *voters* would not have transferred their allegiance to Labour within a very few years '.[27]

Although the issues had changed, the character of Radicalism had changed very little. Radicals were still individuals pursuing causes with a firm dislike for party discipline and a firm respect for the politics of conscience, political frontiersmen blazing trails through the ranks of the irrational, the benighted and the helpless. Each Radical had both his own priorities and his own scheme of values, and was unwilling to compromise either. Again, it has to be remembered that Radical critiques of existing social and economic conditions were not cumulative in their indictments. They did not lead to similar conclusions and in some cases they led to the totally unexpected critique of reform which served as a *de facto* defence of the existing order. This attribute appears with certain of the land taxers who, because of their residual premises, were just as likely to jump back into the middle of the nineteenth century in their views upon government and the individual.

In the context of Edwardian political debate, a most significant book was Hilaire Belloc's critique of the servile state and the new industrial order, which very accurately depicted the current state of the individualist-collectivist argument, and also illuminated both the current Radical confusion between the means and the ends of social reform, and the orthodox despair over the Radicals' seeming inability to comprehend the likely consequences of their actions.[28]

Belloc accepted the existence of instability within a capitalist state, resulting from the discrepancy between the state's moral assumptions in favour of a society of free and equal citizens, and the economic structure of capitalism which produced an unequal ownership of property (particularly in the ownership of the means of production), and allowed one class to increase its own political and economic strength at the expense of another. He postulated two ways in which development might logically proceed. First, towards the wider distribution of property, until ' that institution shall become the mark of the whole state, and until free citizens will possess both land and

---

[27] C. P. Trevelyan, *From Liberalism to Labour* (1921) (emphasis added).
[28] H. Belloc, *The Servile State* (1912).

capital ', which he termed the ' Distributive State '. Secondly, towards the complete negation of private property and the management of the means of production by ' the political officers of the community ' who would hold all such property in trust for that community, which he termed the ' Collectivist State '. While the first, he believed, was nearer to a traditional understanding of the process of evolution, it was towards the second that the progressive society was tending in its extension of public control to services and monopolies.

Both explanations were, however, only approximations of the true course of events. Believers in the collectivist ideal wanted nationalisation as a means for attaining equal living standards and a measure of economic security for all. When such believers encountered resistance from entrenched interests, and when the capitalist conceded the reciprocal recognition of new duties between himself and his employees, and recognised an obligation on his part to contribute towards their welfare, the socialist or collectivist welcomed such concessions as seemingly the first step towards his goal. Yet such a compromise in reality implicitly accepted the continuance of the economic structure in which one (and the larger) class remained dependent upon another (property-owning) class for work and livelihood.

Belloc recognised a further group of collectivists who saw society in mechanistic terms in which a balance had to be struck between social classes and economic interests. This group would, he wrote, be deflected too from nationalisation by the temptation to rely upon legal, regulative and bureaucratic means to attain the balance. Finally, there was the practical reformer who ' takes the world as he finds it ' and whose resort to empirical reformism ' reduces freedom by inches ' and ushers in ' a welter of anarchic restrictions '. The net result of all three groups would be ' to reach a condition of stable equilibrium ' in society, in which a sense of duty and obligation would be enforced upon everyone through the restrictive powers of the state. This last condition he termed the ' Servile State ', in which the mass of men would be constrained by law to labour for the profit of a minority, but as the reward of such constraint, should enjoy a security they did not possess under pure capitalism. The masses would accept this condition because they were so conditioned to a type of society in which they were accustomed to being wage-earners under the control of other men that they had forgotten all about an older condition of economic freedom (to which the collectivists had originally appealed). They were intent simply upon an immediate betterment of their position; their aim was security and nothing more: 'After the long terrors imposed upon them through a freedom unaccompanied by property, they see, at the expense of losing a mere legal freedom, the very real prospect of having enough and not losing it.'

'Servile' legislation would then proceed along certain lines: to alleviate the insecurity of certain sections by, for example, minimum wage legislation to compel an employer to pay a certain rate, or by laying compulsory duties on an employer, under Liability or Insurance Acts. Conversely, there would be provision made for the state to compel a man, lacking the means of production himself, to labour in return for help when unemployed or ill. He forecast the spread of compulsory Boards of Arbitration, of complete state control over both the conditions and the terms upon which a man worked, including the power to decree standards of efficiency and output, below which no man might drop without fear of poverty.

Such a prospect the Conservatives feared was imminent and Liberal Radicals recognised as undesirable. Belloc's analysis illuminated the drift to the collectivist state which combined the worst of both worlds; not only an economically 'unfree' society, but one in which regulation and restriction hampered production and enterprise. Belloc foreshadowed the static society which the Liberals (and many Conservatives) dreaded, a society in which effort was characterised as burdensome, in which a man's work was to be seen purely as the service he owed to society in return for his keep, and in which the individual, bound and delivered to the perpetual mechanism of production, lacked both the means and the incentive to express his individuality.

This was the abiding phantom which lingered within all opposition to the growth of social and collective responsibility, and it appeared also within working-class, especially trade-union, reluctance to countenance the apparatus of the over-mighty state. The unions, also raised within the fabric of a constitutional society, were concerned to see that there should be no power without the means to enforce proper accountability. Specifically, the unions wished for a greater, and perhaps a preponderant share in determining their own conditions and security, and preferred to see this achieved through the extension of their own organisation; syndicalism or guild socialism were equally attempts to resolve the dual problem of securing political accountability and economic security, both essential if the servility of the capitalist society was not to be replaced by the servility of the collectivist state.[29]

The real basis of the trade-union demand for economic reform lay in their criticisms of the nineteenth-century belief in flexible wage rates, in labour as a commodity whose significance did not extend beyond its function in the labour market. This criticism was as much subjective as objective, indeed, it would be virtually impossible to separate the two as regards motivation. The demand for a minimum wage, itself a logical extension of the union demand for the common rule and the standard rate, received little economic support before 1914 apart from under-consumptionist backing, and probably gained most support on grounds of natural justice, as expressed in the phrase ' the living wage '. Working-class antipathy to the market economy was couched primarily in non-economic terms. They were, perhaps, seeking a reform in their style as much as in their standard of living, in which a rejection of commercialism, the factory system and the wages system figured prominently:

Within a remarkably short space of time, working people have become highly socialistic in money matters, though not . . . in other respects. The theoretical aspects of socialism do not appeal to them, and they resent as much as ever any state interference in their private lives. Bureaucrats they mistrust: a chill Fabian efficiency has no attractions for them. What they want is fair play between man and man.[30]

There was too a rejection of the monotony of modern industry, and a concern for the individual's place within vast impersonal organisations amongst ' unrelated specialisms '. Hobson's all-inclusive definition of the ' organic welfare ' of human industry was paralleled by Graham Wallas' emphasis upon ' the organisation of happiness ', both rejecting the orthodox insistence upon a purely quantitative judgement of economic welfare. This was, again, an illustration of the gulf between the social and the economic imperatives, and industrial democracy, as a reaction from the nineteenth-century view of labour as an unintelligent and expendable commodity, paid scant heed to the form of orthodox reasoning; it was enough that the

---

[29] Cf. *The New Age*, 15 January 1914: ' The myth of the state being an objective power above the classes and always meting out full justice deludes the majority of people to be inactive.'

[30] S. Reynolds and Woolley, *Seems So ! A Working Class View of Politics* (1912) pp. 171–2. Also Pelling, *Popular Politics and Society in Late Victorian Britain*, ch. 1.

latter's premises were wrong. G. D. H. Cole recorded that industrial reformers before 1914 ignored problems of economic management, including control ' over investment, of which we were hardly conscious as a problem '. The industrial unionists in Britain paid little or no attention to such details as fixing price or co-ordinating economic development.[31] The rhetoric of *The New Age* scarcely acknowledged the existence of such issues. It was enough that the christian socialist believed that ' the ethics of the market-place are an abomination ', and that ' the universe appears without moral form and void, a sinister, blind machine, relentlessly grinding surplus value out of human beings '.[32]

Such judgements, however, were ' not the birthright of untutored amateurs ',[33] and A. C. Pigou drew a clear distinction between economic welfare, the higher condition which could only be improved through an aggregate increase in the national dividend, and simple, or social welfare. Economic welfare was a study of the most productive use of a society's resources, the direction of all expenditure to the most productive ends. It was assumed that the rich were naturally more productive than the poor, and it was assumed too that investment in machines produced a greater return than similar investment in increasing the social efficiency of the poor : ' attempts to transfer resources to the relatively poor (through enforcing artificial wage rates) stand, as a general rule, condemned as injurious to economic welfare '.[34] The national minimum could only be of use as a physical, quantitative standard.[35] As a demand for wage increases regardless of the after-effects these might have upon production, the minimum was purely subjective and possessed no economic standing; its attainment might therefore be expected to lower the real income of the community as a whole.

With the idea of a living wage, with the attempt to impose social, humanitarian, standards upon hitherto autonomous industrial processes, and with the move to circumscribe the importance attaching

---

[31] Foreword to B. Pribicevic, *The Shop Stewards' Movement and Workers' Control 1910–1922* (Oxford, 1959) and p. 15; S. T. Glass, *The Responsible Society : The Ideas of the English Guild Socialists* (1966).

[32] *The New Age*, 13 June 1907.

[33] A. C. Pigou, *Wealth and Welfare* (1912) p. 487.

[34] *Ibid*. p. 351.

[35] *Ibid*. pp. 393f. The National Minimum was expressed as: ' the direct good resulting from the marginal pound transferred to the poor just balances the indirect evil brought about by the consequent reduction of the (national) dividend '.

to capital as the pre-eminent factor of production, the Radicals sympathised, and Liberalism, in parliament at least, accorded a great measure of tacit support. The Liberals disagreed strongly with Pigou's narrow conception of welfare. Welfare was not, for Hobson, simply a matter of marginal adjustments in the distribution of resources in order to maximise the production of wealth, but a matter of discovering the empirical path to defining in harder terms an abstract criterion of welfare, whereby the costs and pains of production, human and monetary, might be measured against the utilities and pleasures of consumption; the final aim being to impute to every transaction that criterion, ' the utility of vital value ', which would secure for each a just reward for his ' real ' effort. The discovery of the criterion depended not simply upon empirical advances, but also upon the ability of society to develop ' a collective consciousness and will . . . capable of realising a collective vital end '.[36]

The Liberal ideal of a process of distribution in which earnings depended upon the value of the work or service performed, and where such ' value ' was other than the price allocated by the exchange system in a competitive economy, distinguished them sharply from the Conservatives, who preferred a strictly economic measurement of value. Hence both parties came more and more to develop their own premises from which to develop their conceptions of individuality, the social good, social and political responsibility. For the Liberal, social reform was intended to promote individuality, ' to go deeper into the man . . . and to give him that place in the social estimate which his natural powers deserve '.[37] If this involved a large-scale emphasis upon social reconstruction, the redistribution of income by means of progressive taxation and welfare policies, then the language of the social good could be invoked for justification.[38] While in so far as society was viewed in organic terms, so the responsible state would be concerned to see that the rights and obligations meted out to distinct sections or classes bore some accurate relationship to the respective merits and strengths of the classes involved. Individual virtue was a goal to be achieved, not a premise to be taken for granted. Retrenchment and reform were no longer synonymous terms, and the hidden costs to the community by way of low wages and sweated trades had to be countered by way of the

---

36 J. A. Hobson, *Work and Wealth* (New York, 1914) ch. 1, pp. 9, 15, 174.
37 W. Lyon Blease, *A History of English Liberalism* (1913) p. 10.
38 Cf. P. Alden, *Democratic England* (1912) p. 6. Also M. Ginsberg, *Law and Opinion in England in the Twentieth Century* (1959) pp. 3–26.

minimum, expressed through state expenditure in favour of the weak
and unorganised. The Liberals prided themselves on having created
a distinct precedent in the field of the state's relationship with the
market economy. 'Economic Society' was to be 'converted into a
gigantic trade union . . . The most original work of the new
Liberalism has been economic. What most distinguishes the governments which have held office since 1906 is the degree to which they
have interfered with the economic structure of society in order to give
greater freedom to the poorer classes.' [39] If Liberalism was finally to
be restrained in its movement to reform by an inability to conceive of
any radical alternative to orthodox interpretations of market operations and the price mechanism, which prevented any explicit commitment to economic collectivism, still the notion of tapping an
unproductive economic surplus, allied to the exploitation of those
resources which the community possessed in the land, did provide an
element of flexibility for the state which was undreamed-of within
the previous bias of the utilitarian equation in favour of individual
activity.

Such reconstruction demanded the adoption of a new socialistic
principle, the ethical demand for the living wage had to be admitted.
As 'the foundation of Liberty is the idea of growth', and as
Liberalism, historically, had discovered its rationale within evolving
concepts of Liberty, so now Liberalism was called upon to give a
positive expression to a new concept i.e. to developing the conscious
mind of an expanding social will, in order that the many values with
which 'Liberty' had historically been associated, civil, fiscal, local,
national, social and economic, might be conjoined within a greater
policy of social justice. [40] Liberalism would therefore insist upon the
relative character of every privilege and institution, relative, that is,
to the wider welfare of society. It would insist that all property be
understood as a social trust, enjoyed through the protection of the
community, and held for use and not for power within the community; that industrial liberty did not mean either the unlimited
acquisition of possessions or absolute freedom in their disposal; that
society was entitled to appropriate social income, or the unearned
increment of production, in schemes for the benefit of society.
Liberalism would insist that the ability and the impulse within man
to formulate an ideal was both an antidote to man's baser qualities

[39] Blease, *English Liberalism*, pp. 326, 332.
[40] L. T. Hobhouse, *Liberalism* (1911) p. 163.

and the only element on which a rational society might be based.[41] The appreciation and study of such an ideal of social justice would not only be a guide to those who insisted on the primacy of the practical or empirical debate, but would also serve to answer any deterministic (individual or collectivist) attempt to realise ultimately similar goals through the impersonal working of industrial and economic forces. In this context, the fear of servility was mistaken, for Belloc had forgotten 'the larger tendencies' behind social reform.[42]

The progressive and Radical plea was for a raising of the level of political debate, to establish a social ideal, the successful pursuit of which constituted the real criterion for judging a society's development. This was to invoke a conception of politics that was above all constructive and serious. Politics was no longer a game, a dilettante activity confined to the elucidation of the principles governing public affairs and legislation. Politics involved the eager location of all possible sources of discontent, and the continual and deliberate adjustment of the social equilibrium. Of Thorold's *Life of Labouchere*, *The New Age* observed: 'The picture of high politics portrayed in this book is to us the strangest imaginable phantasmagoria utterly unreal and completely unrelated to actual life. The facts of economic development have swept this school of politicians off the stage for ever.'[43] *The New Age* was clear that a distinct Radical section was providing the initiative in progressive matters, but doubted whether they would ever agree to use politics to change the economic structure of society.[44] The new Liberalism was evidently an established force, although for the Liberal party, the 'crisis of the centre' which Hobson had foreshadowed in 1909, was quite unresolved by 1914. However sympathetic the centre might be to specific social reforms, on points of 'practical detail' over 'the effects of social reconstruction' it begged to differ. By the middle of 1914, a tentative prediction might be made in favour of the further progress of Liberal Radicalism, if only because the party had moved too far from the old Liberalism to return, and the new ethical premises were too well-established in Liberal thought:

The theoretical objections of the older Liberalism against the State as an instrument for supplementing self-help and undertaking useful lines of

[41] Cf. G. L. Dickinson, *Justice And Liberty : A Political Dialogue* (1911).
[42] From a review by *The Nation*, 9 November 1912.
[43] *The New Age*, 30 October 1913.   [44] *Ibid*. 4 July 1912.

co-operative activity have almost entirely disappeared. Liberalism may be said to have a really open mind towards the various principles of national-isation, taxation, state regulation of wages and hours, public housing schemes, and other large projects for strengthening the condition of the workers. But . . . there remains a good deal of uncertainty as to what lines of present practical policy can be considered sound and feasible. The time has clearly come when a volume of close thought must be brought to bear upon the problem of the economy, of moving along several converg-ing lines of constructive policy, including state ownership, public regula-tion, state support for special weaknesses . . .[45]

[45] *The Nation*, 22 March 1913.

Bibliography

Abbreviations used in the text are indicated by the appropriate sources.

PRIMARY SOURCES

(i) *Private papers*

At the British Museum:

John Burns (JBP)
Sir Henry Campbell-
   Bannerman (CBP)
Charles Dilke

Herbert Gladstone (HGP)
Sir Edward Hamilton
Ripon (RP)
J. A. Spender

Also consulted: A. J. Balfour, A. Birrell (Add. Mss 49372), W. E. Gladstone (Add. Mss 44648)

At the Bodleian Library: H. H. Asquith (AP), J. Bryce (uncatalogued section only)

At the National Library of Scotland: Haldane, A. O. Murray (Elibank) and A. C. Murray

At the Beaverbrook Library: Bonar Law, David Lloyd George (LGP)

At the House of Lords Record Office: Herbert Samuel (HSP)

Also consulted:

Sir William Harcourt Papers (in the possession of Lord Harcourt of Stanton Harcourt, Oxfordshire)

Walter Runciman Papers (in the possession of the Hon S. Runciman, Elshieshields, Lochmaben, Scotland)

Sydney Buxton Papers (in the possession of Mrs E. Clay of Newtimber Place, Hassocks, Sussex)

At the London School of Economics: The William Beveridge Collection on Unemployment, Henry Broadhurst, Sir Robert Giffen

(ii) *General Committee Minutes and Annual Reports of the N.L.F. (British Museum)*

(iii) *Cabinet Papers, 1892–5 and 1906–14, Cab. 37 (Public Record Office)*

(iv) *Parliamentary Debates*, 4th and 5th series

(v) *Transactions of the Political and Economic Circle of the National Liberal Club* (National Liberal Club)

(vi) *Pamphlet Collections*: volumes of Liberal Publication Department issues at the National Liberal Club; and the Collection at the L.S.E. (including Fabian Pamphlets)

(vii) *Infancy of the Labour Party 1900–1912*. Minutes of the L.R.C., etc. 2 Vols. (L.S.E.)

(viii) *Newspapers and magazines*:

Blackwood's Magazine
Commercial Review (1911–14)
Commonwealth (1896–1906)
Contemporary Review
Cornhill's Magazine
Daily News
Economic Journal
Economist
Edinburgh Review
Eighty Club Year-Book
Financial Review of Reviews
Fortnightly Review
Independent Review (1903–7)
Individualist (1911–12)
Land Nationalisation Society Annual
Land Union Journal (1910–14)
Liberal Magazine
Liberal Monthly (1906–14)
Liberal Year-Book (1887–9 and 1906–14)

Manchester Guardian
Nation (1907–14)
National Review
New Age
Nineteenth Century
Progressive Review (1896–8)
Quarterly Review
Reformers' Year-Book (from 1901)
Review of Reviews
Speaker (1892–1907)
Spectator
Temperance Annual
Times
Tribune (1906)
Westminster Gazette
Westminster Review
World's Work (1902–14)
Year-Book of Social Progress (1912–14)

(ix) *Reference books, etc.*:

Annual Register
Banker's Almanac
Bradshaw's Railways Almanac
D. Butler and J. Freeman: *British Political Facts 1900–1916* (1963)
Dod's Parliamentary Companion
P. and G. Ford: *A Select List of British Parliamentary Papers*, 1833–99 (*Oxford*, 1953)
P. and G. Ford: *A Breviate of Parliamentary Papers, 1900–1916* 'The Foundation of the Welfare State' (Oxford, 1957)
Pall Mall Gazette, Election Supplement (1892–1906)
Reader's Guide to Periodical Literature
Who's Who

SECONDARY SOURCES

All books published in London unless otherwise stated.

(i) *Liberalism and the Liberal party*

W. S. Adams: 'Lloyd George and the Labour Movement', *Past and Present*, 3, 1953

H. Belloc: *The Servile State* (1912)

W. L. Blease: *A Short History of English Liberalism* (1913)

F. Brockway: *Labour and Liberalism* (1913)

J. Butler: *The Liberal Party and the Jameson Raid* (1968)

C. Chesterton: *Gladstonian Ghosts* (1905)

W. S. Churchill: *Liberalism and the Social Problem* (1909)

P. F. Clarke: *Lancashire and the New Liberalism* (1971)

C. Cross: *The Liberals in Power 1906–1914* (1963)

G. Dangerfield: *The Strange Death of Liberal England* (1935)

R. E. Dowse: 'The Entry of the Liberals into the Labour Party 1910–20', *Yorkshire Bulletin of Social and Economic Research*, May 1961

Eighty Club: *The Liberal View* (1905)

Essays in Liberalism By Six Oxford Men (1897)

J. F. Glaser: 'English Non-Conformity and the Decline of Liberalism', *American Historical Review*, LXIII, 2, 1958

R. Haldane: *Constructive Liberalism* (1904)

D. Hamer: *Liberal Politics in the Age of Gladstone and Rosebery: A Study in Leadership and Policy* (1972)

F. W. Hirst *et al.*: *Liberalism and the Empire* (1900)

L. T. Hobhouse: *Liberalism* (1911)

J. A. Hobson: *The Crisis of Liberalism* (1909)

J. M. Hogge: *The Aims and Achievements of Liberalism* (1912)

R. Jenkins: *Mr. Balfour's Poodle* (1954)

J. G. Kellas: 'The Liberal Party and Scotland', unpublished Ph.D. thesis, London 1961

'The Liberal Party and the Scottish Church Disestablishment Crisis', *English Historical Review*, LXXIX, 1964

H. Laski: *The Decline of Liberalism* (Hobhouse Memorial Lecture, 1940)

The Liberal View By Members of the 80 Club (1904)

The Liberal Victory By The 80 Club (1906)

D. Lloyd George: *The New Liberalism* (1909)

Better Times (1910)

H. W. McCready: 'Home Rule and the Liberal Party 1899–1906', *Irish Historical Studies*, 1964

K. O. Morgan: *The Age of Lloyd George: The Liberal Party and British Politics* (1971)

J. Morley: *Liberalism and Social Reforms* (1889)

J. B. Pope: *The Socialism of Lloyd George* (1909)

The Radical Programme: (The Political Manifesto of the Metropolitan Radical Federation, 1897)

A. Reid (ed.): *Why I am a Liberal* (n.d.)
The New Liberal Programme (1886)

J. Roach: 'Liberalism and the Victorian Intelligentsia', *Cambridge Historical Journal*, XIII, 1957

J. M. Robertson: *The Future of Liberalism* (1895)
The Meaning of Liberalism (1912)

P. Rowland: *The Last Liberal Governments*, Vol. 1, *The Promised Land* (1970); Vol. 2, *Unfinished Business 1911–1914* (1971)

C. B. Roylance Kent: *The English Radicals* (1899)

H. Samuel: *Liberalism* (1902)

Second Chambers in Practice: Being the Papers of the Rainbow Circle 1910–11

P. Stansky: *Ambitions and Strategies. The Struggle for the Liberal Leadership in the 1890s* (Oxford, 1964)

Towards A Social Policy: The Speaker, 1905

C. Trevelyan: *From Liberalism to Labour* (1921)

B. Villiers: *The Opportunity of Liberalism* (1904)

J. Vincent: *The Formation of the Liberal Party 1857–68* (1966)

S. Webb: *Wanted: A Programme* (1888)
'The Difficulties of Individualism', *Economic Journal*, I, 1891

T. Wilson: *The Downfall of the Liberal Party 1914–1935* (1966)

(ii) *Historical*

P. Alden: *Democratic England* (New York, 1912)

W. Bagehot: *Physics and Politics* (12th edn., 1900)

E. Barker: *Political Thought in England 1848–1914* (1914)

E. Carpenter: *Civilization: Its Cause and Cure* (1889)

H. Cecil: *Conservatism* (1912)

G. K. Clark: *The Making of Victorian Britain* (1962)
The Expanding Society (1968)

J. Derry: *The Radical Tradition* (1967)

A. V. Dicey: *Law and Public Opinion in the Nineteenth Century* (2nd edn., 1914)

G. L. Dickinson: *Justice and Liberty* (1911)

R. C. K. Ensor: *England 1870–1914* (Oxford, 1936)
'Some Political and Economic Interactions in Later Victorian England', *T.R.H.S.*, XXXI, 1949, p. 17

M. Gilbert (ed.): *A Century of Conflict* (1966)

M. Ginsberg (ed.): *Law and Opinion in the Twentieth Century* (1959)

E. Halévy: *A History of the English People*, Vol. IV (1929)
  The Rule of Democracy, 1905–1915 (1934)
W. E. Houghton: *The Victorian Frame of Mind* (Yale, 1957)
Allen Hutt: *This Final Crisis* (1935)
  Ideas and Beliefs of the Victorians (1949)
Sir C. Ilbert: *Legislative Methods and Forms* (1901)
W. Lecky: *Democracy and Liberty* (1896)
S. Letwin: *The Pursuit of Certainty* (Cambridge, 1965)
B. E. Lippincott: *Victorian Critics of Democracy* (Minnesota, 1938)
N. Longmate: *The Waterdrinkers* (1968)
H. Lynd: *England in the 1880s* (Oxford, 1945)
T. Mackay (ed.): *A Plea for Liberty* (1891)
W. S. McKechnie: *The State and the Individual* (Glasgow, 1896)
S. Macoby: *English Radicalism 1886–1914* (1953)
  English Radicalism : The End? (1961)
P. de Mendelssohn: *The Age of Churchill* (1961)
A. Milner: *The Nation and the Empire* (1913)
S. Nowell-Smith (ed.): *Edwardian England 1901–14* (Oxford, 1964)
A. Ponsonby: *The Decline of Aristocracy* (1912)
B. Porter: *Critics of Empire* (1968)
Property : Its Rights and Duties (1914)
M. Richter: *The Politics of Conscience* (1964)
H. Sidgwick: *The Elements of Politics* (1891)
H. Spencer: *The Man Versus the State* (1888)
W. T. Stead (ed.): *Coming Men on Coming Questions* (1905)
W. Sylvester-Smith: *The London Heretics 1870–1914* (1967)
A. J. P. Taylor: *The Trouble-Makers* (1957)
A. Toynbee: *Lectures on the Industrial Revolution* (4th edn., 1894)
G. Wallas: *The Great Society* (1914)
  Men and Ideas (1940)
A. White: *Efficiency and Empire* (1902)
R. A. Woods: *English Social Movements* (1891)
G. M. Young: *Portrait of an Age* (1937)

(iii) *Political and electoral*

W. S. Adams: 'Lloyd George and the Labour Movement', *Past and Present*, 3, 1953
F. Bealey: 'Negotiations Between the Liberals and the L.R.C. before 1906', *Bulletin of the Institute of Historical Research*, November 1956
  'The Electoral Arrangement Between the L.R.C. and the Liberal Party', *Journal of Modern History*, December, 1956
F. Bealey and H. Pelling: *Labour and Politics 1900–1906* (1958)
P. M. H. Bell: *Disestablishment in Ireland and Wales* (1969)

H. Belloc and C. Chesterton: *The Party System* (1911)

N. Blewett: *The Peers, the Parties and the People: The General Elections of 1910* (1972)

F. Channing: *Memories of Midland Politics, 1885–1910* (1918)

O. F. Christie: *The Transition to Democracy 1867–1914* (1934)

P. F. Clarke: 'British Politics and Blackburn Politics 1900–1910', *Historical Journal*, 12, 2, 1969

Conservative Case Against Radicalism (Conservative Central Office, 1909)

J. Cornford: 'Transformation of Conservatism in the Late Nineteenth Century', *Victorian Studies*, VII, 1963

D. W. Crowley, 'The Crofters' Party, 1885–92', *Scottish Historical Review*, XXV, October 1956

J. Dunbabin: 'Parliamentary Elections in Great Britain 1868–1900', *English Historical Review*, January 1966

P. Fraser: 'The Liberal Unionist Alliance', *English Historical Review*, January 1962

G. L. Goodman: 'Liberal Unionism and the Revolt of the Whigs', *Victorian Studies*, December 1959

V. Grayson and H. Taylor: *The Problem of Parliament* (1909)

H. R. G. Greaves: 'Personal Origins and Inter-relations of the Houses of Parliament Since 1832', *Economica*, IX, 1929

W. L. Guttsman: *The British Political Elite 1832–1936* (1963)

W. B. Gwyn: *Democracy and the Cost of Politics* (1962)

R. Hall: *Liberal Organisation and Work* (Cardiff, 1888)

H. J. Hanham: *Elections and Party Management 1868–85* (1958)

'The Sale of Honours in Late Victorian England', *Victorian Studies*, III, March 1960

'Party Finance 1868–80', *Bulletin of the Institute of Historical Research*, 27, 1954

F. H. Herrick: 'Origins of the N.L.F.', *Journal of Modern History*, XVII, 1945

J. Howarth: 'The Liberal Revival in Northamptonshire 1880–95', *Historical Journal*, XII, 1, 1969.

R. B. Jones: 'Balfour's Reforms of Conservative Party Organisation', *Bulletin of the Institute of Historical Research*, May 1965

M. Kinnear: *The British Voter: An Atlas and Survey Since 1885* (1968)

Liberal Reorganisation, Memorandum on, Copy, British Museum (c. 1900)

J. H. Linforth: *Leaves from an Agent's Diary* (Leeds, 1911)

T. Lloyd: 'Uncontested Seats in British General Elections 1852–1910', *Historical Journal*, VIII, 2, 1965

O. Macdonagh: The Nineteenth Century Revolution in Government *Historical Journal*, I, i, 1958

B. McGill: 'F. Schnadhorst and Liberal Party Organisation', *Journal of Modern History*, XXIV, 1962
'Parliamentary Parties 1868–1885', unpublished Harvard Ph.D. thesis (1952)

T. J. Macnamara: *The Political Situation* (1909)

A. H. H. Matthews: *Fifty Years of Agricultural Politics* (*A History of the Central Chamber of Agriculture*) (1915)

W. Mitchell: *The Political Situation in Scotland* (1893)

K. O. Morgan: *Wales in British Politics 1868–1922* (Cardiff, 1963)

M. Ostrogorski: *Democracy and the Organisation of Political Parties* (1902)

H. Parris: 'The Nineteenth Century Revolution in Government: A Reappraisal Reappraised', *Historical Journal*, III, i, 1960

H. Pelling: *The Social Geography of British Elections 1885–1910* (1967)
Popular Politics and Society in Late Victorian Britain (1968)

J. H. Robb: *The Primrose League 1883–1906* (Columbia, 1942)

R. Robson (ed.): *Ideas and Institutions of Victorian Britain* (1967)

C. Rover: *Women's Suffrage and Party Politics in Britain 1866–1914* (1967)

A. K. Russell: 'The General Election of 1906', Oxford D.Phil. thesis, 1963

C. Seymour: *Electoral Reform in England and Wales 1832–85* (Yale, 1915)

F. E. Smith: *Unionist Party and other Essays* (1913)

D. Spring: The English Landed Estates in the Age of Coal and Iron, 1830–80, *Journal of Economic History*, XI, 1951
'The Role of the Aristocracy in the Late Nineteenth Century', *Victorian Studies* 4, 1, 1960

R. Stevens: *The National Liberal Club* (c. 1900)

T. Tholfsen: 'The Origins of the Birmingham Caucus', *Historical Journal*, II, 1959

J. A. Thomas: *The House of Commons 1832–1901* (Cardiff, 1939)
The House of Commons 1906–1911 (Cardiff, 1958)

P. Thompson: *Socialists, Liberals and Labour: The Struggle For London 1885–1914* (1967)

J. E. Tyler: 'Campbell-Bannerman and the Liberal Imperialists 1906–1908', *History*, 23, 91, 1938

D. W. Urwin: 'The Development of Scottish Party Organisation in Scotland Before 1912', *Scottish Historical Review*, October 1965
'Scottish Conservatism', *Political Studies*, June 1966

R. S. Watson: *The National Liberal Federation, 1878–1906* (1907)

G. Williams (ed.): *Merthyr Politics: The Making of a Working Class Tradition* (Cardiff, 1966)

P. M. Williams: ' From Liberalism To Labour ', *Political Studies* 15, 2, 1967

(iv) *Labour and Socialism*

R. P. Arnot: *The Miners 1889–1910* (1949)
  The Miners: Years of Struggle (1948)
P. S. Bagwell: *The Railwaymen* (1963)
Canon Barnett: *Practical Socialism* (1888)
M. Beer: *A History of British Socialism* (1929)
R. Blatchford: *Merrie England* (1894)
C. Booth: *Industrial Unrest and Trade Union Policy* (1913)
C. Bradlaugh: *Labour and Law* (1891)
  Socialism: Fallacies and Dangers (1887)
K. Brand: *British Labour's Rise to Power* (Stanford, 1941)
A. Briggs and J. Saville (ed.): *Essays on Labour History* (1960)
K. D. Brown: *The Labour Party and Unemployment, 1900–14* (1971)
  ' The Labour Party and the Unemployment Question 1906–1910 ', *Historical Journal* (1971) xiv, 3, pp. 599–616
C. Carpenter: *Trade Unions and Co-partnership* (1913)
J. Clayton: *The Rise and Decline of English Socialism* (1926)
H. A. Clegg: *General Union* (Oxford, 1964)
  A. Fox and A. F. Thompson: *A History of British Trade Unions* (Vol. 1, 1889–1910) (Oxford, 1964)
R. V. Clements: British Trade Unions and Popular Political Economy 1850–1870, *Economic History Review*, 2nd Ser., xiv 1961–2
G. D. H. Cole: *British Working-Class Politics 1832–1914* (1941)
  The World of Labour (1913)
  A History of Socialist Thought, Vol. 2 (1956)
M. Cole: *Makers of the Labour Movement* (1948)
W. J. Davis: *The British T.U.C. to 1916: Reminiscences* (1916)
R. E. Dowse: *Left in the Centre* (1966)
G. Drage: *The Labour Problem* (1896)
A. E. P. Duffy: ' Differing Policies and Personal Rivalries in the Origins of the I.L.P.', *Victorian Studies*, September 1962
R. C. K. Ensor (ed.): *Modern Socialism* (1903)
S. T. Glass: *The Responsible Society. Ideas of the Guild Socialists* (1966)
J. Greenwood: *The Theory and Practice of Trade Unionism* (1911)
R. G. Gregory: *The Miners in Politics in England and Wales 1906–1914*, Oxford D.Phil. 1963 (since published)
R. Harrison: *Before the Socialists* (1965)
  ' The Land and Labour League ', *Bulletin of the International Institute of Social History*, viii, 1953
F. Henderson: *The Labour Unrest* (1913)

L. T. Hobhouse: *The Labour Movement* (1893)

E. J. Hobsbawm: *Labouring Men* (1964)
 Labour's Turning Point (1948)

G. Howell: *Trade Unionism : Old and New* (3rd edn., 1900)

A. W. Humphrey: *History of Labour Representation* (1912)

H. M. Hyndman: *The Economics of Socialism* (1896)

Industrial Remuneration Conference, Report (1885)

C. Jackson: *Unemployment and Trade Unions* (1910)

J. P. Jefferys: *The Story of the Engineers* (1945)

M. H. Judge: *Political Socialism* (1908)

J. A. Little and C. Watney: *Industrial Warfare and Its Aims* (1912)

A. M. Macbriar: *Fabian Socialism and English Politics 1884–1918* (C.U.P., 1962)

J. R. MacDonald: *Socialism and Government* (1909)
 The Social Unrest (1913)

J. L. Mahon: *A Labour Programme* (1888)

A. Morris: *Discussions on Labour Questions* (1893)

C. Noel: *The British Labour Party and What It Wants* (1906)

W. V. Osborne: *Sane Trade Unionism* (1913)

E. R. Pease: *A History of the Fabian Society* (1916)

H. Pelling: *The Origins of the Labour Party* (1954)
 America and the British Left (1956)

P. P. Poirier: *The Advent of the Labour Party* (1958)

R. W. Postgate: *The Builders' History* (1923)

B. Pribicevic: *The Shop Stewards' Movement and Worker's Control 1910–22* (Oxford, 1959)

A. Reid: *The New Party* (1895)

J. H. S. Reid: *Origins of the British Labour Party* (Minnesota, 1955)

S. Reynolds: *Seems So! A Working-Class View of Politics* (1912)

B. Roberts: *The T.U.C. 1868–1921* (1958)

T. Rothstein: *From Chartism to Labourism* (1929)

S. Rowntree: *The Industrial Unrest* (1911)

H. A. Russell: *Constructive Socialism* (1909)

E. Selley: *Village Trade Unions in Two Centuries* (1918)

G. B. Shaw: *The Fabian Society : Its Early History* (1892)
 Fabian Essays (1889)

T. G. Spyers: *The Labour Question* (1894)

W. T. Stead (ed.): *What Labour Wants* (1905)

R. H. Tawney: *The Attack and other Papers* (1953)

B. Tillett: *Socialism and Trades Unionism* (Manchester, 1894)

B. Tillett and T. Mann: *The New Trade Unions* (1890)

S. and B. Webb: *A History of Trade Unionism* (2nd edn., 1902)
 Industrial Democracy (1920)

S. Webb and H. Cox: *The Eight Hour Day* (1891)

J. E. Williams: 'The Political Activities of a Trade Union, 1906–1914 ', *International Review of Social History*, II, 1957

(v) *Social, economic, etc.*

W. R. Adkins, *Liberalism and the Land* (1913)
D. H. Aldcroft (ed.): *The Development of British Industry and Foreign Competition, 1875–1914* (1968)
P. Alden: *The Unemployed* (1905)
  Democratic England (1912)
Argyll, Duke of: *The Unseen Foundations of Society* (1893)
G. Armitage-Smith: *The Principles and Methods of Taxation* (1906)
W. J. Ashley: *The Adjustment of Wages* (1903)
W. Ashworth: *The Genesis of Modern British Town Planning* (1954)
G. Askwith: *Industrial Problems and Disputes* (1920)
H. L. Beales: 'The Great Depression ', *Economic History Review*, V, i, 1934
  The Making of Social Policy (Hobhouse Memorial Lecture, 1945)
W. Beveridge: *Unemployment : A Problem of Industry* (1909)
  Voluntary Action (1948)
T. G. Bowles: *National Finance : An Imminent Peril* (1904)
A. L. Bowley: *Livelihood and Poverty* (1912)
  The Change in the Distribution of National Income (Oxford, 1920)
A. Briggs: 'The Welfare State in Historical Perspective ', *Archives Europeenes de Sociologie*, II, 2, 1961
J. Brown: *Ideas Concerning Social Policy and their Influence on Legislation in Britain 1902–11* (1964) London Ph.D. thesis
M. Bruce: *The Coming of the Welfare State* (1961)
H. Bunbury (ed.): *Lloyd George's Ambulance Wagon* (Being the Memoirs of W. J. Braithwaite) (1957)
E. Cadbury: *Experiments in Industrial Organisation* (1911)
F. Channing: *An Agricultural Policy* (1905)
J. H. Clapham: *An Economic History of Modern Britain 1887–1914* (Cambridge, 1938)
R. O. Clarke: 'The Dispute in the Engineering Industry 1897–98 ', *Economica*, N.S., XXIV, 1957
D. Collins, 'The Introduction of Old Age Pensions in Great Britain ', *Historical Journal* VIII, 2, 1965
A. Davenport: *The Economics of Alfred Marshall* (1935)
M. Dobb: *Studies in the Development of Capitalism* (1946)
Economist (The): *The Budget of 1908* (1908)
  A Centenary Volume 1843–1943 (1943)
Employers' Parliamentary Association (The): First Annual Conference, 1913

T. W. Fletcher: 'The Great Depression of English Agriculture 1873–1896, *Economic History Review* 13, 3, 1961

A. W. Fox: *The Rating of Land Values* (1906)

F. W. Galton: *Workers on their Industries* (1895)

H. George: *Progress and Poverty* (1879)

R. Giffen: *The Progress of the Working-Classes 1834–84* (1884)
    Economic Inquiries and Studies (1904)

B. Gilbert: *The Evolution of National Insurance in Great Britain* (1966)

G. J. Goschen: *Essays and Addresses upon Economic Questions* (1905)

P. A. Graham: *The Rural Exodus* (1892)

F. E. Green: *The English Agricultural Labourer 1870–1920* (1927)

E. E. Gulley: *Joseph Chamberlain and English Social Politics* (Columbia, 1926)

K. Hardie: *John Bull and His Unemployed* (1905)

R. Hawtrey: *Good and Bad Trade* (1913)

F. A. Hayek: *The Constitution of Liberty* (1959)

J. R. Hicks: *The Theory of Wages* (1932)

H. Higgs: *Proceedings of the Political Economy Club 1821–1920* (1921)

L. T. Hobhouse: *Social Evolution and Political Theory* (Columbia, 1911)
    'The Ethical Basis of Collectivism', *International Journal of Ethics*, January 1898
    Democracy and Reaction (1904)

J. A. Hobson: *The Economics of Distribution* (New York, 1900)
    The Social Problem (1902)
    The Industrial System (1909)
    An Economic Interpretation of Investment (1911)
    Work and Wealth (New York, 1914)
    'The Marginal Theory of Distribution', *Journal of Political Economy*, 13, 1905, p. 587

T. W. Hutchison: *Economic Doctrines 1870–1929* (Oxford, 2nd edn., 1962)

T. H. Huxley: *Social Diseases and Worse Remedies* (1891)

K. S. Inglis: *Churches and the Working Class in Victorian England* (1963)
    'English non-comformity and social reform', *Past and Present*, x, 1958

D. C. Jones: 'Some Notes on the Census of Occupations', *Journal of the Royal Statistical Society*, 78, i, 1915

J. M. Keynes: *The End of Laissez-faire* (1926)

K. G. Knowles and Robertson: 'Wage Differentials 1880–1950', *Bulletin of the Oxford Institute of Statistics*, 13, 4, 1951

W. Lecky: *Old Age Pensions* (1908)

H. Llewellyn-Smith: *Some Aspects of State Socialism* (1889)

G. Lowndes: *The Silent Social Revolution* (Oxford, 1937)

B. Mallet: *British Budgets 1887–1913* (1913)

W. H. Mallock: *Property and Progress* (1884)

T. Mann: *From Single Tax to Syndicalism* (1913)

D. Marsh: *The Changing Social Structure of England and Wales* (rev. edn., 1965)

A. Marshall: *Elements of the Economics of Industry* (1892)
The Present Position of Economics (1885)

C. F. G. Masterman (ed.): *Heart of the Empire* (1900)
(ed.): *To Colonise England* (1907)
The Condition of England (1911)

B. McCormick and Williams: 'Miners and the Eight Hour Day 1863–1910', *Economic History Review*, 12, 2, 1959

J. S. Mill: *Principles of Political Economy* (Ashley's edition, 1909)

L. G. Chiozza Money: *Riches and Poverty* (1905)

C. L. Mowat: *The Charity Organisation Society* (1967)

F. Musgrove: 'Middle Class Education and Employment in the Nineteenth Century', *Economic History Review*, 12, 3, 1959

A. E. Musson: 'The Great Depression 1873–96: A Re-appraisal', *Journal of Economic History*, June 1959

E. E. Nemmers: *Hobson and Under-consumption* (Amsterdam, 1956)

J. Orr: *Unemployment* (1908)

H. Parris: *The Government and the Railways in Nineteenth Century Britain* (1965)

E. H. Phelps-Brown: *The Growth of British Industrial Relations* (1960)

A. C. Pigou: *Economic Science in Relation to Welfare* (1908)
Unemployment (1913)
Wealth and Welfare (1912)
(ed.): *Memorials of Alfred Marshall* (1925)

C. W. Pipkin: *Social Politics and Modern Democracies* (New York, 1931)

D. C. M. Platt: *Finance, Trade and Politics in British Foreign Policy, 1815–1914* (Oxford, 1968)

L. Playfair: *Subjects of Social Welfare* (1889)

J. H. Plumb (ed.): *Studies in Social History* (1955)

S. Pollard: *Economic History of England 1918–1965* (1962)

Policy of Social Reform in England: 80 Club lectures (1913)

P. W. Raffan: *The Policy of the Land Values Group in the House of Commons* (1912)

M. S. Reeves: *Round About a Pound a Week* (1913)

Report of the Land Enquiry Committee (2 Vols, 1912–13)

T. Richardson and M. Walbank: *Profits and Wages in the British Coal-Trade 1898–1910* (1911)

L. Robbins: *The Theory of Economic Policy in English Classical Political Economy* (1952)

D. Roberts: *Victorian Origins of the British Welfare State* (1960)

J. M. Robertson: *The Fallacy of Saving* (1892)
  The Taxation of Land Values (1914)
E. Roll: *A History of Economic Thought* (1954)
J. W. F. Rowe: *Wages in Practice and Theory* (1928)
B. S. Rowntree: *Poverty : A Study of Town Life* (1902)
  The Labourer and the Land (1912)
J. Saville: ' Some Retarding Factors in the British Economy Before 1914 ',
  Yorkshire Bulletin of Social and Economic Research, May 1961
D. L. Schloss: *Methods of Industrial Remuneration* (3rd edn., 1898)
B. Semmel: *Imperialism and Social Reform* (1960)
R. V. Sires: ' Labour Unrest in England 1910–14 ', *Journal of Economic
  History*, 15, 3, 1955
W. Smart: *Second Thoughts of an Economist* (1916)
R. L. Smyth (ed.): *Essays in the Economics of Socialism and Capitalism*
  (1962)
P. Snowden: *The Socialist's Budget* (1908)
F. H. Stead: *How Old Age Pensions Came To Be* (1909)
F. Taussig: *Wages and Capital* (New York, 1897)
F. M. L. Thompson: *English Landed Society in the Nineteenth Century*
  (1963)
A. P. Wadsworth: *Newspaper Circulations 1850–1954* (Manchester
  Statistical Society, 1955)
A. Wallace: *Land Nationalisation* (3rd edn., 1882)
J. Wedgwood: *Henry George for Socialists* (1908)
D. A. Wells: *Some Recent Economic Changes* (1896)
J. D. White: *Economic Ideals* (1903)
G. Williams: *The State and the Standard of Living* (1936)
C. H. Wilson: ' Economy and Society in Late Victorian Britain ',
  Economic History Review, 28, 1, 1965
R. Winfrey: *Allotments and Smallholdings* (1907)
R. Woods: *English Social Movements* (1892)

(vi) *Biographical, etc.*

W. H. G. Armytage: *A. J. Mundella* (1951)
H. H. Asquith: *50 Years of Parliament* (1926)
L. A. Atherley-Jones: *Looking Back* (1925)
C. R. Attlee: *As It Happened* (1954)
E. Baker and P. Baker: *J. A. Baker* (1927)
A. T. Basset: *J. E. Ellis* (1914)
W. Beveridge: *Power and Influence* (1953)
A. Birrell: *Sir F. Lockwood* (1911)
H. Bolitho: *Alfred Mond* (1935)
H. N. Brailsford: *Life-Work of J. A. Hobson* (Hobhouse Memorial
  Lecture, 1957)

M. Brett (ed.): *Journals and Letters of Viscount Esher* (1934)

A. Briggs: *Seebohm Rowntree* (1961)

V. de Bunsen: *C. R. Buxton : A Memoir* (1948)

Cecil, Lady Gwendolen: *Life of Robert, Marquis of Salisbury*, 4 Vols. (1921–32)

A. Chamberlain: *Down the Years* (1935)

R. S. Churchill: *W. S. Churchill* Vol. 2 (1967)

G. D. H. Cole: ' J. A. Hobson ', *Economic Journal*, Vol. 50 (1940) pp. 351–60

P. Corder: *R. S. Watson* (1914)

D. Crane: *Sir R. Perks* (1909)

E. W. Evans: *Mabon* (Cardiff, 1955)

H. Evans: *Sir Randal Cremer* (1909)

P. Fraser: *Joseph Chamberlain* (1966)

A. G. Gardiner: *Life of Harcourt* (1922)
  George Cadbury (1922)
  John Benn and the Progressive Movement (1925)

W. George: *My Brother and I* (1958)

S. Gwynn and S. Tuckwell: *Sir Charles Dilke* (1917)

R. B. Haldane: *An Autobiography* (1929)

D. A. Hamer: *John Morley, Liberal Intellectual in Politics* (1968)

E. H. Hamilton: *Life of Henry Fowler* (1912)

J. L. Hammond: *C. P. Scott* (1946)

J. A. Hobson: *Confessions of an Economic Heretic* (1938)

J. A. Hobson and M. Ginsberg: *L. T. Hobhouse : His Life and Work* (1931)

R. R. James: *Rosebery* (1963)

R. Jenkins: *Asquith* (1964)
  Life of Dilke (1958)

H. E. Kearley: *The Travelled Road* (Rochester, 1935)

G. S. Keeton: *A Liberal Attorney-General* (W. S. Robson) (1949)

Sir G. Kekewich: *The Education Department And After* (1920)

J. Kent: *John Burns* (1950)

D. Lowe: *From Pit to Parliament* (Keir Hardie) (1923)

S. McKenna: *Reginald McKenna 1863–1943, a Memoir* (1948)

Sir C. Mallet: *Herbert Gladstone : A Memoir* (1932)

V. Markham: *Friendship's Harvest* (1956)

L. Masterman: *C. F. G. Masterman* (1939)

H. Mitchell: ' Hobson Revisited ', *Journal of the History of Ideas*, July–September 1965

K. O. Morgan: *David Lloyd George's Welsh Radical as World Statesman* (Cardiff, 1963)

J. Morley: *Life of Gladstone* (1903)
  Recollections (1917)

A. C. Murray: *Master and Brother* (Life of Elibank) (1945)

A. E. Pease: *Elections and Recollections* (1932)

Lady Pentland: *Lord Pentland* (1928)

R. W. Perks: *Notes, Privately Printed* (1936)

R. S. Rait: *Memorials of A. V. Dicey* (1925)

Viscountess Rhondda: *D. A. Thomas* (1921)

K. Robbins: *Sir Edward Grey : A Biography of Lord Grey of Fallodon* (1971)

Sir W. Runciman: *Before the Mast* (1924)

G. W. E. Russell: *Sir Wilfrid Lawson : A Memoir* (1909)

S. Salvidge: *Salvidge of Liverpool* (1934)

J. A. Simon: *Retrospect* (1952)

D. Sommer: *Haldane of Cloan* (1960)

R. Speaight: *Hilaire Belloc* (1957)

J. A. Spender: *Sir Robert Hudson* (1930)
  Weetman Pearson (1930)
  Men and Things (1937)
  Sir Henry Campbell-Bannerman (1924)
  Life, Journalism and Politics (1926)

J. A. Spender and Cyril Asquith: *Life of Asquith* (1932)

A. Thorold: *Life of Labouchere* (1913)

E. Wallace: *Goldwin Smith* (Toronto, 1957)

B. Webb: *My Apprenticeship* (1938)
  Our Partnership (1948)

C. V. Wedgwood: *J. Wedgwood : Last of the Radicals* (1951)

J. Wedgwood: *Memoirs of a Fighting Life* (1940)

M. J. Wiener: *Between Two Worlds : The political thought of Graham Wallas* (1971)

L. Wolf: *Ripon* (1921)

Index

315